WHAT EVERY ROOKIE SUPERINTENDENT SHOULD KNOW

Surviving Year One

Robert Reeves

Published in partnership with the
American Association of School Administrators

Rowman & Littlefield Education
Lanham, Maryland • Toronto • Oxford
2006

Published in partnership with the
American Association of School Administrators

Published in the United States of America
by Rowman & Littlefield Education
A Division of Rowman & Littlefield Publishers, Inc.
A wholly owned subsidary of The Rowman & Littlefield Publishing Group, Inc.
4501 Forbes Boulevard, Suite 200, Lanham, Maryland 20706
www.rowmaneducation.com

PO Box 317
Oxford
OX2 9RU, UK

British Library Cataloguing in Publication Information Available

Library of Congress Cataloging-in-Publication Data

Reeves, Robert, 1930–
    What every rookie superintendent should know : surviving year one /
Robert Reeves.
        p. cm.
    "Published in partnership with the American Association of School
Administrators"—T.p.
        ISBN-13: 978-1-57886-376-1 (hardcover : alk. paper)
        ISBN-13: 978-1-57886-367-9 (pbk. : alk. paper)
        ISBN-10: 1-57886-376-7 (hardcover : alk. paper)
        ISBN-10: 1-57886-367-8 (pbk. : alk. paper)
        1. School superintendents—United States.   2. School management
and organization—United States.   I. Title.
    LB2831.72.R44   2006
    371.2'011—dc22

                                                            2005023064

Manufactured in the United States of America.

CONTENTS

FOREWORD

This book is a godsend and guide to any new superintendent of schools. However, it is also a tremendous book and guide for current and experienced superintendents looking for ways to improve their performance. Finally, this book is a wonderful guide for new and current school principals as well. The wealth of knowledge, wisdom, concepts, and practical tips in this book are without parallel in the education industry.

Rarely does a leader in a field, someone who has been there and done that, take the time to organize and share accumulated wisdom in such a systemic fashion as Bob Reeves has done. Written in a series of conversations over 12 months between a new superintendent and his mentor, each page is chock-full of the tacit knowledge and tips that are the result of the school of hard knocks.

Bob has been one of the most progressive and successful district superintendents over the past 25 years. What is unique about this is Bob's approach to his job and to the education field in his systems thinking approach. It is without peer and is much more than just a systematic approach, but one that is in keeping with systems thinking and the natural way the world works.

Rather than theory, this book is about the practical realities that leaders in education face—almost insurmountable odds these days. Surmounting them successfully is what this godsend of a book and guide for new superintendents is all about.

If you read only one book this year, this is the one. Read, reread, and savor each page. Make it dog-eared as you use it over and over again.

Stephen Haines, chief executive office and founder
Haines Centre International

ACKNOWLEDGMENTS

I think it only fitting to acknowledge those that helped make this project possible. I could start with my mother who had faith in me to become a school leader, but I won't.

Trying to capture the depth and breadth of the chasm separating the rookie from the successful veteran was the idea of Dr. Gloria Johnston, a fellow administrator, a doctoral student, and then a first-year superintendent. She encouraged me to write a reflection on what worked in our successful school district. We talked about a joint project comparing her first year to my many years of experience. The collaboration didn't materialize and it took 7 years before I felt confident enough to start out again, but now without her. She went on to write her own first book, *Eight at the Top*. I was encouraged by others to share a nearly three-decade journey—my own trials, tribulations, and triumphs.

Drs. Ken Blanchard and Paul Hersey, former parents in our district, were instrumental in introducing me to the outside world of organizational development and change. In the late 1970s Ken and his wife, Marge, worked with us for a year in five schools. This was our first experience in using consultants and trainers from outside the field of education. Ken's friendship and support over the years was an inspiration to me. Situational Leadership training became a mainstay in the school district.

This opened the door for us to actively interface with William Pfeiffer, former chief executive officer of University Associates in San Diego; Steve Haines, chief executive officer at the Centre for Strategic Management; Richard Lyles, another parent, consultant, and writer; Larry

Lezotte, cofounder of Effective Schools; Peter Block; and last but not least Madeline Hunter, our first educational guru. These folks provided the base upon which we were to build a nationally recognized school system.

For Sam Horn, noted author, teacher, and speaker, who recognized that this book project had a future and helped make it come true, my undying thanks. You are a special friend.

Many thanks to Eileen Haag, communication consultant, who coauthored our first article, *Now I Am One,* which got AASA's attention for publication in *The School Administrator*, November 2003. And to Paul Houston and Claudia Mansfield Sutton, the executive staff and editors at AASA, who believed in the idea that rookies needed mentoring, compiled a compendium on mentoring for state associations to use, and endorsed this work.

In the actual writing many wonderful people were willing to help bail me out, providing valuable guidance. Rae Adams, Charlie Garten, Steve Haines, Dr. Steve Halfaker, Dr. John Keiter, Cindy Marten, and Ray Wilson again are worthy of special recognition.

Douglas Reeves, my son and the family writer and editor, gave me sound creative feedback.

To the folks at Rowman & Littlefield Education, who turned this project into a book worthy of publication, many thanks. The help of Tom Koerner, Cindy Tursman, Paul Cacciato, and Nicole McCullough kept a nervous first-book writer from going crazy with anxiety.

And to Meda Menius, without whom this couldn't have been written, my sincere gratitude and undying thanks. She was my encourager, helper, editor, critic, typist, and friend throughout the project.

INTRODUCTION: WHAT EVERY ROOKIE SUPERINTENDENT SHOULD KNOW

In order to change the culture you must change the conversation.

—Peter Block

It was late in the evening and a rookie superintendent was struggling over the many things that would be facing him in his first weeks on the job. As he became more frustrated, his anxiety level rose. What does he do first?

"What does the board really expect from me? I've never worked with five bosses before!"

Who could he turn to for advice and direction? His mind wandered in near exhaustion as he dozed off watching *The Wizard of Oz* on the old movie channel.

In his dream, like Dorothy, he was swept up by a tornado and dropped into the Land of Oz. He started following a yellow school bus on the yellow brick road in search of the Emerald City and the Wizard, the one with the magical management wand for new school superintendents working with school boards. He was sure that if he could find the Wizard all his problems would be solved.

If he were granted all wisdom and knowledge and returned home to the safety of his new school district office, he would be able to avoid school board issues and problems, subordinates defying directions, more resistance to accountability for high student performance, more negative attitudes about pressing curriculum issues, labor union strife, more daily crises and parental problems, and more anxiety attacks and sleepless nights!

But then, finally, entering the Emerald City, right in front of his eyes on the corner newsstand, he saw the blazing headlines of the local newspaper, *The Daily Ozette*: "Trustees vote not to renew contract of first-year schools chief!"

"Oh no!" he exclaimed. He read that the superintendent only lasted 18 months. Is it that bad out in the new superintendent world? Frantically turning to page two, he saw an article that proclaimed the downfall of another superintendent: "District moves to dump 2nd schools chief in the past 18 months!"

The board released him after only 6 months! "Will I be next? How will I ever get through this first year? I know I need help. Where's the Wizard? Where can I find my magical management wand?"

Suddenly, nervous sweat on his brow, he sat up with a jerk in his easy chair, wondering where he was. The television screen was blank. It was 2 a.m. At first he wanted to thank his lucky stars that it was a dream. Slowly he fought through his grogginess and realized it was not a dream at all. His new job started the next day. Everyone would be looking for answers from the new leader. "Do I have them?" he worried out loud, wiping the sweat from his face.

In desperation he realized that there was no magic wand and he must seek guidance before he became the next headline. "What do I do now? Where do I go for help?" he exclaimed.

Sound all too familiar? The anxiety? The fear? And worrying about being a statistic—one of the short termers! What is it about the job of school superintendent that puts one on the fast track to self-destruction? Do they really mess up their first year? Where do you go for help before you're in way over your head and wouldn't even recognize what a magic wand looks like? Where is the Wizard when you need him? Of course, our rookie realizes, now fully awake, there isn't one! Then, with a shock, he realizes, I'm really on my own tomorrow!

Are you taking on a first-time chief executive officer or superintendent's position with a new district in a different town? You landed the job, but instead of working directly for one boss, you are the boss working for a board of directors—five to seven new bosses—that think you may, or have to, walk on water. Do they really know you're not perfect, even though you had convinced them you were darn near close?

You prepared for the interviews. You sold yourself to the various interviewing panels and the new bosses. You've even signed the employment papers, and now you are suddenly hit with a sinking apprehension.

"Why am I doing this? Can I handle it? What do I do next? What if I let them down? What if I can't measure up?"

Are you starting to lose sleep, waking up suddenly?

You may be wondering, why did they hire me in the first place? What characteristics did they like? Were they rebounding from a bad experience with my predecessor? Or do they see in me hope for improving the productivity of the organization? Solving all their problems?

With the too-often changing of the guard, school boards are faced with the challenge of hiring a new superintendent that will stay forever. But in reality, forever turns into a few short years for a variety of reasons. How can you become, on your own, a successful first-year survivor when often you don't even realize what you don't know?

THE PROBLEM

During my research, superintendents shared some first-year experiences that suggest there's a better way to transition new superintendents with their new school board, organization, and community. While working well with the school board is critical to success, it's not the only reason for not making the grade. In addition, there are problems of not understanding the territory (culture), avoiding early pitfalls, understanding what you don't know but need to, and understanding the change process as CEO.

Here are a few comments on school board relations that don't always appear in textbooks.

- "In my first year the governing board (one member) took out a lawsuit against the other four for trying to control the behavior in board meetings."
- "How can I resolve the problem of an overzealous board member who was trying to micromanage?"
- "My second day on the job I had a group of parents come in to see me about how they wanted me to control a board member who was in their words, 'out of control.'"
- "When the question of my first pay raise came up, one board member approached me to say he would support a larger increase than

the one on the table if I would give him the difference to pay off his gambling debts."

- "I made a veteran board member cry when I told her if she were going to micromanage the system she did not need me. This was in my first month on the job."
- "Being well schooled (via effective schools) in the distinctions between process and product, I assumed that my Board would just love my willingness (eagerness, even) to be evaluated based on data, on student outcomes. . . . Despite a lip-service agreement, I found that they would rather evaluate me on process elements."
- "If I was adequately prepared myself in dealing with board-superintendent relationships, they would need the same understanding (of the difference between governance and management, for instance)[1]—as a result without it, I'm simply out-numbered (and hence often overwhelmed!)."
- " 'We want everyone to love us.' This was a board member's comment to me as to my job expectation. We were broke, no curriculum, no direction, no instructional model. The local college refused to send student teachers to our district. Things looked bleak for the Mudville Nine."
- "I failed to get my board evaluation developed the first year, and even avoided doing one the second. I was gone the third."
- "I lasted only one year. I don't know what happened. The board chair said I wasn't a good fit."

CENTRAL THEMES

The theme of working effectively with school boards is illustrated throughout the 15 chapters. The key to success is to develop a good trusting working relationship right from the get go. A second important theme is seeing the organization as a whole with interrelated parts, a systems thinking approach. Learning about and understanding the people side of the business is also a recurrent theme. Problem solving and decision making are explored in depth. Finally, learning to manage change is faced almost every month.

But there's much, much more to the job to becoming successful the first year—and beyond. It's about becoming an accomplished and effective leader. But first you have to survive your first year.

WHAT'S THIS BOOK ALL ABOUT?

Follow the trials, tribulations, and triumphs of our first-time CEO and school superintendent chronicled over a 12-month period, from late-spring hiring though June the following year. Month by month, he is faced with making decisions the school calendar dictates. These range from learning about the school board and getting to know the territory in the summer to opening school and then working through the many complex issues requiring determination and change throughout the year. He discovers what he doesn't know about managing and leading in a different, more diverse and complex school system. He wants to know what it will take to be successful the first year—or rather, just survive it.

His former university professor, a retired, very successful school superintendent and management consultant is asked to fulfill his previous promise to all his doctoral students that he would make himself available to help them anytime. He commits to serve as a sage mentor and coach during the critical first year.

The rookie is counting on his new coach to have everything he will need—all the skills of a John Wooden, Don Shula, and Vince Lombardi rolled into one.

Also, he thinks that it would be nice to survive and, along with survival, learn some things that would help reduce the time and intensity found along the first-year learning curve.

The fictionalized dialogue in the following chapters between the rookie and the mentor is presented in a way to help make this happen, allowing the rookie superintendent to learn from the competent advisor how to become more knowledgeable and successful sooner than by the old trial and error method.

STAGING THE DRAMA

Written in a novelized conversational format, this book is a case study approach to building basic leadership skills and the accompanying strategies needed to manage well and survive. The situations are drawn from actual occurrences, but the places, people, and described events are fictional.

Applying the various strands of expertise from the nonpublic school arena through time-tested management theories and models, the mentor weaves them into a whole fabric to guide problem solving and decision making for the rookie and his team. As the mentor demonstrates how these worked in his former career, the rookie is challenged to integrate those practices that might work for him in his new school district.

The mentor fills in gaps as the rookie discovers what he didn't learn about leading and managing in the "kindergarten" of the university administrative preparation programs. Also, the system of learning by coming up through the ranks didn't adequately prepare the new superintendent to be able to handle the first struggling year with much practical knowledge and confidence, especially working with school boards.

As the 12 months unfold and new challenges arise each month, the mentor coaches him on survival strategies, effectively working with and developing positive relationships with a 3–2 politically divided board, systems thinking, backwards thinking and planning, strategic management, and the basics of Situational Leadership and Social Styles. In addition, the rookie learns about dealing with financial crises, handling staff members that don't get on board or aren't doing their job, and arbitrating labor union issues. He and the mentor address clarifying the main mission and change strategies and using models to initiate change and student improvement, such as effective schools criteria, accountability, and effective communication planning, along with other practical ways of managing the enterprise.

THE ORGANIZATION

Each chapter, or month, carries issues that are based on real occurrences that need to be thought through or planned for. Each chapter begins with a set of objectives to be covered. The dialogue is in a conversational parable format. After the topic has been established between the two, creating a "what?" scenario, the narrative is stopped for readers to consider where the story and issues are taking them. This begins a thinking process in the "so what?" phase of the adult learning cycle. A question asks if there is meaning for the reader as thoughts play out from the reader's experiences: does this make sense?

The reader is challenged to contemplate whether enough self motivation has been developed to move on to a "now what?" consideration with more questions for back home consideration and possible implementation. Readers are asked if there is enough meaning discovered to make changes in their own workplace.

Finally, a number of "Strategies and Survival Skills," based on the dialogue, the problems, and training, are presented at the end of each chapter, and a Toolbox is provided, listing key references for programs and solutions included in the chapter.

Walking and talking the rookie through his first year, month by month, allows the reader to follow key learnings in various parts of the system as they occur chronologically. Some first-year problems were set up and developed throughout the year and some surprises added along the way. It certainly doesn't cover everything the leader should know or do, but rather how to deal in certain key selected areas—areas for which many textbooks or classes rarely provide adequate preparation.

We often describe the enterprise we work in as a "school system." But do we think in systems terms as we function? As CEO or superintendent, do we operate, manage, understand, and lead our organization from this point of view? Learning about board relationships is critical, and the story begins exploring a real dilemma. This is discussed in chapter 1, "The Beginning."

The challenge to the reader is in sorting, selecting, and integrating various ideas into a personal leadership bank of knowledge and experience. Often we find a particular idea or strategy before it's needed to solve a future pressing problem. I hope the reader can do the same by filing away the concepts and resources presented. If even one good idea comes from this effort, then this project will have been successful.

Is there a more systematic way we could use for training our future school system leaders? I'm not sure, but in my own experience, the school of hard knocks helped prepare me to see the big school system picture in its subordinated role to the state and the state's educational subsystems—school districts—it sustains. It wasn't until after several years that I was able to understand and affect the leadership role in building a high performing organization within this context.

Can others capture the vision, the inspiration and the structure to shape their own success? Some of my colleagues and students have gone on to do so.

Obviously, the decision that this story should be told was made in the hope that, somewhere, someone can take an idea or two, make it better and become more successful in our almost sacred mission of "All students learning—whatever it takes."

THE AUDIENCE

This story is being written for those in leadership positions with special focus on school systems. Most of the principles shared can be true in any leadership position. This work can be shared on the job, in college classrooms, and in training seminars by hopeful, current, and future superintendents and by school board members.

This book can

- be read only as an interesting case study
- be seen as an adventure shared
- be a source for identifying strategies and skills the reader can use on a select basis
- be used as a how-to, self-help manual for both the rookie and veteran superintendent
- be used as a model for school boards in making a smoother transition with their new superintendent.

Often, successful organizational leadership goes unnoticed. Valuable experience over time is not shared beyond those immediately acquainted with or part of the organization.

The successful story is hard to write; so many valuable lessons remain untold. Can successful leadership in one organization be transported to another setting with different players? Can the corporate resistance to change be shortened by listening to those who have been there, done that?

A mistake we often make, when we hear about success stories, is that we want to go see the outstanding practice and try to replicate it back home for a quick fix. This doesn't work! All we can attempt to do here is share ideas and ask the reader to consider these as motivators and tools to use in each of their own situations. While they have all worked well for us, they have to become a part of you, as an individual, and of your organization. You and your people have to make them part of you by creating your own culture and your own success stories.

Focusing on the prime target of this book, the leadership of school systems by the inexperienced CEO or superintendent is an attempt to share successful experiences in an effort to bring aspirant, rookie, or veteran superintendents alike information that may help them do a better job. Properly addressed, mentoring experiences can raise the hope for success earlier in a career and help the rookie superintendent not only survive and shorten the learning curve but catch a glimpse of what it took in one system to bring about a high degree of success.

Too often we read headlines such as those at the chapter beginning as school superintendents are summarily dismissed, negotiated out, or fired as the political climate changes early in a career. Too often the young superintendent doesn't know how to deal with and within the system. Often rookies don't have a clue on the basics of getting off to a good start. Too often the training and experience obtained prior to taking this important first job is not enough. College and university courses don't focus on becoming the CEO. State administrative associations run seminars for training aspirants, usually with visiting veterans sharing their expertise. Helpful, but is it enough?

The American Association of School Administrators should be applauded for taking on mentoring of new superintendents as a challenge and opportunity to improve the chances for surviving the first year well.

How can you do the job by the book if there is no book? This story's "Strategies and Survival Skills," found at the end of each chapter, may help in creating a book to guide you.

Are you now prepared to respond to these and similar situations? Are you able to jump right in and give these folks sound advice? What might you add to the list of first-year crises that would require attention and inspired leadership?

Even though we're focusing on year one, along this journey you need to keep in mind the conflict between career advancement and all that this entails and staying put for a long tenure! Change is not an overnight experience. Cultural change takes anywhere from 3 to 10 years. So when should the leader decide to move on? As you read this story, think about who you are, what you want to become, and what your legacy will look like.

None of the situations we will share have easy solutions. If we had a quiver filled with simple solution arrows, we might have a clue on how to proceed. "Strategies and Survival Skills" should help you in selecting some of the arrows you need and can use to hit the bull's-eye or at least come close.

Maybe, there's enthusiasm and hope, a wizard's magic wand somewhere. But is there a better way to gain experience and shorten the learning curve? I hope you make it so!

Hence, the story of the Rookie and the Mentor unfolds.

NOTE

1. "I bought each of them a copy of Carver's *Boards That Make a Difference*. They didn't want to hear it!"

THE BEGINNING: THE ROOKIE IS HIRED

> What do we do now?
>
> —Robert Redford, *The Candidate*

In this chapter you will do the following:

1. Meet the anxious rookie and the sage mentor as they face real start-up situations.
2. Learn about board hiring tendencies.
3. Begin to define the territory of the new job.
4. Be introduced to systems thinking.
5. Be able to apply the five-phase backwards thinking methodology in different situations.
6. Have the opportunity to apply these skills in your own situation.

IN THE BEGINNING

Rob Moore was sitting and fidgeting in his office waiting for the phone to ring. This was the day Karla Schmidt, school board president for the nearby Paradise Valley School District, was to call candidates to announce the board's choice for a new superintendent. As an anxious assistant superintendent of schools, Rob hoped he had what they wanted. According to the headhunter, the competition was tough, but he had prepared himself for this very moment; the moment that would shape his future.

Ms. Schmidt said she would call by 9 a.m., but when Rob last checked his watch, which he had been doing at 5-minute intervals, it was 10:30 a.m. He didn't know whether calls were first being made to also-rans or whether he was an also-ran.

He couldn't concentrate on the pile of papers on his desk. His stomach was churning. "Will I get this job? Has someone else already gotten it?" It was like a she loves me; she loves me not rhythm running through his brain. He could barely stand not knowing.

Then the phone rang. Suddenly he thought maybe he really didn't want to know.

"Dr. Moore, it's *the call*," his secretary said.

"Okay," he said with a sigh, "put it through."

"This is it," he thought, taking a deep, relaxing, cleansing breath.

"Rob," said the board chairman, "I'm calling to congratulate you on your selection as the new superintendent of Paradise Valley School District. The vote for you was unanimous."

Rob was speechless. "Dr. Moore, are you there?"

Rob's brain was swimming. "Is it real? Did I hear her right? Is this what I really wanted?" Somehow, a couple of stutters later, Rob managed to acknowledge the news with a weak thank you and assured the board chairman that he'd do his best to justify the board's confidence in him.

After hanging up, he slowly absorbed what had just happened. He gathered his thoughts and said to himself, I made it! Then, making sure his office door was closed, shouted, "Now I am one!"

The euphoria didn't last long. Reality set in like a blitzkrieg. He realized he had been so focused on how to get the job that he hadn't spent much time thinking about how he would do the job. "Now what do I do?" he asked himself as buyer's remorse quickly turned into panic. "I really don't know. How do you start a new superintendency? Where do I go for help? Are there special skills for new superintendents? Where would I start looking? Do I really have what it takes? Where do you look for help when you're the boss and a rookie at that? My predecessor there won't be any help with what's been going on with him!"

Rob's one-man roundtable went on for several panicked moments. He paced back and forth, changing direction with each additional unanswered question. And then it hit him; the first really rational thought in the past several minutes: He remembered his doctoral class at the university and its popular professor's offer to help his students in their careers. Rob couldn't think of a better time to test this maybe idle offer. The professor was both an experienced school superintendent and an adjunct professor in educational administration at the nearby university. Rob quickly found the professor's phone number.

"This is Barry Woodson, how can I help you?"

"Hi, it's Robert Moore calling, and I really need some help."

Dr. Woodson remembered Rob Moore. He was a good student and a high school principal when he was taking his doctoral courses. That must have been about 5 years ago. Woodson heard Rob was recently promoted to assistant superintendent.

Woodson's curiosity was aroused. He smiled to himself as he asked, "So what kind of trouble are you in?"

"Big trouble," Rob said, "but good trouble, I hope! You're talking to the new superintendent of the Paradise Valley School District. So, now I am one!"

"Congratulations," Woodson said, but his excited former student quickly interrupted him before he could say more.

"Sure, that's the good news. The bad news is that I start in 4 weeks and don't have a clue about what to do first, second, or even at all. I want desperately to get off on the right foot. I'm unsure of myself, scared, and I want to survive at least this first year. Can you help me?"

"I guess all you learned from me went in one ear and out the other," Woodson teased. But he really knew exactly how Rob was feeling even though it had been a long time since Woodson had gotten his first job as superintendent.

"I really used a lot of what I learned in class when I was promoted to assistant superintendent, but now I'm the boss and supposed to know *all* the answers. I figure since you lasted as superintendent at the same very successful school district for the better part of three decades, you're my best bet to get the help I need," Rob said.

Woodson laughed out loud. "You know, Rob, you sound just like Robert Redford in *The Candidate*. After all the struggle and compromise of winning a campaign, the newly elected senator turned to his campaign manager and asked, 'What do we do now?' So it sounds like you're asking me to play the role of a transition manager," Woodson paused building up the suspense, and then added, "I'd relish the role."

Rob breathed a loud sigh of relief.

"Don't be too relieved yet, Rob. You haven't seen my fee!"

His mentor chuckled at his own joke but didn't wait for Rob to appreciate it before launching into the first lesson, advice he was given by a veteran superintendent when he began his first superintendency. "Rob, let me tell you a story.

"One time, as a new superintendent started his first job, a veteran superintendent gave him four sealed letters and instructed him to keep them handy in his top desk drawer to be opened only when he was desperate.

"When things began to get tough after 6 months, he opened the first letter: 'Blame the former superintendent' was all that was printed on the page.

"At the end of the first year he was so frustrated he opened the second letter: 'Blame the state legislature, collective bargaining, and not enough money.'

"He didn't need to open the third letter until 18 months had gone by: 'Blame the split board, insensitive community, low test scores, and low socioeconomic level of parents.'

"And finally, after 2 frustrating years, everything was in a mess, so he tore open the fourth letter and in bold type he read, 'Prepare four new letters!'

"Rob, as you might remember, I never had to open the last letter! The goal of our work together is to see that you don't get desperate enough to open the first letter."

Rob didn't respond to his humor; it was way too close to home. Dr. Woodson realized that the timing was probably not right for levity. Rob was too uptight and was anxious for answers.

"On a more serious note, Rob, we need to find some time so you can fill me in about the district, tell me what you've been doing, and what you've learned. Why don't we meet for coffee at the cafe around the corner from my office at 4 p.m. on Tuesday? You know where it is. We can begin looking at what a new first-year superintendent needs to think about, plan, and watch out for."

"Sounds good! See you then. Do I need to bring anything?" Rob asked.

"Yes, of course. Your brain and some forethought," the professor-soon-to-become mentor challenged the rookie.

"Ohhkay!" Rob stammered not knowing how Dr. Woodson was taking all of this.

"Think about how you would describe your job as the CEO and superintendent. What do you think it takes? What are you supposed to do and try to achieve the first year? Try to put it in a sentence or two. Let me do some more thinking on first things for us to do and I'll send you something," Woodson said.

After hanging up, Rob went in to see his boss, his not-so-good superintendent role model that he was happy to be leaving. He told him the good news as he handed him his letter of resignation, effective in 4 weeks. The superintendent was congratulatory and wished him well. This was Rob's first experience of acceptance into this new inner circle.

The hard part was walking around his office and telling his loyal staff that he was leaving. Most were happy for him, but then they started to realize the change would affect them. He knew from experience they would be wondering what was going to happen to them with a new boss.

Thinking about his new mentor's previous classroom advice, he did have a ready replacement in mind, if only his superintendent would listen. He wanted to soften the blow and have a well-known and respected administrator in his place to help ease the tension for his immediate staff and, of course, for the good of the district. But, he thought to himself, if he doesn't listen or delays too long I'm going to steal Don Halverson away as quickly as I can. Don was the current high school principal and Rob had worked with him in another school district.

THE MENTOR BEGINS

After Woodson put down the phone his mind began racing, as he thought about the challenges ahead for the nervous and excited new superintendent. The first year is always fraught with opportunities to err and challenges to overcome.

One thing Woodson had learned, sometimes painfully, was that during a change process you can't move faster than your staff, board, and community. He wondered how big the change would be for Rob in becoming a superintendent for the first time—and in Paradise Valley at that! He knew the district recently had made some interesting newspaper headlines.

Woodson went to his computer and prepared an e-mail that outlined what he thought should be covered in the first meeting. He'd give him some basics on school board–superintendent relationships.

Dear Robert,

Here are some ideas for you to think about for our first meeting. Call me if you have any questions.

First Meeting Agenda

1. What was the board looking for in a new superintendent?

What really happened to your predecessor? What were his perceived "weaknesses," if any? Let's review what the board asked you in the interview. We can get some keen insight from this. What did you commit to?

2. What do you know about the territory?

The memory of the opening song on the train in *The Music Man*, "Ya gotta know the territory," comes to mind. The traveling salesmen sang, "ya gotta know the territory, ya gotta know the territory" to the beat of wheels clacking on the rails. We'll have to discuss what you know and what you need to learn about the community landscape, political scene, senior administration, and the schools and their culture. The key issues for your first year include the following:

- board relationships
- administrative staff
- performance of each school
- district-wide standards and achievement
- principal effectiveness
- status of labor relations
- parent expectations
- financial conditions
- community relations and business partners

3. What do you know about systems thinking, setting goals, and survival skills?

Together we should look at the entire system strategically. Before we meet, you should be able to clearly define your personal goals. In one sentence, write your job description. What do you think a superintendent is supposed to do?

You should know what you want to say and do publicly at your first school board meeting. You should establish a reasonable timeline to set the stage for success. You'll survive by revisiting your management skills, adding to them, and being flexible when things happen that you can't even dream of now!

Finally, remember you have been successful and they chose you. Use your talents that have worked well in the past.

See you Tuesday.
Barry Woodson

Woodson reminded himself that he has to go slowly so Rob wouldn't get overloaded. Thinking out loud, Woodson's next thoughts were, "This is an overwhelming starting list. Probably too much, but he needs to consider every area, the entire system, and then prioritize. We can decide where to start by defining each item later in an urgency and importance matrix."

Barry sent these initial ideas off to Rob and thought he should add a "not to worry" caveat, knowing he will anyway!

THE INITIAL MEETING

Two days later Rob arrived at the cafe 10 minutes early and found Barry going through some notes with two cups of coffee on the table.

"I saw you park and I ordered your coffee, since there's no time to waste," Barry said with a welcoming smile. "Well, did you come with a one-sentence job description?" asked the mentor to start the conversation.

"I thought of a lot of things but couldn't put all the ideas in one sentence. I was sure you had an answer anyway," he quickly added with a knowing smile.

"Okay! I guess you know me better than I thought you did. I'll give you a definition that I think best describes what I tried to do as superintendent. It took years for me to crystallize what I thought the job was all about."

Barry tore a page out of his note pad, jotted down a few words, and handed the paper to the rookie.

The Superintendent's Job Description

To provide for, protect, and lead the organization's learning system and create an environment to maximize student learning and teaching excellence.

"Well, that's at least food for thought. I don't remember reading that anywhere. It does put priorities in the right place—on student learning, good teaching, and supporting the system," Rob noted.

"Let's leave this for now. Think about it over the next few months and see if it stands the test of time from your experience.

"Now let's start with what you know. What do you think the board was looking for when they picked you? And tell me what happened to your predecessor!" Barry began in rapid-fire fashion.

"My predecessor, Dr. Albert Branson, definitely did not want to be my predecessor," Rob explained excitedly. "After I talked with you, I got a call from Branson's attorney, who 'suggested' that I shouldn't sign my contract because Dr. Branson, recently fired, wasn't going to leave without a fight. There will probably be some kind of buyout. I hope I can stay out of it."

"What happened?" Barry asked.

"It was a political mess. Apparently, after giving him a great evaluation in January the board, on a 4–1 vote, fired him in March. There was a board election in April and the board chair, one of the majority, was defeated. Then they finally got their attorney looking at the mess, and to minimize their legal exposure they rehired Branson as a classroom teacher for this fall."

Barry observed that Rob might have a pretty unpredictable board. He suggested that they get to that later, but for now they needed to talk about the weaknesses that caused the board to fire Branson after giving him a good evaluation. It's important to know the causes because boards almost always hire to counter the perceived weaknesses of the predecessor. Sometimes they forget that a new superintendent should have well-rounded skills—not skills just for short-term needs. They'd have to devise a strategy to get the board to look forward toward creating a better system rather than backwards and blaming each other for past failures. And that's what he strongly suggested that Rob should do as well.

Rob jumped back into the conversation. "You've just given me my first homework assignment. Let's talk more about that at our next meeting. You are going to stay with me through this critical period, aren't you?" Rob mentioned feeling ever so much better to have someone to talk with.

"Sure, I'll do the coaching and you do the heavy lifting because I've been there and done that. Now, I'm happy to say, it's your turn. Let's change the focus," Barry added. "What do you think the board members found most interesting and appealing about you?"

"Probably not my good looks," Rob retorted nervously and then smiled.

"I would agree with that!" Barry teased. During the three classes Rob had taken with him this light banter was common.

"Now, getting serious for a minute if I may," Rob halfheartedly pleaded.

"Be my guest!" The mentor was trying to quiet the uneasiness he sensed that Rob brought to the meeting, probably unsure of how to fulfill the daunting task he would soon face.

"A big thing I had going for me was that I was prepared for the interview. I analyzed some of the district's publications and its website, reviewed the state test scores, and then made a couple of calls to two former candidates who were interviewed for director jobs there," Rob explained.

"I knew they were looking for a curriculum and instruction leader, so I decided to emphasize this as one of my strengths. My record demonstrated that my team at the high school had really made a difference in student learning. We focused on results and we held ourselves accountable. We agreed that learning was no longer an option. We made it a mandate. We applied equal pressure and support to move the system. I even carried this mandate into the district office and began moving the other schools in this direction."

"How did the board react?" the mentor asked.

"They were nodding along with my explanation," he remembered.

"Good!"

Rob looked up toward the ceiling, trying to collect his thoughts. "Now that I think about it, that seemed to be what people were describing as Branson's primary weakness. He came from a military background and was seen to have fiscal experience strength. I emphasized my 8 months as acting business manager in my last district and the skills I used during one of our frequent superintendent upheavals and subsequent reorganizations. It was probably good to show that I could match his strength there." Rob leaned back and finally took a sip of coffee.

Barry leaned forward. "Sounds like your strategy was sound. You got the job! What was it about Paradise Valley that attracted you?"

"They passed a school construction bond measure in May—even with an acting superintendent and in the middle of the Branson controversy! Despite their unpredictability, I liked each of the board members. I like the challenges, and I'm ready to test my wings," Rob said confidently. "I believe that I can get them working together."

"Passing the bond does indicate strong community support, and that's a real plus. What are the challenges as you see them?" Barry asked.

Before Rob answered, he started to scribble some notes on his napkin. Barry handed him a notebook, "I thought you might need to record some notes from our meetings. Bring this to each meeting so we can keep a record of our thinking and decisions," he suggested.

"There seem to be a few issues. Let me start a list of what seems most critical as of now," Rob said as he wrote in his new notebook.

1. getting the school board working together and working effectively with me
2. building quality staff and positive community relations
3. controlling the budget and knowing where the money is
4. completing labor negotiations in a positive manner

Rob explained, "On the issue of the divided board, it seems to be split on whether the curriculum should be the tried and true traditional approaches supported by the new state assessment program, or whether the district leadership can be open to new ideas, such as using technology effectively, off-site Internet courses, and other creative teaching ideas."

🕐 Time-Out—A What

Take 10 minutes to consider the following:

1. What has been your experience with school boards?
2. Identify any problems you've had or observed like these mentioned.
3. What are the recent issues confronting your school board?
4. Select a current superintendent or board issue and discuss with a colleague how you would handle it.

Rob continued, "I'd like to do more than prepare kids to get good state test scores and make the district look good. Or do well on SAT scores and send the elite to college. What really matters is that kids ought to know how to be effective when they leave high school and college."

"That seems reasonable," Barry replied, trying to reassure him.

"I want to convince both camps on the board that each of them is right," he emphasized.

"Any ideas?"

"Not yet. That's why I need your experience," Rob responded, stating the obvious.

"Okay!"

"Regarding the labor negotiations," Rob said, "during my interview with a faculty group, I gave the teachers' union my commitment to come to the table and negotiate. They don't trust the current management representatives. They said they are not getting good information on the budget."

Barry looked up quickly from his note taking.

"Your advice would be really helpful on the labor stuff," Rob suggested as he put his pen down.

The professor let some quiet interrupt their conversation and then said softly, "I learned a long time ago there is no one best answer for any of the challenges you listed. You have to read each situation and adapt as necessary. There are ways to get to win-win negotiations. That will take time and commitment from you, the board, and the teachers' union. This kind of change is usually slow and time-consuming, but it can be done. Maybe during your first-year honeymoon period you can start working toward this. We can look at a planning-to-plan step when you think the timing is right."

Barry raised his voice and increased its intensity, signaling what he was about to say would be important. "But it always helps to stop and organize what you know. Let's do some backwards thinking," he suggested, remembering how helpful a systems thinking approach worked for him as superintendent.

"What's backwards thinking?" the rookie asked.

"You start with where you want to end up or what you want to accomplish and then plan backwards from that point to the present. For example, where do you want to be at the end of this first year?"

"One thing you taught me that I didn't forget is that I have to make sure to 'keep the main thing the main thing.' My main thing is to keep focused on all students learning," Rob stated emphatically. He continued with a hopeful smile, "I guess we should begin with the end in mind as Stephen Covey (Covey, Merrill, & Merrill, 1994) states and do some systems or backwards thinking like the method we used in class. Can you outline it for me again?"

"Let me share my understanding. Steve Haines (2000), the one I learned this from, of the Centre for Strategic Management, is always talking about going from complexity to simplicity. This is my way of describing how I see systems thinking applying to your situation. Systems appear in all of nature and each has similar properties, so it gives greater insight to more universal big-picture thinking."

The Elephant and the Helicopter

The school district is like the elephant, and the blind men's explanations are the various parts that make it a whole. The parts can't, or shouldn't, act independently.

"First, I'll repeat the story of the elephant and then add a helicopter trip," he began. "There were five blind men in India trying to describe an elephant by touching it. They each had hold of a different part. One had it by the tail and said it was like a rope. Another grasped the leg and said it was built like a tree, a third was stroking an ear and stated it was like parchment paper, the fourth patted a tusk and thought it a spear-like appendage, and finally, the last one believed the trunk he was touching was more like a large snake. Which one accurately described an elephant? Of course, they were all describing their perception of what they were touching, but all were incorrect in describing the elephant as a whole!

"We are trying to consider the entire system and its internal workings along with the environment in which the school district finds itself. Too often the perception of our role or place in the organization causes a silo mentality. We see only our jobs or functions as the main thing. And become protectionists of our own territory!

"Now, picture jumping in a helicopter and flying high above the elephant. What do we see from this height? Even though we don't quite see it all, we see enough of it to complete a picture the blind men separately couldn't create. We may see the elephant walking around in its environment, watching its behavior and interrelationships with other elephants, people, and the territory.

"I hope this gives you a picture of what we mean by a system. In life itself there is a natural hierarchical organization to things, starting with the cell and then moving up to organ, individual, group or team, organization, society or community, and the earth itself—a world view," Barry concluded, pouring another cup of coffee. He continued, "However, each component of the system plays a role in the smooth and effective operation of the larger complex system."

"Problems that are created by our current level of thinking can't be solved by that same level of thinking."

—Albert Einstein

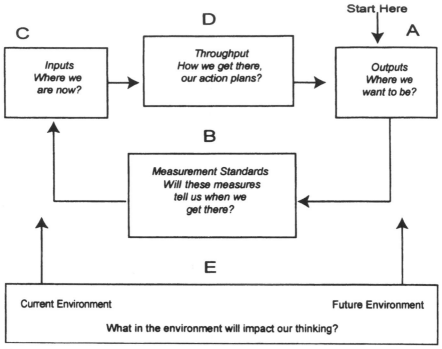

Figure 1.1. The Five-Phase A-B-C-D-E Systems Thinking Model
Source: Haines, 2000.

"So . . . if we generally use analytical thinking we now need real 'Systems Thinking' to resolve today's issues."

—Stephen G. Haines

When the professor arrived, Rob jumped right in after barely taking time to say hello. "I've already ordered coffee. The waitress is on her way now. I'm ready to give you feedback on what you sent. Let me show you the things I don't understand and then I would like you to walk me through one of the situations we've identified."

Wondering where to start, Barry thought, I think Rob is a bottom-line guy—doesn't mess around with too many pleasantries. I think his communication style is that of a results-oriented driving type. I wonder if he remembers what this means in the Social Style model we covered in class. I'll review it with him later.

I better get right to the point with his agenda. I'll listen carefully and I'll make him listen to himself as well. I'll bring this up again as we continue after he gets his feet wet on the job and gets to know the new folks he's going to work with better. Understanding his own style and those of his colleagues and board members is an essential part of getting to know the territory.

"Okay, Rob, what's on your mind?"

"What is a system, as the Centre used the term?"

"Here, let me show you," Barry responded as he pulled a writing tablet from his tattered briefcase. He could think better when explaining things visually. "The seven levels of living, or open, systems go from the cell to the supranational level." He drew and explained the characteristics of a living system.

1. Supranational System   Global systems, continents, regions, earth.
2. Society   States, provinces, countries, nations, regions within countries.·
3. Organization   Firm, company, school district, community, city. This is you as a district.
4. Group   Teams, departments, families, and similar bodies comprising members. This is self-explanatory.
5. Organism   Single organisms such as humans, animals, fish, birds. This is where we put the faculty, the employees, kids, parents, etc.
6. Organ   The organic systems within our bodies.
7. Cell   The basic unit of life.

"Within this list Haines [2000] is trying to focus our attention on levels 2, 3, 4, and 5, the interaction with the 'outside' community and societal systems, the district as a whole, the school and department, and the individual."

After all this was done he pointed out that Rob's school district system is actually part of a bigger state system containing over a thousand districts as its subsystems, which need to be integrated to effectively achieve the main mission. This would be used in developing phase E in the A-B-C-D-E model. The CEO or superintendent has to see the whole collective, larger picture and each of the related interdependent parts that work almost simultaneously. It's the helicopter view of looking at the elephant and its functional parts.

"Begin with the end in mind."

—**Stephen Covey**

"Now let's work through an example. It will be quick and dirty, needing a cleanup later," Barry said as he started on the rest of Rob's concerns for the day. He will not get me to do his work here, he thought, as he reminded himself that he wanted Rob to do the heavy lifting.

Then he said aloud, "Remember that the Outputs box (phase A) is where we start. Remember, Stephen Covey (Covey, Merrill, & Merrill, 1994) tells us to begin with the end in mind, as do some other visionary leaders I know. Now, where should we be, say, at the end of year one? Let's talk about three or four quick ideas and pick one so we can begin to think backwards from year's end to figure out your priorities. I think we can really get a good plan in place by the end of summer on some issues. After you get to know the territory a little better, let's plan for a rough environmental scan phase, getting more information from all the key players involved as soon as possible."

"The first thing that comes to mind," Rob responded, "is that I want the board to recognize that I've done a good job in the first year, so they want to keep me around for at least three more."

"Basic survival is a good place to start," Dr. Barry agreed. "That's why we need to understand this backwards thinking system mind-set. Also, we'll need to review and formalize other survival strategies as situations arise during the year."

THE ROOKIE THINKS OUTCOMES

After ordering another cup of coffee, Rob started writing on his tablet what he thought some Output targets might be:

1. Continue in the job.
2. Bond the board into a positive working force with the best interest of kids as a priority.
3. Assess the current budget, find some money for salaries, and increase the reserves.
4. Successfully conclude teacher negotiations, including a commitment to begin working toward a win-win model.
5. Working through the principals, complete a review of the district's commitment to learning and determine the level of commitment by the schools, administration center, and parents.
6. If needed, develop effective administrative training and staff development programs that would lead to creating a learning organization.
7. Continue planning for the new elementary school funded from the construction bond measure passed in May.

A SURVIVAL PLAN

"I would like to start with my survival need and do a quick walk-through to see how the model might help. I can work on these other goals with the board as we set up my work plan and first-year evaluation process."

"For the Output results, where do you want to be in June?" Dr. Barry started.

It didn't take much thought for Rob to answer. "If I like my new job and work well with the board, I would like to stay here at least 3 more years!"

"Okay, let's put this in box A," Barry suggested (see Figure 1.2).

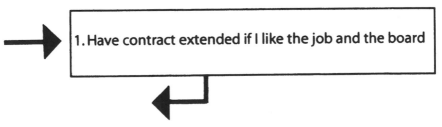

1. Have contract extended if I like the job and the board

Figure 1.2.   Phase A: Where We Want to Be

"Now let's see how we can measure this," he added.

"Well, I guess if I set reasonable goals for the year and get a good performance review I can expect to have my 3-year contract extended by a year. Also, I need to determine how I like the job and board. Any ideas?" Rob asked.

"Rob, what would you be satisfied with?" Barry said, turning the question back to the superintendent.

"Since I am going to be working on board relations anyway as a critical area, why don't I just say that if the board comes together and works without acrimony while staying within the guidelines of good boardmanship as set by National School Boards Association (NSBA) and respecting me as their CEO, they will pass muster. I'll have to consider how I feel about being the superintendent at year's end."

"Let's summarize and put this in box B (see Figure 1.3). Now we need to do a "Where are we now?" piece for box C. Just make a good guess since you haven't had time to get to know the territory. What do you know so far?" the mentor asked him, wondering what he really knew about all the issues, especially the political ones (see Figure 1.4).

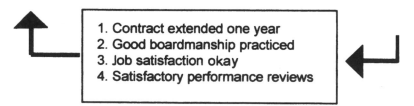

1. Contract extended one year
2. Good boardmanship practiced
3. Job satisfaction okay
4. Satisfactory performance reviews

Figure 1.3.   Phase B: How Will We Know?

1. Board has confidence in me now
2. Took the job with confidence in my ability to be successful
3. Board divided philosophically among its members
4. No performance review process or measures in place

Figure 1.4.   Phase C: Where We Are Now?

"I have a 3-year contract. I think I will like the challenge and I hope I will still feel this way at year's end. I have a sense of where I want to take the district over the next 3 years. I want to put what I learned over the last year to work now. I think I can be a great change agent for this district by focusing on the main thing—student learning. The board is politically and philosophically divided and yet I got a 5–0 vote when they hired me. Why don't I keep the model simple for clarity's sake today and fill in the box this way?" Rob responded with some confidence.

"We are running short of time. I need to beat the rush hour traffic if I expect to get to my administration class on time," Barry said. "We can't do it justice now. Let's just finish the example so you will get a good idea for making the model work. In Phase D is the hard work (see Figure 1.5). We might have you establish goals with the board for approval by the November board meeting. Each month when I meet with you, you can share your feelings about the job. You might even want to reflect and record your thoughts on your daily calendar as you think about them. What do you want to do about the board issue?"

Rob paused and then said, "I need to think about this one. I don't want the board yelling at each other as reported. Maybe holding a workshop to develop my evaluation format and process and first-year priorities could be a start. I might even bring in someone from the California School Boards Association (CSBA) to work with us as a starting point. Also, I want to use CSBA's book on effective boardmanship to review the rules of the game with them."

"Before we leave this, remember that although we have some data from the Phase E we need to do more in this arena. Right now we don't know the political conditions about the split board. Need more observa-

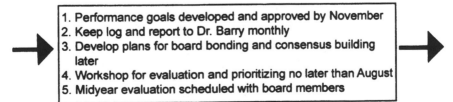

1. Performance goals developed and approved by November
2. Keep log and report to Dr. Barry monthly
3. Develop plans for board bonding and consensus building later
4. Workshop for evaluation and prioritizing no later than August
5. Midyear evaluation scheduled with board members

Figure 1.5.   Phase D: How Will We Get There? (Close the Gap C–A)

tion and homework as you get on the job," Barry said while he finalized the elements of the backwards thinking model.

"I see now how this works," the rookie added.

"Now that we walked and talked our way through this one issue, do you have any more questions?" Barry asked warily. "I'm working through this method of thinking with three of my clients as we speak. It's helped them clarify their thinking on many decisions."

"I do need more time to digest all of this," Rob said in a somewhat subdued tone. "I've got a lot to think about as well as make do on a survival basis. I'll review this, try to work another idea through, and then I'll give you a call to see if I'm on the right track."

"You might want to start involving some of your key staff with you in the process, so they will begin to understand how you think and help in identifying some pitfalls. Getting them involved early will help in building your team and definitely will help in the implementation of what you all come up with," Barry said.

"Coach, thanks a lot for all this early help. Let's schedule some more time in 3 or 4 weeks. I really appreciate your help. I don't think I'll be losing as much sleep as I have been, knowing where I can find you," Rob joked.

With that, they shook hands, and Rob left thinking about what they had accomplished in such a short time. There was much work to be done—a lifetime's worth! This could shorten his learning curve and improve his level of effectiveness a lot.

What have I gotten myself in for, he thought helplessly. I am one! But I have an experienced mentor here to help!

🕐 Time-Out—The So What

1. What meaning do these discussions have for you?
2. How did you feel when you made your first move into school administration?
3. Were you ready, scared a bit, or nervous?
4. How did you manage the first 3 months on the new job?
5. What worked and what didn't?
6. Does the backwards thinking model make sense yet? What don't you understand about it? Try to explain it to a colleague.

7. Pick an issue you have and think through the steps. Write down some ideas. Keep it simple!

8. How would you feel about having someone to talk to you as a mentor?

SUMMARY

In this chapter you were introduced to the rookie superintendent trying to find an answer to the question, What do I do now? The sudden realization hits him—"Now I am one!"—that he is a superintendent and he is unsure how to proceed. He now has to face a new job in a new school district. In somewhat of a panic he goes back to his college professor and friend to get help. Together they start a planning-to-plan effort to sort out beginning priorities.

They share real first-year problems actually experienced by new superintendents.

An examination of school board hiring tendencies is presented as well as a less than harmonious school board. Of course, the new superintendent wouldn't be there unless there was an opening for some reason. Today, this happens far too often.

The professor and coach's successful experience brings an understanding of systems thinking and backwards thinking to the discussion. These approaches will help them as they encounter other challenging situations throughout the year.

🕐 Time-Out—Reflections

1. After you have considered the preceding issues, what do you find relevant to what you are doing?
2. What action could you be taking now?
3. Select another problem you are working on and apply the systems thinking model and share it with a colleague. Have your colleague troubleshoot your plan.
4. Do more research on this topic by reading the references, attend a training session, or obtain additional material.

5. Think ahead about a challenge that Rob is facing and see how you would handle it before reading on. For example, how would you develop a backwards thinking plan for his negotiations problem?
6. Think about using the model to solve a situation of your own.

STRATEGIES AND SURVIVAL SKILLS

1. Why were you hired?
   • Understand as much as you can about the school board's reason for hiring you. Determine the hiring tendencies in order to find out about the strengths and weaknesses of your predecessor, paying especial attention to the perceived weaknesses.
2. Understand what your job is.
   • Clearly understand what you believe in, understand what you will be doing, and be able to articulate it in a few short sentences.
3. Get to know the territory.
   • Find out quickly as much information as possible about board politics, the students, your new staff, and the community.
4. Make haste slowly.
   • Make only necessary changes. Listen a lot and learn.
5. Learn to apply systems thinking.
   • Remember the elephant and the helicopter.
6. Develop a strategic management approach that all can understand.
   • Let your staff know that you begin processing with the end in mind and can use the backwards thinking methodology—The Five-Phase A-B-C-D-E Systems Thinking Model.

TOOLBOX

California School Boards Association (www.csba.org). 3100 Beacon Blvd., West Sacramento, CA 95691.

Covey, P., Merrill, A. R., & Merrill, R. R. (1994). *First Things First: To Live, to Love, to Learn, to Leave a Legacy.* New York: Simon & Schuster.

Haines, S. (2000). *The Systems Thinking Approach to Strategic Planning and Management*. Boca Raton, FL: St. Lucie Press.

National School Boards Association (www.nsba.org). 1680 Duke Street, Alexandria, VA 22314. info@nsba.org.

Reeves, R. (1972). *Ten Case Studies in Hiring a School Superintendent*. Unpublished dissertation, University of California, Los Angeles.

JULY: GOTTA KNOW THE TERRITORY

IN THE GAME OF TRUST THE LEADER
MUST ANTE UP FIRST

In this chapter you will learn to:

1. *Better understand the first steps in working with a new board.*
2. *Continue to apply systems thinking to real problems.*
3. *Go slow but make critical changes as necessary.*
4. *Establish trust right away.*
5. *Use a priority setting model.*
6. *Begin planning for teacher negotiations.*
7. *Reflect on why you got where you are in your career.*

A WAKE-UP CALL

It was only 6:15 a.m. The phone rang on the kitchen extension just as Dr. Woodson was finishing a last cup of coffee. He set the morning sports section aside and reached for the phone. He was almost ready to put his tie on, grab his briefcase, and take the 25-mile drive to the university. Who would be calling this early, he thought? He hoped it wasn't a family crisis.

"Barry Woodson speaking," he croaked with an early morning catch in his throat.

"It's Rob, Robert Moore," a voice said with an anxiety that sounded desperate, even more so than the call last month that led to their first getting together.

"Rob, I recognize your voice," Woodson said with some irritation. "What's going on that demands a wake-up call?"

"It's not too early is it?" Rob sounded worried. "I really need to talk to someone and you did say that you were only a phone call away."

"It must be important, so tell me what happened." Woodson thought a suggestion that "a phone call away" meant during working hours but decided listening was better. Rob did sound frantic.

"When we met in June I only briefly mentioned the call I got from the former superintendent's attorney telling me not to sign my employment contract. I was upset! Then I got mad and told him rather directly that the board legally hired me. I said I had resigned from my current job and I'm reporting as Paradise Valley's new superintendent on July 1st. Even though I could probably get my old job back, I didn't like his attitude. Then I got more upset that my new board hadn't said a word about this mess. I probably should have checked them out better.

"I didn't want my wife more upset than she already is with us having to relocate again and the kids changing schools. In my mind I could hear my dad saying, 'I told you so,' about me being so impulsive. He always admonished me to measure twice and cut once as I helped him build houses. He'd have a field day with this one if he ever found out. This just had to work!"

"This added a little spice to your life, didn't it? I'm surprised you didn't mention it before now," Woodson said with plain annoyance.

"Well, it worked out okay when I signed my contact on the Saturday before the Monday court date. The board's attorney said the federal judge would throw out Dr. Branson's—my predecessor—request to stop any hiring if I was signed up prior to Monday. Being on board was a done deal—but the legal problems aren't going away!" Rob was getting worked up again.

"Slow down," Woodson said softly, but to no avail.

"On top of all this, I just found out last night that the former superintendent and one of my school board members are suing the Concerned Citizen Committee. They claim they were libeled in a newspaper ad about some nefarious dealings with land developers right after they fired Branson. They are going to call me as a witness. What am I going to do? I wasn't even here then! Help me, Doc! I could be in a lot of trouble!"

"The first thing to do is calm down," Barry cautioned. This is an interesting addition to knowing the territory, at least the political territory, he thought.

"But that's not all!" Rob added excitedly. "There's been a petition going around to recall the three majority board members. You remember this past March the board fired Branson rather hastily on a 4–1 vote before the board election? The board chair then got defeated by a formerly recalled board member. Some folks didn't like this and other stuff that's going on so they are going the recall route."

"Okay! Okay! Rob, I know about Branson. You just brought it up twice! Slow down! We can work this through later. I'll give it some thought, talk to an attorney friend, and get back to you soon." Wow! What an introduction to the superintendency. Woodson was thankful most all his protégés had a less traumatic beginning. Thank goodness!

"But that's not all!" the rookie exclaimed, shifting his emotions and attention back to the school board meeting. "The attorney for the district, obviously supporting the board majority, asked the new board member directly if he and the former superintendent had taken kickbacks from one of the developers over a site for the new elementary school. I almost died!

"This was the same attorney who drew up my employment contract that I signed before the judge's deadline to throw Branson's case out of federal court!"

"Rob, take a deep breath. It's not the end of the world . . . yet! And remember, it's too soon for buyer's remorse," Woodson added with a sense of assurance he had gained through experience.

"Any good news from nosing around the territory?" he asked Rob somewhat tentatively, hoping to focus on other issues. What had Rob heard and been going through? This was unique territory! Rob showed his strength by signing on in the midst of this controversy. This either showed his confidence or his stupidity, he mused. I hope he can be coached through this as we work to identify the key issues and problems he's going to be facing. But, Woodson thought, I don't want to push myself where I'm not needed or wanted.

"The community is in upheaval about the firing of Branson. The teachers didn't like him since he kept salaries low. There doesn't seem to be enough management help. Community politics around board recalls and divisive members is a major issue. These are a few things of note. Otherwise it looks like a piece of cake," Rob noted, finally seeing some humor in his outburst. Maybe being an assistant superintendent isn't all that bad, he thought. At least he had the old man fighting his fights with the board and community. Now, he guessed, it's going to be his turn at bat whether he liked it or not.

"I see you might just have a challenge. You can always go back to your old job!" Woodson jabbed him, remembering full well he had resigned even before he signed his new contract.

Ignoring the professor's attempt at humor and with some agitation in his voice, Rob changed the subject and got back on point. "In addition, I got some early feedback about the board that actually worked out well. The two strategies my almost new assistant superintendent, Don, and I prepped for my final board interview session in May turned out to be the decision point for the board."

"Don's an almost? You got the board to agree to hire a new person? That takes some guts. Great going! What did you say?"

"I just told them that in my analysis of the district's management organization they couldn't get done what they were asking me to do without some additional help. I mentioned my colleague, but said I didn't know whether he would leave his district. I got their commitment to go after him."

"Well," Woodson said, "what were the two strategies? Shall I write them down and put them in my class notes as a success story?" Woodson thought Rob now could handle his humor even as stressed as he seemed to be. He was calming down somewhat.

"First, Don and I knew that I hadn't made the first cut for interviews. But after they rejected the first six candidates, I was in the second round of three. We knew that they were split—three that were considered too liberal and the other two were seen as too conservative. Actually, now in retrospect, the majority three were to the right of Attila the Hun and the other two somewhat farther right!

"Based on the rejection of the first six applicants, we knew it would be tough to get a unanimous vote with the board split. We decided to say that I had read research somewhere indicating that even in good times, boards seldom if ever agreed 100% on their final selection. So when they asked if I would take the job on a split vote, I avoided the trap. I told them I would take it if I was at least first or second on each one's list. The chair indicated that's what sold them on me.

"The other thing was about salary. They were paying the acting guy about $4,000 more than they advertised as top salary. If I'd agreed to the posted salary, I'd have to take a slight pay cut from my current job. Don suggested that when they asked about salary I should inquire what the acting was now making. Of course, we already knew! It did come up! When asked, I followed our strategy by saying that I would be comfortable with whatever they were now paying the acting superintendent. One board member blurted out the higher number, so I said that would be just fine. The board chair later just laughed about how that turned out."

"Knowing the territory helps, doesn't it?" Woodson reemphasized.

"I did say a few things at the board meeting but let the staff prepare most of the agenda. Still, I was kind of overwhelmed! Even though I watched my former board in action, with this one I wasn't sure what to expect. A lot of people came to see what the new kid on the block looked like and how he acted. Board meetings had become the best show in town over the past few years with all the shouting and infighting. I made a commitment to myself that this was not going to happen on my watch, so I thought I was ready. But the attorney popping off at the board member took me by surprise."

"Which attorney is this one?" Woodson wanted to know. Maybe Rob should get a law degree.

"The one I mentioned before, the board's attorney."

"For a moment I thought there were more," Woodson replied. "Anything good happen?"

"Teachers were there being friendly, but mentioned looking forward to negotiating with me. I felt like a goldfish in a glass bowl," Rob sighed. It seemed that he had run out of gas for a moment.

"I'm taking notes, Rob. We have a lot to cover when we meet."

"Yes." Rob said, "I don't think I told you that when I was introduced at the board meeting, the night after the board chair called and confirmed my selection, a newspaper reporter from the weekly stuck a microphone in my face and asked about my vision for the district."

"What did you say?" Woodson asked, seeming anxious about the answer. Another potential pitfall he hadn't prepared him for.

"I didn't really say anything specific as I was caught off guard. Never did I dream this would happen! I wasn't prepared. I talked about improving the schools and being part of the community. You know I really don't think in specifics yet. I worked so hard to get the job that I never really looked ahead. I didn't realize that in this town when the superintendent says something it makes front page news. I am meeting my new territory's key players and need to focus my thoughts. I think I could answer that question a lot better now, but I'll need more help."

Woodson tried again to slow the rookie down and refocus his thoughts. "Let's put these crises in order of importance and focus our energy for the moment," he said again, trying to lead the conversation back to some sense of order. "And let's think about these issues on an urgency and importance framework," he suggested as he quickly drew a model on the notepad he kept near the phone. This would help him think through what he was going to describe to Rob. "Got your notebook and a pencil?" he asked.

"I've got one here some place. Just a sec. . . . I'm ready."

"Good, now draw a large square and fill it in as I describe the model."

After Woodson finished talking Rob through the drawing of the model, the diagram looked like Figure 2.1.

🕐 Time-Out

What Woodson was referring to was this simple two-independent-variable matrix that he had seen at a Covey workshop years ago. The model stuck and he used it every week for his Monday morning cabinet meetings to help frame the agenda. Each cabinet member brought in items and placed them on the matrix. Times were set to limit discussion on each. Other administrators in the system picked it up and also used it effectively with their groups.

I. Take a few minutes to reflect on the issues Rob mentioned. Place each in the appropriate quadrant:
   • the attorney's conduct at board meeting
   • reporter and lack of Rob's clear vision of what to say
   • the Concerned Citizen lawsuit
   • the board majority being recalled

2. To this, add from the previous chapter
   - teacher negotiations
   - split board relationships
3. Within each quadrant how would you prioritize these issues regarding their importance and urgency?
4. What advice would you give Rob on each of the pressing matters he's just mentioned?
5. Have you had to deal with a similar problem?
6. Write down what you did and hold it for a later discussion.

THE ATTORNEY PROBLEM

"Rob, using this matrix, we could fairly say the attorney at the board meeting needs to be dealt with first as a very urgent and important matter—at least before the next meeting. Do you agree?"

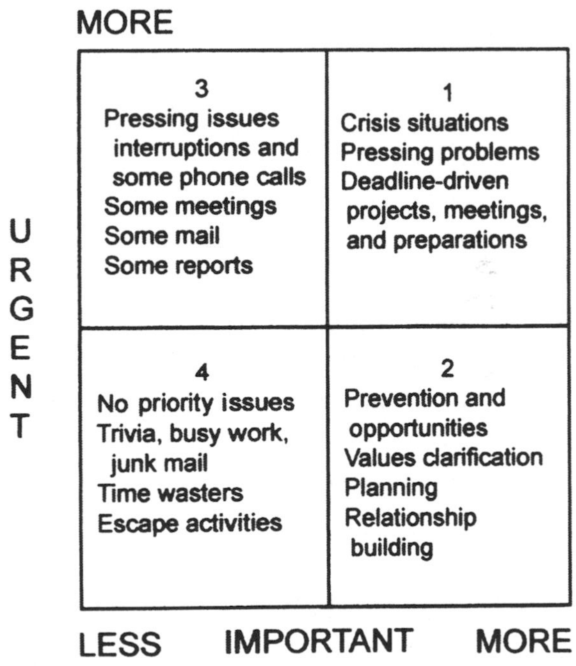

MORE

3 Pressing issues interruptions and some phone calls Some meetings Some mail Some reports	**1** Crisis situations Pressing problems Deadline-driven projects, meetings, and preparations
4 No priority issues Trivia, busy work, junk mail Time wasters Escape activities	**2** Prevention and opportunities Values clarification Planning Relationship building

URGENT

LESS   IMPORTANT   MORE

Figure 2.1. Priority Model.
Source: Covey, Merrill, & Merrill, 1994.

"Definitely," Rob responded quickly.

"I would like to use the backwards thinking model on this one, looking at the desired outcome first, and then developing a plan to work it through," the mentor suggested.

"I need coaching on this real problem," Rob said, somewhat desperately.

"Let's place the other issues on the matrix, and we will talk about these at our meeting next week," Barry continued. "Okay?"

Rob grunted what sounded like agreement. "But getting back to the attorney issue," Rob continued rapidly, as this seemed to dominate his thinking this morning, "my first thought is that I don't need him there and I certainly don't want him there berating board members. I want him to go away but not necessarily with hurt feelings. After all, he still represents the entire board; at least the majority members think so."

After a slight pause for gathering his thoughts, he continued, "I guess I am going to take the bull by the horns and tell him I'll call him when I need him. Then I'll begin to look for legal help elsewhere. After assuring him that he was helpful to the board majority during the last few months, I'll let him know that he can best support me and the district by not attending any more meetings unless I request it. I'm going to be anxious about telling the board this. I'll remind him that there will be a conflict of interest as he was allegedly part of the committee now being sued."

"Sounds like a plan. It will give you a chance to begin influencing the change to a different way of doing business. While it's a risk, I applaud your decisiveness. It will let them know that all this board craziness will not be tolerated and it won't be business as usual with you as the new leader. At least three board members will hear about your decision quickly. The other two will probably applaud you! You might ask the attorney to keep your conversation confidential until you have time to share your decision with the board."

"I'll let you know how it goes."

⏱ Time-Out—A So What

1. Draw the model and list four or five key issues with which you are dealing and place them in the priority boxes.

2. List the desired outcomes you would like from those you placed in the More Important–More Urgent box.
3. Did you put a topic in the Urgent–Important box? What is driving the urgency?

"I'll wait for more information on the lawsuit now that I'm calmed down. I'm glad you were there for me this morning. I guess if I have to testify I'll first consult with a new attorney I'm going to recommend. It'll be a while anyway. I'll put the other things on our next agenda."

"Good. That was a quick processing of the model. We have a lot of ground to cover between now and the start of school. Also, we need to review and integrate the priorities you listed in May and June. Are we still set for next week?"

"Yes. I still have some homework to do. I may send some stuff along for you to review before we meet. It's starting to come together. I'm feeling a little more at home now after being on the job for a few weeks. Being settled in the office, meeting all the district office staff and feeling accepted has made me more comfortable. I'll see you then," he said as he hung up.

Woodson shook his head, as he couldn't believe this was happening in the first month, but stranger things had happened to other rookies and veterans alike, he knew.

THE ROOKIE RESPONDS

Rob drafted his first attempt at using the Five-Phase A-B-C-D-E Backwards Thinking Model in describing his goal for teacher negotiations. Along with this he would send Barry an agenda for their first meeting in his new office and directions on how to get there.

Rob knew from past experience that management controls only half of the bargaining process, and he needed skill and luck to bring this to successful closure before school started. He believed he needed to encourage the teachers' new faith in him as their boss and, he hoped, leader. No real compromises needed to be made out of the legal scope of bargaining yet. Best to wait and see. Perhaps this first time could be used to plant seeds for a different type of relationship. At best he might

"You can put these guiding principles in the notebook for reference over the next weeks and months. This is not an exhaustive list—you can add to it as you go," Woodson advised.

Woodson handed him his list. While it wasn't too surprising, it represented his many years of working with and observing school boards.

Basic Survival Skills for Working With a Board

1. Get to know your board members as individuals and the desires, needs, and dreams related to their position. Schedule one-on-one meetings as soon as possible and listen to understand them as people, who they really are. Find out why they ran for the board, how many kids they have or had in the system, and what expectations they have of the system.
2. Treat all board members with respect.
3. Make sure each board member gets the same information. If one requests information, follow-up and send a copy to all.
4. Good communication requires an early heads-up on critical issues as soon as possible (before the press gets the information), followed by frequent updates.
5. Each member is to keep confidential all issues discussed in closed sessions.
6. Begin setting the stage for a definitive system for determining your performance objectives and evaluation process early in the game.
7. Share with them more about yourself and your ideas. Define what you see as the immediate needs and issues.
8. Don't refer to "how we did it" in your previous district. Be the expert they think they hired.
9. Begin building trust through care, concern, and leadership. Be honest and straightforward with each member.
10. Remember this board is divided and not a smooth working team. As a rookie you are still the CEO—understand your role—establish it early. They hired you to run the district as the main man. You are still basking in the honeymoon halo effect. Use your status with caution.

11. Begin talking about a special meeting this month to set board meeting protocols.
12. Begin with the end in mind, shaping, sharing, and testing issues before they go on the formal board agenda.
13. Make haste slowly! Make only necessary changes immediately. Rather, watch, listen, and wait.

🕐 Time-Out—A So What

1. What would you add to the list?
2. Are there any pitfalls to be avoided?
3. If you are not a superintendent, talk to your superintendent about this.
4. If you are, what do you do to overcome board members' reluctance to meet?
5. List what you do and ask your colleagues what they do. If you are in an appropriate college class or preparation seminar, bring up the idea and get feedback.

Woodson added that these were good points for any superintendent to review once in a while. He continued with some ideas on how to implement these notions.

"For one-on-one sessions, you can meet either formally in your office or have lunch or a cup of coffee, off-site preferably. You need to go slowly, as initially not all board members will want to do this. Only once did I meet two-on-one as a result of the insecurity on the part of one member. I had only two board members in over 25 years that refused to meet with me one-on-one. But that's another story! I will show you later how to maximize this potential as we will say more about your and each board member's communication style. For now, I'll help you look at this through your beginning superintendent's lenses, as foggy as they are now," the mentor said with a smile.

"It seems that there is a lot of ground to cover before school starts," Rob said. "But now I'm curious. What about the two exceptions?"

"The short version or the long one?"

"For now, the short will do."

THE MENTOR'S BOARD STORY

Barry leaned back in his chair, stared at the ceiling for a few moments, thinking what to say, then he related the events as he remembered them.

"Several years ago I'd fired a bus driver for cause—'cause he was a safety risk and not handling kids and parents well. Cost the district two hearings and close to $100,000 in legal fees. Three years later this former bus driver ran for the board. We all said that getting elected was impossible and took it as a joke. But the impossible happened! The joke was on us, and he got elected! Three incumbents didn't decide to run until after he filed. Consequently, they took him lightly and didn't do much campaigning. Two were defeated. However, two of three new members came on board in support of the district and, of course, the superintendent. That made the vote 4–1.

"After a few months the former bus driver decided to meet with me in the superintendent's office. It didn't seem to make a difference. Things got worse, as he was negatively outspoken in board meetings. He was certain he didn't want me as superintendent, especially since we'd fired him earlier! How was this for the obvious?"

"Amazing you survived and lived to tell about it!" Rob chirped, trying to keep a straight face.

Rob's interruption didn't faze Barry. "Finally, he stopped coming in when it was apparent he wasn't going to get me fired, and the board members refused to second his nuisance motions. During the public comments part of the meeting, they all had to listen to his exposés, as well as those he invited to speak. As a result of this, a usually community-friendly board limited all public comment to 5 minutes for each speaker.

"After 2 long years, the next election brought a community activist on the board who was constantly opposing new home development on her side of town. She joined up with him against the administration. Now he had someone to second his motions and for the next 2 years it was a living nightmare. Enter the religious right, of which they were neither! Now even these two had a sympathetic forum as they were used by this new alliance to attack the administration. At this point the superintendent was really fortunate that he could count to three with a five-member board."

Barry paused, looking for a reaction from the rookie.

"I think I can count that high, too," the rookie replied innocently.

"Get off my back! Thinking about it still hurts. We lost all momentum for improving learning for almost 4 years in our reactive protective mode. Playing defense all the time can get to you!"

"Don't get upset with me. You are telling the story!" Rob quipped, trying to lighten things up again.

But Woodson drove home the point. "Now, since you are starting fresh I hope you can count to five, as in 5–0. You don't want to live with this ugly situation you inherited. This is why you will work hard to begin the healing process, of course, with your mentor's help."

"You are my leader and chief advisor for now!" Rob informed him.

"To cut to the chase I did help start a behind-the-scenes campaign to get good folks elected. So the former bus driver was unsuccessful in his reelection and finally, 2 years later, the activist was defeated. As I mentioned, all during this time the entire administrative cabinet was placed in a defensive position to protect the schools and principals from all the crap," he concluded, finally running out of emotional steam.

"That's the short edition!" Rob teased. "I guess we need a couple of hours more for the long version."

🕐 Time-Out—A So What

1. What does this show about trying to communicate effectively with board members?
2. Do you have an incident similar to this in your own experience? How does it relate?
3. What are other dangers that can happen from meeting one-on-one with board members?

"Sorry I got wrapped up in the telling of the tale, but it still brings back a distasteful memory of the wasted time we spent on other issues apart from our main mission of student learning."

"But Dr. Barry, it's right on target for what you had me write down as your one-sentence description of the superintendency. Let me quote, 'To provide for and protect the organization's learning systems and create an environment to maximize student learning and teaching excellence.' That's right, isn't it?" he smiled smugly.

"You left out 'lead'!" Woodson retorted.

"So give me an A– then."

Barry then began to get a little more serious, so Rob listened more intently as if he knew that what was about to be said was important. "This does bring up an area of disagreement in the professional circles. Should a superintendent get involved in school board elections or just let the community send their best and brightest without our help?"

"What's your take on this now that you've been on both sides of this issue?" Rob challenged, not sure how the professor would react.

Barry quickly responded, "I'll cop out!"

"Why's that?" Rob asked.

"It depends on the circumstances. It's situational! Generally, I advise staff to stay out of it. Entrench the mission, core values, and vision so securely in the system so that parents and the community will want only good people on their board. Of course, this doesn't always work out. We got complacent and hadn't yet finished working our mission focus, all students learning, into the vocabulary and infusing it throughout the system. We got blindsided! Even when I mentioned what the first election was going to do to the district, some business colleagues in the chamber of commerce just attributed it to hysteria. They didn't appreciate the fact that I had lived through this in an earlier life.

"Over the next 4 years they recognized what I had been saying was more than true. These things can come out of nowhere and disrupt the organization and its ability to teach. Thank God we were able to keep most of this from the schools!"

"It looks like I may have some similar issues here in Paradise Valley," Rob said.

"We'll work these through, but let me finish because I decided to go against traditional wisdom."

"Before you do—haven't I read about some of the good old boys controlling school board elections over the years as a means of maintaining control and sticking around?"

"It still happens. That's why you need to pay attention to the risks involved." Before Rob could say more, Barry plowed forward. "I decided that with these outside attacks I needed to exert my influence as their superintendent over the past 15 years to keep the ship headed in the right direction—the focus on student learning and quality. I quietly went to war. Surprisingly, a majority of parents and business leaders were now ready to join in. They saw what an embarrassment the board meetings had become."

"So! The correct answer is—?" Rob asked, now more interested.

"Use your judgment. It depends on the circumstances. Make haste slowly. Sometimes you have to make a value decision to either fight or flee," Barry concluded.

"In general the answer is stay out of it. With our core values being violated, I quietly took on the issue of getting good school board members elected. This went against all I had known earlier. In this case I made the right choice, not only because it worked out so well but it had to be done to protect the learning environment!"

"Wow! Quite a tale! Getting back to meeting with board members, ..." said Rob, reminding his mentor where they had been 10 minutes before.

"Why don't you start with the board chair? Explain what you want to do and get her blessing," Dr. Barry advised. "Then once established set this as an expectation. When you do your midyear evaluation you can ask the board members how overall communication is going, including these meetings. Ask them if it's okay."

VISION FOR LEARNING

Returning to other issues, Dr. Barry continued. "There is always more to do than there is time to do it. That's why we are working through this on a priority basis to help you keep focused, trying to use your time both efficiently and effectively."

"Can you give me some help on expressing my vision for learning and other stuff?" Rob asked as he redirected the conversation.

Dr. Barry responded with some emphasis, "You've got to be able to articulate the vision so that people will remember it. Try to keep it simple. It's like an elevator speech. When in an elevator and someone asks what you do, think about what you can say in less than 2 minutes."

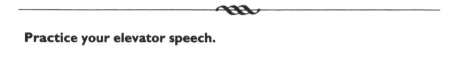

Practice your elevator speech.

"Let's think about what you believe and want people to know about you. What else do you know about yourself? How do others perceive you, what you stand for, and your management style? You need to go back to your basic belief system."

"Sounds like a good place to start. I really haven't thought about it in this context much," Rob admitted. Then he went on to explain that most of his thinking had been confined to graduate classroom exercises.

"I looked over some of the papers you wrote and saw that you frequently address the concept of 'All students learning—whatever it takes.' Do you still believe in the Lezotte and Edmonds 'heresy' of all students having to learn?"

"Yes, of course." Rob said confidently, knowing he had told him this before.

What a dumb question, Rob thought. With federal intervention and enactment of No Child Left Behind along with our state's new push for accountability in student learning, doesn't everyone believe it? Maybe not! Some of the more experienced superintendent colleagues I know are waiting until "this too shall pass." They must figure that with the inability of urban systems to get better quickly the impetus will dry up. There will be too many student failures, especially if graduation standards are going to be part of the picture. Federal standards are higher than or different from most states. The feds aren't giving states the benefit of their own testing and improvement standards. The problem will escalate when too many schools and districts flunk out.

While Rob didn't always agree with the current methods, he sure believed efforts for increasing student learning accountability should be stepped up. Maybe there are elements in this that will acquire account-ability for a higher school performance level statewide.

WHO AM I?

"Okay then! What do you want to say about who you are?" Dr. Barry continued. "You might want to take time to reflect on this. Pull out your notebook." Barry then gave him a few minutes to jot down some notes while he chatted with Diane. He needed a stretch and a soft drink anyway.

Rob thought quickly about some key events that had started him on the road to the superintendency and began writing. He knew he didn't start out to be one, so he titled the journal entry "Now I Am One— Why?"

Should I start when I was in my mother's arms, he thought humor-ously? That would throw Dr. Barry. Why did I go into teaching? After a freshman year at the University of California at Los Angeles I didn't know what to do with my life. I made my career decision to become a teacher during my sophomore year in a small Christian college. It was sort of a calling I felt, so I transferred back to the university. Finally, I earned my teaching credential while I was teaching in a private high school.

I really wanted to help youngsters who didn't have access to good values. By teaching math and coaching them in football and track, I could try to give them a role model to look up to, to help guide kids, especially those who had rough backgrounds. I discovered that I related well with these kids.

Then I started to notice that I might do a better job at leading than some others I saw in high places. That's when I decided to go back for administration classes. Later, I took classes that led to a counselor's cre-dential.

Early on, I pushed my ideas too hard and left for one reason or an-other. I always got promoted to a position of more responsibility. Then I went through the administrative chairs, learning a lot from my mis-takes and those of others, who I observed or worked for. I served under two weak superintendents and a couple of others that had major flaws. I think I wanted to have more control and put what I learned about leading and learning into practice in an entire school system. I felt if I ever wanted to be a superintendent, I had to get a doctorate in school administration. Dr. Barry was really helpful then, both in class and in career guidance.

Finally, I was ready to be in charge and create my own better mousetrap. I started on this path leading to folly and frustration or to becoming a superintendent.

🕐 **Time-Out—A Reflection**

1. Where were you when you decided to become a teacher?
2. What factors led to this decision and why did you make the choice?
3. Now how do you feel about this decision?
4. What about the decision to become an administrator?
5. To what degree have your reasons and values changed over the years?
6. Dr. John Goodlad advocates four moral imperatives: facilitating critical enculturation, providing access to knowledge, building an effective teacher-student connection, and practicing good stewardship. In light of this definition, would you agree or disagree? Explain.
7. How would you go about finding out what you don't know?

Barry strolled back in and resumed where he had left off. "Maybe you had an idealized vision of how you could make a difference. Too often we've forgotten the innocence of those times, our values and roots. Taking this trip down memory lane reminds you of key intervening variables that helped shape growth throughout your career.

"What I would suggest is that you go back and find the critical places where you had to test your values and personal mission, recognizing that these situations are good indicators. They tell you who you are and who you have become. Identifying these now will help shape the responses to the next challenges and decisions and will continue to help you in tough spots.

"Also, reviewing challenging situations that you handled well and not so well is helpful, especially noting why the solution worked or didn't. This is called experience, I guess. Another idea is to think about what upset you and ask why. How did you handle this? We will go over this in more detail after school starts when you won't have so many pressing issues on your plate," summarized Barry as he finished this mini-lecture.

But then he added, "Now why don't you tell me what you want others to know about who you are? Think about your experiences and tell me what's important to you now."

Rob took a deep breath, "I want them to know that

1. I am committed to every child being an effective learner, having the basic skills to move to the next level and then out into the world.
2. I want to make decisions based on the best interests of the students and parents, ahead of administrative convenience of the system.
3. I am concerned about every facet of the whole system, not caring where I hear about problems but committed to having them solved at the lowest appropriate level in the organization.
4. I believe that everyone in the system has to be accountable and responsible for student learning.
5. I believe in excellence in all that we do, but not necessarily perfection."

"That's all?" Dr. Barry teased. "Where did this all come from?"

"You told me to be reflective. Most of this just came together when I was a high school principal. Also, I laid this on the board during my interviews. Just bringing my experience to a new organizational level."

"That's a good starting list. Well thought out."

"I guess I've got a major challenge." Rob ended with a grin. "I'll probably still be working at it when I've been a superintendent as long as you were."

FOCUSING ON PRESENTING YOURSELF

"You've done good work here. Now let's focus a bit on your community reception at the lake next week. Pick the three most important points you want to make," Dr. Barry challenged.

Rob thought for a minute and then said, "I want to keep it simple, but from the heart. First, I want to give them some background and why I chose to come to this community. Second, I want them to know that I believe that each child has the right and opportunity to learn in this system and that learning is no longer an option; it's going to be required. Next, I want to resolve the budget issues, and finally, I'll work toward having an open administration sensitive to the staff and community."

After checking his watch, Dr. Barry looked up. "Good. While it's longer than an elevator speech, it seems to be well focused and simple. Now, let's review what we've covered already."

It was the professor's turn to write, and he tore a page out of his notebook instead of using his favorite writing paper, a napkin.

"Here, take this home, type it up, and keep it with you. These are some more survival skills to be learned as you begin your career as a superintendent." He handed Rob the following list.

Some Survival Skills

1. Know who you are by understanding your beliefs, personal mission, and core values.
2. Identify your predecessor's weaknesses and strengths. (Remember to offset the weaknesses and to emulate the strengths.)
3. Define your own vision based on your own strengths.
4. Know the territory and what is expected of you.
5. Organize what you know.
6. Use a backwards thinking mental model.
7. Set goals.
8. Design measurable criteria for these goals.
9. Decide how to get to your goals from where you are now.
10. Be prepared to articulate your vision anytime and any place.
11. Keep the main thing the main thing.

🕐 Time-Out—A So What

1. Review Dr. Barry's list.
2. Take time to answer these for yourself.

3. Do you agree? What would you add or take away?
4. Do you think this is a good starting point? Why?
5. Keep this list in front of you and observe how you, or how your superintendent, behave against these statements.

"We admire and follow leaders who are honest, forward looking, inspiring and competent."

—James Kouzes and Barry Posner

WHAT ABOUT TRUST?

"And finally, we know the number one thing that followers want in a leader is someone who is honest and is worthy of their trust. Remember, in the game of trust the leader must ante up first.

"Tell people who you are. Be honest and open. You'll figure things out as you go," Dr. Barry said as reassuringly as he could. "Also, don't feel you have to be an expert on everything. Get input from your key people. Listen. Don't be afraid to find or hire those with experience. Use the experts!"

"You're right, I need to go slowly and try not to do everything the first month. I don't want to make any waves at first unless I have a crisis that needs immediate attention." Rob looked overwhelmed. His energy seemed to sag.

Dr. Barry quickly changed the subject, thinking, he's been overloaded. Let's slow down.

"What happened with the conversation with the attorney over his outburst at the last board meeting?" he asked, curious about how it turned out.

"Good news! What I planned actually worked! With your guidance," he quickly added with a smile. "The guy was apologetic when I mentioned that there was a new sheriff in town. He actually wanted to help lessen board friction at meetings. We were on the same page for that.

He didn't realize how others saw him. He understood and would wait for me to call him, if need be."

"Let's hear it for backwards thinking!" Dr. Barry clapped enthusiastically.

NEGOTIATIONS, BUDGET, AND PEOPLE PROBLEMS

"What I would like now is some guidance in setting priorities with the board on teacher negotiations and the budget. The budget is becoming a real problem. The director of finance brings me new budget numbers daily. Each time he comes by there is a $100,000 variance, more or less! I can't get to the bottom line and negotiations are scheduled to start next month.

"The budget final approval is scheduled for the early August board meeting and he just told me he is taking a cruise during the first 2 weeks. This was planned, of course, before his other boss was relieved of duty by the board. I don't think he was involved in much budget planning. The ex-superintendent was really in control of most everything, even rewards and punishment!

"Another thing I thought odd was when the budget director and the facilities director showed up in my office around noon each day during my first week in the district. Finally, my administrative assistant, Diane, told me that she found out they did this because they had been directed to stand by for lunch with the former superintendent every day. I asked her to give them the word that this wasn't the drill anymore. They could go to lunch with whomever they wanted but know that I'm available anytime they needed to talk."

"It sounds as if it was just a part of the old cultural territory that needed instant change," Woodson chipped in.

"I was too busy trying to learn about the district and its problems for lunch most days anyway! But what is this about cultural change?"

"Later. Remember, anything and everything you do will be watched, and sometimes you have to signal what you want in simple ways," the mentor said, reinforcing Rob's quick action.

"Yes, you told me not to make any quick changes, but I'm finding it is impossible to do a budget and settle negotiations without good data. I've no confidence in this director. I'm not sure he can do the job!"

Dr. Barry interrupted, "None of these rules of the game are absolutes. If you have to make a personnel change early in the game, remember that everyone will be watching and wondering, Am I next? You need to do your own assessment of people. Too often some staff members will come to you and try to undermine those they don't like or can't work with.

"If you're going to make a change, you need to lay the groundwork well in a short time. Can you let him down gently?"

"He was promoted from purchasing agent last year. The position is open again. I think I could put him there for a while after he gets back from the trip. I believe he now knows he can't handle the job as I expect him to," Rob explained. "I can also freeze his salary at the current level to assist him in having less to worry about in the change process."

"What do you want to do? Are you ready to make a move?" Dr. Barry said firmly. "Do you have a ready replacement? It's a critical move anytime, but just before finalizing the budget and with negotiations soon beginning, can you afford to do it?"

"I believe it has to be done," Rob said with strong conviction. "I'll talk to him first."

"Think through this. Why don't you discuss this with your cabinet members? Get their take on it. I feel the best way to handle this is with some respect for the individual. Give him the opportunity to go back to his old job. He'll know why, but it will be a face-saving move. You might wait until he gets back from his cruise so you don't spoil it for him."

"Thanks for the advice. Are you sure you don't want to do this for me?" he halfheartedly kidded his mentor.

"I'm not being paid the big bucks! Now that you've solved this major problem, what's next?"

"Barry, did you get the systems thinking model on teacher negotiations that I sent you?"

"Yes, I did. It's a good start. Pretty much complete. Why don't you start putting the plan in motion? Remember, as you learn more and move forward, you can go back to any of the steps and enter the new data and rethink your plans; it's a circular model. This is part of the strategic management notion."

> ### 🕐 Time-Out
>
> Go back to the systems chart (see Figure 2.2) that Rob sent to the mentor about his plans for negotiations.
>
> 1. What would you add that he may have missed?
> 2. Could you do a similar backwards thinking process based on your experience or in a real situation?
> 3. How would this process help keep you focused?
> 4. What advice would you give the superintendent for handling the director developing the budget?

SUMMARIZING ACTION PLANS

As they settled in again with a fresh cup of coffee, Rob said, "Before we leave, let me try to establish some priorities. Some of these items we've discussed previously, but I'll repeat them again. Watch me while I write!" Handing the professor a printed copy of the urgent-important model they had worked on earlier, Rob reinforced and added to it, stating this is the territory as he now knew it.

The Territory Defined: Important and Urgent

1. Dealing with my insecurity
2. Dealing with a split board and my goals
3. Getting a handle on the budget and using this as a prep for negotiations
4. Working through the predecessor thing
5. Determining how to present myself and what I believe in—and maybe even an organized communication plan like we started in my last district
6. Successfully opening school next month

Important and Less Urgent

1. Finding out more about teaching and learning in the district
2. Getting the community's input and involvement in setting the direction for where the curriculum should be directed

3. Developing a long-term, more positive labor relationship
4. Developing a more systematized approach to budget and operations
5. Finishing the first year's systems backwards thinking plan, focusing on the successful outputs we should target

"Yes," Barry replied, "but let me add one or two comments. You've done good work using the model to approach these challenges. You need to think through how you will approach the board to gain its confidence and support. Also, you might want to set some timelines in place and determine who is responsible for doing what."

"These goals need to be part of what you and the board agree to. Are they on the same page about your vision for student learning?"

"I'm not sure they are on any same page for anything!" Rob sighed.

"Well, you now have an opportunity to show them how you are as their leader. You might want to set up a workshop to cover this and a few other things I'll suggest. Check it out with your chair. I'd like to help you both in getting off on the right foot earlier than later," he advised and then reemphasized, "Remember, when in doubt use a systems thinking approach to solving problems."

"Good advice!" Rob replied. "I'll let you know."

"We've done some really good work here," Dr. Barry smiled. "The most important thing is for you to crystallize your vision. I like your focus on student learning. Effective student learning is why you are in this business and the main reason you got the job."

After setting a time for the next meeting Dr. Barry concluded by saying, "Let's save the Important–Not So Urgent for later. Your homework is to begin planning some activities around these goals. Be sure you start getting key staff involved in deciding how to approach the solution to these issues. After all, that's why you have assistants, to do the work," he chided.

On his way out he thanked Diane and said goodbye.

As Dr. Barry got into his car he wondered if there was too much information laid out. But he reminded himself again how important it was early in the game to at least identify those issues that came with the new territory.

Then he remembered a critical situation where he had been hired to work with a second-year superintendent in trouble. After finishing his second year, the guy didn't yet have a clue how the board felt about his performance. He hadn't done much of what Dr. Barry had just discussed with Rob at all in his first year.

The second-year superintendent didn't know that the board dynamics changed when he got two new board members. He didn't even recognize that the board was dissatisfied with his work until he got a midsummer letter listing his shortcomings along with a 120-day notice to improve or else! Six months later they fired him. One day in March the board's attorney came in and told him to move out the next day.

 Time-Out—The So What

1. Write down your belief system about student learning in two or three statements.
2. Walk around your district and identify areas for improvement.
3. Develop a backwards thinking plan and present it to your boss.
4. Review the list of survival skills for working with a board and share with a superintendent or board member to validate the ideas.

SUMMARY

In this chapter emphasis was placed on working with a school board in a new role and district. These ideas should help working with any board group. As mentioned earlier the use of the systems approach and the backwards thinking model elements were used to think through desired outcomes and action plans. The dilemma of deciding when to make change early on was described. When beginning on the job, establishing trust and confidence was indicated as an essential to future success.

A very key point was made about understanding yourself—not only who you think you are, but how people perceive you. This will be developed more in chapter 4, "September."

⏱ Time-Out—Reflections

1. What was a new idea you discovered in this section that you could apply back home?
2. Can you apply backwards thinking to a real situation that would help clarify the issue?
3. With which problems did you identify, if any?
4. How did you handle them?
5. What would you do differently now?

MONTH I—JULY

Strategies and Survival Skills

1. Work with the board
   - Set up meetings with individuals
   - Set beginning evaluation process early in the game
   - Get their support on negotiations
2. Establish your role early
   - You are the CEO
   - Make sure they know what you expect from them
3. Make haste slowly—again a reminder
   - Be careful about changing things too soon unless you have critical problems that won't wait
   - Handle personnel problems with care and class
4. Build trust
   - Involve others in decisions
   - Let them know you
   - Clarify your vision and core values in a clear and concise manner
5. Continue to know and understand the territory
   - Quickly as possible understand the people and issues in this new environment
   - Use the decision and problem analysis models as tools to help in managing the organization

6. Know who you are
    - Clearly understand what you believe in and be able to articulate it in a few short sentences
7. Use others
    - Don't be shy about using or hiring those with expertise, even those smarter than you

TOOLBOX

Covey, P., Merrill A. R., & Merrill, R. R. (1994). *First Things First: To Live, to Love, to Learn, to Leave a Legacy*. New York: Simon & Schuster.

Fullan, M. (1993). *Change Forces: Probing the Depths of Educational Reform*. Bristol, PA: Falmer Press.

Haines, S. (2002). *What Is Learning and the Learning Organization* [Monograph]. San Diego, CA: Centre for Strategic Management.

Kouzes, J., & Posner, B. (1995). *The Leadership Challenge*. San Francisco, CA: Jossey-Bass.

AUGUST: PROBLEMS IN PARADISE

School boards always expect more from the superintendent, especially if what is really expected has not yet been established.

SCHOOL IS STARTING—ARE YOU READY?

In this chapter you will learn to do the following:

1. Set up goals and an evaluation system.
2. Establish meeting protocols with the union.
3. Review the superintendent's role and expectations for school start-up.
4. Define what is important for the staff to know about the new kid on the block.
5. Decide on procedures for administrative cabinet meetings.
6. Learn more about the territory by walking around.
7. Revisit the topic of when the CEO should start making personnel changes.

CATCHING UP

There were scores of e-mails waiting for Dr. Woodson when he fired up his computer. After returning from a too-short Lake Tahoe vacation, he felt like pushing the delete key and dumping them all. After such a great time with his kids and grandkids, it was hard to get focused. But good judgment prevailed. He had a week-old message from Rob. Maybe things had finally settled down in Paradise Valley, he thought hopefully.

Taking some time on his vacation from the tyranny of technology, he did do some thinking about ideas for this week's regular monthly meeting with the rookie superintendent. He believed that superintendents should take work-free vacations without cell phones and e-mail, which he still advocated and tried to practice in his new life as a professor and consultant. Hard to break old habits, but then he didn't want to. They hadn't caught up with each other yet, as he told Rob he would be out of touch during this vacation time.

You don't always have to be available. Turn off your cell phone once in a while. Delegate to a subordinate. Build organizational capacity. Others in the organization should be able to handle emergency problems.

With school starting at the end of the month, he wondered how prepared the Paradise Valley schools were to open their doors? With all the chaos who was responsible? Or did it just happen? How is the district set up to start school, he wondered? If Rob wants to start changing the culture, what he does and says now will impact this greatly.

His mind raced. What do they want to happen that first week? Are they thinking ahead? Does Rob know who is doing what? What should a superintendent with a tight budget be checking on the first week? Where does Rob want to be on opening day? What kind of first impression does he want to make at the before-school teachers' meeting? Of course, the word is out about him already. That's why it is so important to start smart, carefully letting the territory know who you are and what you expect. Now is the time to do some catching up.

Dr. Woodson found he was reliving old anxieties about the first day of school. It was difficult to come off an enjoyable mountaintop experience and focus on this problem-filled valley floor—the Paradise Valley floor.

He double clicked on the first e-mail from Rob and read it carefully. Rob's concerns and insecurities were highlighted by the length of the e-mail.

To: Barry Woodson   August 5

These days and nights have been busy. I can't seem to get everywhere at once. Good things are happening. The board approved Don Halverson as the new assistant superintendent. He's the one I negotiated for during my final board interview. Remember, I told them that one more administrator was needed in the central office. I explained to the board that there were too few administrators to do what they wanted to get done. I used the example of how I had organized my former high school with area responsibilities. Added some of the wisdom we shared in class about school district organization and delegating responsibilities. It worked, of course!

Next, I had a critical problem with a district administrator that surfaced during my interviews and was confirmed by the board chair. I decided to promote this potential problem person as my deputy. Needed to get him out of the personnel office. Gave him an office next to mine. This allows me to closely supervise him and personally watch him work with people.

I better check out the territory before I jump to any more conclusions.

However, he has skills in accounting and budgeting, so I'll have him do the legwork on getting this budget accountability mess sorted out. The change is seen as positive by the board as what he lacks in personnel skills he more than makes up for in business functions.

I picked up strong concerns from teachers and board members about him. Can't believe the board actually made him acting superintendent from April to June 30th with all the complaints from both applicants and employees that they were getting. Giving him the job of straightening out the budget matches his best talents.

I did have to make this critical change early in the game, where you urged caution. He feels good about moving into the superintendent's suite of offices. He had come straight from the classroom, promoted by Dr. Branson 2 years ago to head up the Personnel Department. An interesting promotion at best! Will keep you posted on this one!

Just as you warned, I'm having parents with concerns coming in to test the waters. Although I'm new, I'm smart enough to just listen and play dumb. This is easy! That's a joke! Branson previously had turned down many requests. Many of the issues were handled the way I would have done anyway.

A serious problem seems to be over a split in the parent-teacher group. Most schools are affiliated with the Parent-Teacher Association, and yet five schools have a splinter group of a Parent-Teacher Organization, the one not affiliated with the national organization. I've got some ideas to share about this.

The business manager came back from his cruise and is now the purchasing agent. He seems relieved to be back where he started. It might have been the Peter Principle at work. It makes me more curious about the type of loyalty that was expected by the former administration. Promoting folks based on their loyalty but beyond their capability to do a job often doesn't work too well.

I had to deal with one other personnel issue. The district's public relations person hardly talked to me and she wasn't doing her job. For a small district I didn't think we needed one anyway. Also, she couldn't get over her anger about the firing of the former superintendent and her loyalty to him. Having never worked with a public relations person, I didn't really know how I would keep her busy. After discussing my reasoning with the board members in closed session, the issue was resolved by eliminating the position and giving her proper notice of termination of employment.

I recalled what you'd said, taken from Peter Block's work, that in an organizational leadership change of the CEO the subordinates need to get on board right away. If a toxic relationship builds up early you can expect nothing but trouble! He suggests the subordinate should be the one leaving. Fat chance in most school districts these days!

I made a point to establish with the board that as CEO and superintendent, I expect them to approve my personnel recommendations. If by chance they don't agree, then refer the issue back to me. They have only one employee to evaluate and that's me, the superintendent. If I can keep them in agreement about this, it'll cut down on many problems. I think I established that to not be supportive in this one arena would cause me to rethink our relationship. I need to continue moving them toward a proper board's role and not one of micromanaging. I sense they are looking to me to provide structure to this mess. Kinda letting me run with the ball—at least for now!

These personnel moves, after laying a good foundation, seem to be okay. I got only one negative comment when I moved the facilities planner up to business manager without opening up the position. I didn't want to take the time to advertise with negotiations and the budget mess coming up fast. One board member asked whether we were doing on-the-job training rather than going out and looking for an experienced person. I mentioned that right from the first time I had dealings with him I thought the director could do the job. Since I had some business office experience in my former district, I knew what to look for and I was sure he could do it. Even the former director and purchasing agent agreed he was good and pledged to help him.

I'm getting ready to work with the board on my evaluation. Will you hold the last Saturday this month open for us? Will get back to you ASAP.

That's it for now. I dumped all the notes I had in my journal on you all at once. I feel better anyhow—more later. Hope you are enjoying your trip.

Regards, Rob

 Time-Out

The Peter Principle (Peter & Hull, 1969) is defined as promoting someone beyond the level of his or her competence.

1. What are your experiences with the Peter Principle?
2. Has this happened to anyone you know?
3. How were you affected?
4. How did you feel about the outcome?
5. How did this problem get solved? Or did it?

Even after the mentor suggested that Rob go slowly on personnel issues, he sure moved fast! It sounded like some change was needed. Dr. Woodson liked the way he worked through these issues, trying to maintain the employee's self-respect.

The problem with the woman in public relations must have developed quickly. He hoped that the new assistant and the rest of the administrative cabinet were involved in these decisions. He needed to ask. Since he and the new assistant superintendent had worked together for so many years, they must have collaborated on these kinds of decisions. Two heads are usually better than one and the group most often better than two. Rob had mentioned the new guy was thoughtful and didn't make quick decisions.

He wondered how other cabinet members reacted to Rob's decisiveness. Had his driving style been tempered with some serious listening?

He made a note again to go over effective communication styles with Rob later to see what he remembered.

Barry printed out the first e-mail and then prepared some notes for Rob. Turning to the master calendar hanging on the wall next to his desk, he blocked off the Saturday date. He would plan to use a format similar to one so effective in the past. He hoped this would be an opportunity to do some board team building.

After affirming Rob's handling of these tough personnel issues, he would alert him again to the perils of change early on. Rob should be aware that to go into an area and make change for change's sake is not smart. Some new superintendents believe they have to do so to establish themselves. They may be into power rather than good leadership or just don't know any better. Dr. Woodson listed a few points to cover:

- Can't let the staff influence him to making changes too early in the game!
- Understand the territory and the players first.
- Leave smooth working departments and schools alone.
- Listen and observe.
- Learn when and when not to intervene.
- Readiness and timing are everything!

Woodson was remembering all the training he had had in Situational Leadership with Ken Blanchard and Paul Hersey. He needed to find out how Rob felt about taking some more time to review this material. Maybe he should ask Rob about his doing an introductory workshop for Rob's cabinet members.

As he went searching for a cold drink in the kitchen, he had a sudden thought. He should call Rob right now and get clarity on the board evaluation workshop he wanted him to help with. Didn't want him to get too far in front on the planning yet.

IT'S TIME TO TALK

The mentor picked up the phone and called Rob's private number. "Dr. Moore's office. How may I help you?" came the cheerful answer.

"Diane, this is Dr. Woodson. How are you?"

"Great! Wait a sec and I'll put the boss on."

"Hey, coach! To what do I owe this honor? Isn't this your first day back? How was the trip?"

"I'll tell you more about it when we meet," Woodson responded quickly, as his thoughts turned to something Rob hadn't mentioned in the e-mail. He still needed to cover the workshop planning. "You didn't mention anything on how things were going with you and your staff. What have you done to know the territory better, build trust, and begin to know what's really going on? In other words how well are you putting your listening skills to work?"

"I've been a little busy while you were off playing in the mountains with your grandkids. No rest for the wicked or something," Rob laughed. "What's been going on? Hm. Where do I start? I've been meeting the staff bit by bit. Since our last meeting I've met with each of the central office administrators and supervisors. Told everyone that I would probably cross sacred hierarchical lines and talk to some of their subordinates with key assignments."

"How did that go over?"

"Don't really know, but I'm doing it. The word is out, so I'm sure that they know I'm just asking them about what they do. I'm also asking if they have any suggestions. I've asked the cabinet members how meetings were going and mentioned how I expect them to participate. I do want staff that contributes at meetings. Then I asked them to start thinking about school start-up," Rob said, then paused for a minute.

"Sounds like you're working at getting to know the territory," his mentor said, complimenting the rookie.

"At one of our meetings, when I introduced Don, I asked them to give us a rundown on each principal. That was helpful. None of the principals had a formal evaluation last year.

"As soon as principals reported back to work this summer, I've been going to each school, getting a tour, and finding out what their issues are. I'm cueing them in on school start-up by asking what they've done in the past and then sharing my thoughts. I'm telling them more about me and how, for the most part, I want to keep their problems at their level. I don't care where I hear about problems or issues but will work to have them solved at lowest possible level in the system. I reviewed where I thought we were on teacher negotiations and asked them about union strength at their school. Many of them knew about the budget issues. They couldn't get answers from the 'head shed' either. I mentioned that I had some ideas I wanted to share after school gets started. Started laying the groundwork for higher student achievement," he summed up. "Does this sound okay?"

The mentor smiled a smile somewhere between agreement and amusement, remembering his own early anxieties. "Of course! It sounds as if you are managing by walking around. And you don't need my okay. Just keep up what you're doing. It's part of the territory. Only one question; are you listening to what they're really saying?"

"Yes, I think so. I know you think that I can do better in this area," the rookie added thoughtfully.

"Good. But I need to go over some of your thoughts about the workshop right now," he replied, changing the topic back to the reason he had called. He asked where Rob was in his thinking about his evaluation.

THE EVALUATION PROCESS

"Barry, I have decided to set up my evaluation accountability issues and processes soon. I know there are literally scores of things a superintendent does, but as you suggested I might want to focus on a few priorities. Things I can realistically get done this year."

Dr. Barry agreed. "I think that's a good idea. You could take everything from your job description and list at least 50 things you are supposed to do and it would miss the real target. After 6 weeks on the job how do you see the fit between what you want your performance focused on versus what the board expects?"

"Well, I was about to tell you," he said, chiding Dr. Barry for interrupting. "The areas I want to start with are those that we outlined in May. Remember we listed . . ." Rob then began to read the list he had on his desk.

1. Be continued on the job.
2. Bond the board into a positive working force with the best interest of kids as a priority.

3. Assess the current budget, find some money for salaries, and increase the reserve.
4. Successfully finish negotiations and begin working on developing a win-win model.
5. Working through the principals, begin to review the district's commitment to learning and determine the level of commitment by the schools, administration center, and parents.
6. If needed, develop effective administrative training and staff development programs that would lead to creating a learning organization.
7. Continue planning for the new elementary school funded from the construction bond measure passed in May.

"Good," Dr. Barry said. "What procedures are you setting up to get where you want to go? Do you have the end in mind?"

"Kind of. Now I have the board's agreement to meet on the last Saturday morning this month to put the content and process together. Of course, I had to tell them that you would be happy to facilitate this." Then Rob added jokingly, "But I had to lie a bit in my build-up of you. Told them you were a superstar!"

"Great thinking! Now I'm dead in the water with that endorsement!" Dr. Barry said, a little tongue-in-cheek. "In spite of the build-up I think I can put together a process that will examine their expectations and establish a process and a procedure for the year. It will culminate with positive year-end success!"

"If you can guarantee it, go for it then," Rob replied as if he really believed all the baloney.

Refusing to acknowledge the remark, the coach continued, "How do you want to start? Are we set for the last Saturday?"

"Yes, I've done the groundwork with the board."

"Rob, let me outline what I think will work. But first I need the board's permission for a simple survey before we start. This should help get us talking when we meet."

"What are the questions?"

Barry said, "First, I like to ask why each one decided to serve on the board. Then I ask the following continue, more of, and less of questions:

1. What do you like in your relationship with the superintendent that you want to see continued?
2. What do you want more of or want him or her to start doing?
3. What do you want him or her to do less of or to stop doing?

"This is effective for a reason. I start with the positive, what's working well now, and then move to the helpful, what you can improve on or start doing. By the time we get to the stuff they want you to stop doing this more negative list is pretty small. In the short time you've been with them there may not be anything on it," he explained.

"Will they have enough information this early?"

"Good question. I'll expand it so they can apply their responses to how they see what's going on in the district," Barry said, after reconsidering Rob's suggestion.

"Send me the forms and I'll get them to the board."

"No, let me go directly to them. It keeps me looking more impartial. Have Diane send me their e-mail and mailing addresses."

"No problem, she'll send them along with the consultant forms needed to keep the business office happy. You know, so you can get paid!" he quipped.

"That's a great idea! See you next week," he said as he hung up the phone. He was pleased that the superintendent saw the importance of getting all this in place.

A few days later he got another e-mail and thoughtfully digested it.

To: Barry Woodson   August 8

I've got good news and bad news! I'll tell you the good news first—the budget bottom line is now in place and I know where most of the money is. My newly promoted deputy is working hard trying to get the accounts up to speed. They're not even closed out for our fiscal year that ended June 30th. It's a mess! I still remember your advice that the quickest way to lose your job is to make a big mistake in the budget and financial side of the house. Luckily, he is doing a thorough job.

We are going to set up a special board meeting next month to let them preview the budget and our new accountability system. Here we are 2 months into the school year and we don't have an approved budget!

I keep hearing rumors that my predecessor was a financial genius. Some folks now think we should have two superintendents: one for business,

Branson, and the other for instruction, me! At least it's not the "get rid of Moore and bring Branson back" that I heard last month. They can't let go of the past yet. After we dazzle them with a balanced budget in September, this too may start to go away.

Of course, you recall that I inherited the former superintendent as a teacher this year. The board's attorney told them last April to rescind his March dismissal from the district and reassign him to teaching. We've teamed him with a middle school teaching partner. Don't know if he can teach or not! He came to Paradise Valley from the military business side. Don't want to hurt the kids too much!

Also, I've been up front with the teachers. I am going to let them look at the same budget numbers I've been working with and build trust by anteing up first, as I remember you saying.

And yes, I'm ready to present at the all-teachers' meeting before school starts.

The community picnic social and get-acquainted event went well. I got a sense that they were looking for someone to take charge and stop the in-fighting among board members. A few indicated that there was nowhere to go but up! Seems some want a strong referee to stop the squabbling. The folks were both optimistic yet tired of the crap that had been going on. Of course, these basically were the allies, the supporters.

All five board members showed up. Maybe this is the beginning of the healing process or they didn't want any one-upmanship. They were compli-mentary about me so far. I heard how they believed they outmaneuvered each other to select me. The story is that, since they didn't trust each other, they pretended to like another candidate even to the point of starting off to visit her district 125 miles away. On the way each side said they provoked the other about this lady, so they came to visit me and some community folks in my district later that very same day. My former district was closer anyway. That day I was at the state capital in a meeting. My secretary finally found me. Luckily, at the airport I got the last stand-by seat that would get me home in time. Called my wife to inform her we were going to a dinner interview at the downtown hotel.

I don't think I mentioned that in my first board interview one member was missing, so I hadn't met him yet. At dinner that night I didn't know which side each was on. I assumed that the chair was one of the majority members as she was just named chair after the March elections. Undoubtedly, on a

3–2 vote. The chair suggested that my wife sit between two of the men. I finally came to realize that these were the bad guys and ultraconservatives supporting Branson. All went well as they left that night to go back into closed session in the district. The next day they called offering me the job. And I eagerly accepted. Later, each of the two said, while they didn't like the way Branson was treated, I was their guy and to expect their support.

Now I just have to get through the lawsuit, endure a recall election, and unite a divided board. Then maybe I can begin thinking about student learning. It reminds me what I learned from Maslow's hierarchy of needs. The need for satisfaction at lower levels must be met before one can expect the individual or organization to move to the next level to finally reach its potential.

As you remember, the need levels are as follows:

Physiology—food, water, air
Safety—feeling secure, trusting (this is where I think we are)
Social—affiliation
Esteem—recognition
Self-actualization—becoming all that you can become

Without a sense of security and trust in the people-side of this equation, I'm not sure how I can succeed in rebuilding the organization.

I'm almost reluctant to bring this up after all the help you have given me. Can't seem to figure out the people I work closely with sometimes. A few years ago I had a problem or two directing the work of one of my assistant principals. I thought I was clear on directions, but he never got it right. I figured if I told him and trusted him to do the task it would get done. Never did figure it out. I think they understand what I'm asking them to do, but sometimes they don't appear to get the work done the way I want.

And now with Diane, she seems to be friendly one day and not the next—stays quiet and just answers yes to everything for a few days and then is back to normal. I'm so busy I hardly have time to listen to her concerns. She is very efficient, but the educational vocabulary and system is somewhat different than the business world. Being an assistant to the CEO and defining this role are new to her. I'm depending on the office clerk to help her learn the ropes and get to know the district way of doing business. I just can't find time to deal with this now.

I would like to review with you the way you handled your administrative cabinet meetings. I don't really have a good model to draw from. My old boss was somewhat disorganized and without much of an agenda. Mostly we listened to him complain about the schools and some of the principals. My first meeting didn't flow as smoothly as I hoped, even though I thought I was ready. I think I need a strategy to get each cabinet member to participate more. Of course, with only a few meetings under our belts, they are still cautious about me. I have met with them individually and had each tell me what they were doing and why it was important. It seems much was put on hold during the interim, waiting for a new boss to be hired and come on board. My new assistant attended the meeting but remained quiet. He likes to watch and observe before he commits.

My wife and kids have talked me into letting our athletics-oriented son finish his senior year at his current high school. I plan on getting an apartment in the district. I'm going to ask Don if he wants to double up as he's faced with the same situation. And it would help with the expenses. What do you think?

Finally, the meeting with the teachers' union leader went better than expected. We established an agenda, starting with developing an agreement on the protocols for negotiations. I talked about trying to start slowly and setting up a way we could test the trustworthiness of each party. We're then going to have the group look at ways we should conduct the meetings. We started with the end in mind. This backwards thinking model may work. Using models seems to make the process a little less emotional and gives us a framework to fall back on if it does get heated. I'll review this with you when we meet.

I know this is long winded again, but I'm in the swamp up to my waist in alligators and need someone on dry land to help drain the swamp or at least throw me a rope by letting me sound off some.

Regards, Rob

 Time-Out

1. Should the superintendent live in the district? Make a case for your decision.
2. What would you do first in trying to build trustworthiness with the teachers' union?

3. What would you do to convince the naysayers to forget Branson? Or would you try?
4. How relevant were Rob's thoughts about using Maslow's hierarchy? Explain.
5. Why is he having trouble with his new cabinet?
6. What would you suggest to solve this problem?
7. What do you think is going on with the communication issue with the administrative assistant?

Barry Woodson thought about all that was going on. "I need to focus again on the more urgent and important matters. Rob has never been through this before. It doesn't seem like he had very much helpful district office experience in his previous job. Must have been limited to the Instructional Services Department and was not as broad and comprehensive an experience as I first thought."

For Barry, getting school started efficiently with teachers teaching the first day was most important in establishing the learning environment. He believed there was no reason not to be ready to start teaching on day one. He wondered if Rob saw this the same way. "Hope Rob knows there's a big connection on how others see the first day's learning to what the leader believes is important. Is he walking his 'All students learning' talk?" Barry mused.

As he thought through all the updated information Rob had mentioned, he started to make a list of what he could do to guide Rob. First, he would have to use the important-urgent matrix. They may need an all-day meeting to get everything done!

He needed to ask Rob how he expects to manage his cabinet meetings—the protocols and procedures. This is important to get set right from the start. He wasn't sure what the superintendent's management style was. Did he lean more to the democratic participatory side or more directive and autocratic? It didn't sound like Rob was as well organized as he thought. Setting meeting times, agendas, how decisions are going to be made, developing the board agenda, and so forth need to be reviewed.

They needed to always go back to the list of priorities set in June to see if Rob is on track or needs to adjust. He must keep the main thing the main thing as he tries to resolve all these unplanned "opportunities."

The mentor knew that he would need to ask about Rob's feelings toward the job now after such an exciting introduction into the superintendency. Was he recording his reactions over this busy first summer as he had committed to doing?

THE MONTHLY MEETING

Rob and Barry were once again in Rob's conference room. There was plenty of coffee. With this long, complex agenda, they needed both the whiteboard and the two flip charts stationed ready to use at the front of the room. They could put in writing the development of ideas and record next steps.

After spending time on prioritizing the agenda items, they decided to start with the board workshop on his evaluation—Rob's top goal for survival.

On one of the flip charts Rob listed the agenda items they had decided to cover this afternoon. On the other chart he wrote at the top, "To-Do List." He drew three columns headed by "What," "Who," and "By When." They would record their planning decisions on it.

PLANNING THE BOARD WORKSHOP

"Now let's get to the main issue I forgot to put on the agenda. Are we okay for the last Saturday?" Rob asked hopefully.

"It's on the calendar."

"Did you get any surveys back yet? I urged each of them to get right back to you."

"Not all of them. Once I get the remaining two, I'll work them into the agenda. But basically, I'll explore what they want to hold you accountable for this year using a more open-ended approach."

"With the recall election officially in place for February, I should have a strategic plan to survive a potential loss of up to three members. With these work plans in place, I'll have a better opportunity to persuade any new members that I know what I'm doing right from the get go."

A single change in a board seat changes the dynamics of the group.

"For a rookie—good thinking! I had a similar experience that forced me to improvise and come up with some practical strategies. We can work specifically on this project when we know who's running for the board seats later in the year. Remember that a single change in a board seat changes the dynamics of the group!"

"In the interim you want to continue the role as peacemaker, unifying the board as much as it can be. I must admit that you're off to a good start; you got them to agree to the 1-day workshop," he added

"Where do we start our planning for this project?" Rob asked.

"What should the ideal outcome look like? What do you want to happen?" Barry threw out as a challenge to get Rob leading the conversation.

"I want to establish a board-approved annual work plan and develop a process containing evaluation criteria, processes, and timelines. Can you do this all in one day?" he asked skeptically.

"I don't think we will be able to cover everything. I'm anticipating that with the board disharmony it will take me longer to process," Barry replied without much surety. "So what is the next step?"

"Now you're testing me. I have the answer, of course. How do we know when we get there?"

"Well?"

The superintendent paused for a moment to get his thoughts in order and then he replied, "I see the accomplishment of this effort as a completed written evaluation process adopted by the board, by 5–0, I hope. Then we need a superintendent's evaluation format developed that we can all live with. I would like to have a goals document that I can have the board approve either in October or possibly November. My thinking here is that as I take this idea to each department, I'll ask them to give me their top five targets for the year. After the cabinet helps to prioritize these, I'll work to incorporate them in the document. I'm thinking about adding a section for expected board performance. That's a little scary, but it may need to be done. What do you think?"

"I'm amazed at how well this flowed off your silver tongue!" his mentor said with a smile. "At least the first two steps in the backwards thinking process seem to be becoming a habit now."

As he stepped back from the creation of their new masterpiece Barry asked, "Does this make sense to you? Tell me more about the board members. And are we going to have enough time?"

"I hope I can persuade them to adopt this 8 a.m. to 4 p.m. Saturday schedule with a working lunch," he said with a mixture of assurance and hesitancy. "Do you think there's enough time to develop the content of the evaluation and have it ready for adoption at an October board meeting?"

Barry took a moment to think and then replied, "Probably not! At least we will have done a planning-to-plan process, laying out the work to be done and leaving the hard work unfinished. After we listen to what they need, then you get to take the ball and run with it. We'll have the format done, and then it's up to you do the heavy lifting, filling in the holes. Work it through with them. I can guide you, but I won't own it. You and the board will!"

"I'll make it a top priority—no, I guess it should be the top one for survival," Rob said optimistically.

"Are you sure? In my experience with other well-meaning superintendents, it's kind of an out-of-sight, out-of-mind thing. More urgent matters, such as getting school started, seem to get in the way of planned tedious work. I can push you to meet the timeline we come up with at the workshop if you need this kind of support. We can negotiate for leadership style support depending on how hard you want me to push. It's important that you accomplish enough of these goals to have significant progress by, say, February or March, with the final year-end wrap-up in June. Will this work?"

"I can't see any problem yet. Keep pushing on this evaluation process. This I really don't like to do, so you have permission to bug me about it! But heaven knows there's a lot to do the next few weeks."

"Good! Let's go for it. I'm pleased you are starting off this way. It's the continuation of building trust and openness. They hired you for your expertise and this gives them an idea how you want to be united on district direction. Remember—sincere feedback is a gift and you seldom go wrong considering it as just that! I even gave a small gift-wrapped box to another superintendent as a symbol to use with his board when we were working on this same issue."

"Let's move on," Rob suggested as he looked first at the long list of agenda items on the board and then at his watch. They needed to speed up some.

GETTING SCHOOL STARTED

From the agenda, Barry wrote on a flip chart, "Starting school issues"—what should Rob expect and inspect? He thought that Rob needed to emphasize what's important about student learning at least.

Dr. Barry quizzed Rob some. "You wanted to review getting school started? Why do you need my help on this? Weren't you involved in your previous district?"

"I need some help here. In my past experience we did the schedules, got the place cleaned up, issued text books, and started when the bell rang," Rob said with a smile. "We helped principals prepare. We had before-school in-service meetings. But I can't say we were too well organized. Now I'm the main man responsible. I don't need chaos on the first day."

"Okay. Let's go to A-B-C-D-E thinking again; what are your expectations, wants, and hopes? Tell me what to write."

"Let's see," he pondered, "I want to focus on student learning and have an organized start. I need data to balance budgets, balance classes, and hire or release temporary teachers, among other things."

"Rob, in your case it might be very important to signal that you have high expectations for student learning. Remember I mentioned that Peter Block told us in a workshop once, 'In order to change the culture, you start changing the conversation.' If you want to make a case for learning, then the principals and staff need to know this. At the before-school meeting I would suggest telling them you expect each teacher to be teaching when the first bell rings. You want principals to be out on campus and visiting in the classrooms. You will be assigning district office staff to support each school's needs before classes start. And you will personally visit each school on day one," he said with emphasis, finally winding down.

Rob hemmed and hawed a bit as he absorbed this, and then he mentioned the things he thought were important. He got out his markers and wrote this list of outcomes on the board:

1. Schools physically ready before school starts
2. Teachers teaching when the bell rings
3. Good experiences happening for kids on the first day
4. Don't want kids wandering around during class time
5. Minimize student class changes at middle and high schools
6. Temporary teachers notified of their status as soon as possible

Barry and Rob spent 20 minutes processing each of the objectives.

"Now, what are you going to do with all of this?" Barry inquired.

"Let me give this some thought. I'll share it with the ad cab and put something together."

"Let's put some of our action plans on the to-do list," Barry said, going to a flip chart. He sketched out the following:

What	Who	By When
Talk to ad cab about school start-up ideas	Rob	Monday's mtg.
Schools physically ready before school starts	Ad cab	Day before school starts
Teachers teaching when the bell rings	All adm.	First day
Good experiences happening for kids on first day	All	Continuing
Don't want kids wandering around during class time	School adm.	First day

Classroom observation	District office staff	First day
Temporary teachers notified of their status	Dir. personnel	ASAP
Minimize student class changes 7th–12th grade	Prin./couns.	Review in Nov.
Develop a class-change tracking system	Counselors	Review in Nov.

Barry added, "Using this model, take all this work to the ad cab for them to review."

"Not a bad way to track decisions and action plans," Rob observed.

"I still am old-fashioned enough that I like to see these on a flip chart or screen. An alternative is to have someone with a computer type the list, print it, and send it to each player. I like to put the flip chart up at the next meeting to review progress. All can see it. It encourages completing tasks. If and when schools are completely networked, each member can see the information on screen. It can probably be put on a Palm Pilot."

They talked some more and decided that Rob was off to a good start, and he now needed to discuss this with his cabinet for modification and to add any new ideas. It was a good blueprint for planning. Then the principals needed to work through the steps to make this happen. By this process Rob could answer the A-B-C-D-E model's question— Where are we now? Getting the support of those involved is an essential part of the success of any organization.

They decided it was time for a break. Rob went to check on messages with Diane while Barry grabbed a soft drink from the machine.

🕐 Time-Out—So What

1. Explain why a school's starting smart makes a difference.
2. What did they leave off the list in starting school that you would add?
3. How would you approach your principals to begin the conversation to change the culture? Or would you even try?

> 4. At the all-teacher before-school session, how should Rob present his expectations for first-day teaching without upsetting them?

UPDATE ON NEGOTIATIONS

When they returned, Rob started off. "Next, let me fill you in on negotiations. We've agreed to try a more informal approach. We will start by processing how we want to conduct ourselves in our sessions. Establish meeting protocols. Don will process this for the group. He's new enough so he's not carrying any baggage. Usually he gains trust fast. We'll talk to the union and show them the budget. We will try to work the language issues first and then the big money issues," he explained. This seemed to be going well, so Barry decided not to comment further and went on to another item.

CABINET MEETINGS

"You wanted to review some ideas about working more effectively with your cabinet," Barry reminded Rob as he reviewed the posted agenda. "What are the issues?"

"They are all waiting to see what I'm going to do or say. They seem gun-shy or maybe it's me."

"Have you told them what your expectations are for the part you want them to play in managing the district? Did you explain how they would be participating in decision making?"

"I used the first few meetings to go over crisis issues that we were facing. As I look back I think I was doing most of the telling and not enough listening," he concluded somewhat hesitantly.

Suddenly he realized that he hadn't shown much confidence in them. The composition of the group had changed and, therefore, the dynamics of the relationships. First, he had promoted Peter Paulson out of the personnel office, making him his deputy superintendent. Next, he had promoted Doug Daniels to business manager, and Don Halverson was now effectively on board. The only holdovers were Dr. Susan Jameson in elementary education and Larry Ramirez in secondary. Out of five, there were three carryover players, but one of these was in a new position with a perceived bigger title.

"No wonder there is confusion at times," Rob admitted as he explained this to his mentor. Since there was not any one best way to organize the district, this would have to do for now. Maybe as they get bigger this will change. And Pete's future is still in doubt.

"Coach, can you believe that I've been so busy I haven't even recognized the effect on the cabinet of these group changes? What a dummy!"

"Okay! You are a dummy. Feel any better now? Let's work on the task of what you might do now," Barry said.

"Why don't I listen for a minute?" the rookie suggested, unsure of where to take the conversation.

"Since we're not going to solve all the world's problems here today, let's brainstorm some ideas and remember what we know about decision making," his former professor suggested. "I have some ideas to start with."

"You start and I'll add," Rob encouraged Barry, as he started to think again.

"Since each cabinet member is responsible for a major function, modeling good meeting practices should filter down into each of their own group meetings when they have them. I think I'll go to the board and write down some ideas," he said.

"You forgot that the deputy doesn't have a group. He's still part of the team," Rob interjected.

Not reacting to the obvious, the mentor began to write.

- How are decisions going to be made?
- How will the team know how you are going to decide?
- How will the agenda be made and who will do it?
- How will the agenda be arranged?
- Will there be time limits for discussion?
- How will decisions and action plans be recorded?

As he stopped to think whether he'd missed anything, he decided to talk through these points with Rob.

"I used what I thought was good practice before. I had each member bring in agenda items they wanted to discuss or get a decision on," Barry said.

"That's a good idea. If you have them come prepared to put their items in the decision matrix we discussed earlier, you can sort out the ordering of the most important and urgent. You can have them put an estimate of the time needed to process each of them. Then you might have them decide whether it's an information-only item, whether they need a decision, or whether they want help in solving a particular problem."

The rookie thought this was a good start and then asked, "How is this done?"

"One person could be a time keeper, another the facilitator, and one the recorder. If you use the to-do chart like we did, then someone needs to record decisions, responsibility, and deadlines. This could be a responsibility for Diane, and at the same time she will be more aware of what's going on in the district. Assign her to make sure you follow-up. These cabinet roles can rotate depending on who is presenting an item."

"I need to let them know that I'm in charge and the buck stops with me!" Rob said in a defensive tone.

"Robert, they already know who the boss is!" Barry reminded him sternly. "You only need to signal how you are going to let a particular decision be made. Either let the group decide, let them make recommendations for you to consider, or you decide with their input. Another option is to announce your decision and ask for their help in implementing it. These variations we can discuss later. In fact, I have an old chart somewhere where these variations are listed, from complete leader-made decisions to those totally group made.

"I didn't mean it to sound how it came out. I'm concerned that, with a new group, giving them all this leeway I may be giving up too much control," Rob said in defense.

"Remember something we reviewed in class called Situational Leadership? Well, I think we should review it again sometime soon. I believe this model along with Social Communication Styles are two basics that any good leader needs to incorporate into management practice.

"So much for the lecture! Let's talk about expected behavior among the players. Here I would suggest you use the group to decide on the way they want to interact. One idea I've used before is to ask them to write down the behaviors they like to see in a perfect meeting. Write the results on a flip chart. Then do the same for a poor meeting. From this comparison you will be able to develop your own protocols and meeting norms. It should give permission for any group member to raise his or her hand for a time-out to ask whether the rules previously agreed to are being violated."

"That sounds really good. I believe I have enough to start working with the team. If I bog down, I'll get in touch. Let's take a break before we tackle the rest of the agenda. This is really tough start-up work. I didn't realize the learning curve would be so steep so soon!" Rob exclaimed.

🕐 **Time-Out—Another So What**

1. Explain why a well-organized meeting makes a difference to you.
2. List the characteristics of a bad meeting and those of a very good one.
3. How would you resolve the issue of the superintendent's need for control?
4. What would you add to these ideas that would make the cabinet meetings more effective?

After returning to the conference room they decided to pick up the pace. It was again obvious to each that they needed to split this session into 2 days. But time was short. They could continue for another hour before they had to adjourn.

SCHOOL BUDGETS

The school budgets were out of control. Money was going to the schools irregularly at best. Barry and Rob discussed a plan from Rob's former district called Personnel Staffing Units (PSUs). It gave the principals more local control. Rob decided to talk more about this after school started. He didn't want to change too much too soon and wanted his staff's support.

The coach thought he got a glimpse of Rob's leadership style. "Wants to give principals more control. An interesting contradiction?" wondered Barry.

As they finished this item, the professor said, trying to keep Rob calm, "You look a little frustrated. Don't think you have to find instant solutions. This gives you an opportunity to put a good system in place. Crisis management allows for a direct approach sometimes."

PTA VERSUS PTO PROBLEM

"By the way, the PTA thing worked out. Met with the ladies that were fussing. Asked them what a desirable outcome would be. They wanted only one organization. Using my influence as a 'honeymoon' superintendent, I got them to support the PTA program for now. The PTOs reluctantly acquiesced after I asked which group was state and nationally affiliated. I added my successful experience working with PTA and assured them I would come to their districtwide leadership meetings," Rob said with a sense of accomplishment.

"Good work! You're beginning to think with the end in mind," Barry said proudly.

PERSONNEL AND BOARD

Changing direction, Barry moved on to another agenda item. "I was impressed by your conversation with the board about one of your core beliefs—that of expecting support on personnel recommendations. And reinforcing that they are to evaluate *only* the superintendent!"

"My former boss got in trouble when the board started messing with personnel. I decided I needed to take a stand here," he said with some intensity. "I'll have to do a good job, and if I do screw up, admit it, and solve it, even if I have to let my mistakes go on to other pastures."

Looking up at the clock, Barry thought they had covered enough for one day. "Rob, since we have only one more agenda item, let me suggest that I send you a paper I wrote on how we used the communication styles stuff in the old district."

ADMINISTRATIVE ASSISTANT COMMUNICATION PROBLEM

"But let me ask more about your relationship with Diane. Getting any better?" Barry asked.

"Some."

"What I might suggest for the time being is that you spend more time with her. Acknowledge her need to work with people more. She's sensitive to keeping peace in the family, I believe. And she's still learning. Not until she gets through this full year together with you will she understand the scope of the job. Sound familiar? You are learning together, so be patient. If you are interested after you get the communication material, we can work out a more specific plan to effect a better working relationship."

"Let's call it a day. I'm putting your assignments on the to-do list and expect you to get it done!" Rob chided his mentor. "We have the date for our workshop set and our next meeting in September is on the calendar. Anything else?"

"Well, you avoided my toughest homework assignment."

"Which one?" the superintendent responded, somewhat unbelieving.

"Did you forget the suggested review of the backwards thinking planning for the goals you established in June?"

"Not really. Four hours ago I snuck them in the planning for the board workshop when you weren't looking," Rob said. They both were tired enough to laugh about this oversight.

"I guess I knew you'd been too busy to do a lot of planning these past weeks. When the timing was right, I had faith that you would get to it. It's hard to stay focused on planning when you're new on the job. Or again, just think about that famous cartoon punch line, 'When you're up to your backside in alligators, it's hard to focus on draining the swamp!' I just visited the Everglades and this has a sound pictorial meaning."

They chatted some more as Rob walked Barry to his car. He was pleased to be able to talk with his mentor. It is a lonely job at the top. The buck really does stop with him.

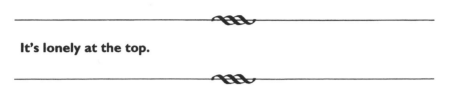

It's lonely at the top.

The mentor's thoughts were on his homework. Most of the material on social communication styles was in his briefcase, but he decided the timing wasn't right to give to the superintendent today. Rob would need some time to digest it before they went into specifics. He thought about how good a tool this had been in the past. Rob might be interested in trying out the program with a small group to see if they liked it. Maybe it could be introduced in a cabinet meeting and then be used to help Rob apply the learning in the situation with Diane.

THE BOARD WORKSHOP OUTCOMES

The board and superintendent workshop was held as scheduled. It went pretty well. They answered the question of where Rob and the board want to be at the end of the year by identifying key goals and knowing how they will get there, Phase A and B. Using the feedback questionnaires, Dr. Woodson took them through a review of where they thought the district was at this time. He then helped them lay out steps to get there. Rob shared the model of the work for negotiation planning he had developed last month so the board would better understand how the backwards thinking process worked.

The follow-up to this workshop was that Rob would submit his goals and work plan to the board at their meeting either in October or November and have it approved publicly. He would ask the various departments to contribute to it. As the superintendent, he would select the six goals that were identified as the highest priorities and the most critical along with their measurements. A second section in the document, reflecting the input from departments, would be included as part of the work plan for the year.

They agreed on a midyear evaluation date scheduled for the first week in March because they were late getting the process started for this year.

At the first meeting next June, he would publicly report the year's progress. Following this public report, he would ask the board members to complete the evaluation forms they had outlined for later development. It may take two or more meetings. The evaluation instrument they developed was in two parts. Part I was the board's most important measure of how well the six goals they agreed to were met. In part II the evaluation was performance based and contained these subjects: board relations, educational leadership, personnel relations, business and facilities services, community relations, administrative services, and personal qualities. In a review of board policy, they found mention of these areas, and the board wasn't ready to give them up yet.

Thinking ahead to the February recall election with its potential change in board membership, Rob thought any new board members needed to see the full scope of his duties and responsibilities. He was proposing that each of the sections would have 5–10 descriptors that defined these areas. A place for comments was included to support the "Exceeds Standards," "Meets Standards," and "Needs to Improve" marking areas.

He would informally share progress with the members when appropriate. When they completed a major step or completed a change, he would be sure to make the point in the write-up on the board agenda. Following this, Rob and the board would meet with a facilitator's help to review the process, format, and progress made, culminating with a written evaluation for the superintendent along with a recommendation to extend (or not extend) his contract.

⏱ Time-Out

1. What do you think the problem is with the administrative assistant and the superintendent?
2. Tell about a time when you couldn't seem to communicate with someone in your organization.
3. If you were able to resolve the communication problem, what did you do?

4. Review the superintendent's evaluation process. How would you improve upon it?

SUMMARY

In this chapter a number of situations were presented that needed to be resolved. The main idea was how to get started with the board in deciding what the superintendent's goals would be for the year. Emphasis was placed on the importance of getting a system in place that should prevent surprises in the superintendent-board relationship. There was a comprehensive review of situations that could and did actually arise during a first summer.

Working to get a better understanding of the district through the insights of the principals was encouraged. Examples of protocols on how to work with the cabinet during meetings were presented. Issues of changing personnel early on, teacher negotiations, a messed-up budget, and ideas about school start-up were covered.

The use of resources and models to help clarify issues and processes were identified, including more of the backwards thinking process; Maslow's hierarchy; and the continue, more, and less of analytical model.

Finally, the importance of working to develop trust with the board and staff was emphasized. Developing trust by understanding the issues and resolving each with a good strategic management approach was demonstrated.

⏱ Time-Out—Reflections

1. After you have considered the issues described in this chapter, what do you find relevant to what you could use on the job? List and discuss.
2. Describe the degree to which the situations and resolutions presented would help you survive as a new superintendent.
3. Think of the three most important things you learned in this chapter.
4. To what degree will they affect your thinking and behavior?

5. What do you agree strongly with or disagree with? Use this as the basis of discussion with a colleague.

6. How would you improve upon what they worked out this month?

MONTH 2—AUGUST

Strategies and Survival Skills

1. Don't need to have your cell phone on all the time.
   - Build organizational capacity. Assign, train, and allow others in the organization to handle key decisions and emergencies when you are not readily available.
2. Be clear with the board on where you want to draw the line between their job and yours.
   - If you want to set guidelines on personnel decisions, early on is good timing. Continue to help them understand the differences by using school board association material, workshops, and opportune events. Remember, this is situational—don't push if they're not ready.
3. Continue to keep the board well informed.
   - Anytime you are contemplating a major change to things, let them know first. In particular, in working with personnel, let them know your thinking. They're going to hear about it, so tell them first. When unusual or emergency situations arise, tell them about it before the local reporter does. Be sure they hear about a crisis before *60 Minutes* shows up.
4. Listen to dissatisfied parents and others who didn't feel they were treated well by the former administration.
   - Doing this will help you learn more about the territory and let people know that you do care. Be aware of the consequences of early commitments.
5. Establish your board-approved goals, your annual work plan, and your evaluation now. Don't put it off.
   - Avoiding these creates more difficulty than almost anything else. While addressing them doesn't assure success, it does give you a way to keep the board focused on what they approved.

6. Don't be fearful of using outside experts and proven management models to integrate into the systems thinking and practice.
   - There is an art to the integration of working models and solution strategies and you should be able to explain them in 10 minutes or less.
7. Continue to seek to understand board group dynamics.
   - Think about how changes in board membership can and will change the board's behavior. More about this in chapter 9, "February."
8. Effective meetings with staff define your leadership abilities.
   - Be sure you can apply the best thinking for group interactions. You need to model what you expect others in the system to do in their own meetings.
   - Plan regular one-on-one meetings with principals.
9. Infuse your beliefs and values in others, especially when given the opportunity or having created the situation to do so.
   - While sudden change in the first year isn't advocated, use any opportunity to clarify how you expect the business to be conducted.
10. Remember to continue to understand the system as a system and consider using a decision process that starts with the end in mind.

TOOLBOX

Block, P. (1991). *The Empowered Manager: Positive Political Skills at Work*. San Francisco, CA: Jossey-Bass.

Hersey, P. *Situational Leadership Material*. Center for Leadership Studies, 230 West Third Ave., Escondido, CA 92025. www.situational.com.

Hersey, P., Blanchard, K., & Johnson, D. (1993). *Management of Organizational Behavior: Leading Human Resources*, 6th ed. Englewood Cliffs, NJ: Prentice-Hall.

The Ken Blanchard Companies, 125 State Place, Escondido, CA 92029. www.kenblanchard.com.

Maslow, A. (1962). *Toward a Psychology of Being*. Princeton, NJ: Van Nostrand.

Peter, L., & Hull, R. (1969). *The Peter Principle*. New York: William Morrow & Co., Inc.

4

SEPTEMBER: LEADERSHIP AND YOU

Leadership is the only thing that really differentiates successful organizations from others over the long-term.

—Stephen Haines

SHOULD YOU BE A MANAGER OR A LEADER?
ANSWER—YES!

In this chapter the following questions will be addressed:

1. *What is it you need to know about being a leader?*
2. *Is there a difference between leading and managing? Does it make a practical difference?*
3. *What do followers want in their leader?*
4. *Are you managing your folks appropriately for the situation?*
5. *Do you understand and are you using models that should become part of your leadership system?*

CATCHING UP

"Is Dr. Moore in today or is he out playing golf again?" was the inquiry Diane heard when she answered the phone about 9:30 on a sunny Tuesday morning in September. "Who is this nut?" she thought, and then it dawned on her.

"Yes, this is the time he plays golf on Tuesdays and Thursdays. He's authorized me to handle all the crank calls while he's on the course, Dr. Woodson!" She smiled as she recognized the mentor, even though he was speaking with a tone lower than his usual cheerful upbeat one.

"I thought I could get you, but you're too sharp! Is the man in—and more importantly, will you put him on the line?"

"Of course, your misbegotten humor brightens my day," she replied, laughing out loud. "I'll put him on. He's working on his superintendent-board goal project for a few minutes between appointments. He's trying to organize the feedback he got from the cabinet."

"Barry, I didn't think they allowed cell phones in your golf cart. To what do I owe the pleasure of this call? To check up on me? I probably need it," Rob gibed Barry, since Diane had clued him in on the attempted humor.

"I hadn't read about any disasters when school started last week, so I thought I'd check in to see how it went."

"Let's see, 2 weeks from today we're scheduled to go over the big stuff, so let me fill you in on a couple of things," Rob said thoughtfully as he tried to quickly recap what had happened since they last met 3 weeks ago.

"Speaking of big stuff, remind me to tell you the big-rock story some time," Barry offered.

"Why not now?"

"I would like to hear what's going on first. That's more important," Barry said.

"We got school started. The kids showed up! So did the teachers! I was pleased to observe teaching right from the start in more than half of the classrooms I visited. This was consistent from the reports of the directors assigned to cover schools. However, two and possibly three principals weren't listening when the directions were given, so some of those teachers, among others, didn't know I was serious. I'll chat about this with them later.

"Along with the help of the assigned district office (DO) administrator, the principals got the campuses and classrooms in good shape. Parent feedback, while limited, was highly complimentary about teaching and seeing some homework on the first day. I was especially pleased at what I saw at the two high schools where I spent some time. The counselors and administration had things well organized with all the kids in class and not wandering around on campus not knowing where to go for help. Even the freshmen didn't look too lost."

"That sounds great! Seems you have a little work to do on effective communication," the mentor said playfully. He was happy after hearing the good news from Rob. "Starting out on the right foot is important, especially if you're sending a message that learning is imperative under the new leader."

"I agree," said Rob. "I believe a critical need is to focus on the schools and what they are doing to improve student learning. After I found much of the system in disarray due to a limited focus and weak leadership, making any change, especially improving teaching and learning, will take a lot of energy and time to make a difference. I need to put this on the long-range agenda for sure."

"I think this is important. But you aren't going to save the world in 1 day. Let's talk about a strategic design we can launch later in the year," Barry suggested.

Rob said, "I am not impressed with the principals' level of understanding about leadership and management. They seem to just react to issues more often than use proactive thinking and planning. For example, in discussing opening school with a little more purpose as you shared with me, some wondered why change? The kids will show up and so will the teachers. It will work! No sense of what school is all about. I'm probably generalizing this now, but it's there. Most of the time this is okay, but I know there is much more that can be done. So I'll want to review what you did to turn your district around."

"I can do that. It wasn't easy and it took time. Lots of time and selling people on the mission," Dr. Woodson replied.

"I'm still a little miffed about the lack of uniformity in the principals' support in opening school," Rob said. "I'll need some ideas about getting my directions across to the reluctant learners. Each seems to have responded to my friendly guidance differently. It may mean different strokes for different folks. I need to look further into this."

⏱ Time-Out—A What

Rob had some problems with getting some of his principals to respond to his friendly guidance.

I. Describe what you think might have happened with the principals in failing to respond to the direction given. List some reasons for their not listening to him.

2. Was Rob fair in drawing the conclusion he did from the directors' reports? Why?
3. Explain what the phrase "different strokes for different folks" means to you.
4. What steps do you think Rob should take at this point in handling the principals who didn't seem to get it?

"Thank goodness the plan for opening school worked," Rob continued with relief. "I don't think I would have considered such strong a position without guidance. It did get the staff's attention and I—."

"What I suggested," Dr. Woodson interjected to slow Rob down, "worked for me in the olden days, but these were your plans and your thinking. Good job! When you said there were a few problems opening school in your previous district, I realized that you needed to get off on the right foot. By the way, how does the board feel about the first day?"

"They were impressed, well, three of them were. They had asked if it would be a problem to visit schools on the first day and I gave them the okay. I think they might have been cautious after I suggested that they step back and give me a chance to manage. The staff needed to see me as the leader. I suggested strongly to the principals that, with the political situation such as it is, they should welcome board members and personally escort them around. I wanted feedback if any member of the board tried to put the principals in the middle of things. You know the role definition, 'provide for and protect'; I want to keep the principals from the political mess. It also sends a message to them. Keep focused on your business, and I'll handle the board."

"That's good thinking!" Barry squeezed in.

"Remember, a few got more money for their schools because they kissed up to Branson. I still don't know where each stood during this political mess. I really don't want to know. They just need to get on board as quickly as possible and show support for their new leader. Still, there are divided loyalties out there and also in the DO. This first year I don't want the board members going around the new CEO on issues. I'm going to make sure that they know what I expect," Rob said.

"That's good. This is the time to clarify expectations," Barry replied. Rob got this idea pretty well, he thought, but he'll have to be careful when and what he "clarifies," because it will help set the patterns of behavior for a long time to come. "Just be careful that you tread lightly and smile as you hit them with the big stick," he said aloud.

Rob then told him how well the special board meeting had gone in presenting the balanced budget. The board members each got a 4-inch stack of paper to go through. The deputy superintendent did a great job in putting it all together. In fact, he helped Doug Daniels, the newly promoted business manager, learn more about the budget accounting process.

The subject then moved to the teachers' contract. It was a done deal pending the necessary approvals. The parties had agreed on a 3.5% salary adjustment, covered the inflationary costs of fringe benefits, and made some insignificant changes in the contract language. The teachers got a fair settlement and promised to meet with the administration throughout the year to try to find some middle ground to work on. The teachers were to vote Friday and then the contract would go to the board for approval the next week.

The board had agreed to give the administrators the same financial deal, so that would be on the agenda as well. The two classified unions were waiting to see what happened. Historically, they had followed the lead of the teachers' union. Don Halverson, the assistant superintendent, was to meet with them to resolve their issues.

"I'm glad I called. You probably haven't had time to play golf," the mentor observed.

Rob wasn't sure of the sincerity of this comment and reacted with some indignation. "Dr. Woodson, sir, as a matter of fact one board member told me in front of the others that I could play golf as much as I liked if the work was done! For the record, Don and I played one round 4 weeks ago. I can't fathom when I'll be free to play another. This work will never be done!"

"Rob, I was just teasing. While you seem overwhelmed now, set time aside to have fun and don't forget your family still needs you."

"I've got to run now. Have a meeting with the bean counters. I'll send you an e-mail about the agenda for our next meeting." As Rob hung up, he did realize that a lot of good things were happening so far in spite of his inexperience. It was good to have someone outside the system to talk things over with.

PLANNING THE SEPTEMBER MEETING AND REFLECTIONS

As Rob sat thinking about this month's meeting and the agenda, he began to lose himself in his thoughts, looking back to signing the deal last May. The first question that came to mind was, Is this where I want to be? Did I really want to be a superintendent? I'm getting along with the board and I like being able to guide the work. The board seems to have called a tentative truce, at least during board meetings. That certainly is a relief! At least they seem to be giving me a chance to referee their interpersonal junk. Yes, I think I made the right decision to be one! The recall and the lawsuit are moving along. Keeping the board's attorney away from meetings helped. The community has calmed down, too. My one-on-one meetings with board members are helping me understand them better and they me. The two so-called ultraconservatives are even more supportive now. It's scary and challenging, but I am beginning to make some headway. I guess I need to report this to Barry as I agreed to when we set up my personal goals last June.

At least the budget is in good enough shape to start some real accountability. Fortunately the district has enough money so that accountability, or rather lack thereof, isn't an immediate problem. But this is going to change soon! Negotiations have worked much better than I thought possible. Starting on the basis of trust made a difference. Now, to maintain trust when we get into serious and tough discussions will test my limits.

I want to review the seven goals I set up in June. I've got them in my top drawer.

1. Be continued on the job.
2. Bond the board into a positive working force with the best interest of kids as a priority.
3. Assess the current budget, find money for salaries, and increase the ending reserve.
4. Successfully finish negotiations and begin working on developing a win-win model.
5. Working through the principals, begin to review the district's com-

mitment to learning and determine the level of commitment by the schools, administration center, and parents.

6. If needed, develop effective administrative training and staff development programs that would lead to creating a learning organization.

7. Continue planning for the new elementary school funded from the construction bond measure passed in May.

I think the first four are in good shape. However, the fifth one, the district's level of commitment to learning about the real mission isn't going anywhere yet—the main thing again.

Also, I need to chat with coach Barry about the communication style stuff he mentioned to improve staff effectiveness. It could help all of us to understand each other better.

While I am somewhat reluctant to bare my soul, I know that in the game of trust the leader must ante up, or declare, first. I need to show that I can be part of the team by being a full participant in training events. Barry mentioned that often in companies it was only middle management that was trained. The CEOs seldom if ever participated.

I think the last topic on the list from our meeting in June, the planning of the new elementary school in the urgent-important scheme of things, while important, has to wait for a while. Too many higher priorities now. The business manager can begin working with the architect on this issue and just keep me informed. I've never been responsible for building a school before and I don't think Doug Daniels has either. I'll need to ask Barry to brief me. I think 20 schools were built on his watch.

After he got back from his meeting with the business office directors, Rob e-mailed the agenda to Barry.

Dear Barry,
Hope the following will work. Let me know soon.

The Agenda

1. Dealing with the reluctant learners, my three unbelieving principals
2. Have a better understanding of leadership theory and practice
3. Assessing what we need for administrative training

4. Discussing my feelings about the job and board relations
5. Progress report on the goal-setting process
6. How to begin the process of improving student learning with the principals
7. Building a new school

Regards, Rob

When Barry Woodson got the agenda, he decided to review what he wanted to say that would help Rob on numbers 2 and 3. The prof seemed to be concerned about how to proceed. There was so much written about leadership in the field, so much in fact that it was hard to integrate it into practice. To bring simplicity to a very complex issue, maybe he should reach back to his own experiences and share how he had tried to sort this out. Putting 30 years of discovery into a 2-hour session would be challenging. While keeping on target, a brief "highlight reel" may be a way to review what's needed.

THE SEPTEMBER MEETING

Dr. Woodson had been doing a lot of thinking as to what a superintendent and CEO should know about the fundamentals of leadership. Actually, he had learned by trial and error that the important thing to know about leadership is how to apply the principles of leadership necessary for the job. He had been able to create an integrated set of ideas, bringing together much of what he picked up outside the field of education. His studies in the applied behavioral sciences in the business world opened an entire new vista for him that had a profound impact on his school organization.

How do I pass this on to a new superintendent? he pondered, as he found a parking place right in front of the restaurant. There is so much. KISS, he thought to himself—keep it simple stupid!

"I thought a long lunch at the cafe where we first started our meetings would work for us today," Rob said as they were led to the large table he had requested. This would give them room to spread things out if they needed the extra space.

"As long as you didn't mind the drive; it's good sometimes to get out of the district. This will work just fine. I brought some material for you to look at later. Why don't we order and get right to it," Barry suggested.

LEADERSHIP THOUGHTS

As they sat down, Barry started out by asking Rob a question before they went on to the prepared agenda. He felt that Rob was more interested in dealing with his management team than doing the agenda line by line. "What have you been thinking about your leadership abilities these past few days, or have you had time?" he probed to open up the topic.

"What do you mean? I'm the leader now. At least the board says so," he responded with a smile. He wasn't sure how serious his mentor was.

"What I mean is that, yes, you have a legitimate position as CEO. In one sense you are the one in charge, the leader, but does that in itself make you a leader?"

"I know you are going somewhere with this line of questioning, so why don't you just tell me what you're trying to say?" he responded with confusion in his voice.

"Let me put it this way, I've known superintendents who've had 1 year's experience 30 times! They just repeat marginal practices, don't know how to lead, and in some cases can't or won't. At best, they didn't understand the components of effective leadership. They do what's natural for them without giving it much thought. And most times natural isn't good enough. Yet many of these folks survive. When they wear out their welcome they just move on. It's almost like coaches in professional athletics. After they get released, they just sign on with another team and repeat the same experience until they wear out their welcome again."

"I've worked for one superintendent that was like that," Rob interjected. "I learned more of what not to do than to do. It was ugly!"

"School boards wonder what happened to the leader they spent so much time on hiring. What went wrong? Where did they go wrong?"

"The Paradise Valley board didn't make that mistake, did they?" the rookie asked, wondering what his mentor's comments would be.

"Not so far," Barry said with a frown, putting Rob on. Then he got serious again. "If you plan to stay the course you must understand the system, its environment, and how to lead it or cause the leadership function to blossom through your subordinates. This includes teachers and leaders in the classroom. Master teachers are usually great leaders."

Rob thought a minute and then answered, "I'm getting a clearer picture of what you are trying to get across. But I've had courses at both the masters and doctoral levels in this stuff. I'm not sure it was something I remembered or was too practical as I think about it now. I probably learned a few how-to skills—the basic mechanics of the principal's job at least."

"That's par for the course in most cases. There's not too much taught in leadership training in many doctoral programs that you can take back to your district and apply. This is especially true about an in-depth understanding of what I'm trying to get across to you." Barry observed.

"I think I'm a good leader based on feedback from my past experience. Generally, I get along well with people. As a high school principal, I ran a good shop and as assistant superintendent I did good things and helped students, schools, and teachers become more productive. What else is there?" he challenged his mentor.

"There's a lot more to it than that if you want to succeed. I think we have some work to do in this area. I hope I can help you grow and develop more as the year progresses. It goes back to the thought, what do you want to do for kids to make them *all* successful," Barry said.

🕐 Time-Out—The What

If leadership starts with you, then can you answer the following?

1. How well do you know yourself?
2. What do you know about your leadership style?
3. What do you know about the major schools of leadership thought?
4. What meaning can you get from studying leadership from a historical developmental view?
5. List three positive characteristics in leaders that you would want to work for and three negative ones you wouldn't want to be associated with. Explain.
6. How do you work with others in giving them direction?
7. Describe what it means to be a successful follower.

Rob continued to question his mentor. "What I'm getting out of this is that I need to make sense for myself out of the complexity of all these leadership theories and find practical tools I can apply to the job on a daily basis. How am I going to pass this along to my folks if I'm not clear on it myself?"

"Remember, a theory is just a proposed explanation whose status is still conjectural, in contrast to well-established propositions that are regarded as reporting matters of fact. A lot of our leadership and management authors are describing what they observe and then draw generalizations from the data," Barry said.

"Do you think I need an elevator speech on this? Something that I can articulate to my folks?"

"Maybe not just one, but remember that to lead you need to know about yourself first. As superintendent you must be able to explain to the troops what is important for them to know about leadership in working with you."

"I've been too busy trying to survive to do much thinking about this. Keep pushing me," Rob said, frowning and looking somewhat overwhelmed.

"Remember, in class we reviewed the work of a number of experts in both leadership and management, sometimes too briefly from a historical point of view, or as a special focused topic assignment. I think my bias at the time was around the use of textbooks with long lists of admirable traits and desired attitudes, which supposedly you needed to adopt to become a school administrator. They never included walking on water and leaping tall buildings, but they could have. The fact is, as a rookie, you were hired to lead just the way you were. That's what the board got in the deal. It's how you grow and develop in the position from now on that counts and is your responsibility."

"I guess they saw something they liked and thought they wanted in me," Rob said, feigning a hurt expression on his face.

"Rob, obviously they did. Now let's get on with it. When I was training with Dr. Paul Hersey at the Center for Leadership Studies, he used the metaphor of picking, one by one, different single-color strings of yarn hanging from a ceiling and weaving them into a whole fabric. This integration process was unique to each individual and had to work for that person as he or she picked from the many colored strands of leadership yarns. No pun intended!" he was quick to say.

"You mean I have to learn a new trade," Rob said with a teasing smile. "I don't weave well!"

"You'd better start soon. It might be helpful for you to understand where you are now and which strands you need to first add to your leadership mosaic. Let me tell you about my experience as I struggled to figure this leadership thing out. It only took me a lifetime!" he said as he took a sip of water.

"That will really help. I've forgotten much of what you covered before. And, of course, it wasn't important then as it is now on the new job. Wish I'd paid more attention. Getting the degree was the only focus!"

"I don't expect doctoral students to remember anything after they pass their comps. Well, maybe for a week or so! At least I didn't! Just an idea here and there!" Barry replied. "Did you integrate any of this into your own thoughts about leadership? Are you actually using these ideas as part of the way you manage?"

"Barry, I especially liked the stuff you introduced about leadership being seen as situational and how you used this to help you more effectively direct the work of the district. You mentioned, as I recall, that having the boss provide structure when needed as well as support at the appropriate time helped people. Another factor was that you used that model as a filter for all the other 'new' leadership programs you were bombarded with over the years. You indicated that too many new programs requiring change don't take into account the readiness level of the individual or group, therefore creating a real unfortunate mismatch and often failure. I think about trying to use it every once in a while, but I don't remember the model well enough."

"I can fix that, the expert that I am," Barry kidded Rob. "When you have the time we can do it not only for you, but for your key staff by introducing them to the idea of continuous learning and change."

"Well, I try to learn from my mistakes, so reviewing this won't be a problem."

"The art of leadership is the integration of necessary concepts into a consistent way of doing things, starting with a clear definition of what is meant by leadership."

"For example?" Rob said.

"If I tell you I believe that *leadership* in general is anytime one attempts to affect the behavior of an individual or group regardless of the reason, what would you say?" Barry said, giving the definition he liked from his Hersey and Blanchard training.

"While I think I'm okay with it, is it enough? What comes to mind is someone like an Adolph Hitler or Saddam Hussein. They were leaders by this definition! And I don't think the definition fits, because of that."

"Did I say anything about the quality or purpose for this event? So yes, Hitler and Hussein were leaders, but up to no good and downright bad guys!" he said with strong emphasis to make the point. "When I try to capture the definitions from prominent writers in the field, they usually add that it is directed toward a goal or objective achievement in a given situation. Even this doesn't make leadership good or bad, because if the purpose is immoral then the result is also. We're talking about its use for the right reasons."

"That makes more sense."

"Before I forget it, Hersey and Blanchard define management as a special subset of leadership. They say, 'management is the achievement of organizational objectives through leadership.' Now I'm leaning toward a different practical understanding, one more operational. What counts is how effective and efficient the leader and organization are in both the short and long run. What I'm going to tell you next, you haven't heard before. I just came across a set of tapes from Dr. Ichak Adizes called *Adizes Analysis of Management*. After coming to the United States from behind the Iron Curtain, Dr. Adizes went to work at UCLA's Anderson School of Management. Ken Blanchard gives him a nice intro at the beginning of the tape series."

"Is there a way I can get a copy?"

"Sure. I have an extra I'll bring next time," he said before returning to his thoughts. "Adizes describes the role of management as making decisions and implementing the change. To survive, the organization must become effective and efficient in both the short and long run. He defines effective as making good decisions that work in both time frames. The efficient is defined by 'is the decision cost effective, timely, worth the effort, and lasting?' again in both the short and long haul. There's more to it than this and when we get to styles training I'll fill you in."

"That all sounds interesting. I don't have time to go into another year of study, but the tapes will help," Rob said, trying to interject a bit of humor into this too-serious sounding conversation.

"I agree. But you can get an education by listening to the tapes as you drive to and from work on the days you commute. A couple of hours a day just to listen and reflect. But I'm actually trying to set the stage for you to consider starting out with one or two plans to use in a very practical way to help your people manage better. You have most of the technical skills, but learning how to better use human skills in the workplace is a major leadership improvement task for everyone."

"I remember that usually management functions were defined as planning, organizing, motivating, and controlling. However, I still keep wondering about this difference between management and leadership," Rob said, reflecting on what he had just heard.

"I picked this up somewhere along the way about leadership," Barry said. "Learning to be a leader is somewhat like learning to be a parent or a lover. Your childhood and adolescence provide you with basic values and role models. Books can help you understand what's going on, but for those who are ready, most of the learning takes place during the experience itself. Another wit said that learning how to lead a school district is like learning how to play the violin in public."

"There's a lot of truth in that. And I'm not a musician either!" Rob laughed at the thought.

"In my way of thinking, the writers on this topic get confused with the words *managers* and *leaders* and *management* and *leadership*. The majority seem to think that there is a clear-cut difference in what a leader does and what a manager does. Or what the art of leadership and the practice of management are. There may be a case for this in theory, but in a practical way it's not worth worrying about. Yet as a school superintendent, you not only have to lead, you have to manage. Peter Drucker is credited with saying that managers do things right and leaders do the right thing (Covey, 1989). I like what I've used before: great leaders do the right things right! Using Drucker's statement, several authors add their wisdom seemingly without much analysis of the real meaning and impact of the words. To limit the functions of leading and managing to these clichés is nonsense!"

"Barry, you are starting to get emotional about this," Rob teased, to slow things down. It didn't faze Barry as he rolled right along, ignoring the interruption, and continued to debunk conventional wisdom, saying, "It seems one 'expert' coins a phrase and then it gets parroted without any real thinking to determine whether it really makes any practical sense."

Great leaders do the right things right most of the time consistent with their vision and mission.

"To suggest that managers never do the right thing is preposterous or, for that matter, that leaders always do the right thing. In my opinion there are leaders in every level of an organization in our business, even teacher-leaders. Each and every one has to learn to manage the assignments given to us as well as provide leadership for our subordinates and the organization itself. We often have to lead upward in the organization. The bottom line is that great leaders do the right things right most of the time consistent with their vision and mission. Sometimes extraordinarily well! So from now on let's use the terms interchangeably. It's not worth the time to debate. Identify the skills you need to do the job better and work on those first to be sure competency is attained. You will become a lifelong learner, setting a role model for your team."

At this point it was time for a break. Barry asked the waitress for more coffee, while Rob checked in with the office.

Rob jumped right back in as soon as they were seated. "Barry, uh, I forgot to mention that I really messed up with Diane the first week of school."

"A convenient memory lapse, perhaps?" Barry observed. What now he thought? "Tell me about it."

"I blew it! There's no other way to say it. I was frustrated about not getting the first-day information out to all the principals. I jumped all over her for forgetting two of the schools. This really got her upset. Two days later, I found out it wasn't her fault. Her office assistant had left the names off the mailing list."

"How did she behave after the blow up? I bet I can predict it!"

"The phone call to the office just now reminded me of her pouting behavior. After 3 weeks she's just staring to come out of it."

"I'm not surprised! Let's continue and I'll make a note to talk about a way you can learn to deal with different communication styles effectively. You've heard me say this before and we need to get on with it before the relationship really gets in trouble," Barry said.

"That works for me. Now, why don't you put some other ideas together that you used as superintendent so that we can review those later. I really want to pick your brain on these ideas, but not today. I need to get my feet on the ground first."

"Okay. I'll put some ideas together and send them to you."

REFLECTIONS ON REAL PROBLEMS

About this time Dr. Woodson realized he might have gone too far too fast, but he believed that a better understanding of the concepts and tools available, properly used, makes a significant difference.

He then asked Rob, "Tell me again about the problems you are having with your folks."

Rob thought about this for a few minutes and then replied, "Well, we've already talked about the business manager, the communications person, and my new deputy. I mentioned the two principals and their 'forgetting' to make teaching a priority on the opening day of school. These were not the ones we didn't send the packet of materials to.

"Then in a principals' meeting, a seasoned veteran took me on over a site-based management issue that I was describing. We had a give and take for about 10 minutes. I found out later that this friendly confrontation was misunderstood by some of the others and my passionate exchange intimidated them. I enjoyed the friendly debate, but it didn't come across that way. I really respect the principal for challenging me. Reminded me of myself in that role. Now most of the others are afraid to speak up at meetings."

"Sounds like you need to work on your bedside manner. You need to realize that some people are intimidated with seemingly loud verbal exchanges. But don't stop the debate. Explain yourself. After the social communication styles material sinks in this will become clearer," he said.

"I guess I still don't realize the power of a new leader. The perception of power, at least. I've learned that I have to deal with their insecurities first. I need to be more careful on how I come across in meetings or I won't have anyone to follow my lead," the superintendent wisely observed.

"Learning how to become more productive in communication relationships may well become a major training issue for you and your team. Through training and practice we can get you all on the same page. If you want to get into this soon, then we need to decide right away. If we use a computer-generated response format, then I need to make arrangements with the publisher. It takes 4–6 weeks to set up the diagnostics. I can do the training and feedback in 1 day with follow-up later," Barry said. He then quickly described the Social Style Program.

"This sounds good. We can talk costs later. I think we can handle it. But for now I want to get back to the Situational Leadership stuff you are so high on," Rob answered expectantly.

"I'll tentatively put the communication Styles program on the calendar for, let's say, November."

"That should work," Rob replied, thinking ahead to a workshop he was planning with the principals and cabinet.

"Putting Situational Leadership and Social-Style training too close together will confuse us all, if they aren't separated by a month or so. They can be integrated, but it's too hard to conceptualize for the beginner. You need to learn and practice each set of skills separately before trying to do too much integration."

"At this point in time, let's keep it simple," Rob pleaded.

"Keeping this simple then, let me give you a quick review of Situational Leadership in 10–15 minutes before we get back to the main agenda. But before I do, let me suggest that we consider putting your management team through a briefing on this first as we previously discussed. I would like them to understand what this all means, and how it can be most effectively used. It can be a beginning for team building, skill building, and learning a new organizational vocabulary for safely describing behavior."

"I'm okay with this also. We just can't overload them too soon—or me, for that matter. I agree that we should use this one to help with team building first. But I want to go over the model now to see if that's really the best place to start," Rob said cautiously.

"Okay, then."

"Barry, I remember at one of our first meetings at the cafe you said something to the effect that if you couldn't describe the essence of the concept in 10 minutes after two cups of coffee—or was it two drinks in a bar on a napkin?—no one would remember it well enough to use it in the workplace. I assume that was an exaggeration?"

"First, I don't want to be quoted as doing business in a restaurant that just happens to serve drinks stronger than soft drinks," Barry stated. "But the simplicity element must be there. Basically, it's all common-sensically organized!" he said, a little defensively.

THE SITUATIONAL LEADERSHIP MODEL AT WORK

"Let me begin discussing the Situational Leadership concept. The value in the training is that your own self-perception of your leadership style is described. If you choose, there is a way to get feedback from others on their reality about their leader. Now you have data you can work with, even if it deals with perceptions. But that's how we operate much of the time in real life."

"That seems to be a good starting point," Rob said.

"The model describes the relationship between the leader and follower, with the leader giving directions to the follower about how the work or a task should be done. This ranges from giving explicit directions and closely checking on results to discussing the task and letting the follower run with the ball with only casual monitoring."

"Situational Leadership teaches you to put your brain in gear before your mouth starts."

—Dr. Paul Hersey

"Their model uses the two independent variables so common in many models. In this case they are the style of the leader, from directing to delegating, and the readiness of the follower to handle the work or task, ranging from needing a higher level of direction to lower direction as relationship behavior from the leader increases. It is easier to draw this (see Figure 4.1) and then I can explain it."

"That's fair enough."

Barry explained that the Effective Leadership Styles model theorized that the curvilinear function moving through each quadrant represents the best fit between task-relevant maturity and appropriate leadership styles to be used as followers move from low to high readiness. It's really face validity.

Task behavior is defined as the extent to which leaders are likely to organize and define the role of the members of their group. Basically, it explains what activities each is to do and when, where, and how tasks are to be accomplished.

On the other hand, relationship behavior is the extent to which leaders are likely to maintain interpersonal relationships between themselves and members of their group. This is done by opening up channels of communication and providing social interactions, emotional support, psychological strokes, and facilitating behavior. An example might be when someone does well on a new task making sure it is recognized by a specific comment—"John, you did well directing the meeting. I especially liked the way you allowed each one to speak without being interrupted."

Remember, the behavior of the leader is still the focus at this point. However, the authors, as well as Posner and Kouzes, point out that there is no leadership without a person or a group to follow the leader. Reminds me somewhat of the game of follow the leader we played as kids. We had to follow exactly what the leader did. Probably not totally good advice today.

To complete the relationship between follower and leader, the characteristics of the follower need to be described. This element can be defined as either the maturity or readiness of the follower to do a specific task. Maturity or readiness is defined as the capacity to set high but attainable goals, willingness and ability to take responsibility, and the level of education or experience of an individual or a group. Readiness

In using Situational Leadership, keep in mind that there is no "one best way" to influence others. Rather, any leader behavior may be more or less effective depending on the readiness of the person you are attempting to influence. The following model provides a quick reference to assist in diagnosing the level of readiness, selecting high probability leadership styles, and communicating styles to effectively influence behavior.

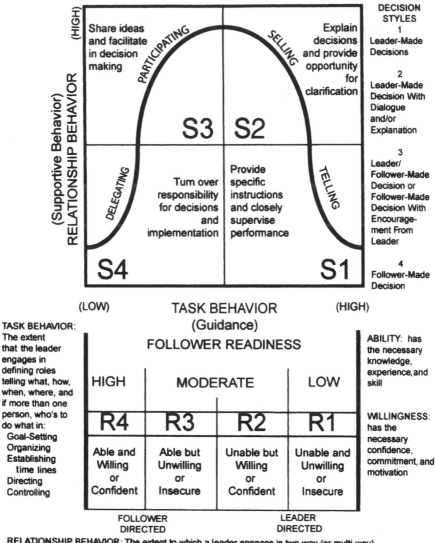

Figure 4.1. Situational Leadership.

Source: Hersey, 1985.

of the follower is made up of two components. Simply stated, the first is willingness and the second is ability. Ability is the knowledge, experience, and the skill that an individual or group brings to a particular task or activity. Willingness is the extent to which an individual or group has the confidence, commitment, and motivation to accomplish a specific task.

In the Effective Leadership Styles model, the maturity or readiness box is designed to describe the follower as mature to immature or more ready to less ready to do a specific task.

Barry took up the conversation again, "To understand how to use the most effective or high probability leadership style, we first must start with the diagnosis of the readiness level of the follower."

"I see and hear what you're saying about this model. But how the devil does it work?" Rob asked, somewhat confused.

Barry reached in his briefcase and handed Rob a copy of the completed model. (See Figure 4.1.)

Rob saw that, to determine what leadership style is appropriate in a given situation, a leader must first determine the maturity or readiness level of the individual or group in relation to a specific task the leader is attempting to accomplish through their efforts. Once this maturity level is identified, the appropriate leadership style can be determined by constructing a right angle from the appropriate readiness box on the continuum that represents the readiness level of the follower to a point where it intersects the curvilinear function in the style-of-leader portion of the model. The quadrant where that intersection takes place suggests the appropriate style to be used by the leader in that situation with the follower at that readiness level.

"Let's go back and recall how you handled the communication person's situation. How would you see her readiness level from what I've just shown you?" Barry challenged Rob.

"Well, looking at the model I guess that she was an R3, able but unwilling."

"If you draw a perpendicular line to where it intersects the leadership curve, you will find that you are in the S3, or participating, quadrant. This suggests that you needed to focus on the relationship and should have tried to find out what was going wrong. But as you explained to me, when you spoke with her she wasn't even willing to respond to that friendly gesture and didn't follow through on what you asked. That probably put her all the way back in the R1 position because the psychological effect of being unable to adjust caused her to become both unable and unwilling. When you draw the perpendicular line now, it cuts the leadership line in the S1, or telling, quadrant. I don't remember you saying that you faced her or even told her about her unacceptable behavior."

"No. I took the easy way out. I listened to another veteran administrator and then I decided, since this was a protected position, we would have an easier go at it now if we just eliminated the job."

"I am not trying to be critical here. The model shows us you should have given her specific instructions and closely supervised her performance before you took that step. If you were making a case for just-cause termination you would have to do this. Although I realize that you didn't have the time to deal with this, since you felt that you couldn't effectively use her anyway," he added apologetically. "Let's take a look at the business manager situation. What did you do with him? And where do you think he was on the readiness scale."

"I think he had to be an R2."

"Why?"

"Because he was unable but seemed to be willing. This seems to fit appropriately. So if I draw the line up, this means I should have given him direction and provided an opportunity for him to ask questions."

"Right on! So what did you do?" Barry encouraged his colleague.

"Well, each time he came in to me, I told him to recalculate the numbers. Each time he assured me that the numbers were correct. But come the next day, they would be wrong or he would add something new to the bottom line. After 6 weeks of this, I concluded that he couldn't do the job. He just didn't have the knowledge or skill for this position, which requires a clear understanding of budgeting and accounting."

"Rob, I think you're beginning to get the hang of how the model works. For me, it was invaluable in working with individuals and groups. The real power of the model was diagnosing in retrospect after we really messed up. This was especially true when I tried to delegate to an individual who wasn't at the readiness level to be able to handle an assignment. I wondered why the work never got done even when I thought I was an experienced Situational Leadership administrator. Looking back now, I'm amazed how quickly we lose it. If the new learning isn't constantly being used and reviewed, its out of sight, out of mind!

"Even with a school community it applies. For example, don't ever announce as if it were a fact that you're considering putting a new high school on double session with the old one to relieve overcrowding until the new high school is finished. This is especially true when you haven't told the school board or the community that it was just a brainstorming idea to relieve overcrowding in the first place."

"What happened?" Rob asked curiously.

"It took 6 months and scores of meetings to work this issue through. The final solution wasn't the one I'd mentioned. They wanted to participate, S3, and they felt I was 'S1-ing' them. A real mismatch! The solution was finally accepted by all and was much more expensive. These diagnostic skills can really prevent you from repeating mistakes.

"What I haven't explained really well is how the model is used for developing people to a higher readiness level or how to handle them when they are not doing so well. This is called either the developmental cycle or the regressive cycle. The latter is what you described with the communications lady. We will have to save this for another time."

"Well, that was a few more minutes over the 10 you allowed yourself. I get the idea."

"Rob, I think you're getting the gist of it. The simple way I remember the model is that you need to do for the follower what he or she can't or won't do for him or herself. If they need direction, give them that or more socioemotional or high relationship strokes if that is called for. Be careful as this is task specific."

You need to do for the follower what he or she can't or won't do for him or herself.

"That's sure easier to remember."

"Let me list several questions that might help outline the thinking here."

1. What objective do we want to accomplish?
2. What leadership action should be taken?
3. What was the result of the leadership intervention?
4. What follow-up, if any, is required?

"This is a preview on how to perform Situational Leadership. With some training all your managers can be on the same page with the same vocabulary using it to make better leadership decisions."

 Time-Out

Think of a situation you're in where this new learning can be applied.

1. What does it tell you now that you didn't realize before?
2. What interventions can you make that will help?
3. How will you know if it did? Keep the desired outcome in front of you.

Barry then opened his briefcase and handed Rob a copy of the sixth edition of *Management of Organizational Behavior: Leading Human Resources*, written by Paul Hersey, Kenneth Blanchard, and Dewey Johnson.

"I want to set a time to have you brief my cabinet members and get them involved in a training session. I'm excited about putting situational leadership skills in my toolbox."

Barry, whose forte was integration of ideas into a systems format, said, "Let's think how this plays a part in organizational life. As we look through our new lens of systems thinking, the management and leadership role is the key to holding the system together. It's the people working together for a common goal effectively and efficiently that creates excellence in organizations."

"How does systems thinking work here?" asked Rob.

"Rather than a piecemeal approach, you might want to do the helicopter view again, looking at what the entire school system's need is for the development of knowledge and skills. What do all employees need to know about the strategic mission after one is developed, for example? A systems assessment of what different folks need can be extremely helpful in deciding where you want to be in 3 to 5 years. How does the development of leadership and followership play a role in this, the bigger picture? There is more to consider."

"I would like to share more of these ideas with my management team for starters, and then move on to help the principals as they get to know me better. I am beginning to form in my own mind how I want to begin working directly with them starting in October. I've scheduled an all-day Friday and half-day Saturday retreat near the end of the month to begin hearing what they need to know to manage more effectively. Also, I want to use this as an opportunity to start them thinking about improving student learning."

"Let me know how I can help," Barry said.

"Also," Rob added, "I am hoping to determine how they feel about taking on more site responsibility for making decisions. After this intro to Sit Lead, I'll be sure to find out their willingness and ability to take this on."

"As you do, note that each will be in a different place on the changes you might make. Don't implement anything until you find out where they are. If you wait until we do more on this, you should have a clearer understanding of their readiness," Barry said as a warning note. "Too often a huge change is implemented without regard to readiness and the initiators wonder what happened when it failed."

Rob said, "There was little thought about these things in the past. We could use part of this time for processing the communication styles feedback material you keep bringing up. Before, things were run more on a day-to-day basis, using a crisis approach to managing. You can't blame the staff, as the district was simply trying to survive all of the political distractions going on."

"How do you want to proceed?" Barry asked.

"What would you suggest? You have more of an outsider's point of view. I'm still trying to keep one step ahead in a survival mode!" he said with a smile, but not too humorously.

"The way I like to lay out a new team-building process is to follow up with what you and the board started to develop as the governance team when we looked at goals, roles, procedures, and relationships. It's best to make sure you have their collective wisdom and commitment to the vision and values you are working toward from the onset. Taking this wisdom to the management folks and helping them see their role should help shape your notions as to what is needed. Be sure you look at their readiness level before you jump off the cliff!" he again reminded Rob.

"Help! Help! I've had enough leadership to last me a lifetime or maybe a week. I need time to think about what we covered today," Rob said, throwing his hands in the air in surrender.

"Before we go any farther along this leadership path, let me ask The Question. What is the end you have in mind?"

"What do you mean?"

"What do you need? I don't want to overload you more than I have already, but a survey of these basics now will be extremely helpful as various new situations arise later."

"What I would like to see as your homework, Barry, is more of the leadership stuff in writing or references to it so I can go over it at my leisure. I then can decide what my next steps need to be. Try to define what you discovered that worked for you in your district. I know I can't directly experience what you did, but it will give me one picture of success to consider. You could even lead me to some resource material I could look over later."

"I guess this wraps up another exciting chapter in the rookie's life. The good news is that you are doing the beginner's 'right things mostly right'!" he said as a verbal pat on the back. "Call me if anything comes up that you need to chat about."

"I'm going to definitely pick your brain before I start to work with the principals. I need all the secrets for success you developed with your principals over the years," Rob pleaded.

"If I tell you all my secrets, I won't have anything to advise you about."

"That will be the day when you don't have something to say about anything," Rob teased. "One thing I do know is there are always challenges to face. Let's call it a good day so far."

"Here we go again, almost completely forgetting the real agenda. Where do you want to go with it?"

Surprised at the time they had been sitting there, they took a look at the agenda and decided they had covered most of it. Rob gave Barry a positive 2-minute update on how well he liked the job and working with the board. The goal-setting process was still in the hands of his assistants and directors with the deadline for completion coming up soon. Rob thought that with the briefing he could better process the concern about the reluctant three.

"Why don't I review my notes on leadership and all? I can send you some material for us to review in a week or two. We then can sort and select what fits your situation for this year. Then maybe we will be in position by year-end to do some multiyear planning to keep the group growing and developing," Barry said, finally winding down.

THE BIG-ROCK STORY

"Wait a minute," Rob said quickly. "I've waited 3 weeks for the big-rock story."

"It's not that big a deal."

"I want to hear it anyway. There must be a point to it or you wouldn't have brought it up."

"Remember the context? We were taking about priorities with the big stuff on your plate. I heard a way to better manage work priorities during a Covey workshop I attended, where he used his *First Things First Workbook*. The story goes that there is this large tub to fill with sand, smaller stones, pebbles, big rocks, and water. The object was to get as much in the tub as possible. Most folks weren't able to fit all of the items in it. Many put the sand in first and didn't leave room for all the big rocks. One enterprising person put the big rocks in first, and then shook the small rocks around them, then the pebbles, and so on. Finally, the sand was poured in and then the water last. Now the tub was full and there were no leftovers. Can you guess the moral of this story?"

"It seems obvious now. You have to deal with the big rocks first or you won't get to them. All the little stuff will get in your way. The most urgent and important needs your attention first. Leave the least important until last."

"Does this remind you of a project you're supposed to be working on?" Barry pointed out.

"You really know how to hurt a guy! I am going to get my evaluation and goal stuff done! I've committed to the board that it will be on the agenda in November."

"You got it!" Barry cheered. "The story really isn't a big deal, but I always remembered it, especially when we were doing the agenda at our cabinet meetings. Someone usually asked if we had all the big rocks in front of us to consider. Lest we forget! It became a working reminder for putting 'first things first.' "

As they parted, Barry felt that the ideas generated would keep Rob focused for years to come. Of course, the hard part was still ahead of him: getting others to buy into these ideas and instilling them in the corporate culture. Even more important than acceptance was permanent adoption of the ideas. Barry thought that Rob was beginning to understand the notion of changing the conversation to get a desired change in the culture. It would take at least 3 to 5 years for any change to take hold, he knew from past experience.

🕐 Time-Out—A So What

1. Think of a change you want to make and assess the readiness level of those involved.
2. What leadership style does your assessment indicate?
3. How would you go about putting the issues and decisions you are now faced with in big-rock order?
4. What leadership skills do you need more work on?
5. How will you approach closing the gap?

BARRY'S REFLECTIONS ON HIS OWN DEVELOPMENT AS A LEADER

Sitting in his office the next day, Barry thought about how best to cover Rob's request in a meaningful way. He leaned back in his chair, looking up at the ceiling, and pictured the leadership journey he had traveled for more than 40 years. He believed he had a good handle on this leadership thing and that he could teach and coach it.

He decided to tell Rob some of the story of his journey. He could only define the milestones, the key incidents that got him to where he is now. Using his experiences to create another very successful organization would be the proof of the pudding.

Understanding the big picture first and then adapting it to your own values about working with people was critical. This was one reason it was important to understand the history of management and leadership thought. He believed that without a personal vision to view the future there can be no effective leadership.

When he first started as a high school principal, Barry was introduced to Abraham Maslow's hierarchy of needs theory. This was the first model he felt he could make sense of and use. Soon after this he was challenged through the doctoral program at UCLA to look at leadership from a comprehensive historical point of view. It was here in a class led by professors Lucio and McNeil that he was asked to write a comprehensive course paper on the history of management, from Machiavelli to the then current thinking. This paper laid the foundation for development of his dissertation, as well as to his realization of the significance of the contributions of experts in the field of leadership and management.

At the university, he also studied the writings of Argyris, Simon, Barnard, Griffiths, Fayol, Weber, Taylor, Dewey, Follet, Sears, Mayo, Lewin, Rogers, and Lippitt. At that time, he saw little relevance to the job in this reading and research. Like most graduate students, he was working full time, as a high school principal, and he was just trying to successfully pass the course. Strangely enough this study was a milestone.

From time to time as an assistant superintendent, he picked up different leadership- followership interrelationship designs, such as that by Tannenbaum and Schmidt. This was the first insight he really had on how to operationalize the relationship between leader and follower, using a democratic-authoritarian relationship model.

In his second year as superintendent two coincidental events happened in the same week. First, one of the high school principals approved a request for a student's father to speak about leadership to the student council. The other significant event occurred on a United Airlines flight home from a meeting in Chicago, where his assistant superintendent of business services had a seatmate who excitedly drew a leadership model on a napkin. Independently of each other, both the principal and the business manager rushed to tell Barry about their discoveries.

The high school student council had just heard Ken Blanchard speak, and the business manager sat next to Paul Hersey, also a district resident. As a result, this started a partnership between the school district and these two outstanding applied behavioral scientists at the Center for Leadership Studies. Their book *Management of Organizational Behavior* became required reading in the district. This book gave them a comprehensive history of the development of behavioral thought. Many of the gurus he had just thought about were mentioned in this work.

This led to the use of the very comprehensive Situational Leadership model and then the integration with other current fields of thought. Leadership training was now required for all administrators with an emphasis on skills developed through Situational Leadership. From this relationship, a door was opened to work with University Associates of San Diego. This gave the administrators in the district access to other great thinkers in the field.

Another milestone was reached through a casual conversation with a high school counselor. She introduced the superintendent to workshops on communication styles conducted by Performax in Minneapolis. This program was so successful that more information from a value-added program developed by the TRACOM Group in Denver was included. This also was required in the district's management training program.

The bottom line was that this established a culture of learning and inquiry. Many other gurus were invited to speak at district workshops. This inspired other departments to reach out and learn more about their own work. Teachers were encouraged to go to conferences, present programs, and train other teachers.

As mentioned earlier, the notion that the leader can't exist without followers was first introduced by Hersey and Blanchard and then reinforced later by the work of Kouzes and Posner. In the latter's research they summarized what followers wanted in a leader: honesty, competency, being forward-looking, and inspirational. As followers, this should not come as a surprise to us at all, Barry thought. They went on to describe what leaders do, when at their best: challenge the process, inspire a shared vision, enable others to act, model the way, and encourage the heart.

The irony of all of this was that Woodson and his administrative team were doing most of these things before they read the books or before the books were even printed! Over the years this happened time and time again.

Vision can't be copied. It must be experienced.

It seemed to be the right thing to do when you were fulfilling a clear vision and were guided by core values. An example of this floated through his mind. When Peter Senge's *The Fifth Discipline* (1990) introduced the characteristics of a learning organization, his folks had already created one using very similar notions. This, he thought, would be important to mention to Rob. He would have to live it himself. As a mentor, he could only point him in a direction. Rob and his organization will have to experience this journey together. They must create their own vision, because a vision journey can't be copied. It must be experienced.

THE SUMMARY FOR ROB

After all this reflection and knowing that he left so much out, Barry needed to provide a summary for Rob.

He went to the whiteboard in his office and began to outline what should be covered. He thought a moment. He didn't want Rob to think he wasn't a good leader or unknowledgeable. He just wanted to revisit the basics so they could be on the same page when they laid out a management training program for the district.

He said to himself, I have the Hersey and Blanchard material I used from way back when. I can tell him about the impact their thinking made on me and about the follow-up work they each have done. It's commonsensically organized. I'll add a few things about the debate over the definition between leadership and management, which doesn't really matter because both work. Need to refer him to Adizes, Bennis, and others to do some thinking.

As he continued to write the background for Rob, he added,

Remember, individually we don't generally have top-drawer skills in all areas of desired management skills. You should continue to learn, grow, and develop into a lifelong learning individual and, from this, transform yourselves into a powerful learning organization. You need to be able to integrate all these ideas into your leadership behavior—at least those you believe are the most important. It's not easy and needs practice. Most of the areas where we do not have strength can be improved, and when these improvements are well learned they are sometimes more effective than our natural behaviors.

The real skill is finding either leader potential or highly skilled leaders in your school principals. Your central office administrative staff needs to be balanced in leadership skills to effectively work as a team.

"Who the superintendent is, what the superintendent values, and the style of operations supported by the superintendent will be manifested throughout the school system."

—Phillip Schlechty

I believe you should start on skill training now to move the focus toward more effective student learning. You can work with building the management team now—later we focus on the skills for all those other systems and subsystems that have a piece of the action.

I'll close with what Phillip Schlechty wrote in *Working on the Work*. "In the long run, therefore, who the superintendent is, what the superintendent values, and the style of operations supported by the superintendent will be manifested throughout the school system."

Hope this isn't too overwhelming. Read yourself to sleep with it. See you soon.

He edited the essay and sent it to Rob.

THE PROMPT RESPONSE

Rob's response came almost immediately after he received the overview from his mentor. Yes, he wanted to review what he had learned and experienced as a leader with Woodson.

He then sent the following e-mail.

Dear Barry,

I just received the information that you put together on leadership and followership. Why don't we get together sometime soon to review some key ideas? I have a few questions about what I need to know. I really like sticking to one or two book resources that I can use when I need them. Right now I don't have time to do much more. When we do the briefing with my administrative cabinet, I hope you will go over some of these ideas and concepts more thoroughly.

I will add time for you on the cabinet agenda. We hope to go off site on the last Friday of the month. Hope you are free. More details to follow. Thanks for everything.

Sincerely, Rob

Time-Out—So What Do I Do Now?

1. If you see value in Situational Leadership, what next steps do you need to take to make it part of your skill bank?
2. Review Kouzes and Posner's work on the leader-follower relationship. What is there that you should add to your growth and development?

SUMMARY

In this chapter Rob reports on the opening of school, problems with principals not getting the right message in time, how he handled board members visiting schools, and the settlement of teachers' negotiations.

Part of the chapter was spent on a discussion of some historical aspects of leadership and development. A number of key players were identified as contributing to various schools of thought. A variety of definitions centering on leadership and management were listed for your consideration. Then the focus centered on the role that Situational Leadership can play early on in learning how to manage people. Examples of how Rob handled or mishandled three employees early on in the game were reviewed using the model. You were given an opportunity to try out your understanding in four situations. What followers want from leaders and what leaders can do to be more effective was mentioned as part of Kouzes and Posner's contribution to the topic.

The chapter ended with the thought that there was so much in this area to cover that they should keep it simple and just work on two major management models this year—Social Styles and Situational Leadership.

"From the same strokes for the same folks, to different strokes for different folks, back to different strokes for the same folks."

—Ken Blanchard

MONTH 3—SEPTEMBER

Strategies and Survival Skills

1. The leader needs to know about leadership and followership.
   - Review who you are in the leadership scheme of things.
   - Reflect on how you made decisions in the past.
   - Keep learning and listening and pay attention to what is written and said about leadership.
2. Try and find leadership training models that work and that meet the needs of your administrators.
   - Be careful not to move too fast in introducing these models. We did so early on only to get the content into this chapter.
3. Model the leadership that you expect from your followers.
   - Remember, your subordinates are watching you all the time.
4. Remember what followers want in their leaders.
   - Your followers want you to be honest, competent, forward-looking, and inspiring. Be reminded again that to change the culture you have to change the conversation.
   - Understand the role that power plays in an organizational setting.

- Power is one of the least considered aspects in the organization. Yet each and every person in the organization can describe the many aspects, both good and bad, seen in the organization.

5. As you start a change process, be sure the necessary parties are with you, especially if you need the board's support and commitment.
   - Buying into ideas, committing to them, and understanding them are coins of the realm.

6. With your protector-of-the-schools hat on, in an uncertain board climate, try to insulate the schools from the politics.
   - In a new situation it will take time to determine loyalties. Let the folks know up front what you expect. Let the board know also whether your new-guy-on-the-block halo is still on straight.

"Leadership is the process of translating intentions into reality."

—Peter Block

"Successful leaders begin to believe that a key to the task is to re-create themselves down through the organization."

—Peter Block

TOOLBOX

Adizes, I. (1993). *Adizes Analysis of Management*, [Cassette]. Los Angeles, CA: Adizes Institute.

Covey, P., Merrill, A. R., & Merrill, R. R. (1994). *First Things First: To Live, to Love, to Learn, to Leave a Legacy*. New York: Simon & Schuster.

Covey, S. (1989). *The Seven Habits of Highly Effective People: Powerful Lessons in Personal Change*. New York: Simon & Schuster.

Hersey, P. (1985). *Situational Selling*. Escondido, CA: Center for Leadership Studies.

Hersey, P., Blanchard, K., and Johnson, D. (1993). *Management of Organizational Behavior: Leading Human Resources*, 6th ed. Englewood Cliffs, NJ: Prentice-Hall.

Hersey, P., Blanchard K., & Natemeyer, W. (1961) *Situational Leadership, Perception, and the Impact of Power*. [Monograph]. Englewood Cliffs, NJ: Prentice-Hall.

Kouzes, J., & Posner, B. (1995). *The Leadership Challenge*. San Francisco, CA: Jossey-Bass.

Senge, P. (1990). *The Fifth Discipline*. New York: Bantam Doubleday Bell.

OCTOBER: DO YOU KNOW THE PRINCIPAL PLAYERS?

There may be schools out there that have strong instructional leaders, but are not yet effective; however, we have never yet found an effective school that did not have a strong instructional leader as the principal.

—Ron Edmonds

SHARED VISION + FOCUSED MISSION + EFFECTIVE PRINCIPALS = EFFECTIVE SCHOOLS

In this chapter you will be presented with the following:

1. *Elements of Effective Schools research, including the Effective Schools correlates.*
2. *Ideas and components for delegated site-based management.*
3. *Thoughts about vision and mission.*
4. *One way to get feedback from your principals.*
5. *Being part of a Situational Leadership workshop follow-up.*

REVIEWING THE SITUATIONAL LEADERSHIP WORKSHOP

On this lazy fall afternoon the scenic view outside was causing them to lose concentration. Their lunch table had an unobstructed view overlooking the beautiful and challenging island green at the 18th hole. Rob and Barry were just finishing a late lunch in the English Pub at this secluded north county resort hotel. Their table overlooked the lake that framed this famous last hole. It was close to 2 p.m. and they were relaxing after finishing the cabinet meeting and workshop. Two of the group, deputy superintendent Peter Paulson and administrative assistant Diane Menius, had eaten quickly and left to get back to the office for late-afternoon meetings. Diane decided that next time she wouldn't schedule meetings immediately following retreats. There were too many follow-up things that needed her attention. Live and learn, she realized.

Barry had recently discovered this great meeting spot. Actually, Diane told him about it. She was trying to be more helpful and show more initiative. When she heard the meeting place discussion in a cabinet meeting she volunteered to set something up.

Two weeks ago Diane had arranged a visit for the two of them to meet with the resort's sales manager and they drove north to check it out.

The rookie and his mentor again looked longingly at the temptation right in front of their eyes. To work or to play, that was the question. More effective planning would have let them join the other administrators frustrating their egos, or in plain talk, golfing. During the session there had been so many questions that the group decided to work straight through lunch time and try to catch a bite after they finished and before golf.

They were both tired. Rob, the superintendent of schools, worked as hard as each of the other six administrators in trying to better understand the Situational Leadership model and, more important, how it could be best applied on the job.

The management team had decided to escape the district and their regular day duties to do a Friday away from the office, looking into the efficacy of the leadership program. This was the program so heavily touted by Rob's mentor. Of course, meeting here also allowed for some recreation. If there was time! They all had been working hard these first 3 months and needed some R & R. Team building was a secondary objective.

What had started out as the half-day, 8 to 12, workshop had gone until the 1:30 tee time and hunger intervened. Barry had done most of the hard work in presenting the system from the ground up. The remaining four of the group decided to adjourn to the prearranged small group seminar session on the course. When Barry and Rob decided to debrief instead, this left only one foursome. The four golfers had to eat on the run to make their starting time as it was.

Rob and Barry had wanted to take advantage of the glorious view, the pleasant surroundings, and the time available to go over some of the conclusions drawn from the session and consider next steps.

As they finished reading the administrative team's feedback that Diane had collected, they were smiling. This gift of positive feedback would support the superintendent in laying the groundwork to move forward with a full-fledged training program for the other administrators in the district later on in the year. The cabinet's support was a necessary first step. This would help in building a real learning focus in the district. Also, it met one of the annual goals he had decided on right after he was hired by the board in June.

THE ROOKIE AND THE ADMINISTRATIVE ASSISTANT

After a few minutes of pleasantries, Barry's usually cheerful smile was replaced with a serious looking frown.

"It didn't seem to me that you and Diane were too friendly. You were both very professional, but I felt the tension and Don Halverson, your new assistant superintendent, even commented casually, almost offhandedly, about it during the break." He hoped the topic was safe to bring up as she had just left and, if he was to help them both, he first needed to get Rob's point of view.

Now he watched Rob squirm as he struggled with an answer to the direct question about Diane.

"Well, uh," Rob stammered, "Things were better until last week. I don't know what triggered it, but we seem to be having more problems. I don't think she's gotten over her moodiness yet or maybe it's just me. She's been awfully quiet and withdrawn this week."

"Tell me what happened," he asked curiously.

"It seems to me that I haven't been paying enough attention to her needs and concerns. I've been running around like crazy and haven't taken time to meet with her to discuss how I want things to be done.

Sometimes I don't even know myself. I have just been quickly giving her directions and assignments without much explanation or thought. I assumed she could manage it by now. But after watching her in today's training session, I think much of the job is still too confusing and somewhat overwhelming. I've expected too much too soon. I need to talk to her and go back to ground zero on communicating my expectations and how I can better explain this to her. She seems to need a lot of friendly conversation and support. I need to mention to her that I am learning how to explain my working style. Maybe I erred in not giving her enough step-by-step direction on new tasks. She may be at a readiness level that isn't appropriate for the way I am giving her directions."

"Is that all?" Barry commented. "Surely you realize that as tasks come up for the first time throughout the year, each will be new to her. You may need to go back to ground zero as each new task arises. Do you understand the various jobs well enough to explain them to her?"

"Maybe not. I'm not taking the time. I know she is working hard to appropriately schedule staff and others who want to meet with me. She seems to like to make sure that people around her work harmoniously and are friendly," Rob quickly added as he thought more about it.

"She's even suggested that maybe we could take time away from the office, so that we could go over all the stuff that I can't seem to find time during office hours to cover with her. Apparently this was acceptable in her previous job. We had occasion to discuss this when I met her husband last week at a TGIF district office function, which included spouses and friends. Her husband supported the lunch idea as he knew Diane was frustrated when I wasn't available to work with her on some of the assignments and projects I ask her to do. What advice could you offer me on the situation? Is this a good way to build a better boss-secretary relationship?"

Woodson reached back in his memory bank and then said, "After a few years on the job in my former district, especially after we grew to over 20,000 students, I started using the time after work to meet with people I couldn't squeeze in during the day. Sometimes this included my secretary of 15 years. Also, I met with principals, directors, and assistant superintendents in this informal manner singly and in twos. I had a favorite restaurant with a classy lounge where the business community gathered regularly. This was extremely effective for me. Away from the office we could relax and share information while winding down the day and before rushing off to another night meeting or going home."

"It sounds like you worked 12 to 16 hour days a lot," Rob said, stating the obvious and then wondered about his own commitment. It may be easier now without the family, but next year?

"I really enjoyed meeting with people on an informal basis and I realize that meeting with the CEO from their perspective may not seem informal. It's just another way to build trust over time. However, in your district I would be very careful. A working lunch at a popular restaurant might be okay. Now, with sexual harassment in the forefront these days, I would be extremely careful, even in your community where most folks wouldn't give it a second thought. Protect yourself! It's too early in the game to take this risk."

⏱ Time-Out

1. What do you think about Rob's approach to getting acceptance from his cabinet about using a training-team building process such as Situational Leadership for the rest of management?
2. Would you get acceptance from your group differently? List three or four suggestions.
3. What is your opinion about going off site for management meetings or training?
4. Would this be possible in your district? Explain.
5. What is your advice for Rob about lunch meetings with his assistant or spending more quality time helping effect better communication? How would this fit in your community?
6. Explain what you think the problem is between the administrative assistant and the superintendent.
7. What advice would you give Rob for improving the relationship between him and Diane?

Rob replied, "Good advice! First, I need to concentrate on finding more time during the day to work with her. Maybe the last 30 minutes of the day, so we can do a quick review and plan for the next day?" he declared, as if he just discovered the fount of all wisdom.

"Remember, even initially, if you don't take quality time to train your administrative assistant, it will come back to haunt you—as it's already doing. The time taken up front pays off in spades later on as you will find out as you start over with her, soon I hope."

"However, I like the idea of a working lunch in a very public place away from phones and other interruptions," Rob continued.

"It's your funeral!"

"I guess then I shouldn't wait until after the Social Style workshop next month to work this out?" Rob had heard enough about finding time to repair the damage already done. Feeling as guilty as he did, he would try to start fixing the relationship first thing Monday morning.

Barry wasn't ready to let it go as he had a deep concern that Rob still didn't quite know how to deal with this effectively.

"Talk to her about your concerns. I always found it hard to bring up sensitive matters with my secretaries and assistants. I didn't want to hurt their feelings. Much of the time I just avoided the situation, hoping that it would solve itself. And most of the time it didn't," Barry admitted.

"Having a compatriot in my misery isn't going to solve my problem."

"Well said. I may even have another good idea. Why don't you invite Diane to be part of the Style training? You might ask her to give you feedback on whether or not the training may be valuable for all administrative assistants and secretaries. Since they and their administrative counterparts work closely, they should learn more about handling their bosses."

"Great idea! Send her the forms and I'll ask her to expedite them back to your associate," Rob said with relief.

Then they began talking about how to get started implementing management training. Barry jumped right in with a solution strategy. Sometimes he was impatient to share things that had worked well for him in the past. In fact, they were things that still worked well with other clients. But he did have to practice attentive listening and wait for Rob to initiate solutions, so that he would take on more ownership in his new leadership role.

"Coach, are you getting the results back from the social styles material you sent out to the ad cab and the principals?" Rob asked, abruptly changing the topic as he tried to cover everything on his mind. Woodson was going to have to get him refocused soon.

"My assistant is working on this. Since she's very competent I am sure everything is coming along okay. They've had the questionnaire for only 2 weeks. She has a computer printout from the scoring company and will follow up. We still have about 4 weeks until we present it. I'm going to use the first day to focus on the model, and then for the next day I'm scheming up a practice session that will involve practical problem solving within the context of styles. I hope this will augment the backwards thinking process," Barry said.

"That takes a load off my mind," Rob responded with a sigh of relief.

WRAPPING UP

"So what's the end game you are seeing in your mind now?" Barry asked, trying to push Rob to think both systemically and backwards simultaneously.

"This is easy. We need well-trained effective principals to lead the change process toward higher student performance and then creating more effective schools for the system," Rob responded, almost as if he was quoting from a textbook.

"Speaking of effective principals, you never did tell me how it went with the three that didn't get the message about teaching on the first day."

"It went pretty well with two of them."

"How so?"

"One situation was very plausible. It was a rookie principal and a new secretary at the school. It was lucky that they got school opened on the right day. I did do some constructive and corrective criticism. The second one just didn't remember to focus on teaching. He apologized profusely. I really believe that he thought it wasn't important."

"What about the third?"

"That one could be a problem. He didn't really seem to care. His director told me that the school was disorganized and he was a weak leader and not very responsive to coaching over the past 2 years. In a meeting with both the principal and the elementary director, Dr. Susan Jameson, I reviewed what I expected him to be doing to get the school in order sooner rather than later. Laissez-faire leadership was no longer acceptable.

"Once we get the Effective Schools plan in place, I'm going to really push for improvement. In the meantime, she'll be watching all three of them closely. We put our one reluctant leader on our watch list."

"Susan seemed to understand the training today. Might be a good time to strategize with her using the model as a tool for next steps with him," Barry suggested.

"That's a thought! I'll talk to her about it. Maybe work together on it," he said, thinking of the advantages of this idea.

"It sounds like you're on top of these three situations. So you think these two management training programs will give the principals help in leading more effectively?" Barry said, testing the water again.

"Of course, I can see that. But more than that, I want to understand what I can use from Larry Lezotte's approach and then work toward more site decision making and, definitely, more accountability. I want to have the top schools in the state!" Rob declared with conviction.

"Why? What do you mean by top schools?" Barry challenged.

"I don't want to go there now. Maybe at another time," Rob said, rejecting the path his mentor was leading him down.

"Okay, then."

🕐 **Time-Out—A So What**

1. Is Rob on the right track using the Situational Leadership learning to help change the performance of the principal? Explain.
2. What next steps would you now take with Diane to increase the office effectiveness?
3. Think of a poor communication interaction you are having. What have you learned so far that would help you resolve it?

RAPPIN' WITH ROB

Rob then switched back to another big-rock concern. "Let's get back to planning for this month's challenges and opportunities. Things are going pretty well. When we spoke last week, you suggested I find ways of opening up communications with the principals. I took your suggestion and announced that one of our two monthly principal's meetings would be on an informal volunteer basis away from the district for them only, chatting with the chief. I dubbed it 'Rappin' with Rob.' No other administrators!"

"How'd your ad cab take this? Mine were upset when I tried this years ago!" Barry interjected. "Some liked it so much they began calling it 'BS-in' with Barry'! It must have been in loving affection!"

"Yeah! Sure! They loved you! Same reaction from my ad cab as you had. I had to reassure them that we would not be doing anything behind their backs. I said I would go over the outcomes with them at the very next cabinet meeting. My rationale was that I needed to bond sooner rather than later with our school leadership folks. Don helped smooth the way. In our previous work together, he saw its effectiveness. He assured them this would work okay.

"I hope to build trust with some people as a result," Rob said. "I need to hear from them directly, so they will know that I will support them. Also, I mentioned I was inviting Diane as I needed help in coordinating and taking notes for the rappin'. By including her, I wanted to signal to the principals that she was indeed my confidential administrative assistant and could be trusted with keeping what was said in the room confidential. In this way, she would also get to know both me and them much better and be able to help them in their relationships with me. She's very good at this."

"Good thinking! And, of course, she keeps you organized and handles the follow-up for the cabinet?" Barry replied.

"Certainly! She does like to be part of this. After work last Tuesday, we had the first session at the Paradise Valley Country Club. Diane coordinated and made all the arrangements. The club manager gave us a meeting room without charge in exchange for our order of beverages and light hors d'oeuvres. I mentioned that we were planning on doing this five or six times a year.

"As the principals started arriving, I offered to buy the first glass of wine or a soda and then said after this they were on their own. The district paid for the food and sodas. Remember, this was an after-work meeting and voluntary. After hours, of course, is a thinly disguised joke as the entire management group is considered by the board to be on duty 24/7."

"Sounds like you're off to a good start with them."

"I told them we're going to be rappin' with Rob a lot throughout the year. That I still saw myself as a frustrated high school principal and was still thinking like one of them."

"What was your point?" Barry queried.

"Well, in my previous principalships, I wanted the superintendent to tell me what he expected, give me enough resources, leave me alone, and I would deliver at the end of the year. I wanted them to know that I understood what they are going through. So to be most helpful, I would like them to be as candid with me as they felt comfortable being."

"That comes across a little cocky!" the prof observed. "How did your new group respond?"

"I'm not sure they believed me," Rob said as he smiled, knowing it would take more than one meeting to break through their cautious resistance.

"So, what happened then?" Barry asked. This had worked so well for him he hoped it would be an effective clone for Rob. Cloning doesn't often work that well, he knew from past experience.

In his old district Woodson had expanded the process to other groups, including the directors, the supervisors, and all the administrative assistants and school secretaries. It provided an opportunity for him to listen to concerns and explain where he thought the district should be headed. The vision he had was being reinforced through both the district's informal and formal influential leaders.

"So after about 30 minutes of food, soda, and wine, they were more relaxed as they finally got seated. I started with an introduction about why we were there. I challenged them to ask anything they wanted, since this was an open forum. Then I asked them to work in groups of three and write down what they thought were the key issues facing the district."

"You mean a critical issues list?" his mentor questioned.

"Exactly! I wanted to keep the questions anonymous. Of course, I worked in my agenda appropriately. I had them post their items on a flip chart. Then I asked clarifying questions to get them more involved. This was followed by my input on each topic, trying not to declare too early. It worked moderately well."

"How do you know?"

"By their active participation and by the fact they would like to do it again next month," Rob responded, thinking Barry was trying to trap him.

"Good!"

"Since my friendly debate in the earlier principals' meeting with Charlie last August, they're still cautious," Rob said.

"This activity should continue to break down those barriers," Barry observed.

"The board situation finally did come up. I was able to reinforce my desire to keep them out of the mess. Most of the other items centered on less volatile and minor school issues, so I won't bore you with them," Rob added as he paused to finish his dessert. So much for his Atkins Diet today! It is probably the stress, he rationalized. After they finished here, he was seriously considering going on a 5-mile run before dark.

During a pause to watch the golfers and finish another cup of coffee, Rob tried summarizing the new rappin'-with-Rob experience in his head. He got the feeling that most principals were willing but needed help on determining the areas he was targeting for accountability. There hadn't been much discussion of this in the past, he realized. He wanted to lay the groundwork for moving into a more site-based, delegated management model requiring more decision making by the principals and staff. He knew that not all were ready to take on more decision making in every facet of the job, but he wanted to start on one or two ideas now.

To make this work he had to involve both the elementary and secondary directors. Since the principals reported directly to him, it would work only with the support of the directors. They were in the best position to monitor the process.

They needed to learn about the changes the superintendent wanted to make in providing resources to the school—staff and supplies. In his former district he had used a program called personnel staffing units (PSUs). As a principal himself, he had liked local control over how he wanted to staff his school.

🕐 Time-Out—A So What

1. What have you observed in your district on how the superintendent gets information from the field?

2. How would the principals in your district react to a "voluntary" principals' meeting after hours?
3. What do you think of Rob's idea to have one meeting a month be voluntary?
4. How would you improve on this practice?
5. Would you think seriously about implementing this practice? What would be the pros and cons in your district?

EFFECTIVE SCHOOLS AND OTHER CONSIDERATIONS

Coming out of his reverie, Rob continued, "However, I did get a chance to introduce a conversation on Effective Schools research and giving them more decision-making ability in their schools. That's why I need your wise counsel now, instead of going out and hitting the little white ball this afternoon!"

"I'll be happy to oblige. When I was in your shoes years ago, I had more fun with this and thought it made one of the biggest improvements in performance," the mentor remembered fondly. "It only took about 6 years! Hope you have the patience and staying power! This organizational change stuff isn't easy. I think what I learned still works in today's climate."

"Okay. Where should I start?" Rob sounded lost.

"What do you know about the Effective Schools correlates?" Barry asked, hoping that he wouldn't have to start at the beginning. But after all, he wasn't sure that former high school principals even knew this material existed.

"I never even heard about it until you brought it up last month. I'm just concerned about the performance of my schools," Rob replied honestly. "That's my end in mind. Now what do I do?"

"Well, funny you should ask!" Barry said with a knowing smile. "Now we go to work. I'm going to send you some more material, so you will have something to reference as you go through the rest of the year."

Before they delved into the topic further, Rob stopped to review with his mentor what he had discovered over the past few months.

During his first two rounds of visiting with the principals at their schools, he had centered discussions on listening and answering questions. Along with the two directors, he reviewed the schools' state test scores, finding only two elementary schools and one of the three middle schools way below expectations. However, the schools appeared to be all over the map on how they were approaching the teaching—learning process. The two high schools weren't too bad, one slightly above average and the other slightly below. It looked like they were doing their own thing without much coordination or guidance from the district office. Student focus on learning was noticeably different among the secondary schools.

From comments made, he realized over the past 3 years each school had been allowed to go their own way, mostly due to the focus on the political problems between the board and superintendent. The superintendent seemed to have been spending more time trying to survive than lead. It became more obvious that principals loyal to the former superintendent got additional resources. Some of the principals figured out how to play the survival game and then did what they thought was best. Focusing on students and the learning process wasn't a high survival priority.

Most schools had pretty good teachers. But with the district projected to grow significantly over the next few years, he needed to review the entire selection, training, and development process. Maybe he should chat with the head of the teachers' union, Margaret Muele, and see where she stood on this issue of teacher quality.

As he summarized what he had learned, he knew some schools were just limping along, neither hot nor cold. A few needed a lot of work. What the superintendent and the prof were about to discuss further should head him in the right direction.

"Okay. I'm ready to listen. I thought you and I needed to be on the same page as we begin. Remember, these are just first impressions," the superintendent was quick to add.

"I'm not going to hold you to it, yet," Woodson shot back.

"Good."

"Rob, to better understand how we discovered the Effective Schools concepts, I'll tell you some of the story, the journey that we took early on.

"Somehow I got interested in improving our learning skills and creating better student learning results, probably through our project with the Madeline Hunter folks out of UCLA.

"I had just gotten to know a successful Arizona superintendent. With his encouragement, I took a group of administrators to his annual workshop presentation in Scottsdale. In the keynote session, not quite knowing what to expect, we ended up being mesmerized by Dr. Larry Lezotte. Even staying fixed in a position behind the lectern, Larry got our attention. He was dynamic, capturing and holding our attention all day long. Feeling like a kid in a store offering free candy, I was taking notes furiously for the next day and a half. This was our introduction to 'all students learning' and a method for school improvement. Lezotte backed up what he said with sound research."

"This is the Effective Schools Lezotte?" Rob asked.

"Being good is the enemy of being the best."

—Dr. Larry Lezotte

"Yes," Barry said and then continued, "About the same time, an administrator in our county Department of Education was working with a nearby school district using the Effective Schools criteria. However, we were in our better-than-thou mentality in those days. We didn't believe that we needed to do anything to continue to get better. It would happen naturally. Not so! One thing we learned from Dr. Lezotte was that 'being good is the enemy of being the best.'

"After recognizing that we had so much data we weren't using to measure student progress, we decided to be serious and pay attention. We were in the doldrums as we had just finished our strategic plan and didn't know how to measure student learning—only learning processes. Remember, this was prior to the standards and accountability movement. In fact, from this stumbling start, by developing our own aligned curriculum with our new standards, we got ahead of that flood stream swamping other states.

"From this time on we paid close attention to what Larry Lezotte was trying to teach us. I attended many of his meetings and encouraged the staff to do likewise. Eventually, I became associated with the Lezotte-led Superintendency Institute of America (SIA), a group of reform-minded superintendents trying to make a difference in the learning of students, a radical difference. We also brought Larry into the district, where he spent one morning talking to the elementary teachers and then, after lunch, to high school and middle school teachers. This made the most significant difference in teacher attitudes toward the importance of focusing on student learning.

"Getting back to the correlates, while we didn't really know about them, we had developed our own core values, the way we were going to do business, that pretty well paralleled the elements contained in the correlates. Remember, I am describing years of history in a few simple statements."

"I'm getting to like your history lessons, or at least am learning to tolerate them," Rob said to slow his mentor down a bit.

"Starting with a 2-year implementation of our strategic plan, then a 4-year hiatus getting through the two malcontents on the board, which I mentioned before, not knowing how to measure student learning, and then beginning the development of our own standards, we finally started to make significant positive changes in teaching and learning. When we started to disaggregate our test results, we made more headway along with stronger teacher support," Barry said, ending his travelogue through the past.

"That's quite a story," Rob said when they were distracted by a shout as a golfer made a 30-foot putt. "I get that it has to do with teaching and learning as the bottom line, has some research-based correlates, and that you used something like them, but what did you do specifically? Or rather, what can I use to make a difference? You're not coming across too well!"

"I guess I got carried away some. I'm excited about what a process like this can do for all students and the equity it provides for them."

"Can you explain the school improvement process in a sentence or two?" Rob asked, trying to get the prof to simplify.

"I'll try. First, there has to be in place a commitment to 'All students learning—whatever it takes.' This has to be the driving vision. The focused mission is a strategic implementation of this vision guided by core values—to make it happen! Effective principals along with teachers need to lead a process to get this done. Larry Lezotte suggests that it is a five-step process: preparation; focus; diagnosis and interpretation of data; plan development; and implementation, monitoring, evaluation, and renewal. The correlates are each proven leading indicators of student and school success. Got it?"

"Well, I'm not sure. We're certainly going to have to talk about this more. Rather than do it now, why don't you just outline the correlates for me. Send me the paper about the developmental history and more detail about the correlates later. If they are as effective as you suggest, then I really want to understand them fully."

"That seems fair enough. Let me see if I can remember them. Hand me a piece of paper from your journal notebook so I can list them for you." Barry said as he reached in his coat pocket for a pen.

Barry wrote the following outline.

1. Clear and Focused Mission
2. Instructional Leadership by the Principal
3. High Expectations for Success
4. Opportunity to Learn and Time on Task
5. Frequent Monitoring of Student Progress
6. Safe and Orderly Environment
7. Home/School Relations

"I want to emphasize something," Barry added. "In my opinion, unless there is a clear and compelling vision from the leader that the principals and staff can begin to identify with, an improvement in student learning isn't going to happen. While some hold that change starts with the principal, I don't quite see it that way. The schools belong to a system, and unless the system has the will to change, not much will happen at the school level. It has to start with the chief. Of course, principals can make progress in their own schools, but it can only be effective locally and usually can't, on its own, transform the entire system.

"Without system commitment, it will last only until the principal leaves. State test scores will get their attention for some improvement. Only some students at some schools will benefit. If we believe in equity and equal access, then the entire system must change for the better. This vision, learning for all, must be compelling to each principal. They must believe. And more importantly, they must have the superintendent's and board's support."

"It seems to me now that there is a lot of preparation before this can be addressed with some hope of improvement," Rob pointed out.

"If real progress is to be made, the district's prime mission, which you might want to consider as 'All students learning' for now, has to be driven like the energy from a laser. I'm not saying that lightly," he added with a smile at his play on words. Then he added, "Adizes says that the implementation phase in a change process must be highly directive to ensure the desired results. I've come to believe this myself."

Referring to the list in front of him on the table, Rob commented, "This sure is a challenging list. No wonder it took years to get your district schools in shape."

Rob began realizing how formidable the task was that he would soon be taking on and wondered how long it was going to take him to get the same or better results. Doubts about his ability to bring this off were making him anxious. There is much work ahead to do this right.

 Time-Out

1. Review the Effective Schools criteria. List what you believe the descriptors of each should be in your frame of reference.
2. Look at your system or school and rate it against your definition.

"The way the waitress is looking at us, I think she wants to close up lunch service. Either we need to find another place to sit, or maybe we should meet again after I send you Lezotte's material. We don't need to spend all our afternoon in covering the subject," Barry said, thinking they had almost done as much productive work as they could for the long day, but he knew Rob wanted to know about his approach to site-based management.

"That's okay with me," Rob agreed readily.

"I know that you want to chat some more about the elements of site-based management, or rather delegated site-based management. I'll tell you what I can do if it will speed up our work together. Why don't I just outline what I think is valuable about site empowerment and send it to you as a basis for our next discussion? Remember what we just learned about Sit Lead. Not every principal will be ready at any given time to take on more responsibility and accountability. You will have to diagnose each principal every step of the way to get the most effective results from the change."

"Well, I guess I would have predicted what you would say after 5 hours of Sit Lead training this morning," Rob said smugly. "Since it's now nearly four o'clock, let's pack up and get out of here. If you want to relax a few more minutes, we could have a libation," Rob offered. "It's on me!"

"Let's take a rain check on that. I have plans for dinner tonight and need to get going," Barry said.

"Okay, then."

"So in review, I have just let you lead me upward! I'm so gullible. I am doing the heavy lifting and you're smiling, driving home to your family up north. I hope you have a good weekend," Barry said somewhat halfheartedly.

"I think we're both tired. But if I understand correctly, you're going to send me two sets of materials before we meet again later this month. I had hoped to avoid another meeting, but it looks like I'm trapped. I need to get a better understanding before I go before the staff and act like an expert."

"Sounds good!" came the reply from his mentor.

"Seriously, I hope the golfers are enjoying the afternoon as much as I did. You always are a great help. Drive carefully and safely," Rob said appreciatively as he reached over and shook Barry's hand enthusiastically.

DOING HOMEWORK ON THE EFFECTIVE SCHOOLS AND SITE-BASED MANAGEMENT

On Monday morning bright and early Dr. Woodson was going through all the materials he had on Effective Schools. Also, somewhere in his files there were copies of comments he had asked principals for about the freedoms they had experienced in their delegated site-based program. With this data and a brief overview, he thought Rob would have enough homework to mess up another weekend at home. Taking much of what he had learned in person from Dr. Lezotte and from several of his books, he sent Rob a summarized history and explanation of the correlates. As he hurried, he decided not to send material on the site-based program. It might be better to talk that through face-to-face.

Subject: Effective Schools Material and Stuff
Dear Rob,

Enclosed you'll find material that comes from a number of Dr. Lezotte's resources and books. In this summary I will list the resources so that you may refer to them at your leisure.

I'm still looking for some information on the components of our old site-based program. It became a reality over the years so it wasn't a consciously developed plan. We went with what we thought they could absorb year by year. What we did grew out of our value system about letting the folks at the primary levels in the organization take on more responsibility for managing their affairs. I was partially influenced by the interaction I had with Peter Block, both from his books and several times in person at SIA conferences with Dr. Lezotte.

I'll try to get a better handle on this when we get together next.

Attachment: Effective Schools History and Criteria

I would like to start with some beliefs that are held by Larry Lezotte and addressed on page 17 in his book *The Effective Schools Process*, which you have by now.

"I don't believe that any student ought to have to take a seat in any classroom in America unless the teacher in that classroom can make it clear what results, outcomes, performance, and achievements are expected of that child.

"I don't think any teacher ought to have to take up a teaching station in any classroom in America unless the principal of that school can make it clear what results are expected of that teacher.

"I don't think any principal ought to have to take up a post anywhere in America unless the superintendent, operating as an agent of the Board and as an agent of the state, can make it clear to that principal what results are expected from the school.

"I think the superintendent and local Board have a right to expect the state to define the essential core learnings."

These statements set the stage by defining the ultimate purpose of why we would use any system to reform our school system.

Basic Beliefs

There are several basic beliefs or assumptions that are the underpinning of the "All students learning" mission. Rob, I am putting them in a format that you could use to indicate where you and others in the organization stand relative to these belief statements.

Mark the following survey indicating whether you (1) strongly agree, (2) agree, (3) are undecided, (4) disagree, or (5) strongly disagree.

Beliefs Survey

	1	2	3	4	5
All children can learn and come to school motivated to do so.	○	○	○	○	○
The individual school controls enough variables to assure that all children do learn.	○	○	○	○	○
A school's stakeholders are the most qualified people to implement the needed changes.	○	○	○	○	○
You and your colleagues are already doing the best you know how to do, given the conditions in which you find yourselves.	○	○	○	○	○
School-by-school changes are the best hope for reforming the schools.	○	○	○	○	○
There are only two kinds of schools in the United States—improving schools and declining schools.	○	○	○	○	○
Every school can improve.	○	○	○	○	○
The needed capacity to improve your school resides in your school right now.	○	○	○	○	○
All of the adults in the school are important.	○	○	○	○	○
Change is a process, not an event.	○	○	○	○	○
Existing people are the best change agents.	○	○	○	○	○

This should give you a flavor of a sound belief system and it certainly helps in forming the mission context and use of the criteria.

"The effective schools process is a proven path to learning for all."

—Lawrence Lezotte and Jo-Ann Pepperl

 Time-Out—The So What

Reread the belief statements.

1. To what degree can you support them?
2. Examine those you can't support. Why is that?
3. Take the survey. What do you understand about yourself based on your scores?
4. Now review the Effective Schools criteria. To what degree do you think all administrators have to buy into the criteria to have effective schools?
5. Think of a school with which you are familiar and measure it against the criteria.

Beginning of Effective Schools

In reacting to the Coleman study of July 1966, "The Equal Educational Opportunity Survey," Ron Edmons concluded that these programs focused on changing student behavior to compensate for their disadvantaged backgrounds but made no effort to change school behavior (Lezotte & McKee, 2002). From this position rose the Effective Schools movement. The researchers, Wilbur Brookover, Ron Edmons, and Larry Lezotte among them, developed a body of research that supported the premise that all children can learn and that the school controls the factors necessary to assure student mastery of the core curriculum.

The first task of the Effective Schools researchers was to identify existing effective schools—schools that were successful in educating all students regardless of their socioeconomic status or family background. Examples of these schools were found in varying locations and in both large and small communities. From these studies the correlates were derived.

"We can, whenever and wherever we choose, successfully teach all children whose schooling is of interest to us. We already know more than we need to do that. Whether or not we do it must finally depend on how we feel about the fact that we haven't so far."

—Ron Edmons

Correlate Short Summary

Rob, the following can be found in the material I'm recommending you read. I have an extra copy I'm going to enclose in the mailing.

Clear and focused mission: There is a clearly articulated mission of the school through which the staff shares an understanding of and a commitment to the school's goals, priorities, assessment procedures, and accountability.

Instructional leadership: The principal acts as an instructional leader and effectively and persistently communicates the mission of the school to staff, parents, and students.

Safe and orderly environment: There is an orderly, purposeful, business-like atmosphere, which is free from the threat of physical harm.

Climate of high expectation: There is a climate of high expectations in which the staff believes and demonstrates that all students can obtain mastery of the school's essential curriculum.

Opportunity to learn and student time on task: Teachers allocate a significant amount of classroom time to instruction in the essential curricular areas. Students are actively engaged in whole-class or large-group, teacher-directed, planned learning activities.

Frequent monitoring of student progress: Students' progress over the essential objectives are measured frequently and results of those assessments are used to improve individual student behaviors and performances, as well as to improve the curriculum as a whole.

Positive home-school relations: Parents understand and support the basic mission of the school and are given opportunities to play important roles in helping the school achieve its mission.

To sum up we can say an effective school is one that can, in measured student-achievement terms and reflective of its "all students learning" mission, demonstrate high overall levels of achievement and no gaps in the distribution of that achievement across major subsets of the student population.

Rob, I will refer you to *Assembly Required—A Continuous School Improvement System,* by Lezotte and McKee, for further reading and a more complete and thorough explanation.

Eventually, you find the right model to use with your schools. However, we need to make haste slowly on this one. Such a challenging change too soon may blow the whole deal. Try to keep it simple. Plan for the long haul. Come up with a process with an easily achievable first step. Orientation and discovery works well.

Call me when you want to meet to discuss this further.

Sincerely, Barry Woodson

 Time-Out—Now What

Given the challenge and opportunity for helping low-performing schools and using this material, what would you do?

THE AFTERMATH

The phone rang as Dr. Woodson was walking into the house a few days later. He had stopped off at the neighborhood supermarket on the way home to pick up something for dinner. The baby back ribs looked good and he enjoyed barbecuing them. He was rushing. He had gone off his diet, buying a half-gallon of so-called low-fat ice cream that he needed to get in the freezer before it melted, but he decided to answer the call as it might be important.

"Dr. Woodson speaking!" he said as he grabbed the phone just before it went to automatic answering.

"Barry, this is Rob Moore calling—"

"The Dr. Robert Moore! Rob, hold a minute—got something I must do," he interrupted, then tucked the phone under his chin and slipped the ice cream into the freezer.

"What is the crisis?" asked Rob.

"Just saving my dessert! What's on your mind?"

"I've got a problem! I need to chat with you about Effective Schools and other material you sent. Well, not really chat, but to set up an appointment so we can get together and review the material. At first glance it looks like it's the material I can use or rather make use of in the workshop next month as I start changing the conversation. But what's the best way to present this? I want to jump right in and begin discussing it with my cabinet as soon as possible."

"I am glad you think it will help," his sage mentor responded.

"Can you meet at the Pancake House next Friday at 7:30 for breakfast? Also, I need to explore more about your delegated site-based management ideas. This is going to be something I want to introduce and encourage the cabinet and principals to seriously consider taking on later this year. I need to go over your thoughts on this some more.

"I have the e-mail you sent me with the Lezotte input. I have a few questions about implementation. Such as when and why now? I'd like to have you review my latest thinking on moving forward in setting up a get-on-board plan with the principals. This may well include an implementation system and a user-friendly feedback system.

"I did start with the end in mind and I think I have a description of how I'm going to know when we arrive at or meet our targets. The cabinet is mostly with me on this. The business side of the house is still troubleshooting the ideas we came up with. Doug Daniels, finance and business, just doesn't find it easy to commit without all the data in front of him."

"If you're going to lay this on the principals as you plan, then why haven't you involved them yet?" Barry questioned.

"I met with two already and they seemed to understand. They even want my help and support in their school improvement process. These two were from higher performing schools."

"I would be cautious then. You realize, don't you, that they have little to lose since they are already doing well. You should begin planning the phase-in carefully. Don't lay too many expectations on them this year. It takes time for real lasting change to take hold."

"I'm excited to have some criteria to work from, and I want to get it done yesterday."

"All right then. Let's plan for just these two topics. I'm sorry that I got bushed and didn't send anything on site-based management, but we will cover it at breakfast," he promised.

AT BREAKFAST

Dr. Woodson hadn't done his homework as well as he would have liked. He had just come back from a trip to the northern part of the state, where he had worked with another rookie superintendent. Planning to work on the plane coming back, he was so tired that he just succumbed to reading one of the two popular novels he had brought, a real cliffhanger. So much for good intentions! The flight was delayed 2 hours, so he'd gotten home late last night and now was hurrying on his way to meet Rob for breakfast.

He didn't expect Paradise Valley to change much this year, as it takes a long continuous process if the change is to last. Rob had mentioned earlier that he might want to consider a process in the spring involving a task force to begin shaping the mission, vision, and core values to begin setting the focus on learning. This would help in getting the principals and teachers on board.

This process Woodson mentioned had a parallel process that had worked well before in getting large-scale acceptance. While Rob was committed to having all students learning, he had yet to determine where the principals and teachers stood in this belief.

Rather than make any wholesale changes right away he did want to change the ground rules for the future. He knew they couldn't afford to keep the status quo. Again he thought about Peter Block's statement that "to change the culture you have to begin to change the conversation."

Rob on the other hand had arrived at 7:10 to grab a quiet booth and outline what he remembered about the site-based management, or rather delegated site-based management in Woodson's terms. He got out his ubiquitous notebook and began listing points he wanted to discuss with his mentor.

First, he wanted to ask him to describe the key program components he used. After he got a better handle on this, he wanted to talk about how to begin implementing some of these ideas. He wondered how the principals who had worked with his mentor felt about the program, the strengths and weaknesses. He hoped that Barry could give him some specific feedback.

Next, he wanted to share with his mentor the Personnel Staffing Unit (PSU) plan he had used in his last district to see how that would fit in the overall picture.

Finally, since he knew that he would surely be asked what his ultimate goal was, the end in mind, he better write something down quickly before Woodson arrived. Well, he thought, I'm basically lazy, so I like to delegate the work appropriately to the folks that are hired to do it. Well, that wasn't totally true. Controlling the situation was his cup of tea, but as he trusted staff more, he would feel better about delegating more. He really believed that effective change in the schools happened when the staff, the principal and teachers, caught the vision and had more to say in the process.

Just as he was finalizing his thoughts, he looked up and saw Woodson hurrying toward the table.

"Sorry I am late," Barry said. "There was more traffic around the high school than I anticipated. I had to wait for three signals before I could get here. It seems like all the kids have cars or have their parents driving them to school."

"That's okay. It gave me a chance to pull my thoughts together."

"By the way, how are the wife and kids handling the commuting arrangement?" Barry asked with some curiosity. He knew that Rob had an 85-mile drive and that Don Halverson had just moved into the condo as his roommate, being in a similar situation with a long commute.

"Things are going well. We each try to get home once midweek, but on different nights. Keeps one of us in the district for night activities throughout the week. Getting to know the territory thing," he reminded his mentor, looking for approval.

After the waitress took their order, Barry began firing more questions at Rob.

"Rob, before we begin I need to ask you what you want out of the move to more site-based responsibility? What do you want to accomplish and why?"

"I knew you were going to ask, so I'm ready for you," Rob responded and then shared his belief in empowerment as a way to begin creating the much-needed effective schools in the district.

"This means you should do some Phase A thinking for this strategic planning project, so you had better use the Backwards Thinking model again. You'll find it makes it easier to explain your ideas to others and then work together to process them."

"I got it! You just handed the task back to me. Okay. I'll work it out. And this time I'm going to do it as an ad cab project involving the team, as they're going to be part of the solution."

"Now that that's settled, what else can I do for you?" Barry asked, just as the waitress was refilling their coffee cups for the second time. She mentioned that their orders would be there soon.

"I would like to hear again about how you explained this issue and how your principals reacted to it."

After the waitress brought their breakfast orders, with eggs sunny-side up and a side of sausage, Barry reviewed in his mind what he thought were the keys to success.

"Before I start on my experience I would like to hear more about the PSU plan you used in your last district, Rob," Barry said.

"It is simple and yet complicated to describe. It's a system providing equity to schools based on school level and preset standards. To begin, we just looked to what they were spending on average at each level and their staffing numbers. Basically, each staffing unit is equivalent to 1.0 teacher unit. This 1.0 cost factor is an average of the teachers' salaries from the previous year. The units for all other staff members for whom the principal is responsible consist of a ratio of the average salary in each classification.

"Due to the variation in the size of the schools, each principal got a secretary and one custodian without charge of any units. Assistant principals, counselors, and other support staff were given their equivalent fractional value. For example, an assistant principal's average salary might be equivalent to 1.35 units of the average teacher salary."

"Let me interrupt a second," the mentor said. "I'm sure you aren't doing this, but don't tell them you did it this way back home in your old district. This may shut them down. Many people don't like and aren't ready for suggestions about doing things 'my old district way.'

"If you think the PSU plan is a winner, sell it on its merits. It makes you sound more like an expert anyway."

"Good thinking."

"I think I'm following your 'lecture' okay," the prof joked at their role reversal. "Go on."

"When we started the program," Rob said, "the existing resources at the schools were used in determining the schools' total allocation. There is much more to this, but basically it gave the principals a total number of units assigned to their school. Then they could configure the school personnel almost any way they wanted to within certain limits but couldn't exceed the units given to the school. Are you following this okay, coach?"

"Yes. I've heard about similar programs and I'm glad this worked for you. Is this something you want to consider here for next year?" Barry said excitedly. This sounded very good to him. Rob was moving in the right direction on his own.

"Yes, I think so," Rob said.

"If you're serious, probably the next step for you is to plan how to get where you want to be. I could share some other ideas I used that you might want to consider."

"What can you add to this?" Rob queried.

"I think installing your PSU plan for next September may work. The Effective Schools strategy probably needs a lot more time. Why don't you just order some of the material and have your principals read it? Then you can set up a session where they can discuss it. You may want to use the beliefs questionnaire to find out where they are."

SOME EMPOWERING COMPONENTS

"Now let me review the elements of what I thought was enabling for the principals that worked with me. They had boundaries, first of all. These boundaries were the core values. They had to stay within this belief system, which was driven by the focus on all students learning, whatever it takes," the mentor began. Barry then discussed some other ideas he had for giving the principals more responsibility in their schools.

"*Financial accountability:* The question here is whether you want bottom-line accountability or line-by-line categorical accountability. You might want to go slow on this. You already have a bad example in the high school principal diverting library money to football equipment, which you told me about a few weeks ago.

"Additionally, you need to review how resources other than staff members are assigned to the schools. Since equity has been an issue, you might want to set up a formula, an amount of dollars per pupil by school level, for student supplies, books, and other support material. This then gives the school more decision making if you provide for bottom-line accountability, allowing them to transfer from one category to another as they choose.

"*Teacher selection:* To what degree does each principal have leeway in the final selection of the teaching staff? Can and do your principals involve other teachers and department heads in the selection process? How much central office control do you want to have in this selection process?

"*The PSU plan:* If the average teacher salary is $55,000, are you going to allow transfers from personnel funds to cash to buy other materials? Can a principal take a half unit, $27,500, and spend it on science equipment?

"*Guaranteed site carryover of funds:* Unused funding for things could be carried over to the next year. Also, some PSU dollars could be carried forward. One PSU at high schools, 0.75 at middle schools, and 0.5 at elementary schools. This is how we enabled long-term planning, funding big projects over 2 years, staff decisions on priorities, and a feeling of controlling expenditures. We partially limited carryover so the schools would spend their budgets given them for that year.

"*Special challenge grants:* Each year we set aside money that teachers, schools, and other departments could apply for to fund creative ideas. These were 1-year grants and usually involved technology-related programs."

After hearing this, Rob directed a question to his mentor. "What did your principals say about what you were able to delegate to them?"

"Actually, I do have some statements from a survey I conducted a few years ago. In general, here is what they thought they were able to do on their own. Most were very positive. They liked having control. At first, having to work through a teacher site committee was difficult. Now one principal turns the staffing and budget over to the team of the whole faculty. They have grown to accept this responsibility. Knowing they didn't have to spend frantically before May to use up the budget has given them a better way to plan over the longer term."

"This sounds good. Where do I start?" Rob said excitedly.

"Not so fast! Readiness is everything. Planning for change. Don't rush in!" Barry cautioned.

"I'll get with cabinet and explore some of these ideas."

Barry needed to caution Rob on another point. "Remember, I used the term *delegated site-based management*. Let me explain why. First, the core values and the mission define the boundaries. Second, we didn't allow each and every principal the absolute right to control their own destiny. For instance, one principal couldn't balance his staffing and support budget so the assistant superintendent had to continually oversee his monthly spending. He was held on a tight rein on money issues.

"I had one principal that required no more management than saying hello in September and then thanks for the great job she did in June. She understood the mission and her students were continually improving in the learning process as measured by our assessment program. In most everything she did she would be a good role model for other principals.

"Just one more example. Another principal who was excellent in most things didn't hire teachers very well. The assistant superintendent in the personnel support service had to keep a close eye on her recommendations for final approval. He even had to reject some of the recommendations from the school," Barry concluded.

"I see what you are trying to tell me here. It seemed that you actually used your situational leadership expertise in managing the site principals. Is that why you call it 'delegated site-based'? Tell me, how did they feel about the program over time?"

"Exactly, Rob, you don't turn the class over to the kids without them being ready. And yes it went well. Of course, not everyone was consistent in using the concepts. Over time we didn't reinforce it enough. But when we were debriefing a situation gone wrong we used it as a tool to understand how to be better next time. We tried to instill this as part of the corporate culture."

 Time-Out—A So What

1. Review each of the suggestions for empowering the schools.
2. What would you be able to use? What would you add to the list?
3. How far should the superintendent go in giving schools more autonomy?

Barry, trying to pick up the pace, asked, "What else is on the agenda for this morning's session?"

"Just to report that the board recall is creating some interest on the editorial pages of the local papers. I'm offering no comment except to say something about the community having an opportunity to decide who they want representing them on the board."

"And do you plan to stay out of it?

"As much as I can."

"Anything else?"

"The community tone now is to just have one superintendent and try to settle out on Branson, who many think got an unfair shake," Rob added.

"You must be doing something right!" Barry encouraged Rob.

"This month has been chock-full of stuff. Are we going too fast?" he questioned.

"What do you mean?" asked Barry.

"I just feel overloaded with new stuff."

"Remember, what we are covering are proven practical techniques demonstrated in successful schools and districts. I'm putting them in front of you for your consideration only. This, of course, excludes the two management training sessions you already scheduled for your management team to bring them closer together," Barry summarized. "Remember our prime mission here is to help you survive this first year and meet those goals you defined earlier."

"Yes, I see that. I need someone to pop off to and I guess you are better than dumping it all on the wife and kids when I do get home," Rob said with a faint smile.

"I think we can go back to our respective jobs knowing you are still in good shape for survival. No one seems to want to vote you off the team yet!" his mentor kidded him.

"Thank goodness!"

"Rob, before I forget it, thanks for sending me a copy of the board goals document you're putting on the agenda for approval next month. I like the format and I think it will be interesting to see their reaction."

"As you can tell, it all came from the superintendent's cabinet. We each had a part in it."

"The board's reaction?"

"I did get some input from individual board members," Rob said.

"You were right on target with improving student performance and developing a plan for aligning the curriculum," Barry said. "You had to include improving the budget and accountability processes since that was such a major project this year. Of course, you have to build a new elementary school or the community will come unglued. What I liked best was when you stepped up and included a goal for the board to work more effectively together. I'm anxious to see how that's going to work out, especially with the measurable criterion of having them not shout at each other during board meetings."

Rob said, "While I believe the honeymoon is still going strong, I decided to set the agenda so that the board and community would know where I want to go. If the board approves this, it'll give us a green light to move forward."

"I really admire the work you've done. Is there anything else to discuss today?"

"That's all I can think of. Why don't we call it a day? Keep in touch," Rob said.

They arranged to get together and do more planning for the November workshop and drove away, each with his own thoughts about next steps in this challenging situation.

🕐 **Time-Out—Now What**

1. Is delegated site-based management a possibility in your district? If so, how would you start introducing the change?
2. If not, why not? Explore the reasons.
3. Is Situational Leadership an option for you to consider? Why?
4. Are you ready to use the ideas from Situational Leadership in negotiating for leadership style? How would you begin?
5. What do you think of the correlates? Do they make sense?

SUMMARY

In this chapter we started with a briefing session between Rob and his mentor on the situational leadership material just covered in the cabinet workshop at an off-site location. During this time the continuing problem between Rob and his administrative assistant came up again. Out of this arose an age-old issue of finding time to get the work done involving the right people. This led to a discussion on the effective use of late-afternoon and early-evening time in getting to know the staff, including the notion of informal scheduled voluntary meetings with principals.

The second of two agreed-upon management training topics was planned for a November training session with the cabinet and principals. The two programs would lead to creating a new culture of continuous learning expectations for administrators.

The balance of the chapter was spent on a brief history of the Effective Schools movement with a listing and definition of the Effective Schools criteria. An assessment tool was provided for the reader to compare beliefs with Dr. Lezotte's belief system.

Delegated site-based management was explored through the use of several tools that would give principals more say in decisions at the site.

The chapter closed with an update about the anxiously awaited school recall election set for late February. Moving forward and survival were still two unresolved challenges.

"There is power in the vision of excellence so long as some of us share in the dream and believe in our hearts that we can make a difference."

—**Anonymous**

 Time-Out—Reflections

1. Review the learning points in the chapter. Which material would you like to implement in your setting?
2. Why?

MONTH 4—OCTOBER

Strategies and Survival Skills

1. Try off-site meetings as long as the board approves.
   - These meetings need to be away from phones except for emergencies.
   - Designate one person to stay in the district as the acting chief.
   - Invite board members to observe or even participate as appropriate.
2. Involve your cabinet and gain their support in key decisions affecting both them and others in the district.
   - It pays to get acceptance early in any change attempt.
3. Continue to look for management and leadership training materials and systems that will both bond the team and provide a better basis for leading people.
   - Consider a method such as "Rappin' with Rob" as a vehicle to get your principals and other groups involved in informal communication and issue-resolving processes.
   - Use this method to access your principals' leadership potential and their vision and mission understanding.

- Review the Effective Schools methodology and see if it fits your organizational needs.

4. Be sure you consider all three components of shared vision, focused mission, and effective principals as you move toward more effective schools.

5. Be sure you have a system in place and know the readiness level of your principals before you try or increase use of delegated site-based management.
    - Without a system and well-thought-through steps in moving to site-based management, you will have a disaster on your hands.
    - Remember "to make haste slowly."
    - Analyze your principals using the readiness criteria from Situational Leadership to help better understand where they are now.

6. Sound out your ideas on a few people who will be involved later. Listen and then listen some more.

7. Have a fair system in place for allocating resources to the schools, by school levels, such as a PSU plan.

8. Look to the Effective Schools research to diagnose where your schools are.
    - Consider the entire process if timely. At least understand the leading indicators that affect student performance.

TOOLBOX

Block, P. (1993). *Stewardship: Choosing Service Over Self-Interest*. San Francisco, CA: Berrett-Koehler.

Lezotte, L., & Cipriano Pepperl, J. (1999). *The Effective Schools Process: A Proven Path to Learning for All*. Okemos, MI: Effective Schools Products.

Lezotte, L., & McKee, K. (2002). *Assembly Required: A Continuous School Improvement System*. Okemos, MI: Effective Schools Products.

6

NOVEMBER: MAKING
STYLISH DECISIONS

HOW DO OTHERS PERCEIVE WHAT YOU
DO AND SAY?

In this chapter you will:

1. Learn more about yourself and how others perceive you.
2. Understand more about the TRACOM Social Style Model.
3. Learn more about the concepts in the development of the model.
4. Begin planning to integrate these concepts into the organizational culture.
5. Learn about another decision-making model.

THE WORKSHOP—FRIDAY

The second day of a 3-day workshop was nearly over. Twenty of Paradise Valley School District's finest and brightness had gathered for an emotional, revealing, and sometimes gratifying experience. It was after 10 p.m. and Rob Moore was pacing in his hotel room. At the end of the day, like other participants, Rob received a challenging assignment from the group's facilitator and his mentor, Dr. Barry Woodson. Barry handed out the individual personal profiles and a banner exercise for each just before the group broke for the social hour and dinner.

His homework was to fill out his banner. The exercise was designed to help each participant pictorially interpret the feedback from their

computerized personal profile. The banners were to be drawn as creatively as possible on a single flip-chart page. They would be sharing the
results in small groups the next morning.

But only Rob got a bonus, a second assignment, one he couldn't avoid
any longer. Slowing his pacing somewhat, he looked thoughtfully out
the window at the light playing on the darkened ocean in the distance.
Now he knew how others, the five respondents he and Diane had separately selected for their individual feedback, perceived each of their
communication styles. This gave him the necessary information to work
out an action plan to help the two of them resolve the continuing nag-
ging problems that resurfaced every so often. In his reflection, he worried whether all this effort would be worth it.

Barry and Rob had gone over the computer printout for each participant's Social Style the night before, just after the cabinet group stopped
for dinner. They now knew the style of each participant. As he got more
into the program, he was finally beginning to recognize the differences
among the four styles.

Rob's hope for the outcome was beyond learning about new tools to
help them manage more effectively. He wanted to watch the administrators working together as a team, applying what they had learned to
solving problems, or rather developing plans to resolve them.

Actually, he and Diane were getting along much better now. Barry
had given him some helpful suggestions. He was spending more
planned time with her. They tried to get away for a 2-hour working
lunch every week or so just to catch up. These lunch meetings helped,
and now in spite of his better understanding of her Amiable Style, there
were still times when something triggered a cool atmosphere. Overall,
her work was excellent and she was learning more about the school business each day. She handled irate parents extremely well and the district
staff really liked her. More and more the principals were calling her first
and checking to see if the superintendent was in a good mood for a yes
on a creative request, usually involving more money.

REFLECTIONS AND REVERIE

Rob couldn't get started on his banner or the Diane project yet.
Whether it was simple procrastination or needing a little more ground-
ing, he let his thoughts drift back to earlier in the month, when the

agenda details were finalized for this 3-day workshop. After establishing goals for the meeting, Rob wanted time with the cabinet to go over further implementation of the recently board-adopted "Superintendent's Goals." The cabinet members needed to learn better techniques in managing. Even though the CEO would be directly supervising principals and some of the other directors this first year, the entire group needed to understand and learn these skills to be used with their direct reports.

After the Situational Leadership work with the cabinet had gone so well, he jumped on Barry's suggestion that this material could be equally important and serve well as a good team-building opportunity. Barry even mentioned including a few support services directors as part of the mix. It was never too early to recognize the importance of these folks, he had strongly suggested. Too often, they had been neglected in favor of the credentialed staff.

Once the goals were established, the meeting format was the next task. They had decided to meet on Thursday at the resort hotel that Barry had used before. The hotel condos would work just fine. They slept five each. Smaller double-room condos were available for the overflow.

Barry had suggested an informal folksy way to team build. The cabinet would take turns playing chef for the group with the exception of the second night's dinner in the hotel's main dinning room. The cabinet, checking in around 11 a.m., was to start with lunch in one condo and then meet until around 5 p.m. Following a break, the dinner duo charged with that menu would prepare the feast.

After Friday's prepared breakfast, this time with Chef Rob in the kitchenette, there would be a continuation of wrestling with more "big rocks" until the other members of their team joined up around 10 o'clock. The introduction to Social Style was the first thing on the agenda for the big group.

Later, lunch would be prepared by another two directors. Following lunch the facilitator, Dr. Woodson, was to continue presenting the Social Style Program, with the individual results handed out just before the social hour. This should be good timing because the feedback was not always easily accepted. At times there was a large gap between an individual's self-perception and the consensus of the five others that filled out the behavior-based checklist responses. Relaxing in a social setting would allow informal sharing of the results. This should support the team-building goal for the workshop.

Rob was still avoiding his homework assignment. His wandering mind returned to the memory of calling Barry to arrange a session to chat. He had wanted to have more guidance in working out the backwards thinking model, especially the outcomes box. After board approval, he needed to assign tasks for his cabinet to carry out work they had committed to doing. With the big-rock story stuck in his mind, he was seeking a better way to begin processing challenging opportunities, the current euphemism for serious problems.

Rob, lying on the bed and propped up against the headboard, had his eyes closed now and could almost see and hear every part of that conversation as a movie playing on his mind's "screen."

"Rob, how do you want to approach this interpersonal communication stuff between you and your assistant that we spoke of before? Also, it should be helpful for you in working with the board and administrative cabinet," Barry said, more formally pushing the conversation back to the tough part of the agenda. They'd been all over the place again, avoiding the obvious.

"Can you walk me through it?" Rob replied, thinking that he would soon have to face dealing with Diane in a more thorough manner.

"Yes, of course. Let's try keeping me on a shorter leash. The last time I ran away with the explanation on Sit Lead," he smiled, knowing that these skills learned in the previous workshop were starting to be applied.

"Well, give me a shorter version, and then I'll check for understanding as Madeline Hunter would insist on."

Barry then began. "When I first discovered the communication style concepts in the 1980s, it was through Dr. John G. Geier. In the format he used, adjectives describing behavior were selected and marked with a special pen to raise an image in the blip selected—pre-high-tech era. These responses were then tallied and used to fit patterns in 16 sets of researched preselected styles.

"I remember clearly even today what he described as the basic tenets key to understanding the underlying philosophy. In fact, I still use them to set the stage for the TRACOM Social Style training in class and in workshops."

Then he listed the six basic statements on Rob's office board.

1. You can't motivate people. You create an environment in which people motivate themselves.
2. All people are motivated.
3. People do things for their reasons, not yours.
4. An individual's weakness may be an overextension of his or her strengths.
5. If another person understands you better than you understand him or her, that other person may control the communication.
6. If another person understands you better than you understand yourself, that person may enslave you.

"That sounds rather powerful. Did he overstate the case?"

"I don't think so! Let me give you a quick developmental history of these concepts. Actually, styles were mentioned in medieval times in interpreting the moods people were exhibiting. There may have been a problem in the scientific method in those days as these four temperaments, based on our inner juices (humors), were identified. They named them for our body fluids—sanguine (blood), melancholic (black bile), phlegmatic (phlegm), and choleric (yellow bile). They seemed to dominate the person, so the resultant behavior was codified.

"It's interesting to me, without benefit of research and development using the usual two independent variables, how close they came to what we know as the four behavioral communication, or Social Styles as further developed today."

"I didn't know I was going to get an ancient history lesson today!" Rob cried out as if in pain.

"Stick with me and you'll never know where I may lead you. I hope astray is not an option!" Barry laughed.

"Lead on and I will follow," Rob replied dutifully.

"As far as I know it started with the work of William Marston in the late 1920s. He wanted to know more about normal people, since Freud was focusing on the abnormal. At least that was the story handed down to me years ago."

"When you and Freud were colleagues?" the smart-mouthed response came back.

"I refuse to comment," Barry said with a straight face.

Then, paraphrasing David Merrill and Roger Reid's work in *Personal Styles and Effective Performance*, Barry continued by saying, "By the 1960s, these groups were developing theories, writing books, assembling materials, producing video segments, creating adjective-based questionnaires, and developing feedback systems, testing them over and over again, to allow others to observe the similar behaviors.

"David Merrill started by using a structured adjective checklist developed by Dr. James W. Taylor. Merrill then expanded this by having five others describe the individual's behavior. Then a factor analysis method was used and three clusters, or scales, emerged."

"This has been around a long time. I first heard about these ideas 5 years ago in class," Rob vaguely remembered and then asked, "How many times have you gone through the training?"

"Counting being a participant, leading seminars, and teaching this material, I would say between 20 and 25 times."

"And you still think it's good?"

"Of course, or I wouldn't recommend it. Knowing style makes a big difference," Barry said without a doubt in his voice. "How do you think I get along with you so well? And am I starting to be successful in coaching you with Diane?"

"Got it! I'm more in tune now!"

"Now can I get back to the explanation?"

"Okay."

"The four possible styles are created when the two independent variables, assertiveness and responsiveness, are combined into a four-quadrant model you've seen many times before.

Barry then did a quick review of other, similar work. Rob inquired as to why they even got into the program.

The prof explained that the why came from watching others in the cabinet behave and communicate differently. There had to be a better way to understand each other than by chance and experience. If they wanted to become more effective they needed to understand the similarities and differences in the way they related and reacted to each other. Beyond more effective interpersonal communication and better meeting skills, this helped in conflict resolution and team building. It can be fun. Also, he mentioned that it can be integrated to augment Situational Leadership, and that was helpful, too.

"That's a start at the why. What about the material you decided to use?" asked Rob.

"The one we settled on was the TRACOM program. It's easier to administer and they're easy to work with and helpful. Their updated adjective checklist has been improved by using behavior-based statements. This is more reliable over time, provides greater detail regarding versatility scores, and is more easily deployed in multiple languages.

"The perceptions of three to five colleagues create the feedback for identifying your Style and in creating a Versatility, or Endorsement, scale. At first, I liked another system earlier, as the graphing of results was easier to visualize, but it wasn't computerized. We started using the TRACOM process and my old district is still using it today as we speak," he explained. "I even use it in my consulting work, as you know. I will mention more about this in the training session."

"What's an Endorsement, or Versatility, scale?" Rob asked.

Barry answered, "The questionnaire measures the impact, or effect, your behavior has on others. While the assertiveness and responsive results seldom change over time, new input or changing situations can drive this scale up or down quickly."

"Stop! That's enough background. Can you tell me how the Style process works and how I can use it? Sounds like you were delivering a lecture to the choir," Rob chided.

"Thanks for the feedback!" Barry said with a smile. "Let's look at the board while I go over the model. Ask questions along the way," he added.

THE SOCIAL STYLE MODEL

Rob could see Barry going to the whiteboard in his office and saying, "If I didn't mention it before, this model is based on how you see yourself and how others see you. It is based on behavior we exhibit, what we can see and what the person says or does. Let me remind you that this is based on 'normal' people, if there are any of us left. The test-group results are divided into quartiles for each of the two variables.

"This is explained further in each participant's Social Style Profile with both a description and scoring analysis on it. It places you where you think you are and then where the majority of your five 'friends' see you. This isn't necessarily the same place. Your own self-perception and the averaged perceptions of others you selected are going to vary, unless you really understand how you affect those around you. That's why the feedback is so important in changing behavior—especially your own!"

"Did your Social Style change over time?" the superintendent asked with a little hesitation in his voice, wondering what he was agreeing to. Then suddenly he had cold feet and thought, Am I ready for this? But he remembered what his coach was doing to help him with Diane. Guess he'd have to bite the bullet. He worried that his Style would be put on a flip chart in front of God and everyone. What if he got a low Versatility score? Oh well!

"I've been profiled over a dozen times and no, my Style didn't change even though I used different people each time."

Barry decided it was time to walk Rob through the model. He erased the Geier list after noticing Rob had copied it. Then he drew a model in its place (see Figure 6.1).

"Now reflect on the words in each quadrant. The use of these terms tends to have a labeling effect. However, each term does have its own set of characteristics. It's also important that we learn the strengths, weaknesses, tendencies, and backup styles that we have in common and, most important, how to use this information to produce better results in our communication efforts."

"That's another mouthful," Rob quickly inserted.

"For example, the person with a Driving Style is seen as being more assertive and yet more controlling of their emotional behavior and so on."

"I think I'm starting to see where this goes."

"I'm only giving you an overview here. During the workshop we roll up our sleeves and wade right in. The video tapes will help you see the behaviors portrayed that will illustrate what we're talking about. Are you ready?" the prof challenged.

"I'm game," Rob responded hesitantly, without much conviction. Did he really want to reveal more about himself to others? Do I need to change? Do I want to? He remembered these were the first questions asked when change was imminent. He was trapped, but maybe that's

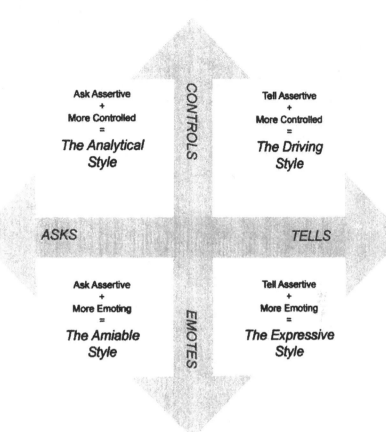

Figure 6.1. The TRACOM Group's Social Style Model.
Courtesy of the TRACOM Group.

okay. Commit now or forever keep old behaviors; go forward or stagnate.

"Rob, let's see how much you've picked up. I'm going to give you your first challenge. Diane will be a real live test. Is she generally warm and friendly with people, somewhat animated, or seemingly unemotional?"

"She is very friendly and open most of the time, seems to like people."

"What about her assertiveness? Does she seem to tell more or ask?"

"She seems slow to take action or even ask questions. I thought she was unsure of herself," Rob replied with some hesitation.

"Probably she is and maybe her communication style needs to be identified and you need to take that into consideration," Barry suggested.

"What do I consider?" Rob asked.

"Hang on a minute. First, what about you? Can you be characterized the same as she is? How do you see yourself?

"Rob, your behavior with me would indicate your scores are in the A and the 2 columns, we could say you are an A-2. Now locate that box on the model and write in your name. This shows how you see yourself, what is labeled a driving style (see Figure 6.2).

"Well, I'm really focused on getting things done. There's no question about assertiveness. I tend to tell more than lead by asking questions. My assistant is the opposite on this measure it seems!"

"Duh!"

"It's that obvious?"

"Of course! I'll place her name where I'm guessing she'll be. That's what I've explained these past 2 months. And do you have trouble listening to others, and are you usually three steps ahead trying to get your response ready? Not really listening! Sometimes do you pop off without thinking and then forget about it? And wonder why others avoid you at times? Right?" he chided the rookie.

"Well, now that you mention it, probably so. Are you some kind of wizard?" Rob replied.

"Only experienced in observing behavior more closely after having gone through training, I'm afraid." Barry said. "As you can see, if I'm right about Diane, you are in opposite quadrants of the model and don't have many style characteristics in common. You have the Driving Style characteristics and she has those of an Amiable Style, which are diagonally opposite. Look at the chart. You're more tell-oriented and she's more ask-oriented. You tend to control your emotions and she tends to show them. The good news is that you can learn how to maximize the communication between the two of you with some more training and practice. And especially for you, learn to be more patient!"

Barry then took the time to explain more in detail about their style differences. When he asked Rob if he wanted to go forward with the training, the answer was yes. Rob said he wanted to use this training both as a team builder and for more effective personal interaction and

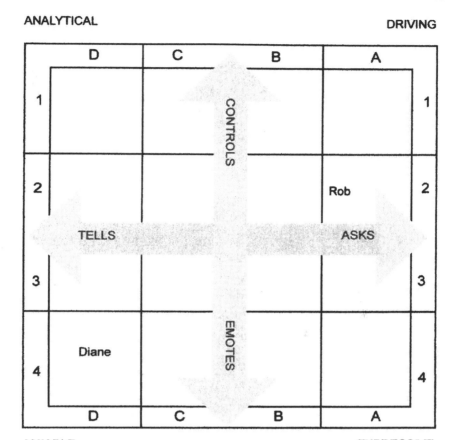

Figure 6.2. Self-Perception.
Courtesy of the TRACOM Group.

better productivity with his staff. Also, he had in mind to practice problem solving with real problems, integrating the Backwards Thinking Model. Barry suggested that Rob consider looking at board members through the lenses of this model.

THE REVERIE ENDS AND HOMEWORK BEGINS

Rob came suddenly out of his reverie. It was only getting later and his assignments were still spread out on the bed. Then he thought to himself, I had better finish now so I can get some sleep. The action plan for working more effectively with Diane had the highest priority. First thing now was to meet and share profiles—perhaps we could find time tomorrow. Once we see the differences, together we can build a better relationship. I'll use the TRACOM chart Barry handed out today as a guide to the conversation.

Rob's mind started in high gear as he thought through a course of action. Since I believe that I have a Driving Style, I need to look at how this affects the Amiable Style. I seem to need support for conclusions and actions while Diane is more into feelings and relationships. I'm going to keep my action plan simple. I'm going to surprise Barry by suggesting that Diane and I get together and jointly work out a plan after the workshop is concluded. Knowing that Diane is concerned about feelings and relationships, I'll ask her opinions first. This will be a good way to begin practicing what we learned in the session today and will be finalizing tomorrow morning. According to Barry, each of us will be sharing our banners with the entire group or at least in small groups, which should give us insight into each one's particular style.

When I get my mentor alone, I think I'll startle him by saying I finally got it and this is how I'm going to start a conversation with Diane. "Good morning Diane. How is your mother?—and now why aren't you getting the work done? Oh yes, quit pouting when I shout at you!" Maybe he'll smile or maybe get upset. He does have to go along with my sick humor sometimes.

I'll begin with my banner, and she and I will share each of our own characteristics. Having seen a few others on the profile analysis, I think we will be able to share each other's printed feedback. I will be patient and understanding when listening to her point of view. I hope she will better understand my need to get results and that I can be very directive at times. I think I'll set up an agreed signal for a time-out to be called when the tension builds up.

To build trust, I'll ask her to say the keywords "you're driving too hard," and mine will be "you need to initiate." This should make me stop in my tracks and consider what's going on. I hope she will be sensitive to the mood she sometimes gets in and will let me talk to her about it. When I'm going about like a roaring lion she can call a time-out. It's really probably more my problem than hers, because I won't make the intervention timely. I guess I just don't want to hurt her feelings.

One more thing came to mind before he could turn out the light—the #@%/! banner assignment. This was ridiculous. He knew he was not an artist, but he had to do it. After all, as the leader he was supposed to model the desired behavior. At first he couldn't find it in his stack of materials and notes, but there it was waiting. He luckily found an old magazine with enough pictures to cut and paste to make his banner. This was what he was to share tomorrow. Finally done! The light went out at 11:45.

THE SUPERINTENDENT'S BANNER

Using the numerical key that follows, select a word, short phrase, or symbol to describe yourself in the areas listed. You will want to refer to both your Social Style Profile and report for guidelines (see Figure 6.3).

Numbers 1–4   Create one picture, drawing, or symbol in each space representing your understanding of your Social Style. Do these in order of value or importance (number 1 being most important; 4, least important).

Use written statements to describe the following:

Number 5   What is my Social Style and Versatility?
Number 6   What are three behavioral strengths of my style?
Number 7   What are three behavioral weaknesses of my style?
Number 8   What growth areas would I like to work on?
Number 9   What style slogan would I use to describe myself?
Number 10   What recommendations does my report suggest?
Number 11   What is one thing I have to remember constantly when interacting with others?

INTEGRATING STYLES AND LYLES

A week before the 3-day workshop was to start, right after he let his four o'clock class go, Dr. Woodson was in his office planning for the Paradise

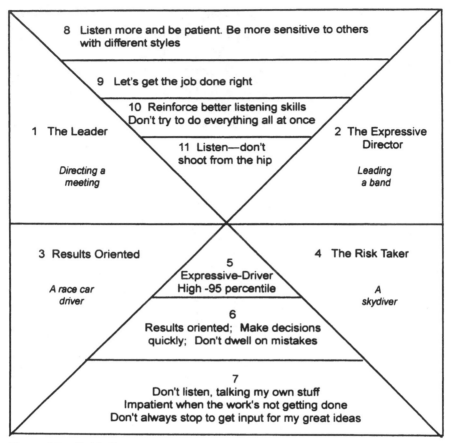

Figure 6.3. Rob's Banner.
Courtesy of Geier Learning International.

Valley event. Rob wanted to start with the cabinet Thursday around lunchtime and deal with some big rocks, including the implementation strategy for the goals just approved by the board. Thursday night would be a social join-up affair. On Friday morning the 14 principals and directors would arrive around 10 a.m.

The styles workshop would take up all of Friday and 2 hours on Saturday. Around 10:30 on Saturday he would set up the fun part using three problems the cabinet wanted to explore. The team would be practicing what he taught them in late October about the Lyles problem-solving, decision-making approach during a 2-hour briefing. They would have one problem-solving session before lunch and two immediately after.

His task now was to develop the integration of styles and Lyles he had promised Rob earlier. There would be a debriefing just before closing time on Saturday, and then Woodson would go home to try and salvage the weekend. He was pleased that Rob's folks jumped at the chance to be part of the workshop even though they had to give up the best part of a weekend. Given the option, most of the team had decided to stay overnight Friday rather than commute. It looked like they might become party animals, or maybe they already were!

In late October, Woodson had worked with Rob's cabinet on integrating some thoughts about the five-phase Backwards Thinking model and with the Problem-Solving and Decision-Making model, written and developed by a parent in his former district, Richard I. Lyles. He thought that there was value added and would try it on for size with the group. Lyles's material had more of a how-to nature and provided some very practical advice in dealing with each of the seven or eight steps.

Organizations can be successful only if there is a reasonably accurate understanding throughout the organization of its purpose and desired results.

DECISION MAKING AND PROBLEM SOLVING

Always the teacher and lecturer, Barry just had to go over some more background material. This time it was what he had learned years ago from Dick Lyles, whose Problem-Solving and Decision-Making Model (see Figure 6.4) encompasses more steps than many of the others and is much less complicated in its approach.

Barry then explained in detail how to work through each of the steps in the problem-solving and decision-making model. He gave them several examples to work through, both the obstacle and deviation situations. He asked them to practice using these strategies so they would be

THE LYLES METHOD

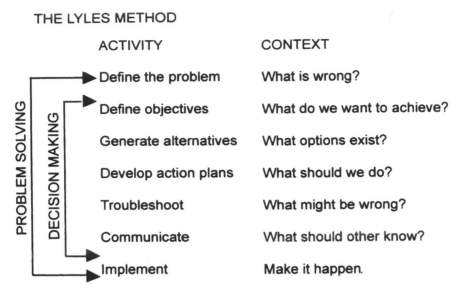

ACTIVITY	CONTEXT
Define the problem	What is wrong?
Define objectives	What do we want to achieve?
Generate alternatives	What options exist?
Develop action plans	What should we do?
Troubleshoot	What might be wrong?
Communicate	What should other know?
Implement	Make it happen.

PROBLEM SOLVING

DECISION MAKING

Figure 6.4. Context for Problem-Solving and Decision-Making Activity.
Source: Lyles, 1982.

prepared to work on some real district problems during the workshop next month.

 Time-Out—A So What

1. Is the Lyles model practical for you in your position?
2. What type of problems would this be helpful for?
3. Run through a problem using the model. What did you learn?

LATE FRIDAY NIGHT, THE HOMEWORK CONTINUES

At the same time that Rob was playing with his banner assignment, Dr. Woodson was in his room reviewing the setup for tomorrow. He was using the Saturday late-morning and afternoon session to further develop the group's problem-solving skills. To this mix he was planning to demonstrate the value of understanding and application of the various styles within the group and the affect on effectively working together. If he could set it up right, they would be experiencing dysfunctions in style orientation in their small groups of five. He hoped that then they would better understand what they had experienced about Styles today and would learn by sharing their banners in the morning session. It would be a start toward reinforcement of the skills learned.

While Woodson didn't think too many of them would figure out the group assignments early on, he expected some to catch on to what he'd done before the exercise was completed. He had taken the three big rocks the cabinet had identified and was going to have each of the four groups work on the same problem simultaneously for about an hour and then post the results on a flip chart.

THE THREE CABINET ISSUES TO BE USED

Session 1: Should we move forward with implementation of the Effective Schools Correlates?

Session 2: To what extent could we move toward more site-based management?

Session 3: How can we determine the commitment level of the district to all students learning?

Since the time allocated for each session wouldn't get the job done, Rob and Barry had decided to just begin the problem-solving-process steps. For each group in each session they would process these questions:

1. What is the root cause that would lead us in the direction posed by the question?
2. Provide three strategies that you believe would lead to a solution.
3. What would the outcome look like if your solution were implemented, and how would we know the outcome had been achieved?

A review of both the Backwards Thinking model and the 8-step Lyles Problem-Solving models would be used in this exercise. He would spend a few moments having the group review each, so they would have a better understanding before they began. He would use the master printout of the feedback profiles showing where each participant's style was on the chart to set up the groups. They would be mixed and matched so each one would get a chance to work with different folks and styles in each of the sessions (see Figure 6.5).

The four groups for session 1 would be made up as follows:

Group 1: 4 Driving Style and 1 Expressive Style
Group 2: 5 Expressive Style
Group 3: 5 Analytical Style
Group 4: 5 Amiable Style

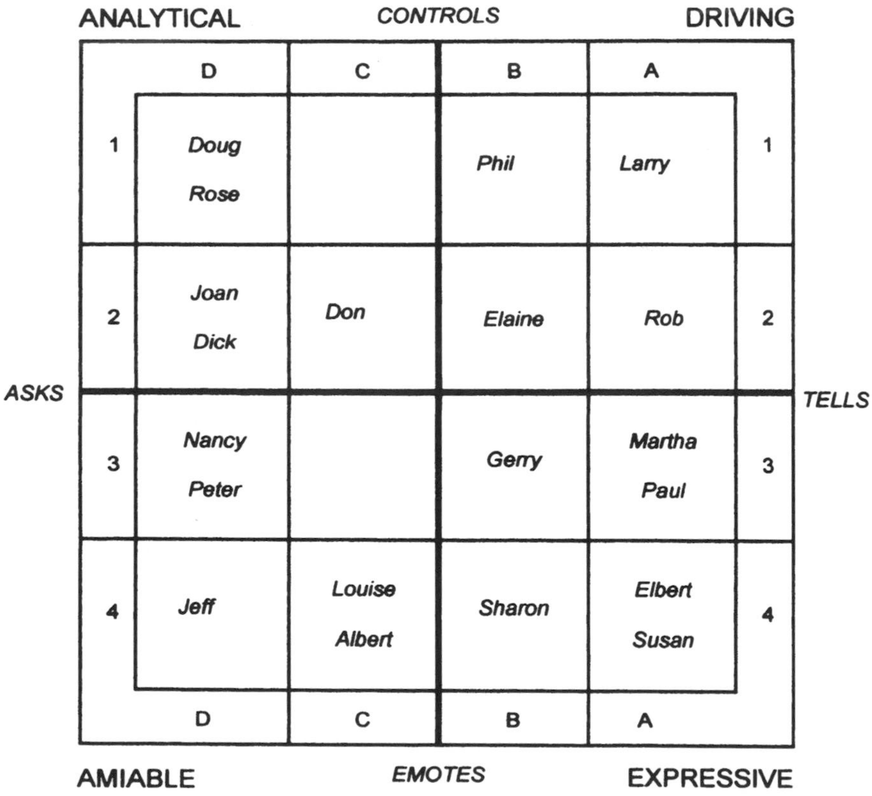

ANALYTICAL		CONTROLS		DRIVING	
	D	C	B	A	
1	Doug Rose		Phil	Larry	1
2	Joan Dick	Don	Elaine	Rob	2
3	Nancy Peter		Gerry	Martha Paul	3
4	Jeff	Louise Albert	Sharon	Elbert Susan	4
	D	C	B	A	
AMIABLE		EMOTES		EXPRESSIVE	

ASKS (left side) TELLS (right side)

Figure 6.5.   Four Groups.
Courtesy of the TRACOM Group.

> **⏱ Time-Out**
>
> 1. On the basis of the characteristics of the styles represented in each of the four groups in session 1, can you predict how they approach solving the first problem?
> 2. Which group do you predict will come up with the best solution? Explain your reasoning.

Hoping he knew his stuff, Woodson predicted that group 1 would be done under the time limit with two or three solutions. The second group would still be talking and proposing solutions with very little written down on their flip chart. Within the first 10 minutes the Analyticals would be coming to him asking for more information. He needed to remind himself that he should listen to group 4 at the Amiable table. He predicted that while they would start the assignment they might be found talking about working together as a team or even what was going on in their own lives, maybe even sharing their personal profiles.

Session 2, right after lunch, would be designed to create the most frustrating experience and could get negative over time. This would be done by pairing individuals that have the fewest matching style characteristics on the assertiveness and responsiveness scales, those in the opposite corners of the model. While the group didn't work out with an even number of people in each style category, he would do his best to match, or rather mismatch, them, so they could maximize learning. He would put two Driving Styles with three Amiables in one group, the three Expressives and two Amiables in the second one, two Expressives and three Analyticals in the third, and three Driving and two Analyticals in the fourth.

In the first group, he would expect the two Driving Styles to dominate the three Amiables and some friction or clamming up would be developing. He might have to intervene in this group to give each one a chance to have a say. The second group was designed to illustrate the highly emotive behavior of the Expressives and Amiables. Group 3 has both Expressives and Analyticals in it, which are located diagonally across from each other in the model, having very little in common. The Expressives will be sharing grandiose ideas, and if the Analyticals participate, they will be challenging and asking for more data. The Driving-Analytical group will be relatively functional with the Driving Styles pushing to get the assignment done and again the Analyticals will be dragging their feet, saying they don't they have enough information or time to make an intelligent recommendation.

The groups for the final session, before debriefing this activity and wrapping up the entire 3-day workshop, would have at least one person from each of the four style groups. If the model works, and Woodson knows from his experience it does, he could predict that the participants would overwhelmingly recognize these as the most functional teams. This session should have produced the best work of the day.

The superintendent was planning a short wrap-up session with an evaluation of the time spent together. After the troops had headed home, the superintendent and the mentor were going to spend an hour or so working on next steps.

THE 3-DAY WORKSHOP DEBRIEFING

It was a few minutes after 4 p.m. and they had just finished packing all the materials and checking out. The rest of the group was on their way home, so Barry and Rob adjourned to the lounge for a welcome beer and serious debriefing.

"Well, what did you think?" Rob started with a question aimed at Barry.

Barry decided to dodge the question, responding, "It's more important that you share your feelings about it since it's your workshop and your people." They had already gone over the evaluation sheets and had a pretty good idea of what the participants thought. The ratings were high and the feedback was mostly positive.

"Certainly there was a lot of content covered during the 3 days. The cabinet was able to do some big-rock work. Everyone had the opportunity to learn more about their communication Style. We each survived the shock of seeing the interpretation of our individual Style and the resultant loss of the five so-called 'friends' we'll never speak to again— just kidding—for the way they described our behavior. Finally, all that we learned about Social Style and groups in the second part of today's practicum was amazing," Rob gushed, hardly pausing to breathe.

"One of your goals was for the group to come closer together through the interaction in group management training," Barry stated. "Looking at the evaluations and your own observations, did we meet that goal?"

"Yes! We scored high marks in this area. I don't think there was much of that going on over the past 2 years. Also, having good content to work with made the day."

"What did you think of the casual comments about Style that seemed to permeate the conversation during the cocktail hour?" Barry asked curiously.

"In some ways, that was probably the best learning that we did during the 3 days," Rob reflected. "There is no question in my mind that we have created a real internal vocabulary that we can use for creating better conversation and communication among us."

"How did you think the banner exercise worked out as an activity for the participants to 'self-declare' their own style?"

"At first I thought it was a pain you know where, but after going through it, I think we all learned more about each other—how we are perceived by others in our communication. In that single exercise we learned more than we could have anticipated," Rob said.

"How are you planning to process the three big rocks we used as content in the exercise?" the mentor wanted to know, since the staff had a good start on planning for the future.

If he didn't convince Rob that he needed a follow-up plan, what they had accomplished could be lost. Often, after an emotional high from a great workshop, landing back on your feet at the office Monday morning facing a stack of routine work would severely dampen their enthusiasm for change and the initiative would be lost.

"This is too motivating to lose the momentum that's been generated. The flip charts are going to the cabinet meeting next week and be used for planning the balance of the year. This work meshes with the board goals, anyway," Rob added with surety.

"Did you understand the relationship of the individual styles to the work I ended up sharing from Adizes's insights?"

"I forgot that for a moment. Understanding that the four functions needed for a successful organization are very similar to the four individual styles was mind-boggling. The match up of relationships with his Producer/Driving, and then Entrepreneur/Expressive, Administrator/ Analytical, and Integrator/Amiable expanded my understanding from the individual to an entire organizational function. Now I know what he meant when he said that, to be effective and efficient in both the short and long run, the organization has to have each of the four functions represented at the top level. That was really a great insight," the super-intendent emphatically stated.

"I appreciate the sharing of your work plan as you move forward with producing better results with Diane. Now that you know her style more completely with the backup analysis, the two of you should be able to work out a way to communicate more effectively. If you need any help later on, I'll be happy to sit down with you both and give you some feed-back on how to further a better work relationship."

"Thanks for this feedback," Rob said sincerely.

"Before we get on our way, there is one thing you haven't mentioned. How did the board handle their goal of dealing with their public con-duct?"

"It went well. Even that section went without objection. There wasn't much comment on the others. One board member came to me after the meeting and told me that since he voted to support these goals, he was not going to give the three majority members any more verbal trouble during board meetings."

"How did you word this item?" asked Barry.

"I included the statement 'The board members will treat each other with respect and courtesy during board meetings.' It looks like it worked. I think my goal of working with the board effectively is paying off. The one-on-ones are giving me clear insight into what they need and want."

"Sounds good!"

Then Rob concluded by saying, "I really appreciate all that you've done for me over the last few months. I can't say it enough, but having someone from the outside to dump on and to get advice for this first-year beginner has been fantastic. I really don't know where I would have been without it. Thanks again and especially for the beer."

"Let's pack up all our notes and junk and head for home. Since you're driving the farthest, be careful. I wish you and yours a very happy Thanksgiving. I already packed my calendar and cell phone, but I know we have our next meeting scheduled for the second week of December on Wednesday around 2 at your office. See you then," Barry said to Rob as they separated to head for home.

⏱ Time-Out—Now What?

1. What issues or problems in your job could be wholly or partially solved by using any of the problem-solving designs that were introduced?
2. Consider selecting a situation on the job where you seem to be having a communication problem similar to Rob and Diane's. Can you develop a plan to improve the situation or do you need more help?
3. What would be your best thinking for resolving it?
4. What value would you find in your workplace in having your group experience a similar training?

SUMMARY

In this chapter you were introduced to the planning of a workshop for integrating the application of social style with two problem-solving models. The effective use of an informal setting for a team-building exercise was demonstrated.

The four styles of the Social Style program were introduced, both from a historical perspective and current usage. The styles were identified as Driving, Expressive, Analytical, and Amiable. These four styles were developed as combinations from two independent variables, assertiveness and responsiveness. In the process, there was an opportunity to get an idea about an individual's Social Style. Ways of working more effectively with the three other styles were shown in the chart. Also, there was an opportunity to review how the superintendent attempted to resolve the communication problem with his administrative assistant through his application of this training.

The workshop highlighted the dysfunctional and unwary use of some style groupings. The most favorable model was used for group effectiveness and was briefly analyzed. The similarity between social style for individuals and organizational functions from Dr. Adizes's work was discussed briefly.

The valuable processes for debriefing a workshop and planning next steps concluded the chapter.

(🕐) Time-Out—Reflections

1. Now that you have had a taste of Social Style, how would you use this material on your job in organizing training for improving understanding in communications?
2. What did you think of the notion of integrating the solving of the 'big-rock' examples the cabinet identified with the learnings from the Social Styles Model?
3. How would you develop workshops for your group that would enhance team building?

MONTH 5—NOVEMBER

Strategies and Survival Skills

1. Be on the lookout for proven effective management-enhancing programs used elsewhere that can be appropriately used in your staff-development programs.
2. When you commit to a program, commit to it full bore—it's not a one-shot deal.
3. Plan to integrate the learning into the culture for everyday use or don't even start.
4. Learn to carefully plan team-building events with a clear sense of purpose and with the desired outcomes thoroughly thought out.
5. Recognize that a systematic approach to decision making and problem solving is a valuable tool in making better decisions at any level in the organization.
6. After training, when you better understand the Social Style model, practice using the information yourself to be a role model for others.
7. Consider using Style intervention language in your cabinet meeting protocols.

8. Make it safe to call a time-out and discuss Style in a nonemotional manner.
9. Share the Style basics with those in your office to help them better understand you at least. Better yet, provide an opportunity for them to be trained also.

TOOLBOX

Geier, J. (1984). Disc Profile Workshop. Maple Grove, MN: Geier Learning International.

Lyles, R. (1982). *Practical Management Problem Solving and Decision Making.* NY: Van Nostrand Reinhold.

Lyles, R. (2000). *Winning Ways.* New York: Penguin Putnam.

Marston, W. (1979). *Emotions of Normal People.* Minneapolis, MN: Persona Press.

Merrill, D., & Reid, R. (1981). *Personal Styles & Effective Performance.* Radnor, PA: Chilton Book.

TRACOM Group, 8878 S. Barrons Blvd., Highland Ranch, CO 80129.

The Social Style Model was originally developed and is managed by The TRACOM Group, which provides a variety of educational materials and training courses based on Social Style. For more information visit www.tracomcorp.com or call 303–470–4982. Social Style Model is a registered trademark of the TRACOM Group.

7

DECEMBER: LET'S GET PERSONNEL

You can either hire winners or develop them.

—Paul Hersey

HIRE WINNERS OR DEVELOP THEM?
ANSWER—YES!

In this chapter you will gain insight on the following:

1. Some components of the personnel sub-system.
2. A beginning-teacher induction system with a second-year follow-up.
3. Strategies for working effectively with the teachers' union.
4. A tenured-teacher assistance program.
5. A management-union program for alternative teacher evaluations.
6. A value-driven perspective defining staff expectations.
7. Developing the accomplished teacher and some ideas about motivating employees.

THE PHONE CALL

"Barry, I followed your advice. I met with the union president in your former district—and wow, did I get sold on some great new ideas," an excited superintendent said as soon as his mentor and coach picked up the phone.

"I am glad it was a worthwhile trip. I figured that you would be impressed with some of the things we were able to do through a positive long-term relationship with our teachers' union. What happened? Did you take anyone with you?" Barry responded, very interested in what Rob was telling him this cold and rainy afternoon in early December.

"Well, I did ask Don Halverson, our assistant superintendent of personnel, to accompany me to answer your last question first. We even talked two of our union leaders into joining us, although they represent a different national union group."

"Who did all of the sweet talking to get them to join you?"

"Actually, Don did. Recently, he has developed a good rapport with them. There have been some personnel issues that Don and Margaret, our union president, have been working on. They seem to be building a more trusting relationship the past several weeks following the conclusion of negotiations. I know you remember that, as part of the settlement early this fall, we agreed to explore ways of doing business differently. So we challenged Margaret, and she agreed to the visit, but she wanted her vice president, Harry Bailey, to join her. Harry will become their chief negotiator next time-out. The four of us went."

"Now, I remember that was your major breakthrough! Still some carryover from giving the store away earlier this year?" he teased his protégé.

Rob's face clouded for a moment, and then he got it. "Okay, enough! You know we did a good job and cut a fair deal. It was one of my goals, remember?"

"Just teasing! Well, are you going to tell me about what you found out? Who did you talk to there?" the mentor asked curiously.

"You often lead me off point. Is this part of your Expressive-Driving style perhaps? Isn't one of your growth goals to listen more effectively?"

"You did learn something after all from participating in the styles workshop," Barry shot back. "I probably said too much about my style weaknesses and growth needs!"

Ignoring the entire off-topic banter, Rob responded, "We got to meet with union president Dave Rascalle, and an assistant superintendent, Devon Smyth."

"Good, because Devon was a part of developing the programs over the past 15 years."

"There were several program ideas that I thought were really good. Your Dave was both excited and proud to have been a part of the long-term program development. The union and the district even had longitudinal data for the past 10 years. It was really exciting to hear it all."

"I thought you might like to hear their story," Barry commented.

"There was one interesting situation. No one seemed to remember your name even though you were there for over 25 years. Did I visit the correct district?"

"If the programs were great—probably. If not, no!" Barry quipped and then laughed, "Well, that just proves the point that good leadership gets the job done, while everyone else takes the credit."

Good leadership gets the job done, while everyone else takes the credit.

Rob said, "Getting serious for a minute, I think some of these programs would fit very nicely here in Paradise Valley."

"Why don't you tell me which ones you might be interested in working toward and then maybe I can share more about how we got there," Barry said.

"Devon first reviewed with Halverson and me alone the systems blueprint that you folks developed. He said this was the framework around which the programs evolved. He gave me a copy which I am sure you have."

Woodson was sure that he had a copy somewhere on his desk. He asked Barry to hold a minute to give him a chance to find it. While talking on the phone would not be the easiest way to describe the complex document, he felt that they could at least be looking at the same diagram as they spoke (see Figure 7.1).

"Just looking at this you might think it rather complex. Have you had a chance to study it yet, Rob?"

"Not really. I like the idea of the entry point looking like the roots of a tree with the system branching outward and upward. Also; the critical points seem to be the entry process, training toward a tenure decision, continuing staff development toward the fifth year with alternative eval-

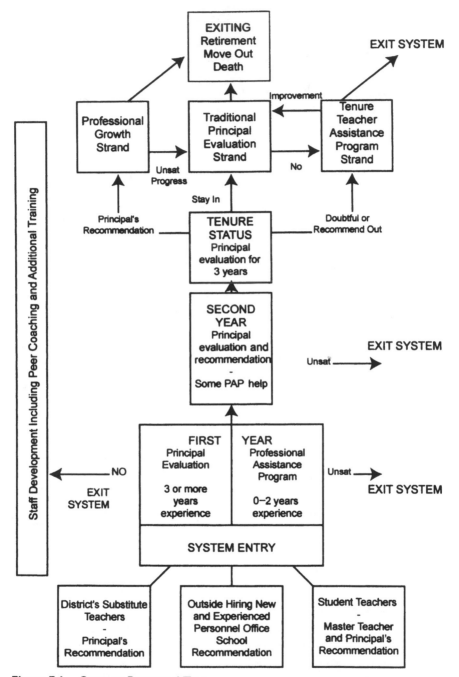

Figure 7.1. Systems Personnel Tree

uation as an option, and finally, dealing with exiting at any branch in the system. Added to this last piece is improvement or the removal of tenured teachers who have been around a long time. Some have 'died on the vine' or should I say 'branches' now?"

Woodson was pleased with Rob's quick take on the Systems Personnel Tree. "Rob, the secret is rather obvious. You need to take people where they are in the system and then develop them. This requires good assessment, support, and ongoing diagnosis. The better you hire the easier and quicker it is to get the teacher performing well. These programs that were developed over time have attempted to do just that."

You need to take people where they are in the system and then develop them.

"Barry, let's be sure that when we get together we talk more about this. The other programs I liked appeared to be key parts of the system. The more I see what you've done here, the better it helps me understand the big personnel picture. I know the nuts and bolts of it, but this puts it into the systems context," Rob added with more confidence. "But one more question. What are the essentials that you measure them on?"

 Time-Out—A What

Take a look at the Systems Personnel Tree.

1. What does this model suggest about systems?
2. What should be added?
3. Examine your own district. What programs do you have for helping all teachers grow and develop at the key decision levels?

"Many folks think the components of evaluation are competency, commitment, effort, and results, and these are the bases for rewards, whereas others think it should look more like competency, commitment, and effort plus results equals rewards. I suggest that focusing on results is a better way to become more effective," Barry said.

"It seems to reinforce what Lezotte says," Rob observed.

"Which of the other programs caught your eye?" the professor then asked.

"Probably the most interesting one is the program used to develop teachers who came to the district with less than 3 years' experience. This is the one that has provided the most data. The union folks were really proud to have made a difference with the district's first-year and second-year teachers."

"What else did they show you?"

"A part of what they covered was a continuation of the program I just mentioned to include tenured-teacher help and support in dismissal. The management team said this was the toughest one to get the union to buy into. Since they were affiliated with the American Federation of Teachers, it was easier to implement. They had done just what you're doing now, visiting other districts. Also, they had another district visit them to discuss the pros and cons of getting into the beginning teacher program. Their management told Devon's people to be sure that any agreement should include a program for working with the union to help improve tenured teachers or to start a process that would separate them from the district. This also looked promising."

"Was it still working?" Barry asked.

"Yes. In addition, we especially liked the teacher evaluation program they were developing. They were taking some innovative steps by including student performance data as part of the evaluation process."

"That's a tough commitment on the part of the teachers. It must be leading edge!" Barry declared, rather surprised by this development after he had retired.

"Harry and Margaret got excited about the professional-development program the district has had in place for the past 18 years. As we discussed later, this looked like a point where we could start working together without too many barriers. We plan on meeting in early January to talk about this some more."

"Did the management people say anything about creating a better evaluation system for administrators?" Barry wanted to know. When he had retired he knew of some discussion going on about this. Devon was talking to principals and assistant superintendents about some of Doug Reeves's work on improving the evaluation system for them.

"Nothing was said about it at our meeting," Rob said.

"Rob, if it's all right with you, can we put the rest of this discussion on hold until our regular meeting next Tuesday?" Barry asked. "I know it's the week before Christmas vacation, but I think it would be a good idea to capture your experiences and try to determine where you're headed. I think it would be helpful if you would go back to Phase A of the A-B-C-D-E Model and decide where you want to be relative to this subsystem in the next 5 years. Don't just jump in and try to lay other district's successes on your own system. Remember what I said before, you can't take the successes of others, developed over time, and expect your own people to readily accept them.

"It was good that your union folks got to see what we were doing in my former district," Barry continued. "We need to sculpt this out next week. So why don't you think this through, talk to your cabinet, and, if Halverson is as enthusiastic as you are, maybe you might ask him to take the lead with the other folks."

You can't take the successes of others, developed over time, and expect your own people to readily accept them.

"I guess you're right," Rob said. "On occasion I do get excited about some great new ideas. I'll get together with him, review what they told us about the four programs we're interested in, and be ready for you next week."

"Sounds like a plan. I've got some old material from the district, so I'll bring it along. I'm pleased that you found the experience worthwhile. I'm looking forward to next week's meeting. See you then."

"We'll be ready," Rob replied as they said their good-byes and hung up.

Immediately he buzzed Diane and asked her to set up the necessary meetings so they wouldn't lose the momentum.

THE DECEMBER CONSULTING SESSION

"Dr. Woodson, it's so good to see you. I suppose you have all of your holiday shopping done by now," Diane said. Rob's administrative assistant recognized and appreciated the intervention that the mentor had made in improving the effectiveness of the relationship between her and the boss.

"You know me better than that! At least I've finished my Christmas list. I hate to shop! Usually I send gift certificates. How are you doing? Have you finished shopping yet?"

"Almost. We still have some stuff to buy for the kids."

"By the way, I really like how you decorated the office. The Christmas tree creates a warm and friendly atmosphere for the holidays." Woodson had decided he also needed to spend time modeling behavior that was consistent with Diane's Social Style need of feeling appreciated. Of course, he was often trying to practice his styles-growth goal for those with a Driving Style by practicing his listening skills.

"Thank you for noticing. You're getting better at sharing the growth needs of your style," she commented, showing off the effects of the recent training. "And before you ask, yes, I think Rob and I have been successful in more clearly understanding the differences in our styles. I feel free to call a time-out if I see that his style is creating too much tension in my life. And now he can do that with me too," she volunteered with a sense of accomplishment.

"I'm glad to hear that, Diane. How much time do I have with the big guy today?" he added.

"I've got you booked from 2 to 4. Why don't you go in? He's free now."

"Great! And many thanks."

As he walked in, Rob greeted him with a warm handshake. The superintendent grabbed a stack of papers from the corner of his desk and escorted Barry to the informal corner of his office. Rob had learned to create different environments within his rather large office. In one corner he had his desk placed diagonally facing the windows with two chairs directly across creating the most formal environment with the desk as both a physical and psychological barrier—the power position. In the center of the room he had placed a circular table that would seat four. This was the office's small group workspace. In another corner he had placed a small couch with a coffee table and two comfortable armchairs. This was his casual corner. Rob had learned a long time ago that by establishing these three areas he could create an environment that would help set the correct tone for the various types of meetings he would have. He often used the informal corner to try and defuse confrontations with irate parents. In addition, he could stand in the doorway, blocking entrance to the office, if he needed to redirect the individual or keep a conversation short.

After a few pleasantries they got right into the first topic. It started out as a catch-up conversation. Before they had a chance to begin, Barry got up and walked to the whiteboard and pointed to a social styles model drawn there (see Figure 7.2) with Rob's and Diane's names along with the five cabinet members on it. "Rob, I see you've been thinking. What's the significance of this?"

"I was looking at the styles patterns of the cabinet. Interesting data? If you notice, we have a well-balanced team with at least one of us in each quadrant. Maybe this is why we're working so well together. When I promoted Doug Daniels to business manager it kept the balance, and I didn't even know it! I guess a lot of what we do happens by accident

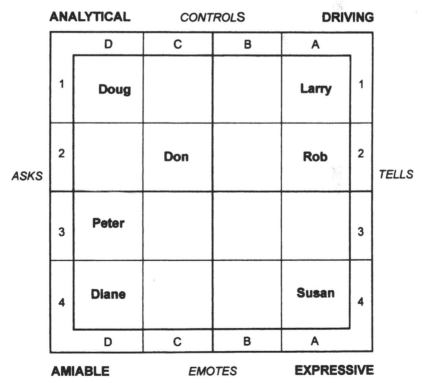

Figure 7.2. Four Groups.
Courtesy of the TRACOM Group.

rather than by design," Rob observed. "I just need to process what I'm learning!"

"That's my life's story," Barry agreed. "Fortunately, with more experience you begin to clarify what you believe, your core values, and then apply it to the emerging patterns in the system."

Rob had some additional thoughts. "I am reviewing this with the team. We started to practice, and we're beginning to incorporate it in our meeting protocols and making it part of our new language. We've been doing the same with Sit Lead. If we can effectively model at this level, we then can start using more training in other parts of the organization."

"I like it!" Barry exclaimed. "Are you also working with the principals to make sure it sticks?"

"The directors are asking each principal to put together some ideas for their own staffs. This will be part of our training program later," Rob responded.

"As I mentioned, we've been practicing. We spend 20 minutes or so at the beginning of each meeting talking about our own style experiences on the job. We are actually helping each other with individual problems that we've been faced with. One of us shares our own situation and our strategy for improving it."

"What a creative way to practice! Hopefully, you will appreciate the team's differences and strengths, using them to your team's leadership advantage," Barry observed.

"We're trying hard anyway. I don't want to lose this. We're even thinking about involving more staff in the training," Rob excitedly told his mentor.

⏱ Time-Out—A What

1. Discuss what you know about the styles relationships between Larry and Peter, Susan and Don, and Rob and Doug (see Figure 7.2).
2. What are the implications for managing the district?
3. What did you think about the follow-up training the superintendent is promoting?
4. Discuss how effective you think it will be.
5. What would you do differently?

CATCHING UP

"Good!" Barry said. "And moving us on, there are a few things we haven't talked about for a while. You haven't mentioned lately how Dr. Branson's doing in the classroom. And how are both the lawsuit and recall elections going?"

"According to his principal, he is just barely making it. Without a teaming partner he would be really lost. I'm working with the board and attorneys to get it settled. Just by chance, the business manager found that the insurance company had set aside a reserve of $100,000 for settlement of his false-termination lawsuit. That means the district has to come up with only $50,000 for what I think we owe the former superintendent. That's what I'm using for a bottom-line settlement number in our negotiations with his attorney.

"The school board, being divided as they are over this issue, has given me direction to settle this as soon as possible. They won't even discuss dollar amounts because the majority is afraid that the two minority members will tell the former superintendent what the bottom line is. I feel like I'm earning my Perry Mason law degree and diplomatic credentials over this fiasco! I can't imagine how this is going to work out, especially with the recall staring us in the face just 2 months from now."

"I can understand that you might want to change professions before this year is over," Barry suggested without cracking a smile.

"There's more. I go to court on January 22 in the libel and slander lawsuit against the Concerned Citizen Committee. As you remember I've been called to testify on behalf of the former superintendent and board member. I still have no idea why. I wasn't even here when it all started," Rob responded with a certain disgusted tone in his voice. He didn't like the position he was being put in, between a rock and a hard place.

"Just answer the questions honestly, try not to elaborate. This too shall pass!" Barry counseled.

"I have another challenging personnel issue arising—it's been apparent since September that my one problem principal is not going along with the program. And he's only in his second year! After the holidays I'm going to have a 'Is this career in your future?' conversation with him."

"As I said when you started back in July, the unexpected will be with you always. This is called experience." Barry quickly added, "What do you plan to do?"

"I'm going to discuss his attitude as it relates to us working together. I hear that he's not happy here and wants to leave anyway. I may have to help him along. He's a climber and wants to be a superintendent by year three." Rob added.

"What else?"

"Good news! Even since our last phone call, I found out that the principals are really getting into the new Social Style habits. We have entertaining principal's meetings now where we are practicing our newfound skills on each other. Many took the material home and shared the model with their spouses. I know you warned them it could be trouble if not handled delicately. However, I haven't heard of any pending divorces yet. Many are sharing this with their staffs. I'm going to have to figure out a way to pay for more professional development—which is good!"

"Just let me know how many are interested and when you are ready," answered Barry.

"Finally, I think I'm running out of updates. This one I've saved for last. The follow-up meeting between Diane and me went well. We've worked out a way to signal each other if we feel the tension building. We've each called two time-outs this week already. It works!" Rob added enthusiastically.

Barry just smiled to himself. Definitely, he wasn't going to share Diane's comments about this with her boss. Often as a consultant and trainer, he wasn't around to watch the positive results of a training experience. Working with a rookie for a year gave him the satisfaction of seeing some change happening for the best. Sometimes there was none. Change doesn't happen easily without commitment and direction from the top—that is, change in the desired direction.

Change doesn't happen easily without commitment and direction from the top—that is, change in the desired direction.

BACK TO PERSONNEL

"Now we can get back to the results of my visit to your former district last week. I've done some thinking and now have an end or two in mind," the superintendent said proudly.

"Let's see. You mentioned three or four. Which ones will meet your end in mind?"

"Barry, I need to share my thinking first. I want to have highly trained teachers who are effective—this means the students can demonstrate what they have learned, how well they have learned, and that the prescribed curriculum is being met. Dave Rascalle gave me a copy of the core values they were using," Rob said, handing Barry a copy. Rob picked one about the staff that he liked for Paradise Valley.

Competent and Caring Staff

We are committed to selecting, developing, and supporting the best possible staff, one that can do the following:

- understands and contributes to the learning process
- cares about students
- performs at a high level
- respects and supports others
- acts in an ethical manner
- seeks improvement through continual learning
- communicates appropriately and effectively
- values the uniqueness of each individual

"This does look familiar," Barry observed. "We developed this as part of our strategic planning effort years ago. It was one of our strongest core values."

"Don Halverson and I both liked it. We think it's a good point for starting a conversation with those of us who are in the hiring process and even more with Margaret and Harry's group."

"Good thinking! Agreement on this would be a basis for future work together," Barry suggested.

Continuing, Rob added, "The bottom line is student learning. However, good teaching and good supervision of teaching are now required there. We need to strategize how to get there. Better understanding of each of the components in this subsystem should help."

"What are the components I can help you with?"

"Let me list them," Rob said as he moved to an unused section of the whiteboard near the sofa and wrote the following:

1. Teacher Assistance Program—helping first- and second-year teachers.
2. Permanent-Teacher Intervention Program.
3. Alternative Teacher-Evaluation System.
4. Staff Development Program, including the Accomplished-Teacher Program.

"Now tell me where you think they fit in your situation." Barry said, moving Rob to another level. He asked, "What they are going to do that's different, and I mean better-different."

After taking a few minutes to think this through, Rob tentatively began to respond, as he looked at the systems model. He could see what the parts were at each critical change point.

Starting with the system entrance points, he made a list of questions.

- What do we need to do on the recruiting scene to ensure getting winners or at least potential winners?
- How much and what kind of training do we need for those new to teaching?
- What do we do to support the experienced teachers we hire?
- How will we know how well they teach?
- Can I get the union to buy into helping weak tenured teachers or eventually helping them change careers?
- Should we start honoring and recognizing teachers as well as others? Will this help motivate them?

"This brings up some interesting thoughts to consider. I haven't even begun to look at what needs to be done with all the nonteaching staff. I'm going to hold off on this until next year." Then the superintendent paused, waiting anxiously for his mentor's reaction.

"You're thinking systemically again, looking at the bigger picture. That's good! Now the hard part begins," Barry challenged.

"I know all my wishes aren't going to happen without the support and approval of the teachers' group. There's a lot of work to do. Dave Rascalle, meeting with our two teacher reps when we were there, told them to go slow and get it in writing. This means we have a lot of talking before anything really emerges that we can implement."

"Remember, as I've mentioned before, this took years and years to happen. You can't just drop this into your system and make it work. Start slowly. Get them to buy into it to be able to maintain the acceptance over time. Find those good teachers who want to make the system better and who are the natural leaders now."

"How did you get it to happen?" Rob asked more apprehensively.

Barry took some time in thinking back trying to find a single starting point. So often in his experience, when faced with a problem or an idea, he started working things out on a trial-and-error basis. The beginning-teacher training program was the first major breakthrough with the union. He described to Rob what Rob had already found out in his visit. Dave Rascalle had come to him with an idea for a personal-mentor project. It was supposed to last for 1 year but actually turned into a 2-year project. Rascalle visited several districts, and as a result, the program got started the third year. He told Dave that it was his responsibility to sell the board on this new program at a board meeting. Of course, as he was trying to teach Rob, Barry already had this board wired in.

Barry then reached in his tattered briefcase and handed Rob a copy of the program elements.

"Rob, did you get a copy of this material when you visited?" Barry asked.

"Yes. I got this document but haven't taken the time to read it yet."

His mentor put his copy on top of the pile of papers as a reference and suggested that Rob read through his copy of the description of the new-teacher support program and then ask questions.

"I think it sounds good, especially the results of having one consultant working with 12 beginning teachers," Rob said and then read from the report.

In the first three years only ten of the over 242 new teachers served by the program have not been recommended to continue service for the second probationary year. It has not been unusual to find the consultant spending over 100 hours of classroom observation, assistance, and support time for teachers experiencing difficulty. But even more dramatic are the observations of principals viewing the program graduates in their second year of teaching. They are seeing second-year teachers with poise and expertise that belies their experience.

"Rob, to summarize then, the federation and the district entered into a joint governance structure that uses peer review to assess the progress of each new teacher. The teacher consultant has the responsibility of induction and the first year of evaluation, subject to a system of checks by the Peer Review Board. The benefits to the profession are many, but it is the students of the school district who will ultimately reap the rewards of these efforts," Barry concluded.

🕐 Time-Out—A What

1. What do you think of this program?
2. What conditions would be favorable in your district to start on a similar path?
3. What obstacles would have to be overcome to even start talking with the union about this concept?
4. What alternatives to this need have you implemented or could you implement to meet the same end in mind?

"Now that you've read about this program, do you have a clearer picture of what they were doing?" Barry wanted to know.

Quickly, Rob assured Barry that they hadn't missed much as far as he knew. "I think that it was pretty clear in the way they explained that during our visit. This gives me a record of the program in writing. One thing not mentioned was that some teachers were weak in the first part of the fall semester, but then came on strong the second half as a result of the consultant's hard work. These marginal, improving teachers created the need for the program to extend into the second year."

Barry reinforced this insight by saying, "We did find this to be true, especially, with brand-new teachers. A side effect was that we choose to have heart-to-heart talks with the local schools of education and their student-teacher supervisors about what we expected from them. We even told one to change the training for elementary teachers or we wouldn't hire anyone from their university. We did so for 3 years. They got the point finally and changed when a new dean came on board."

"It's obvious to me that it all starts with the cooperation of both the teachers' group and management," Rob said thoughtfully.

"Another thing I forgot to ask," Barry said. "Did they tell you, when making recommendations about new teachers, the joint Peer Review Board managing the program never voted? To protect the district, we created a necessary four-vote majority to pass any action, so that management could veto the acts of the three-teacher majority. Originally, we feared how the teachers would deal with this new power. To date it's been all consensus decision making. In fact, visitors to the process can't tell who is who on the board."

"Yes, we thought that was significant. But let me ask something. What's this about the trust agreement that was mentioned in the document?" Rob wanted to know.

"I really don't want to take the time today to go into much detail, except to say that after 2 years of discussion, we decided to put our agreement in writing. It was put into a side agreement, or 'trust' agreement, that could be canceled by either party at the end of each year. Maybe we can go over the whole process the next time we meet," his mentor said, anxiously trying to complete their makeshift agenda. He then suggested that they cover the other programs that caught Rob's interest. Again he handed Rob an outline of another new program—one focused on supporting more experienced, yet ineffective teachers.

The Permanent-Teacher Intervention Program is a joint union and district program for assisting tenured teachers in serious professional jeopardy.

Permanent teachers rated as overall unsatisfactory in classroom instruction are candidates. The specific deficiencies must be given in an improvement plan. The program is governed by the Peer Review Board.

After a first overall-unsatisfactory evaluation, the permanent teacher may enter the program voluntarily. If the teacher does not enter the program, the second overall-unsatisfactory evaluation triggers a requested intervention by the review board. Teachers may refuse all assistance, but then they are on their own without union support.

"While it looks good, I'm going to stay far away from this at the moment," Rob said with a sigh of relief. "How long did it take for this program to get off the ground?"

"You don't even want to know! Remember, I suggested you go visit only to find out what was possible, not to implement it at home in the next 6 weeks," the mentor responded with a rather incredulous look on his face. "For the record, over 15 years there had been 12 teachers who took advantage of the program. Of these, 9 were reclaimed and became better teachers. One thing I haven't mentioned is that because of our commitment to quality teaching, the teachers' union has behind-the-scenes counseled many more teachers and helped them change careers without going through the process," Barry said.

"At least I know it can be done. Now that you've made me more curious about trust agreements and a better union-management relationship, when can we talk about this more?"

"Why don't we save that discussion for next month?"

"Okay. What can you tell me about this alternative evaluation program for experienced teachers?"

"Here is an outline of the program. Read this too and then we can discuss it."

This alternative evaluation program for permanent teachers encourages teachers to continue their professional development and personal growth. The program offers teachers who have consistently demonstrated a high degree of competency an alternative to the traditional evaluation process. The program is flexible to encourage teachers to grow in self-chosen areas of interest that will enhance professional growth and affect student learning. These goals and established criteria serve as a certificated evaluation in lieu of the traditional process. The program is structured to strengthen collegial relationships and collaboration and decrease teacher isolation. The program is also governed by the Peer Review Board.

🕐 **Time-Out—A So What**

1. Discuss the elements of these two programs.
2. What does your district do to meet the goals indicated?
3. What would keep you from developing similar ideas with the union?
4. What other methods for training new teachers are you familiar with?

5. Does your district have the will to fire a tenured teacher?
6. Can you develop a documented plan to terminate an unsuccessful teacher? What data would you use to make sure your decision was supported by the school board?
7. Critique the elements of the core value, competent and caring staff, found in this chapter. What do you like? Would you add more to it? Take anything out? Why?

"What kinds of improvement and evaluation programs are accepted from the teachers?" Rob quizzed his mentor.

"I think I can remember a few good ones that caught my eye. Let's see," he said, gazing out the window trying to see a picture of what he knew. "Oh yes! There are three or four that come to mind. They generally fall into the following areas: improving instructional strategies, developing curriculum, studying learning theory, development of alternative assessments, and infusing technology into the classroom."

"This surely gives me a clearer picture. Margaret and Harry will probably be ready to support this in a couple of years. I'm not even going there now with the principals! This reminds me, I haven't set in motion any processes this year for ensuring the teachers get evaluated in a timely manner," Rob muttered to himself as he made a note on the whiteboard.

Barry explained patiently for the 10th time, "Be reminded again that what I'm doing is simply giving you exposure to a variety of programs for you to think about. File them away. Remember where the resources are. If and when the time comes, pull out your notes and begin planning."

"Okay."

"What next?" Barry continued.

"There was so little time we really didn't get into staff development and the accomplished teacher bit."

"If I can compact 20 years into a few paragraphs, I'll give it a shot.

"This program takes various shapes and forms. It is more of a process than a program. It includes staff involvement on release time during the day, evening courses at a nearby hotel from 4 to 7 p.m. followed by a district-supported dinner and encouragement to attend or present at local, state, and national conferences.

"Sometimes teachers will go to their professional associations and get themselves invited to speak. In my experience, they came to the superintendent to ask for release time and funding. This was encouraged. It's well worth it both in the short and long run. In the short run it turns the teacher on and then the teacher is respected as a professional.

"Instead of taking teachers away from their students for training during the day at a cost then of about $95.00 per substitute day, we decided to use a four-star resort within the community. We got the meeting rooms without cost in exchange for buying dinners at $50.00 a head. Can you imagine how this influenced teacher esteem? They were in workshops at the same venue as employees from Hewlett-Packard, IBM, Bank of America, NCR, and others. They realized that they were being treated as highly valued first-class citizens! The program was open to all teachers in the district. The teachers' kids benefit, the teachers at the school feel one of theirs is making a difference, and in the long run we moved toward our strategic goal of becoming a learning organization."

"Sounds good to me!" Rob exclaimed.

"Let the staff go even though it might be difficult sometimes. Take a risk to invest in your people. I sent two people reluctantly to national workshops for 3 years in a row expecting very little. Four years later they had established a nationally acclaimed middle school nontraditional individualized PE program.

"This means you need to work with the school board and community. But once you get the commitment for becoming a learning organization, you can reorganize the budget to support this. You can even take it out of the proposed funds for next year's salary raises by justifying it as going to the professional development of teachers. Stand tall and make a statement. Of course, not on your first day! But if you see this as a strategic objective and core value then figure out the future and sell the concept and practice.

"Practical on-site training is a clear responsibility of the leadership team. If system change is to take place, having key players buy into the process is a necessity or it won't happen. A best-practice concept here is to involve teachers in the planning. Even if you are in a state-mandated new program, get the teachers involved in the planning and implementation stages," the professor concluded.

"It seems the teachers had your number. They must have been smiling behind your back at what a pushover you were to support them financially for out-of-district speaking engagements," Rob said cheerfully.

Again ignoring the rookie superintendent's attempt at humor, Woodson continued, "When the federal program was introduced to create National Board Certified teachers, it took about 5 minutes of discussion to decide whether we would support this effort. More than just encouraging this, because we had a teacher champion advocate already in the district, we decided to pay the $2,300 program cost if the teacher went for the gold—pass or not. This meant completing the program and taking all the required tests.

"We even decided to financially support those going through a second time. This program was validated and then strongly supported by the first five National Board Certified teachers. They in turn helped others. It ended up with over 100 of our 1,500 teachers being recognized in just the first few years.

"And getting back to your earlier barb—I let them come to me for funding because I wanted them to know that I supported these activities," he added with an I'm-a-teddy-bear-really shrug.

"What else do you have up your sleeve?" Rob asked.

"I could probably go on all day mentioning everything we did. We had teachers at every level working on curriculum standards and assessments. It was up to teachers' groups to recommend textbooks and supplemental material. I see this as staff development. At one time we had nearly 100 mentor teachers working in various projects; including the one Dave Rascalle did to bring us the beginning-teacher support system."

"I know we are doing a lot of what you mentioned here in Paradise Valley. I just don't think it's organized too well. I'll talk to Susan and Larry to bring me up to date. Maybe this would be a good planning project for them to develop, starting next September."

"Maybe so, but go slow!" Barry reminded Rob.

Barry then added another important notion. He told Rob briefly about several ways they had recognized staff. The professional staff was recognized with specially designed pins for each 5 years of teaching. When teachers got permanency they were invited to the Tenure Tea celebration, originally held at the superintendent's home, but as the group grew it was moved to a larger venue. And similarly, when support staff reached their 5-year anniversary they were honored. At every opportunity staff was recognized.

To coincide with the conclusion of the teachers' five-session evening course at the hotel, a management training session was scheduled on the final night. After which they joined up with the teachers for dinner and celebration. The principals handed out diplomas to their own teachers in recognition of satisfactory course completion. Many of these were displayed proudly in teacher classrooms or on office walls.

"Well, I'm off to the district PTA meeting tonight. When I got them to agree to the peace treaty, I committed to attend each month and to give a district update. I think it's paying off," the superintendent shared with his coach.

"Did you have the Superintendency Institute of America winter conference in Scottsdale on your calendar for January? Or, more important, are you planning to go?"

"I think Diane has taken care of all the details. Why do you ask?"

"If you want to drive over together we could have some time to chat. It's only 6 hours. Or we could fly over and find some quiet time to have our monthly meeting," he suggested, not knowing Rob's preference.

"Let's fly over so we can talk on the plane. We can find more time if we need it there."

"Sounds like a plan. Let's do it. I'll have my assistant call Diane and get me on the same plane with you."

"Great! Anything more?"

"Not from me. Hope Santa gets to your house for Christmas okay," Barry added as he got up to leave Rob's office.

After talking a few minutes with Diane on the way out, he headed to his car. He thought it went well and was pleased that Rob had already decided to join him at the conference. He knew listening to Larry Lezotte and Peter Block would give him some great information and inspiration.

SUMMARY

This chapter started with the teaching staff seen as part of a subsystem, describing the career paths available to them and what can happen in between. It indicates various pathways to exit the system. There was an update on some of the more mundane daily things facing the superintendent, as well as an implementation plan for workshop follow-up.

The concept of a trust agreement between the district and the teachers' union that allowed these changes to be made with low risk to either party was mentioned. Assistance programs for both the new teacher and the unsatisfactory senior teacher were described as well as an alternative evaluation program and a program designed to support National Board Certification. The importance of a vibrant staff development program and the ongoing recognition of teachers and their accomplishments was advocated.

⏱ Time-Out—Reflections

1. Review the chapter and list any good ideas you think could work in your district.
2. How would you use systems thinking in developing a strategy to begin such a process of either improving staff development or beginning a conversation with your teachers' group?
3. What would you say in discussing the value of such a program with management, teachers, and the board?
4. Is the risk worth the reward?
5. As a leader develop the steps in an action plan for moving toward one of these goals or set your sights on improving what you see in your district. Start with the outcome in mind.
6. Do a quick environmental scan and assess where you are now. List five or six things that would have to be in place to start moving toward the outcome you listed.

MONTH 6—DECEMBER

Strategies and Survival Skills

1. Understand the district's subsystems, especially those critical to student learning.
2. Work on the positive with your union leadership.
   - You are the leader and have bottom-line control of the gold, or you should have.

- Work on the positive even in the face of adversity no matter how hard it is or how angry you are.
- The reality is that the teachers work for the district, not the union.

3. Don't overdo one-shot training events.
   - Start with the end in mind.
   - Have an implementation plan in the beginning.
   - Stay the course until the application is in place.

4. Be open to new ideas and seek them out.
   - Consider how your private office is organized for effectively setting up the right meeting environment.
   - Be careful of new ideas that appear to be quick fixes.
   - Don't overload the staff.
   - Keep the system in mind—the helicopter view.

TOOLBOX

The California New Teacher Project. (1991, April). *New Teacher Success: You Can Make A Difference*. California Department of Education.

Personnel Support Services. Poway Unified School District, 13626 Twin Peaks Road, Poway, CA 92064. www.powayusd.com.

Poway Federation of Teachers. Don Raczka, President. 11011 via Frontera, Suite B, San Diego, CA 92127. www.powayteachers.org.

8

JANUARY: SHOULD YOU WIN-WIN?

DO YOU TRUST THE UNION? DO THEY TRUST YOU?

In this chapter you will do the following:

1. Learn to apply the principles of a win-win strategy.
2. Consider ideas for handling a board-recall election.
3. Learn about labor-management trust agreements.
4. Review a model for establishing and managing a non-adversarial labor union relationship.
5. Gain an understanding of the labor subsystem and its intersection with that of the school system.

TAKING OFF

Woodson was anxiously pacing back and forth in front of Gate 26 in the terminal when finally he spotted Rob stepping off the escalator. Rob was casually strolling toward the gate area with just a few minutes to spare and hadn't noticed his mentor yet. They had agreed last month to travel together to attend the Superintendency Institute of America's winter conference in Scottsdale.

Barry was nervous. He liked to arrive at the airport early in case of delay with the new security measures.

Since Rob had gotten his group A boarding pass online, he wasn't in a hurry. Barry got his boarding pass nearly 2 hours before scheduled departure time when he checked his bag and golf clubs curbside. With group A boarding passes they had a better chance of sitting together as planned, to get some work, or at least talking, done. Being early wasn't a problem for Barry because he always brought work with him. For this trip he had two chapters of his new leadership book on his laptop to edit and maybe rewrite, so he had plenty to do.

Rob had sent him an e-mail covering a few things he wanted to discuss before the 3-day conference was completed: unfinished business about trust agreements, a review of Barry's experience in developing a win-win relationship with the union groups, and some clarity needed for the union subsystem being part of the school district system. Barry knew there would be other issues that Rob would be dealing with soon that would be critical, including getting ready for his midyear evaluation.

The board-recall election next month, to determine whether his three majority members would stay or go, was really troubling Rob, as it would any rookie superintendent. The ballot would be in two parts. First, the voters would choose to recall any of the three individually. Then, whether they cast a vote to recall or not, the electorate would vote for one of the candidates running for that seat. All seats had three hopefuls to choose from as backups. Any combination of things could happen—mostly all bad for the superintendent.

"I was getting worried," Rob's mentor shared as he walked over and shook his hand. "I was beginning to think that I was on the wrong flight on the wrong airline."

"Never fear when Rob is near!" Rob responded with a broad smile on his face. "I know that's not too funny under the circumstances, but I grew up saying that to relieve tension. I'm sorry I'm late. Had to go by the office at the last minute and pick up some material that I had almost forgotten Diane left for me. She knows how much I can get done when I'm flying," he explained.

"I thought with nearly a 3-week holiday break you would be all caught up," Barry said, knowing better.

"Early on, you said not to forget that I had a family, so I didn't. The week after Christmas we spent skiing at North Star in Tahoe. It was really great. As you know I wasn't at home much except weekends for the last 6 months. I came back charged up, but cooled some when I started thinking about those challenges you predicted that would always be there. You were right, of course. This election thing is worrying me somewhat—well, really a lot."

"I expected as much. I have some ideas we can talk about later."

Boarding first with the A passes, they found an empty row of three seats and hoped that no one would sit between them. To discourage this, they piled some material they were going share on the middle seat. The excess fit in the seat pocket in front of them. Luckily, the plane wasn't full and no one was brave enough to disturb them.

Barry realized quickly that on this short flight and with Rob's concerns it would be impossible to get any work done on his book, so he put his laptop in the overhead bin. They chatted for a while about family and holidays before the superintendent opened up with some pressing concerns.

LABOR RELATIONSHIP AND TRUST AGREEMENTS

"I've been thinking more about my teachers' union folks over these past weeks. I want to know more about trust agreements," Rob began.

"I brought a copy of one agreement and am prepared to review what happened to bring this about."

"Fire away! Just let me get my trusty notebook ready."

"Since I have a captive audience for an hour or so, you may hear more than you ever wanted or needed to know!" Barry warned him and sat back as the plane accelerated down the runway lifting off and banking in an easterly direction into the rising sun.

"No. I really do think retelling your story might be helpful, if it's not too painful!" Rob teased.

"Okay. Here we go. I'll start with the background and then finish with the development of trust agreements. As I told you when we did the styles workshop, I am a results-oriented driver and I always seem to want to be in control. I was good at win-lose. I seldom, if ever, lost! For the first 10 years, I settled on the financial issues for less than the board authorized. Then we ran out of money!"

Woodson went on to tell Rob that when he started as a superintendent in California it was before collective bargaining became law there.

Since he also started with turmoil in a district, he found the teachers were ready for a positive change in leadership. This created an atmosphere that allowed him to work with the board to get the teachers and other groups a fair raise his first year. Early in the game Woodson learned from veteran principals at national conferences what to do and what not to do, based on their early experiences with collective bargaining in the eastern industrial states, where the teacher's union movement had its beginnings. They had more than 10 years of experience to draw upon.

He was encouraged to be tough and never give in to issues that were controlled by seniority. This is the issue many gave in to, as the unions argued successfully that it made decisions easier for both parties. Through his experiences he realized that management and most teachers wanted a say in the decision when it came to interschool transfers. They already had seen good close-knit faculties broken up. In urban districts it further handicapped those schools in less desirable locations. The students ended up being hurt by a lack of high quality experienced teachers. The learning gap continued to widen.

In those days, binding arbitration and agency fees, that required all members to pay dues, were to be avoided at all costs. If the district had money, they could "buy" a contract. If not, it would be extremely difficult to settle short of a strike, without giving up language. This meant loss of control, and he didn't want to go there. He was advised by those with unfortunate experiences not to fight to keep teachers in class during a strike. Fortunately he never had to test this advice during his 20-plus years.

In some districts after an intense labor strike, splits in faculties sometimes were never healed, even 10 years later. He soon began to understand the forces pulling on teachers from two directions: their dedication to the kids and union leadership peer pressure.

As he continued, Woodson related how in the beginning he had tried to be open and trusting but found that his trust in his first union president was misplaced. She tried to use almost everything they had discussed in confidence against him in open negotiations and in flyers to teachers. He had trusted her twice, but not a third time. His early experiences with those from established collective bargaining districts coupled with his assumed betrayal, caused him to develop a hard-line approach.

Being the competitor he was in his early career, his naivete and this loss of trust shaped the position that he was going to win and they were going to lose. He would get a fair deal, but on his terms. The board, basically promanagement, was very supportive, which made it easier. Obviously then, the community that elected them was of the same conservative bent. They frowned on labor action aimed at disrupting their child's education. Therefore, acquiring effective communication skills to inform the community about negotiations was on his early agenda.

Woodson made a strong point made about contract language. Lack of trust required close watching to ensure the written language was accurate. Both groups spent thousands of dollars for attorneys to create the legalese necessary to protect their clients. Woe to the party that signed off on a mistake! The signed-off printed word was etched in stone! It would be the basis for future grievances. No changes until the next contract.

Management felt, after years of developing contracts, they were always giving up power and money with no givebacks. They didn't want to make anymore changes. Control had slipped away. They knew best and those teachers' union leaders had little to offer. Not always were the best and brightest teachers on the negotiating team or serving as building reps.

Resentment mounted over how the union coerced teachers into working to the contract during prolonged and sometimes stalled talks. The revelation that even good teachers couldn't or wouldn't stand up to union pressure really ticked Woodson off over the years. They were friendly and warm after it was over, but they did things that he believed hurt the students' learning and were inexcusable in his way of thinking. Holding the education of students hostage was beneath contempt. There had to be a better way!

Neither party wanted to give up anything. Woodson believed he was the one protecting the real interests of most teachers. Giving all the available money to salaries and fringe benefits didn't help if it left little money to support classroom instruction. As soon as the contract was signed, the teachers wanted the resources necessary to do the job the other 180 days of the school year. Often, he used this argument to reach settlement. It was one that the teachers on the negotiating team couldn't argue against too effectively.

Generally, management has nothing else to give up after giving too much to teachers so has to survive by managing well. He believed that it was the years of insensitive boards and the patriarchal, top-down leadership system that drove teachers to organize in the first place. He wanted to keep the balance of power between labor and management slanted toward his side, but it wasn't easy. After all the smoke cleared, he and his management team had to pick up the pieces and continue directing the district. He knew that during the process he shouldn't do anything dumb that would give the "bad guys" a cause to rally the troops further. They always found something in this win-lose, or rather lose-lose, environment to put him in a bad light. He didn't always keep his emotions in check and took issues personally.

 Time-Out—A What

1. Reread the preceding and describe in your words Woodson's early attitude toward collective bargaining.
2. What would you suggest he should have done differently?
3. Share your experiences in collective bargaining, either as a teacher or administrator, with a colleague.
4. What did you learn from your experiences?

The flight attendant interrupted the conversation for a few minutes as she brought two soft drinks and some pretzels. This break gave Rob an opportunity to comment, "It seems like you weren't headed in a win-win direction. How did you change direction?"

CHANGING THE WAY OF DOING BUSINESS

"We were challenged to 'walk our values talk.' But more accurately, I was challenged to do so by our negotiations facilitator. He emphasized that we had a core value of 'excellence in all we do' and yet had an acrimonious relationship with our teachers' union and, adding fuel to the fire, noted that I had a particularly negative attitude. This observation and initial shock launched me into thinking about a new way of doing business. As a result, we began to develop protocols for our negotiating sessions that would keep both parties from acting badly. Behaviors and relationships began to improve on both sides.

"A couple of years later, a second incident pushed us further along toward a more positive relationship. When three new board members endorsed by the union swept into power, they challenged our approach, suggesting that I bring peace to labor negotiations. I insisted that it would be impossible.

"As parents the new board members had seen all the public commotion and disruption in schools every year before the contract was settled. They hadn't had time to be briefed on labor-management progress over the previous 2 years. They didn't realize that, to settle, things had to get to such an emotional state that good teachers had to demand that their leaders reach an agreement. When teachers approached me while I was visiting schools, in the market, or by sending me notes hoping to convince us to settle, I knew the end was near. Most of them were ready to get back to teaching! The strain wasn't worth it any longer and they saw how much money was usually on the table. Most often, it was enough to settle.

"Basically, they were good people caught in a dilemma. Their leadership had gone to a win-lose school similar to mine. The industrial model for negotiations set education back for years. Fortunately for us, the AFT group didn't control their locals as closely as did the NEA folks."

"I heard that, especially here in California," Rob observed. "Please continue."

"I still wasn't a believer and held out! I thought I had time to change the new board members' position, after they got to understand the real behind-the-scenes stuff going on. I said, 'not labor peace in my time, at any cost!' making a play on the infamous words of former British prime minister Neville Chamberlain in 1938 about a promise Nazi Germany made prior to the invasion of Poland in World War II. Selling out to union pressure wasn't in my vocabulary. Management rights were going to stay management's. However, my attitude was soon to change again!"

"Now you really have my interest. What happened?" Rob asked.

"Actually, at times things went well between the union and management. I spent a lot of time with teachers, visiting schools and encouraging them to participate in decisions through scores of committees at their schools and districtwide. I encouraged them to present at state and national conferences. Our own staff development programs were well received."

"Seems to me you were trying an end run!" the superintendent observed.

"Yes, that's somewhat true. We valued teachers' input but didn't like or want the union telling us what to do. The teachers were doing well, but it was the union that was the pain. We were recognizing teachers' great efforts and successes regularly, slowly building better relationships. Just before this board changeover, we jointly picked a mediator to help moderate our negotiation sessions. We were all trying to do things better."

"What did he do for you?" Rob asked, thinking ahead to his own problems.

"Our facilitator, Steve Haines, kept us working together despite angry and anxious moments. I don't think I've mentioned it before, but a few years earlier when Steve was with University Associates in San Diego, we had used him to help us develop our strategic plan. He was well known by union leadership. With Devon Smyth representing the teachers on the district steering committee, we began to build a somewhat better relationship. Remember, Dave was doing his beginning-teacher-assistance research during this time and then soon after was their chief negotiator. Although I didn't realize it, the trust between us was building."

"So what exactly did the mediator do for you?" Rob repeated. "I mean at this time. I'll hold off on asking about strategic planning until a better time."

"After a stormy session off site at our local country club, we almost lost it. He made us work through a key belief I wouldn't let go of. I wanted to establish my strong and, of course, correct belief that the teachers were ours and not his, meaning the union president, as they worked for us, not the union. On the other hand, I was willing to acknowledge reluctantly that the union had a legitimate role in the affairs of the district, those that dealt with the aspects of legal representation.

We finally reached consensus. Dave's group had the teachers as members of his subsystem and he finally agreed that the union role was to enhance the working environment through wages, benefits, and working conditions. In addition, they would be able to join the work of instructional committees with a representative of their choice—but they understood that the district had the right to establish committees even without collaborating with the union. Without the mediator pushing so hard and Dave's own team pressuring him to accept, it wouldn't have happened. This was a turning point."

"What then?"

"Steve got us to accept this disagreement and strongly advised us not to mention the topic again. We stopped."

"I can see you really are a Driver—a strong one at that," Rob observed, seeing a reinforcement of his newly acquired Styles knowledge.

"I have some material showing how this developed into something quite good. I'll share it when we get to the hotel," Barry offered. "There's a little more to tell in our work and I'm not ignoring what really changed my attitude. This was part of it."

"So say more," Rob urged, just as the announcement came over the loudspeaker to fasten seat belts as they rapidly approached Sky Harbor Airport in Phoenix.

"As I mentioned previously in our conversation, 2 years earlier both groups had agreed to go off site for several days, hoping to resolve the unsettled contract issues. We decided to meet at the old Seaview Motel on the bay near Pt. Loma in San Diego. The district agreed to pick up the cost of meeting rooms and meals, and for obvious reasons, the union would take care of any other refreshment bills. At the end of each day we adjourned for a social in the large two-room suite reserved for this purpose. This helped defuse any of the day's sharp rhetoric.

"It was during this time we set up meeting protocols that facilitated our sessions. Still, it didn't keep me from getting frustrated and angry when they attacked my integrity. I retaliated with a jab at their sore spot and got them excited when I said these were our teachers, not theirs."

"Again!"

"I didn't ever say I was perfect!" Woodson said, smiling. "The mediator took me to task, so I apologized and we moved on."

"Which protocols did you start with?" Rob said, remembering some Barry had suggested last summer.

"Some of the ground rules included the following:

- Things agreed to in writing stayed agreed to during the entire process—no more 'you sign this if we sign that' quid pro quo stuff.
- Until there is a signed agreement, anything said through brainstorming or developing alternatives isn't binding—it is not regressive bargaining.
- What's said in the room stays in the room—both parties must agree on joint press releases.
- Mistakes in data or the basis for a decision will cause that contract section to be automatically reopened.
- If discussions deteriorate, we would resume paraphrasing the previous speaker until we understood him or her.

There were others, but these come to mind now."

"Do you have these written down someplace? I'd like you to give me a copy," Rob said.

"Not a problem," Barry responded, making a note to do so. "Well, over these periods we agreed on several other things still worth mentioning. We worked on interests and verifiable data as much as possible, looking at alternative ways of meeting these interests. As I just mentioned, this led to the ground rule that if either team made a mistake in numbers, dollars, or percentages or in the details of a signed-off contract section, the disadvantaged party could immediately reopen the issue to correct it or withdraw it—especially if it involved dollars. This did happen a couple of times and we did reconsider. This helped with the trust issue."

"That was progress, in spite of how you described your attitude?" Rob interjected.

"Now don't get personal," Barry retorted. "Even as the good guy I thought I always was, I found myself moving from win-lose to more acceptance of the new process. I didn't then recognize this was leading to win-win as a viable way to do this trying and time-consuming business. I guess I was slowly changing!"

"Continue, now that I have hope for you," Rob kidded his coach.

"Our referee used to tell us to take a walk along the bay to reflect, pairing us up with a member of the other team to talk about ways of solving a particular dilemma we were facing. We had become allies against the mediator as we hated to have to look each other in the eye when we were still fuming over some point or another. But it worked after all."

"Give me an example."

"We were deadlocked over agency fee. They wanted the security that came from requiring all teachers to pay dues and not be able to leave the unit in protest at any time during the length of the contract. This would allow the leadership to take risks in trying more new things with us through trust agreements. Or so they said! More on that later. We firmly believed that an individual had the right of choice. I told them that in my union past, as shop steward for 2 years with the International Association of Machinists, we were hoodwinked by the union to give up a raise one year to get a union shop. I didn't like it then, and I don't like it now!" Woodson said with not a little emotion in his voice.

"So you went out to do your two by twos and came back with a third alternative?" Rob guessed.

"Generally it worked pretty well, as the union vice president and I built up trust over the dollar numbers and moved the process forward significantly on salaries. Trust was building!"

"Give me an example of how this third alternative worked," Rob asked.

"After listening more actively to their need for agency fee and them listening to our position, we solved the problem by agreeing to support them in recruiting new teacher members. By including the union's presence at the August before-school luncheon, we gave tacit endorsement for new teachers to join the union. The union had a leadership role in coplanning this event. The idea was to show management support for a strong union. We let them put handouts on the luncheon tables where both teachers and administrators where sitting together. At the conclusion of lunch, management was excused for the union follow-up session with the new folks.

"After we realized they had 92% membership already, we were able to discover the real reason for this contract challenge. As I mentioned, they wanted the security to be able to do things their own members would not be able to effectively challenge them on, even to the extent of stopped payment of their dues. So they dropped their request and trusted us to abide by the agreement. We did and they did. It worked well," Barry concluded.

"Sounds like you were really learning a new way to do business. Changing and still didn't even realize it," Rob observed, again right on point.

"Finally, we were moving to a better relationship by setting up ways to work through the acrimony that had characterized our earlier relationship. This was the first step toward our win-win thinking development," Barry said.

There was a smooth jolt as the wheels touched down on the runway. Rob couldn't contain himself, even after the loquacious and detailed detour his mentor had again taken in response to what Rob thought was a simple question. He asked again, desperate for the answer, "Before we reach the gate, tell me, what got you to go along with the new board's request to find a better way to negotiate?"

"It was really quite simple. They wrote in my annual evaluation that this was a primary goal to try to reach during the next year. They at least expected me to try other strategies. So I did, or rather we did. I was probably more ready than I thought but still predicted to the cabinet that there was no way this would happen. Again I was wrong, but also right. It worked well with every aspect except money issues.

"However, even here we learned more from a later training session on win-win. We agreed to use a new framework to solve the money problems in the final settlement. Finally, it came down to give and take. But with the data in front of us and agreed upon, our joint task was easier. We had learned to be civil to one another through this process. Much later they told me that they knew I never misspoke, had given them accurate budget numbers, and that I would not falter in my support of classroom instruction, stopping short of taking that money for salaries."

As the plane reached the gate, Rob said, "We've arrived safe and sound, so it's to be continued. Don't forget to pick up where you left off about the new insights you were getting."

"I'll get the car if you will get the bags off the carousel. It's about 35 minutes to the hotel. Let's enjoy the drive," Barry suggested.

🕐 **Time-Out—A What**

1. Review the ground rules. What did you like or dislike about them?
2. What would you add?
3. What interpersonal issues have you had with your union leadership that would block developing a systems approach to solving your differences?
4. What success stories can you add to the one Barry described?

RECALL ELECTION WORRIES

As they pulled out on the interstate heading north toward the Embassy Suites, Rob decided to tell Barry more about the recall election. Each incumbent had tried to ensure keeping his or her seat in the hands of someone with similar views by persuading a backup to run for their spot in case they were recalled. The two ultraconservatives couldn't agree between them on three candidates to replace the majority. Each put up a separate slate of three candidates in opposition urging the recall. Rob remembered what his mentor had said about a majority of the board losing their seats in an election and the predictable short-term future for the superintendent.

"What do the candidates know about the district?" Barry asked.

"I don't really know. A strange thing is happening though. One by one, as I ran into the candidates, they assured me that this was not about me, but rather they were supportive of what I've been able to do in such a short time. All but one has spoken to me about their support. I expected this from the three backups, but not the other six."

"That sounds like good news."

"Now what else can I do?" Rob pleaded.

"In a similar experience I took the bull by the horns and invited all the candidates in for a 2-night workshop. During the campaign I wanted each candidate to have the facts and be present when we shared what we were all about to the entire group."

"What did you do for 2 nights?" Rob asked.

"The first night we had each cabinet member share what his or her function was. Unlike the systems approach, we emphasized the complexity rather than the simplicity of what we did. Of course, you realize this was before I completely understood systems and backwards thinking. We did this for two reasons. First, to show off our leadership team's expertise, and then to encourage candidates during the campaign to go to the right person for information. I didn't want the incumbents attacked through misinformation. We were committed early on to be an open system, so this met the test.

"The second night was set up for us to answer questions that we had them write down at the first session. This gave us an insight to their agendas. Also, we made the point that we would remain neutral throughout the campaign and election."

"Barry, how did the incumbents feel about this? Did they believe you?" Rob asked tentatively, not really sure what to believe.

"I mentioned to them what I was going to do and why. They agreed and thought it would be helpful in stabilizing the election rhetoric. They realized it was not in my best interest to change horses in midstream, so to speak."

"Were incumbents invited?" asked Rob.

"Not this time. We probably should have. Remember, this was a recall and they were being severely criticized and attacked at every turn. They didn't need more exposure. These board candidate information sessions were so well received that we did it in each subsequent election and even invited the incumbents running for reelection to join in. I had the board's approval, of course! One by one, I had obtained their acceptance of the idea. They saw an advantage in getting to better know their opponents," Woodson said, adding, "and so did we!"

"Since some folks were, and probably still are, unsure about me, I think I'd like to give this a try," the now more seasoned rookie replied.

"Let me know if I can help," Barry answered as they were met by the bellhop under the hotel overhang.

🕐 Time-Out—A What

1. What advice would you give Rob about his personal involvement in the recall process or for that matter any school board election?
2. Should he endorse the three who hired him? Remain silent? How

> would you respond to a board member who came to you asking for support?
> 3. If you believe that one should not become involved, can you conceive of a time when you should?
> 4. What are your experiences in providing information to school board candidates? How effective was it?

TRUST AGREEMENTS

On Friday afternoon, following Dr. Lezotte's talk about the processes described in his and McKee's book *Assembly Required*, they agreed to meet in Barry's suite to finish the conversation on the trust agreements, the teachers' union subsystem, and an approach to a win-win system that Barry had added to his repertoire. They had 2 hours before the traditional predinner social hour and decided to make good use of the time.

"What do you think of the conference so far?" Woodson asked.

"I liked Peter Block's presentation yesterday on empowerment, especially the interaction with the superintendents that Larry co-led with Peter in the afternoon session."

"Where do you want to start?" Barry wanted to know, referring to Rob's issues. He had three stacks of paper on his sitting room table ready to be referenced.

"When did trust agreements come into the picture?" Rob wanted to know. This was his first major item and would require further discussion.

Barry told Rob how he was first introduced to the notion of trust agreements at an AFT-management joint conference in a presentation by the Claremont Graduate School's Charles Kerchner. This trust agreement concept was aimed at creating a bridge between the two parties outside a labor contract and in the full meaning of a trust.

A few weeks later, Kerchner was invited to the district to talk more about an implementation plan for these agreements. Barry believed that Kerchner was not only interested in establishing the concept with them, but also was interested in a consultant contract to be the referee for union-management trust relationships.

"An Educational Policy Trust Agreement is the negotiated compact between a school district and teachers, represented by their union. Trust Agreements are intended to specify educational problems of joint concern and establish mechanisms for working on them. Trust Agreements also set aside money, time, and authority. And they create structures that allow union and management to resolve disputes as they work toward joint goals."

—Charles T. Kerchner

Barry continued, after being interrupted by a phone call from the conference coordinator telling them about a time change for the social hour. "To make a long story short, we took his idea and came up with a unique result. We decided to do some things differently without changing our basic union contract language. We agreed that our definition of trust meant trusting each other in our spoken, given, and, of course, our written word. We agreed to try out new practices by developing side trust agreements aimed at single issues that were not precedent setting and could be canceled by either party within a specified period of time. Some went for a year, often less, and some could be canceled at a moment's notice."

Then Barry reached over to the first pile and handed Rob a copy of a trust agreement he had brought along. Since they had discussed this program last month, he thought it would be helpful for this discussion.

Agreement
Permanent-Teacher Intervention Program
   This agreement is entered into between the Federation of Teachers and the _____ School District.

1. The parties desire to establish a system for managing assistance provided to permanent teachers employed by the district who have been identified as having classroom performance that places them in serious professional jeopardy.
2. The district and the AFT have established a trial Permanent-Teacher Intervention Program (PTIP), in which the services of a

teacher-consultant from the Professional Assistant Program will assist participating permanent teachers in achieving a satisfactory level of performance and in furthering pupil achievement and the instructional objectives of the district.

3. Recognizing the trial nature of each step, the district and the AFT agree to continue the PTIP by mutual consent only, with each party having the right at any time to terminate the PTIP by giving written notice to the other party. Should the PTIP terminate for any reason, neither the district nor the AFT may assert any aspect of the creation or operation of the PTIP as a past practice or having any impact on the parties' duty to bargain over matters relating to the PTIP.

Date:	Date:
District:	Federation:
By:	By:
Title: Superintendent	Title: Union President

Attached were six pages describing the program in detail, along with a flowchart illustrating each of the steps, many of which they had covered already.

Woodson then showed him three other agreements; the first was the Alternative Teacher-Evaluation Program mentioned in the previous chapter and the second was called Flexible Spending Accounts. It provided for setting up dependent-care accounts limited to $5,000. The third one was an agreement to assist probationary teachers. This one also contained the provision that the program was by mutual consent only and each party had the right to terminate the program at any time by giving written notice to the other.

"I like this very much," Rob declared. "I think this has real promise down the road a ways."

"Keep these copies to use in any way you want to," Woodson said.

"Where would I start, if I wanted to move forward?"

"Why don't you start on a trial basis by offering to settle low-risk issues by varying from the contract through trust agreements? Include language that allows either side to cancel at any time. Second, why don't you or you and Don Halverson continue monthly meetings with union reps to discuss pebble problems before they become big-rock issues? It will take time, but if it works out, you will gain time and less trouble in the long run. If you start with relatively noncontroversial issues, and the agreement works, you will have built up a small reservoir of trust."

"Have you ever had problems with this entire trust agreement situation?" Rob inquired.

"I hoped you wouldn't ask that embarrassing question. Before we really got engaged in the win-win environment, I said something one year that upset them so much they canceled 7 of the 10 agreements that we had painstakingly agreed upon.

"In a way, it was sad since these agreements directly benefited teachers. They wanted to show me or to get even! It's like biting off one's nose to spite one's face," Woodson stated with some emphasis. "It was a setback for a while."

"Sounds to me like the 'willingness' quotient described in Sit Lead reverted to zero! Time for an S-1! What happened?"

"Really not too much negative fallout," Barry answered. "Most of the things were so well entrenched it didn't change practice much. Worthy of note is that the three agreements we hammered out, and that were primarily union created, didn't get set aside. Too much vested interest, I think."

🕐 Time-Out—A So What

1. Do you have any form of trust agreements in your district? If so, describe.
2. What do you think of this notion to move forward without having to negotiate or reopen the basic contract?
3. What favorable factors would have to be in place to enable you to move toward this strategy?
4. What in your district would prevent you from even discussing trust agreements?
5. Identify two or three areas that would benefit from the development of a trust agreement in your district.

THE TEACHERS' UNION AS A SUBSYSTEM

"Why don't you tell me about your ideas for the union as a subsystem," the superintendent suggested, looking at the top of one of Barry's piles of paper. He was intrigued by the paper with a bunch of circles drawn on it.

Barry handed Rob a copy of the material he had put together a few years back. "You remember on the trip over, I shared with you that one year I had to fight with the union to develop, define, and agree on the legitimate roles and responsibilities of the union and the school district. You remember that union leaders usually insist that the teachers belong to them and, therefore, they won't acknowledge who should direct them. Sometimes they even seem to forget where they receive their paychecks," Woodson said, still with some ire in his voice. "Actually, the teachers' negotiating team forced their president to see the light—my light—with my persuasive reasoning."

"What light?" Rob asked.

"The notion was that we each had a role in the system and theirs wasn't to direct the work of 'our' teachers. Theirs was to protect the working conditions as prescribed by law."

"Got it! I remember our conversation on the way over."

After clarifying that there might be a little duplication of what he had just shared with Rob, Barry then read more of what happened as described in his paper.

"As we concluded, by fussing over whose teachers they were we came up with a way to crystallize our thinking. We started with two circles representing our separate interests and our basic missions (see Figure 8.1).

"At first in my innocence, I thought that the circles could be concentric circles. However, one of my analytical assistants reminded me that we couldn't ever make that subsystem and the district system concentric circles, because we had different missions. Also, there are other employees and employee groups in our circle, creating additional subsystems. We are interrelated systems, but not the same. We have fundamentally different missions!" (see Figure 8.2).

"This intersection of circles is so represented because the school dis-

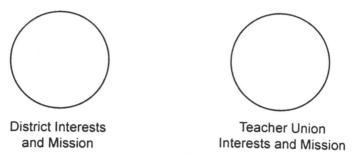

Figure 8.1. **District Interests and Mission Versus Teacher Union Interests and Mission**

trict contains all the people with other subsets, while the union subsystem contains only the teachers, and with a limited legal function with them at that. Another key difference is that the district works with teachers in many ways that the union does not. The issue I emphasized was that these are teachers working for us and the board and we directed their work. They finally agreed that their role was to represent our employees to protect their employment and some legal interests. This was a major concession and a major breakthrough, leading to better understanding and even better relationships later on (see Figure 8.3).

"Most of these issues dealt with teachers' needs and were basically contained in the contract language. How we both were responsible for treating staff fairly under the contract language, and in my case well beyond, was clearly known. After a few months we expanded and then narrowed our thinking.

"I came up with the notion that we needed to continue to overlay and expand the intersection of these circles to indicate more area of com-

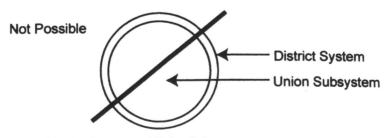

Figure 8.2. **District System and Union Subsystem**

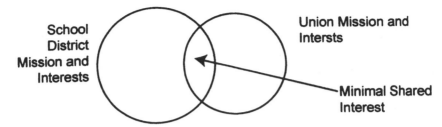

Figure 8.3. Shared Interests

mon interests that we could develop that had been not specified in the contract. This was the beginning of our new era of win-win thinking (see Figure 8.4).

"This difference in mission can be found in the definition in the lines of business found in our mission statements and core values. Basically, the district's stated and functional mission is to educate children, while for the union this may be a secondary desire as their main mission is to represent the interests of the union and their teacher members.

"Finally, both parties agreed we could never share all the same system space but could work to expand the common ground through our trust agreements and begin to try new ideas on a 'trusting' basis without

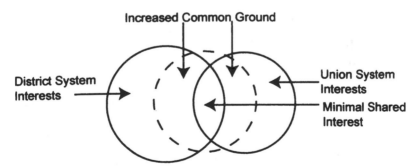

Systems can intersect and find increased common ground.

The area expanded by the broken lines encouraged teams to find more and more common ground, develop more trust, and do further collaboration. One way was through the use of trust agreements.

Figure 8.4. Common Ground

making long-term commitments. Both union and management usually do not move forward because new ideas create new territory to explore and most of us don't embrace change readily. Being fearful and untrusting, we end up doing the safe and traditional things.

"Surprisingly, after 2 or 3 years we agreed that we would have an open contract. Either party could bring up any necessary changes as needed. Most often this was put in a side agreement until a new contract was negotiated," Barry finished, looking for a reaction from his colleague.

"This is good stuff," Rob said. "And I understand it! I really hadn't thought about this from a systems approach. I especially like the diagrams. This information you have been giving me about systems all year is finally getting into focus, especially with the help of your circles."

"We can go over more of this in greater detail as you have need. I realize neither you nor your union is ready for this kind of change. File it away until you can use it," Barry suggested.

After a moment's reflection, he suggested that Rob talk again to Dave Rascalle, the teachers' union president in Barry's former district. Dave might have some insight into things Barry didn't remember or had selective memory about. Of course, Barry noted, this didn't happen overnight and was not without gnashing of teeth, anger, frustration, and only a grudging willingness to change on the part of both parties.

A WIN-WIN SOLUTION

"Why don't we move on and talk some about the win-win program that you folks came up with?" Rob suggested.

"Rob, early on we decided we had decisions to make, rather than see the issues as problems. We then needed to find what win-win bargaining outcomes would look like. Some of these were accepting that it might not work, that it was important to have equal representation, getting a timely settlement prior to the beginning of school was important, that the parties would feel the outcomes were fair, that trust would be increased, that the focus would be on task and not negotiations, and in the end students would win.

"Then the group worked on what would be considered ground rules for positive relationships, including the following:

1. No cheap shots, originated by management, would be used in either the union newspaper or in the local newspaper. Instead articles appearing as joint press releases would be used.
2. There would be no misuse of statistics that the business manager submitted.
3. There would be budget openness and agreement on data; arguments would stop about the size of the pie and focus on how to divide it.
4. Each player would speak the truth, without the usual rhetoric.
5. There would be no impugning of motives by either side.
6. Teachers would gain financially and professionally.
7. Neither side would feel beat up when it was over.
8. A time-out could be called if any of the preceding rules seemed to be violated.

This was modified by our realization that, as we concluded, each side felt disappointed by giving up something they really didn't expect or want to reach compromise."

"These all look like great ideas. But how did they work?" Rob wanted to know.

"Over the next 3 or 4 years, this process took hold and became very effective. However, we still weren't there yet. Dave Rascalle wanted to move the process forward. He introduced us to another program developed by William Haney, a retired mediator. He led us to yet another level beyond which I didn't think we could go."

"What did he bring to the table?" Rob asked.

"Haney called it Interest-Based Problem Solving, or IBPS. The philosophy of this process is based upon open, honest sharing of information and the accompanying education that is required to make the information shared meaningful to the receiving party. It is a problem-solving process based on a set of principles, implemented through a series of steps and facilitated by a set of tools, which trained personnel may use to achieve the best solution for the team—*at that time*. Nothing is etched in stone!"

"How extensive was the training before you got down to real problem solving?" Rob asked.

"I can't remember now, but I think it was several sessions. One condition Haney set was that the superintendent had to be there throughout the training. I was reluctant at first, but in the end I was pleased to have been trained. It was an essential component to the process. He then supported us for about 2 years, as a facilitator and trainer, as we worked on real problems. We met 1 or 2 days a week when in the heat of battle—open contract time. He coached us through the model's steps. Finally, he decided that we didn't need him anymore, since we were then able to use the win-win process without much help."

Rob was curious enough to explore this further, asking, "Can you give a quick overview?"

"Better than that, I brought along for you a copy of the training manual we used in our work. But first let me share a few more important things. The first of these is that you have to make a commitment of time and personnel. The process takes hundreds of hours and many people to make it work," Barry warned.

Then Barry outlined the barriers to group problem solving. There are at least four: competition, communication, assumptions, and trust. Beyond this most of those in leadership positions want to be winners and get their way. To overcome this, egos have to be kept outside the doors. It's too easy to fall into the trap of one winner and one loser. This makes it difficult to identify what the parties can find to agree upon. Not everything can be done this way, as the company at times may need to say no, even *hell* no! But give the reasons why. The union leaders need reasons to defend themselves when they go back to their folks. Select an agenda on which there is an agreement of topics. A good mediator makes all the difference in the world. But both parties have to commit to the mediator process.

Another factor Rob needs to consider is the lack of effective communication. Listening with attention and respect is almost a lost art in this process. Covey covers this in his *The Seven Habits of Highly Effective People* (1989)—"Understand before seeking to be understood." Some experts have found that we speak at 125 to 140 words per minute, are capable of hearing 400 words per minute, and can process 1,000–1,400 words per minute. For effective communication we need to concentrate. Concentrate on the speaker, message, body language, and tone of voice. Clarify in writing what you want to say.

After this summation, Barry continued by saying, "In the labor-management arena, negotiations are based on a series of assumptions, a great number of which are acted on without being written, stated, or identified, creating a continuing lack of trust in the relationship. To overcome this, each side needs to peel back the layers of the onion to find the inner root causes. By forcing the issue, asking Why? Why? Why? clarification can be accomplished."

"Sounds like a systems thinking to me," Rob noted.

"It does now, doesn't it?" Barry agreed.

Finally, Barry suggested that trust is not a barrier. Mistrust and lack thereof are what cause serious problems in any relationship. To make this system work, it had to be built on trust. This was an on-again, off-again issue for years, but eventually they were able to trust each other in the negotiations game. They may have disagreed as to priorities or values, but they trusted the legitimacy of what was being said. But at times more data was required to identify the truth.

"I think a wise counselor told me that back in June. Something to the effect of 'in the game of trust the leader has to ante up first.' Did I get that right?" the superintendent interjected smugly.

Barry smiled and gave Rob another handout.

In IBPS the basic assumption states that to successfully use the IBPS process, the parties must agree to, and internalize, five principles:

1. Focus on the issue, not the people.
2. Focus on the future, not the past.
3. Openly and honestly share all information.
4. Focus on interests, not positions.
5. Evaluate and rank options with standards, not power position.

Woodson then mentioned the instructions in the manual for preparing each group, preparing teams jointly, and learning the team problem-solving steps.

Rob said, "In my limited experience, we've not been able to reach consensus with our union folks on anything. How do you define consensus, or rather, how does Haney define it?"

"Good question, Rob. Let me give it a shot. I can tell you what it is not. It's not voting. It's not being happy. It's not horse trading. And it's certainly not averaging. I think this is what it is: It's the situation reached when all members of a group understand a decision; understand the conditions and viewpoints that drove it; have had an opportunity to air their opinions and viewpoints; and even if they don't wholeheartedly agree with the decision, accept and support it. This was hard to come by sometimes. Later it became almost commonplace."

"Well, I asked for a spoonful and instead got a mouthful," Rob said, surrendering to the wisdom of his mentor.

"Since you're so curious, let me add just a few more things. After training, we got right into the process. As this evolved, we used it to do our one big thing—the annual negotiations ritual. We even brought our former negotiation positions in as interests. The big barrier in using this process throughout was that it didn't work well with money items. The accountability for all funds to manage the overall system was not the union's responsibility, they argued, and indicated that this was our problem, not theirs—a big difference in interests!"

"I guess they didn't see too clearly or want to see their subsystem affecting the whole district's system negatively. So how did you end up resolving the money matters?" the superintendent asked, somewhat disillusioned.

Reading the look on Rob's face, Barry counseled, "No system has all the answers. Human beings have to work at finding ways to resolve differences in an acceptable manner. Now to answer your question, we tried to bring all the facts to the table and share them. As I mentioned previously, we didn't want to unnecessarily increase class size, take away teachers' supplies, or not provide student books for a 1% additional raise in salaries that was approaching $1.4 million at the time. It certainly wasn't chicken feed! We did use the process steps we had recently learned up to the final agreement—and most often the process was built on trust, accommodating each side's points of interest as funds permitted. A warning here! You can mess up the trust easily. Only one betrayal will probably do it," Barry cautioned his charge.

"I think you keep making that very clear," Rob said seriously then asked, "What did you do to keep the process going?"

"We had a full-group steering committee and a small group of two leaders, one the AFT president and the other the assistant superintendent of human resources, to ensure that follow-up and implementation occurred. To this small group we added two or three administrators and teachers. They met monthly to consider all the issues that had come to light during the interim. The full body would meet to resolve crisis situations."

"Give me an example of such a crisis situation," Rob asked.

"A district administrator bypassed a joint management-teacher district committee for the quick implementation of a process, even refusing to back down when confronted by teachers on the committee who felt betrayed. The union reps brought the issue to the big group for resolution. In this case, the teachers were correct. We revisited the process. I did have a heart-to-heart talk with this administrator, who didn't seem to get the point of our win-win relationship. She had a strong Driving Style and had a hard time listening to—I mean even hearing—the point I was making!"

"What was included on the steering committee meeting agenda?" Rob asked.

"To start each meeting, we agreed to have cofacilitators, one from each group. Generally, it started with what was called a check-in, where each member shared what was important in their life the past week or so—a join-up activity. Previous decisions were reviewed and new topics added. A parking lot, or a to-do list for unfinished business, was kept indicating what was left to do, who was to do it, and when it was to be done. In discussing items, the list of interests on that topic was posted to refer to in discussions. Most of the time was spent in working the steps in the process."

"I'm really looking forward to reviewing the training manual," Rob said.

"Not a problem. But now, it looks like we just have enough time to clean up before the cocktail party," Barry observed, "so why don't we meet downstairs in 15 or 20 minutes?"

"Sounds like a plan," Barry responded as he picked up his stack of materials and headed for his room.

🕐 **Time-Out—Another So What**

1. Review and critique the steps presented.
2. What did you learn from this that could be applied in your situation?
3. Discuss the pros and cons of implementing such a process in your district.

CONFERENCE FEEDBACK

During the conference Rob was introduced to many other superintendents. Most of these were seasoned veterans, so he learned a lot just by listening. He was fascinated by the information that Dr. Lezotte shared with the group. It was up to date and challenging. His analysis of the impact of the No Child Left Behind act was very informative and gave the rookie superintendent food for thought.

Leaving late on Saturday afternoon after the conference concluded was not a problem. When they finished playing golf on the course adjacent the hotel, they just had to toss their clubs in the car and race to the airport. They really hoped that no one had to sit by them and their well-used, mud-splattered golfing clothes.

They had continued to talk about the strength of the conference. Building a network of contacts was going to be valuable for Rob, and he wanted to become part of the organization. It was one of the best sessions he had ever attended. Hearing from Peter Block and Larry Lezotte added a lot to his understanding about leadership. This encouraged him to look at the leading indicators of effective student learning that would help measure the effectiveness of his schools.

PLANNING FOR A COLLABORATION SESSION

For their last 1 1/2 hours together on the flight home, Dr. Woodson thought Rob Moore should think about his next steps. There were still loose ends that had to be tied up, such as trying to find time for planning to plan and decisions about building a new elementary school.

"What do you think next steps are?" Woodson asked.

"When we get together next time, let's meet with my business guy, Doug Daniels, and go over some ideas for planning the new school. I also could set up a meeting for you to talk to the cabinet about planning for an Applied Strategic Management training event. These two items seem to be timely now," the rookie suggested, almost thinking out loud about next week's agenda. He looked up, seeking Barry's confirmation.

"That makes a lot of sense to me," Barry affirmed.

"I think I'm ready to do that. I'll have Diane give you a call and set something up."

Barry then asked, "What did we leave off that we wanted to talk about? Anything you can think of?"

"What do you think about this as a plan for moving forward with the union folks? Why don't I take Margaret and Harry to lunch and talk about some of these new ideas? I'm sure they have some ideas we could share that I could encourage them to broach. I don't want to get into the debate about who's the boss. They know that already. I'll show them that I'm trying to be the problem solver—not the problem. We can set up an agenda to work on the rest of this year."

"What are you going to include?" his mentor asked.

"I guess I have to decide where I want to go in this arena?" Rob said uncertainly, looking for support. "I like your idea about trust agreements and expanding the area of overlap indicated in the circle models. Also, I want to have them comfortable enough to bring up issues before they become crises."

Woodson replied quickly, "Okay, why don't you list some agenda items?"

"I'll write so you can see the list and you can help me fill in what I miss," the rookie suggested.

They developed the following agenda:

- Start by celebrating what's working. Remember that we both were able to settle a fair agreement in September, and I got a commitment to meet more regularly.
- Agree to have monthly meetings and review meeting protocols.
- Brainstorm an agenda.
- Have in mind where our team wants to go. It sounds crass, perhaps,

but he who has the gold rules! Remember not to flout it, because they know this already.

• Suggest setting up a rap session with the union building representatives from each school to meet with me for lunch followed by an afternoon update and question-and-answer session.

As they left the terminal and walked toward their cars, Barry asked, "Are you going to make the 2-hour drive home or are you going to stay over in town this weekend?"

"In all the trip excitement I forgot to tell you that my wife is coming down here this weekend, so that we can look at three houses she's picked out. She's probably already at the condo. I'm going to give her a call as soon as I get on the road. The drive is getting to me, so I'll be real happy to move. When I talked to her last night she thought we had a buyer for our place. However, I am not going to finalize anything till after February 17th. I'm confident, but I'm not going to do anything stupid until after the recall election."

"So then, if you need any more help give me a holler. And remember to let me know the election results," he added, as they tossed the bags in their cars and drove off.

SUMMARY

This chapter considered the elements of a case study describing the change in attitude over time of a school superintendent concerning labor relations. Elements surrounding school board elections and the superintendent's desired position were introduced. There was a special concern on how to deal with board candidates and board members during a recall election. The idea of a board candidate briefing night was introduced.

During this change process the union subsystem, as it intersects with the school district system, was described and displayed in a series of figures. Finally, the idea of trust agreements was introduced and its virtues were then described. Several problems that the superintendent was facing were described.

Interwoven around a new learning experience for the rookie superintendent was the conversation and description of a successful win-win model. A general description and some of the steps in a process were described.

🕐 Time-Out—Reflections

1. Looking back through the entire section, list the new ideas that you would like to explore later.
2. With whom would you share these ideas?
3. How would you go about introducing some of these ideas to your own administrative team, the school board, and the teachers' union?

MONTH 7—JANUARY

Strategies and Survival Skills

1. Identify what you know and what you don't know about the negotiation process.
   - Check your attitude and determine whether you're ready to develop better relationships with your union people, if you aren't already there.
   - List the steps that would improve these relationships, even if they are in good shape now.
   - Consider taking a chance to develop a win-win relationship in all that you do.
2. Take opportunities to go to worthwhile conferences and workshops.
   - Find people there that you can learn from.
   - Don't waste your time going to meetings where the agenda isn't focused on what you need.
   - File away the best and brightest ideas you come in contact with. You will be surprised when they come to the fore later in meeting needs.
3. Find a way to educate board candidates.
   - Consider using the board candidate briefing process as one means to do so.
   - Try to treat all candidates fairly, even when you really don't want to.

- Remember OHAB—always try to be open, honest, and above-board.

TOOLBOX

Block, P. (1991). *The Empowered Manager: Positive Political Skills at Work.* San Francisco: Jossey-Bass.

Coser, L. (1956). *The Functions of Social Conflict: An Examination of the Concept of Social Conflict and Its Use in Empirical Sociological Research.* New York: Free Press.

Covey, S. (1989). *The Seven Habits of Highly Effective People: Powerful Lessons in Personal Change.* New York: Simon & Schuster.

Fisher, R., & Ury, W. (1983). *Getting to Yes: Negotiating Agreement Without Giving In.* New York: Penguin Books.

Haney, W. (October 1997). *Interest Based Problem Solving: Path to Creative Solutions.* Unpublished manuscript.

Hart, L. (1981). *Learning From Conflict: A Handbook for Trainers and Group Leaders.* Boston: Addison-Wesley.

Kerchner, C., & Koppich, J. (1993). *A Union of Professionals: Labor Relations and Educational Reform.* Teachers College, Columbia University, New York & London: Teachers College Press.

Lezotte, L., & McKee, K. (2002). *Assembly Required: A Continuous School Improvement System.* Okemos, MI: Effective Schools Products.

9

FEBRUARY: WHAT BUSINESS ARE YOU REALLY IN? DOES IT MATTER?

If you can dream it—you can do it.

—Walt Disney

DO YOU UNDERSTAND THE MISSION, CORE VALUES, AND VISION OF A SCHOOL SYSTEM?

In this chapter you will do the following:

1. Consider the role of the superintendent in school board elections.
2. Understand the business you think you are in.
3. Reaffirm your main mission.
4. Understand the roles and relationships of mission, values, and vision and their power for change in the organization.
5. Understand an effective strategic thinking model focusing on change and improvement.
6. Begin the planning-to-plan phase to achieve an organizational mission.

INTERRUPTED SLEEP

The rain was slamming at the bedroom window and there were intermittent flashes of lightning followed by rumbles of thunder. Dr. Barry

Woodson had just slipped into bed and was preparing for his usual countdown to sleep. It was just past 11 p.m. The open New Testament was by his side as he propped himself up under the reading light. Each night he reread a chapter. This night he had reviewed the second chapter of Acts. His ritual was to ponder the scriptures for a while and then turn to a bedside novel to help him drift off. He was enjoying the final book of Tolkien's *The Lord of the Rings* but was becoming frustrated because he could get through only a few pages until the words started blurring. Would Frodo survive? He wouldn't find out tonight. Quickly he dog-eared the page, turned out the light, and hoped to be fast asleep in a few minutes. It was not to be this stormy February night.

Shortly after, as he was drifting into a sound sleep, he was startled by the ring of his bedside phone. Reaching over to the nightstand, he grabbed it on the third ring.

"Hello," he grumbled.

"Were you up waiting for my phone call?" a cheerful voice asked.

"No, Dr. Moore, I wasn't exactly holding my breath," he shot back in a grumpy voice. "I was almost asleep, if you really want to know. What can I do for you at this late hour?"

"I'm disappointed. Don't you know what day this is?"

"What's left of it is Tuesday, February 17, I think," Barry said with a grumble still in his voice.

"They won! Or rather, we won!" the rookie exclaimed. "Our three good guys won! This means my chances for survival have increased 200%!"

Cheerfully, and now wider awake, Barry responded, "That is good news! Congratulations! It looks like the voters didn't want to change horses in midstream, so to speak. How close was it? What do the results mean?"

Rob, still excited, gave his analysis. "The results are not certified yet, but the margin of victory seems to be great enough so there shouldn't be any problems—until next year! It seems that when my two conservatives couldn't agree and each supported their own slate rather than joining forces, it split the vote and probably took the wind out of the total recall effort. Even if recalled, we still had the good-guy backups elected. One could conclude that the community didn't want any changes at this moment in time. Or they think I'm great!"

"Oh, sure! What's this next year stuff? Are you future minded all of a sudden?"

"Well, Dr. Woodson, these same three board members' 4-year terms are up in just 13 months, and I would like to think if they choose to run they would be reelected."

Woodson thought for a moment and then replied, "Rob, you have to get through this year, but I like your future thinking. A great new end in mind! Survival the second year! What are you going to say to the unsuccessful candidates?"

Rob was on such a high as a result of the victory that he hadn't thought about it. Then he said with sudden insight, "I'm going to send everyone a thank-you note. Since they've shown interest in the district, they may run again. I may even encourage each to get involved on a citizen's advisory committee. You just never know!"

"I'm glad you called. And congratulations again! I'd like to see the results. Why don't you e-mail them to me? I'm not sure my morning paper will pick them up."

"Consider it done. I'll say good night so you can go back to sleep."

"That may be easier said than done," Barry said, thinking he would get a full chapter of the book read before he got sleepy again.

"We're going to celebrate some yet. The two sessions we planned last month are scheduled. I'll tell you more then. Good night," Rob said, hanging up.

Another bolt of lightning flashed and then thunder roared seemingly right outside Woodson's window as he wondered if he would ever get back to sleep this night.

MEETING AT THE PARADISE VALLEY SCHOOL DISTRICT

"Greetings, Dr. Barry," Diane said with her usual pleasant smile. "Dr. Moore will be with you in a minute or two as soon as he gets off the phone with a board member. You will have about 40 minutes before the cabinet meeting. I'm looking forward to it."

"Thanks. How is everyone feeling now that the board will be together for another year?" Barry asked.

"Just great! You can't realize the strain on each and every one of us.

Insecurity was evident. We knew the devil we had and didn't want a more disruptive change," she smiled, amused at the thought. "Staff kept coming by to see how Dr. Moore was holding up. A lot of support was being shown."

The intercom buzzer sounded. "Dr. Moore is ready to see you now."

Rob warmly greeted his mentor and then quickly his face took on a self-satisfied look. "That was the board chairman," he said. "He wanted me to know the three winners are feeling vindicated. He thanked me for the idea of backup candidates, who each won, incidentally. The idea of the board candidate workshop you suggested worked. It seems as there were no dirty tricks used. Then he went on to say how pleased they were with my leadership."

"Did you ask for a raise right away?" Barry joked.

"No. I just thanked him and hoped the entire board would pull together now."

"How strong was the board pressure to get you involved?" the professor asked cautiously.

"I only had mentioned to the board chairman what happened in my previous district, where I got branded as an active supporter in a recall election when my boss was the target. I told him in the best interest of the system I was staying out of this community issue and so would all of my top team. However, I did mention that one strategy successfully used was to argue that there was no real point to change horses midstream, since the three would have to stand for reelection when their terms expired the next spring. He then thanked me and thought he would be okay with my position."

"Well it looks like you have a guardian angel or the good Lord is smiling down. Do you realize with the split of the two conservatives that the recall didn't have much of a chance?" Dr. Barry reminded him.

"Not really. As I mentioned on the phone, I was too excited to listen."

"Now my best advice is to continue with our timeline and planned projects. You still have the guiding strength of the Superintendent's Goals they approved in November and you are going to report these results informally next month in your evaluation and then publicly in June. I'm sure you used them in the board candidate workshop to show that you were on top of things?"

"Yes, I did," Rob responded proudly. "I used them to outline the staff presentation."

"What have you learned from this recall election of the board?" Barry asked, pushing Rob to closure on the election.

"Well," Rob started, "I think there are three or four learnings I want to remember. First is to decide up front my level of involvement, if any. Next, I want to keep my key staff apart from the politics of it all. I can't control what others in the organization do. Third, I want to hold a board candidate forum each election for all candidates, including incumbents. This will indicate that it's the community who selects their leadership group, not the staff. Finally, I feel secure in using the annual board-district goals as a platform, if the board adopts them early enough in the school year. There's word going around in the state legislature that the elections may be moved to November. No matter when they are scheduled, we can give them a public forum to declare what they believe. It sets a more professional environment."

"I agree. Remember, there may be times when the danger to the main mission may mitigate this position. I had to break with this belief as I told you before. Sometimes you may have to risk it all to protect the learning environment. Many times your own personal values are in conflict," Barry reminded Rob.

"I try to keep this in mind," Rob agreed.

Barry then moved on. "Are we set for the cabinet presentation at 10?"

"Yes. Thanks for changing the subject and getting us back to what I need from you this morning. But first I need to report on some results we planned last summer. I've been recording my feelings each month, relating what I like about the job and the board. Despite the election, I am really enjoying bringing the team together, trying to keep the board focused on the students and learning, and still believe I can make a difference here."

"Sounds great," Dr. Barry said with a smile. "You are crazier than I thought. You will fit right in with the rest of the superintendents I know. What else is on the agenda?"

THINKING MORE ABOUT STRATEGIC PLANNING AND MANAGEMENT

"Well, I've been wondering about one thing. What did you do when you were superintendent that made that system so good? Or is that too simplistic a question?"

"Rob, the truth of the matter is, there is never simply one thing that makes a change process work in developing a top organization. It's never that simplistic. But I'll give it a shot. You know I'd never stopped to consider that single question before until a new superintendent asked me this at dinner a couple of years ago. I stumbled around in my mind for a single answer. I hurriedly mentioned three things without much thought behind them. I think I mumbled something about our strategic planning and values, having good people, and a long-term commitment to student learning."

Rob stopped the dialogue and said, "It sounds like you've identified some critical pieces."

"Since then, I've thought about it more, especially trying to recapture the elements to determine whether my adventure can be replicated. Just recently, I've seen evidence that convinces me that there was one key but also recognized other multiple factors that made this work. My one-factor answer is a total system commitment to a set of powerful core values driving the system. Measured by a sampling of principal and teacher feedback, along with continuing improved state test scores, I'm convinced now more than ever that the development, belief in, and enculturalization of powerful core values will keep the schools on course to do wonderful things for kids," Woodson said with a sense of both conviction and pride.

"Sounds like you have given this a lot of thought," Rob commented and then asked, "How does this play out for us? You've convinced me we can't just step in and copy any program, adopting it lock, stock, and barrel. Change doesn't happen that way!"

"Bravo! Certainly what I'm going to share with your cabinet will be part of what this process could do to help your district, including the impact of change. For us things just started improving, our team got better at what we were doing. We kept a semblance of a vision in front of us. When I first started I told the board that we were going to put the kids and their learning first and ahead of the administrative convenience of the system. This is not what you are asking exactly, I realize."

The development, belief in, and enculturalization of powerful core values driving the system, will keep the schools on course.

"I'm sure there's a lot more to it," the rookie responded.

"The one thing that really helped to establish a collective focus occurred after an 8-year journey and discovering what our 'business' was really all about. I've mentioned this before. We're all about emphasizing *learning*, not teaching! I'll elaborate on that later today.

"Then it took us a long time to learn to measure results rather than process. However, remember that the Effective Schools criteria (clear and focused mission, opportunity to learn and student time on task, frequent monitoring of student progress, climate of high expectations for success, instructional leadership, safe and orderly environment, and good home-school relationships) are leading-edge indicators that can be used as a framework to improve the conditions to enhance student learning. However, in my opinion this alone won't move a school to great heights. The entire system has to be considered along with any school improvement plans. There is much more to do to get at this readiness level, along with a serious commitment to the time and task. Maybe we should spend more time developing this concept later in the spring. We can cover some more ideas in a wrap-up today."

Rob reiterated the obvious reason for Dr. Woodson's meeting with them. "I'd like very much to understand how all of that worked for you folks. That's why you're here today. I've heard you tell pieces of your adventure. I want to hear more, so we can decide if the process would work here and, if so, the best timing for me to propose it. Most everyone in the state I talk to is very complimentary about your former district and the job that was done. They give you a lot of credit."

"Let me correct you. It was a 'we' job that was done. Lots of staff got on board to make it work."

STRATEGIC PLANNING AND MANAGEMENT

"Can strategic management change and recharge a school district's mission?" Barry stated and then told Rob the following.

What business are you really in? Driving trains or the transportation business? While this question is sometimes asked and answered in the private sector, the answer is not as clear in the public education instructional business. In the past 5 years a partial definition has been developed, but not all that students are expected to learn in a school system is included.

"Insanity is doing the same things the same way and expecting different results."

—Steve Haines

Most states, and even more recently the federal government, are demanding accountability at least in the reading and mathematics basics by setting standards and testing them. These assessment systems are limited at best.

However, does the organizational system charged with these outputs really know what business they're in? Are they going to be able to pull this off? For example, if the organization believes its main focus is teaching rather than student learning, does it make a difference? It sure does!

"A good deal of the corporate planning I have observed is like a ritual rain dance; it has no effect on the weather that follows, but those who engage in it think it does. Moreover, it seems to me that much of the advice and instruction related to corporate planning is directed at improving the dancing, not the weather. I have no objection to the inclusion of aesthetic considerations in planning; to the contrary, I insist on it, but not at the expense of the proper function of planning—creation of the corporate future."

—Russell L. Ackoff

This paradigm shift that changed a high-performing district into an even better one leads to this conclusion. Can it work for everyone? Probably not, but this methodology provided the framework for achieving outstanding performance well above state and national standards.

The systems approach to system management is used with an applied strategic model developed for the private sector. Continued commitment is an essential component. In our example even with new leadership the mission is still driving student learning and accountability to even higher levels.

"This is a good teaser. Let's use it and see what happens," Barry said.

"Thanks," Rob replied. Looking at the clock on his desk he added, "Let's take a break and meet in the conference room in, say, 5 minutes."

THE CABINET MEETING

The cabinet was seated around two circular tables, so that they faced two flip charts on either side of the projection screen. The magnificent seven included Diane, who now was a regular in the group. The others were the deputy and assistant superintendents, the directors of business and personnel, and the two directors of instruction.

"Barry, you know everyone I believe?" Rob asked.

"Yes, of course," Barry responded as he greeted them warmly. He wasn't sure how eager they were to consider another project just yet. It seems every time he showed up he was bringing or suggesting more work than they were used to doing under Branson. With the new superintendent, their plates were overflowing it seemed.

"I'm glad that you're here to explore the planning process some more. I'm sure you all want to take on more work this year?" Then he paused for effect. "From the looks on your faces I can see the eagerness," he said tongue-in-cheek. There were a few eyes rolling.

Barry went on to set the tone for what he thought was important. He reminded them this was just an exploratory meeting to give them more information. He wasn't selling anything. Then he added, "I wouldn't be here if I didn't believe that to improve your schools you need a strategic management plan. I won't recommend that you jump into a new change process until you're ready," he said with sincerity. "And I won't let Rob go overboard about this if I can control him." This broke the ice with some chuckles and a few smiles. After all they had been in three training sessions with Barry since September.

The first activity he asked them to do was to read and prepare to discuss five assumptions.

On the screen he projected a list of assumptions, or rather false assumptions, that he had picked up somewhere along the way.

Assumption 1   The top management shares a common understanding of the organization's strategy.

Assumption 2   If something is longer range it is strategic and if it is shorter range it is operational. (This strategy is, in fact, measured in terms of impact on direction.)

Assumption 3   If a business unit's strategies are clear, the organization's strategy is clear.

Assumption 4   We have a long-range plan. So we know where we are going. (Operational trap.)

Assumption 5   Our top team has the experience to think strategically.

The discussion that followed got the cabinet members in a lively debate about the historical lack of planning in the district. They weren't even sure they understood the differences between the two types of planning mentioned in the questions. Barry assured them that he would get to this very soon.

Then Barry led them through the agenda, handed out the short paper for them to read, and followed this up with a join-up activity that got them thinking more about what outcomes they wanted or expected from the meeting. Rob had done a good job in prepping them all. The predominant outcome was to know more about strategic management, especially the planning part. Second, they had discussed the need to have enough information to make a decision about what their next steps should be, if any.

In answer to the question posed earlier, Woodson began by describing the different types of planning. The three types he identified were incremental, long range, and strategic. Incremental was just that—an add-on to what was being done piece by piece or incrementally. This has no real alignment with what they should be doing over time, even if they knew. The second, long range, was what most districts seem to be practicing, believing that this was strategic planning, but usually it was not. They look at what they are currently doing and then decide what they want to change for the next year. They would add on to what was working well and work on some improvement needs. They seldom abandon anything by choice.

If you always do the same thing the same way, you will get what you've always gotten.

Finally, he addressed strategic planning as part of strategic management, tying it to the systems model they had covered earlier in the school year. He suggested that this is the process by which the guiding members of the organization envision its future and develop the procedures and operations necessary to achieve that future. Simply stated, the shift is to start with an idealized future state and plan backwards from there. He then displayed a slide on the screen, pausing a minute for them to think about it.

Which method of planning is critical to the success of an organization? Incremental Planning—or Long-Range Planning? Or Strategic Planning?

 Time-Out—A What

1. What answer would you give? Why?
2. What do you believe?

He displayed the answer at the bottom. "Yes." He went on to say that each had its place, but for organizational change that impacts the culture in the long term, he was going to focus on the strategic position in today's deliberations.

Don Halverson, assistant superintendent of personnel, wanted to know why this particular process was being used. He'd been part of an effort where the plan ended up on a shelf gathering dust. Why should they put out the effort? This reflected some of the early skepticism obvious in the group.

Woodson agreed this was true but promised to offer more insight. He reiterated that at the end of the session he would come back to this question and summarize the input for the team. He asked Doug Daniels from the business department if he would write it on the flip chart next to the one indicating the desired meeting outcomes they had developed earlier.

Desired Outcomes

1. Learn more about strategic planning
2. Decide if they wanted any part of it
3. Learn more about Barry's successful experiences
4. Determine if it would help with the No Child Left Behind (NCLB) bill requirements

Barry asked them to look at the backwards thinking model on the wall. "Right now you are dealing with the current state, Phase C. You have to decide if you want to go through a focused improvement process. If so, then go to the end in mind and describe what your future should look like through your mission, values, and vision.

"The tough part comes next. Determine the elements of the critical success indicators. This is a sampling that provides indicators of success. You have, or will have developed, more extensive measures of student learning to meet state and federal requirements. These need to be identified and integrated.

"At this point, the decision is about how much you can do in a year or two, including all of the planning needed before you begin. A beginning structure for this decision can be built around the Effective Schools criteria. From this each school can identify their greatest needs and develop plans to close the gap.

"However, if you want a systemic change, then consider the rest of the system as part of the plan. Remember, it is critically important that the school board and each and every employee, not just those at the schools, be part of the change toward the powerful and compelling mission you will identify as your driving force.

"Get back in the district helicopter and be reminded about the other departments and their direct or indirect impact on student learning. Also, look outside the system from this view and identify what you will be affecting by this effort. What outside factors are supportive and how should those opposed be reckoned with?"

Susan, director of elementary education, asked Barry to give an example as she wondered how this would impact the schools she supervised.

Barry replied, "In our case, we determined that student learning was our primary mission. Then we concluded that most learning of the prescribed curriculum took place or was supposed to take place in the classroom under the direction of a teacher. From this we concluded that everyone else in the system had to be part of the support system for learning. So we all became the supporters and reinforcers of this new learning-teaching paradigm. Even the superintendent was identified in this support category. Even our central office departments changed titles to reflect this change of focus. The Instructional Division changed to Learning Support Services and the others did similarly."

Douglas then asked, "Do you mean all the staff in the business division has to be part of this effort?"

"It all depends on you, but we did, and it made a huge difference," Barry replied. "You all have to determine whether you are a state compliance teaching system or a learning system is the way I see it. If you just want fair scores on our state test, just meeting the minimum on the federal level, don't expect to see the system change much. Remember what a system is. It's not only the schools. It's the entire district system, its piece parts, and how it interfaces with its external world."

"Barry, why is this process different than what we've seen in the past that usually started with a bang and went out with a whimper?" Don, assistant superintendent, asked, unconvinced.

Barry then went on and explained more. Why this could be different was that when a process management plan was added for implementation, regular quarterly meetings were scheduled, more stakeholders were involved as part of the initial process, including those from all elements in the system, and the plan was simplified to no more than two pages.

Failure, he explained, was due to one or more negative forces that blocked the effort to stay the course over time. Lack of initial commitment, overwhelming resistance to change, too complex a plan, weak leadership, poor implementation planning, little follow through, a weak or nonexistent assessment of outcomes system, and change in leadership at the superintendent or board level during the multiyear implementation process were among those forces.

To relieve some of the uneasiness and encourage all the trailblazers in the group, Barry now set forth to tell his success story to give them more information on what it took to make a significant difference in his former district. If this leadership team was taking this on only because it was politic to do so, he noted, then they shouldn't waste the energy. They needed to decide if, and when, they were ready to commit to the long-term consequences.

Then he reviewed some of the objectives of using Effective Schools research as a basis for creating improvement plans that do include the mission, values, and vision components.

At this point, Rob stopped him and wanted to know why Barry was trying to force their course of action before they first established their end in mind. The staff looked relieved at the intervention. The boss was not going overboard. Barry agreed that he had jumped the gun, and would stage a strategic and quiet retreat. But he did have their full attention!

After a brief discussion among the group about the ideas presented, they wanted him to continue. They would hold up the final decision until they had all the facts. This is what Barry had hoped for.

Looking directly at Douglas, the director of business, Barry asked, "What do you think would cause a food service director to change the logo on the school food delivery trucks from 'You Can't Teach a Hungry Child' to 'A Hungry Child Can't Learn Well'?"

A hungry child can't learn well.

"Obviously something significant happened. I see what you're getting at," Doug replied.

"Even our grounds department changed their early-morning schedules for mowing under elementary school classroom windows so as not to interfere with core reading time," Barry mentioned.

After a brief discussion they realized these were paradigm shifts of some magnitude. As Madeline Hunter might say, this was a good anticipatory set. Now they showed even more interest.

⏰ Time-Out—A What

1. What do you think happened that caused the logo and mowing changes?
2. What do you know about paradigm shifts and thinking?
3. Why is the impact of this thinking on the groundskeepers significant?

Walking the Talk

Barry then began his story about effectively transforming a lower performing district.

"Most of us, when we think about or hear about strategic planning, shudder, laugh, or say, what a waste of time. Why? Our experiences have been negative about any meaningful results. Most often we see this as another management-directed plan of the month. Another bright idea developed by a board member, the superintendent, or a management team.

"However, there have been many successes, and we are one example. Companies in this day and age have to be able to respond quickly to changes in the business environment and so should we. We need to do strategic thinking and have an effective and efficient implementation system to make changes as fast-paced circumstances dictate."

Rob again interrupted Barry's flow as his curiosity got the better of him. "Were you ready for the NCLB mandate?"

"Fortunately, I retired at the right time," Barry said with a sense of nostalgia, but with a smile at the thought. "Over the past 40 years, I've seen reform come and go. However, our system in place was, for the most part, ready when the mandate hit. The required data was available. You realize from what you've read that the students now perform at high levels on mandated tests. A high percentage of the schools have been nationally recognized."

"I see what you mean by being ahead of the curve," Rob replied.

Barry continued. "Our experience starting with a district of about 20,000 students, 1,600 teachers, and 2,000 other employees, was one we can look back on and see many positive results for our students over the ensuing years. We changed our thought process from strategic planning to strategic thinking, or backwards thinking, and renamed the process strategic management."

Barry handed out a paper he had prepared for a talk he had given tracing the experiences they went through.

THE PROCESS

Nineteen administrators and a secretary representing the district office and the schools were selected from a volunteer pool to spend 16–18 days during the year in the process. This was our F team in Ken Blanchard's parlance. Later, a teacher representative was added at the suggestion of the union.

Meetings were planned for 2 1/2 days at a time, off site, in a pleasant out-of-town environment. The group agreed to do this in addition to their regular duties and assignments. They decided to start the sessions either on Sunday afternoon or finish on a Saturday to reduce the time spent out of the district. Over and above planning requires extra time and a steadfast commitment. It helps if the time spent is enjoyable and fun. A not-so-obvious benefit, at least to us, was the sense of team that was so powerfully generated.

Progress was initially slow for two reasons. The first was that the newness caused us to spend a lot of time questioning it and ourselves. Also, we drove hard for consensus, not only in the group at first but later among those stakeholders we identified through what we dubbed our Parallel Process. This included other administrators, the PTAs, the board, the teachers' union leadership, and any other group one of us had connections with. It was a creative addition to the model we were using. The side benefit we didn't realize at the time was that the groups buying into the process at each step of the way led to them staying in it. We even started talking about learning and core values before we had board approval.

When we got to creating measurement standards or critical success indicators, we didn't have a clue (this was before the standards and accountability movement). We used our annual state test scores for academic measures and counted attendance days for simple baseline data. We were trapped in measuring process rather than product. It wasn't for 4 more years until we began making decisions on what we wanted students to know (knowledge), be able to do (skills), and how to act (attitudes). We called them our KSAs. With more experience this now can be done in a much shorter time.

Four years later, the core values were revisited and consensus changes were made to reflect more inclusiveness for parent participation and diversity issues not clarified previously in our mission. Our mission statement was adjusted and core values modified. Almost 10 years later, with a majority of the curriculum aligned to our standards as well as those of the state and using a new assessment system, good feedback was now available. Now it can be said that we are measuring the results of our work toward our mission of "All students learning—whatever it takes."

"What did you change to include parents?" Rob asked.

"At first we included them only as a resource supporting their children in the learning process. A majority of the schools had included in their own core values something about expanded parent roles in the schools. So we decided to enhance the district's core values. With the addition of parents-as-partners language, we went to the PTA presidents and showed them our newest proposal. It stated, 'Parents should make a difference.' They changed it to 'Parents do make a difference.' They know that a difference can be either for good or bad."

"What's this about schools having their own core values?" Larry Ramirez, director of secondary education, asked, wondering how this would affect his high schools and their need to be unique.

"I guess I'd better finish the story. I do have a handout I'll leave that illustrates what I've been trying to explain," Barry said, hoping to relieve their anxiety. He referred them to his handout.

ROLLING IT OUT TO THE TROOPS

When the 2-year initial work was done and the plan printed, we decided that to make it known and usable we needed to get others involved in a rollout process to the schools and every nonschool department. We had 37 of these areas to train, develop, and then help implement their local plans. We gave ourselves 2 years to do this.

As far as this implementation strategy went, we decided that Adizes was right. Have stakeholders involved in critical decision making, but implement the changes almost autocratically. In my inimical style, I told the leaders of each group that they would go through the miniprocess we had developed. The principals and department heads could decide during the 2-year rollout period when they wanted to take their group through the process. The first group of volunteers was easy. Most of the first wave came from within the planning group, showing the power of participation and buying into the process. However, at the end of the cycle, two department heads had to be directed to join up.

This training consisted of a miniprocess of the work we had gone through. Three representatives from approximately six areas were trained in 2 days with the final afternoon devoted to developing a local-site planning-to-plan document. Each group was then given a 3-day off-site opportunity to develop their own mission statement, core values, and vision with 15 to 20 of their own staff members depending on unit size. We needed a critical mass to tip the teeter-totter toward total systemic change. Overnight lodging was provided for those who chose to do so. Making this financial commitment by the district leadership and the board made this a highly valued activity to each group. They realized that we meant business. The opportunity to go off site like real businesses do boosted morale considerably.

The rules were to focus on student learning, or the support of it, for nonschool areas and that the districts' core values couldn't be excluded, only added to. In fact, in just such a session the food services logo was generated.

"What other significant things happened during the process?" Rob asked expectantly.

"Good question. Let me continue and I think you will have an answer," Barry said.

The first "ah ha" the team experienced occurred in the first 3 days. When we were asked what business we were in we quickly said teaching, of course. There was no opposition to this notion on day one. However, after sleeping on it, one of our principals came back and declared she thought we were in the learning rather than the teaching business. She believed the other eighteen of us were wrong and she was right! It took several more hours discussing the matter before we saw the light—our organization was in the learning business, not the teaching business. Attitudes were changed and a new sense of commitment was developed. Using our consensus model we made sure everyone there was on board. This changed the world of our unified school district over the next 15 years.

CONSENSUS

It's not voting; it's not being happy; it's not horse trading; it's not averaging. Consensus is the situation reached when all members of a group share the following:

1. Understand the decision.
2. Understand the conditions and viewpoints that drove it.
3. Have had an opportunity to air their opinions and viewpoints.
4. Even if they don't wholeheartedly agree with the decision, accept it and will support it.

Are our customers the kids, or are they the parents, or both? We decided to focus on the KSAs for students with their parents in a supporting role. As you review our mission statement and core values you will not see the words teaching or education—only learning.

Barry then handed out a copy of the mission statement to illustrate this. He clarified that there were good criteria for developing one and then cautioned that almost every school system had similar words. The big difference is what you do with it. Does it drive change or gather dust?

Mission Statement

Our mission is to ensure that each student, to the best of his or her ability, will master the knowledge and develop the skills and attitudes essential for success in school and society.

To fulfill our mission we provide comprehensive K–12 programs, complemented by early childhood and adult programs, which include a wide variety of learning strategies, experiences, and support services to promote student learning.

The learner outcomes were defined as follows:

Knowledge—what should students know?
Skills—what should students be able to do?
Attitudes—what should students feel or believe?

A second paper was handed out as Barry put the next slide on the screen (see Figure 9.1).

Barry then gave a short overview on the components for effective mission statements.

Ten Criteria for Evaluating Mission Statements

1. The mission statement is clear and understandable to all personnel, including rank-and-file employees.

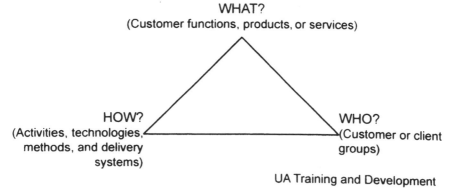

MISSION DEFINED
A mission defines an organization's "reason" for being now and into the future.

THREE BASIC ELEMENTS OF THE ORGANIZATIONAL MISSION

WHAT?
(Customer functions, products, or services)

HOW?
(Activities, technologies, methods, and delivery systems)

WHO?
(Customer or client groups)

UA Training and Development

Figure 9.1.   Mission Statement.
Source: Pfeiffer, Goodstein, & Nolan, 1985.

2. The mission statement is brief enough for most people to keep in mind.
3. The mission statement clearly specifies what business the organization is in. This includes a clear statement about the following:
   - What products or services will fill customer or client needs
   - Who the organization's primary customers or clients are
   - How the organization plans to go about its business; that is, what its primary methodologies are
4. The mission statement should have a primary focus on a single strategic thrust.
5. The mission statement should reflect the distinctive competence of the organization.
6. The mission statement should be broad enough to allow flexibility and implementation but not so broad as to permit a lack of focus.
7. The mission statement should serve as a template and be the means by which managers and others in the organization can make decisions.
8. The mission statement must reflect values, beliefs, and philosophy of operations of the organization and reflect the organizational culture.
9. The mission statement should reflect obtainable goals.
10. The mission statement should be worded so as to serve as an energy source in a rallying point for the organization.

"Well, this is interesting," Rob commented, and then looking at the cabinet members he asked, "Do any of you know if we have a mission statement?"

⏱ Time-Out—A So What

1. Put the preceding mission statement through the three questions found in the Triangle diagram (see Figure 9.1). How does it meet the three learner outcomes questions?
2. Do the same with the 10 criteria. What did you find out?
3. Do you have a mission statement in your organization? If so, what is it doing for the organization?
4. If not, find one and run it through the two tests. Does it measure up? If not, where does it miss?

5. What drives the work of your organization?
6. What did you learn from this exercise?

Larry Ramirez offered a comment after some hemming and hawing, "We weren't really focused on instruction with all the board and community fighting going on, so if we decide to move forward it will be from scratch. Maybe there's one around somewhere, but starting over I think would be a breath of fresh air for us. We are becoming a new organization."

Rob then confessed, "In my innocence when I was hired I didn't even think about asking for one. Since then, as you all know, we've been just fighting fires so far this year."

The deputy superintendent, Peter Paulson, wanted to know what role the core values play in an organization.

"I couldn't be fed a more timely question to answer," Barry observed. "And tell the group that I didn't cue you."

"Of course not! I'm curious to know more, since I've done some reading about this," he replied in self-defense.

"Let's take a break, say about 15 minutes, and when we come back we'll go over values and vision."

When they returned and got settled in again, Diane's assistant finished taking lunch orders so they could work through until 1 p.m. to finish the discussion today. Some had appointments later.

CORE VALUES

"Core values tell your folks and your customers—students, parents, the community—how you are going to do business or manage the organization. We like the four-question test to determine if a value is really a core value," Barry offered and handed out another page.

How Does One Know if a Value Is Really a Value?

1. It permeates the organization.
2. It drives decisions.

3. There's a strong reaction when it's violated.
4. It's the last thing you'll give up.

"What does this mean operationally? Do we still believe? How do we know?" Barry seemed to question himself.

⏱ Time-Out—The So What

1. Can you identify your own core values? Your organization's? Do the written values reflect how your organization does business?
2. What is your vision for teaching and learning?
3. If you could use a crystal ball and wave a magic wand, what would you want your school or system to look like or be doing differently in 5 years?

"There were originally six core values that we got acceptance on from the various segments of the organization through our parallel process of stopping at each major juncture to get feedback. If we didn't have unanimous support from the development group we didn't include the idea for the stakeholders to consider," Barry said.

"I've told you how it affected other areas when they did their rollouts. Even the bus drivers changed their attitudes after recognizing that they were the first school representative 10,000 kids saw each morning. They decided to work on being friendly and helpful as youngsters climbed aboard their bus. They became the opposite of Ed, the retired bus driver in the *Crankshaft* comic strip, who left kids behind at the bus stops and enjoyed insulting parents."

He passed out more paper with the reminder that the parent core value had been added 2 years later.

Core Values

1. All students learning
2. Parents as partners
3. Competent and caring staff
4. Staff participation in decision making
5. Safe, orderly, and attractive environment

6. Effective management of resources
7. Excellence in all we do

The mentor then went on to explain how these were operationalized throughout the system. Each value had descriptors to clarify the original intent. Each word was thoughtfully considered and sometimes fought over before being accepted. There was a long discussion on whether to use the word *all*. The issue came down to commitment to every child regardless of station in life. For us *all* meant all, he emphasized.

Director Ramirez stopped him with an interesting observation. "In looking at your core values, I noticed that there may be some conflict."

"What do you see? And that's a very good observation!" Barry declared.

"Well, if I am committed to 'all students learning' how can you recommend expulsion for a student who is doing drugs at school? Isn't that a value conflict?" Larry remarked.

Barry was quick in his reply, "More than once, parents asked the same question at the school board meeting when their child was being expelled. Let me explain."

Barry put a slide on the screen. He said that he had come up with the notion from his work as a football referee. The idea was to let the schools and departments make decisions within the boundaries defined by the values, but if a line was crossed, the guilty party would be flagged or the whistle blown (see Figure 9.2).

He asked them to draw an imaginary line between the two core values of "all students learning" and "safe, orderly, and attractive environment."

"Do you see a similar conflict here?" Almost in unison they answered a rousing yes.

"But how did the board respond to the parent whose son was being expelled?" Don wanted to know.

"To say the least it was tough, but the board chair was prepared. There really isn't a good answer for the parents to make them feel better, if they can't accept the fact that their child did wrong, or to others who just want to exercise their rights. The answer was that to protect the safety of all students the boy would no longer have access to school

All Students Learning

Staff Participation in Decision Making

Value

Competent and Caring Staff

Effective Management of Resources

Conflict

Parents As Partners

Safe, Orderly, and Attractive Environment

Excellence in All That We Do

Figure 9.2. Core Values: The Playing Field—Value—Conflict

for his education. He had forfeited it by his actions. Further plans for schooling were being made at an alternative school run by the county."

Douglas commented, "It seems the parents knew the core values pretty well."

"Barry, these two examples really bring to life the need for a well-crafted set of values," Rob stated the obvious again.

"One benefit of the process used was that the representative and workable-sized group of 19 was able to develop each step with plenty of time to argue, debate, sell, and convince each other of the 'truth' and values they should stand on. After these 2- or 3-day sessions members were assigned the task of getting feedback from the various stakeholder groups. From their input the work was modified as necessary," Barry clarified.

He then went on to mention that every time he spoke in the district or in the community his focus was the core values. In all manner of writing they were included. New administrators were briefed before school started. "All students learning" became the driving force behind almost everything. It created the synergy to develop district learning standards, another laborious part of the process.

"I now see why you are so set on 'to change the culture you must change the conversation,'" Rob said, remembering the Peter Block quote that Barry had repeated on so many occasions.

"Yes, we really lived it and saw the powerful changes these values created when followed. Often decisions were screened through them," Barry said and then quietly added, "or we debriefed our screw-ups afterward to see which value we violated or Sit Lead clue we missed."

VISION

Moving on to creating a vision, Barry began, "This part of the essential triad of mission statement, core values, and vision was the hardest for us to define. The vision is the ideal implementation of the mission. We ended up our first cut by making a list of statements on what we wanted our students to be like 5 years hence. What should they know and be able to do? Two come to mind. The graduate will be a user of knowledge and be a contributor to society. They each had a list of descriptors attempting to define them.

"Even 10 to 12 years later we were struggling to create a better vision concept. From the work of Dr. Larry Lezotte, one of the district's and superintendent's gurus, a statement emerged from our mission statement, 'All students learning.' A couple of years later we added 'whatever it takes.' This became our driving force. This drove another team vision for describing how the new high school should be different.

"This simple statement of a vision has had tremendous impact on student learning over these past 15 years," Barry told them.

They took a break as their sandwiches had arrived and sodas were distributed. Barry and Rob huddled at the back of the conference room trying to come up with the next steps for Paradise Valley. Rob decided that he would like an outline containing questions they should be answering before heading blindly down this path. Barry had prepared one and would make appropriate comments in an attempt to clarify. They agreed to stay away from the details of the process until a decision was made. However, Rob was intrigued by the dramatic changes in student learning Barry had mentioned and wanted to know more. They set aside some time in March to go over these ideas.

After Rob got the group's attention again he told them what the two had talked about. Not having been involved in that conversation, pesky Halverson asked that Barry review the positive outcomes for his system. Barry added another sheet to their growing stacks.

Learnings

1. By immersing the entire organization in applied strategic planning, a solid basis for change was developed. The focus on "All students learning" and "Excellence in all that we do" became the bookends of success.
2. Schools and school districts need to be driven by student learning, not student education.
3. Schools and school districts both need to focus on measurable learning outcomes defined by the leading, not trailing, indicators.
4. The mission shouldn't include platitudes that can't be measured with respect to student learning, such as "we shall provide an opportunity for an education. . . ."
5. Even when the process loses its luster and we forget to follow-up, the ingrained values still should be able to drive the organization.
6. Changing faces in key places means that the message needs to be repeated and repeated some more.
7. Hiring new leaders must include an assessment of their commitment to mission, values, and vision process and the strategic management of it.
8. Keeping the "new" conversation going by the leader and CEO and pushing for better results has to happen to show the importance of the change.
9. Early on schools set 3 to 5 improvement goals. This was before student-learning measures were in place. This became busy work. Now schools set where they would like to improve on a variety of measures. The district maintains the direction and resources, insisting on progress on those targets that were by and large developed at each site.
10. When the critical mass for the organization has bought into the new paradigm and the new values take hold, questions such as

"All students learning; what and how well?" take on new meaning
and emphasis. The state of California's drive to raise the bar by
having statewide tests and a test for graduation eligibility now set
the results-oriented focus in concrete. They had a 5-year head
start on establishing and aligning curriculum in some areas.

11. Train and retrain—don't lose good staff except to promotion.
12. Annual and quarterly reviews of progress need to be built into
    the annual calendar and strictly reserved for this follow-up.
13. The use of top consultants such as a Larry Lezotte keeps the fire
    going. Send people out in groups or bring the people to you.
14. Network with other learning organizations with similar beliefs.
15. Integrate the plan within the budget priorities.

🕐 Time-Out—So What

1. What are your district's core values?
2. Does dynamic tension exist between them?
3. Review Barry's list of learnings. Which did you like? Disagree with?
4. How would you begin a conversation about this process in your
   district?

WRAPPING UP

Barry reiterated a stern warning to know why they were going down this
particular path. Remember, don't use Yogi Berra's advice: "When you
come to a fork in the road take it!" Everything needs to be part of your
strategic thinking. Before considering a major effort, first several questions need to be asked and answered.

"When you come to a fork in the road take it!"

—**Yogi Berra**

Barry went to another flip chart and wrote down some key questions.

1. Why are you doing this or thinking about doing it?
2. Do you know which plan, or model, to use and why?
3. Do you understand the key elements?
4. Do you really understand organizational change and how hard it is?
5. What is the level of commitment to start and continue the journey?
6. Can you keep the main thing the main thing?

🕐 Time-Out—A Reflection

Review the preceding questions.

1. What would your answers, relative to your system, be on these six questions?
2. Select one thing to start changing in your district and use the list to outline some ideas in response to the questions.

Barry was asked to review in retrospect what they had done on the six items. The staff was still in need of more reinforcement. He went to the questions on the flip chart and did a quick review of how they responded to them.

"I can answer most of the questions for my old group, but you need to answer for yours. That's why I'm here today. A couple of years ago a system lost the driving force behind this focus through the retirement of a veteran CEO and superintendent. They faced the challenge raised previously here. Would the organization move away from the existing mission, values, and vision? As I mentioned earlier, if the values are deeply entrenched, even when a new leader tries to change the culture, it would take 3 to 8 years. The good news is that the emphasis is still on all students learning—and they're doing well."

🕐 Time-Out—A So What

1. Review the preceding questions and discuss them with a colleague. Do they make sense? Which ones need more reflection?

2. Can you apply this to your system? Where do you think your system is with regard to planned strategic change?
3. What did you learn from reviewing these questions?

WHAT NEXT?

Barry said, "Can the system maintain its values and belief system yet press for all students learning—whatever it takes? Even with the added state and federal pressure for accountability so far what the state wants is accountability measures in the basics only. But think about other areas: PE, music, art, and all the rest that are not tested. What is your vision for these areas? What is your definition of a comprehensive opportunity for learning now? Have you changed, surrendered, or are you fighting to keep the learning experiences for kids comprehensive?

"What are we directing our work toward, what is the body of knowledge, the skills, and attitudes we need developed? With a focus on results—can the organization be focused in a backwards-thinking or strategy-thinking mode most of the time?"

Barry then commented, "If you decide to move forward, we can map out a process that will take less time, but not less commitment. Going through the process and staying the course makes the difference between success and just another flavor-of-the-month experience with the staff thinking and saying, This too will pass. We can wait this out.

"Remember what I told you before. You can't pick up a plan and try to implement it. It won't work until you make it yours with your people and stakeholders buying into it. Even very successful pilot projects often fail to be replicated due to the lack of ownership.

"All I can do is share the process we used. You can take the best of it, modify it to fit your circumstances, and then get your staff working on the answers for your district. I can help with this or I can give you the names of some people I know that will do a great job for you."

You can't copy other's results. They have to be your own.

Rob then got up and spoke for his group. "Thanks. You've given us a lot to think about. With NCLB, we better get moving or I might be replaced," he joked. "We may follow your suggestion and develop a planning-to-plan team to get more folks involved for the initial decision—to go or not to go. We have so much on our plate this may take some time. We really appreciate all that you've shared with us."

Barry handed out a packet of information containing the definitions he was using. He then directed the team to websites to check out some programs and facilitators should they be interested in moving ahead sometime in the future.

They adjourned the session after reviewing the desired outcomes flip chart and the next steps they put on the to-do list. Even though they were still somewhat unsure, they decided to make a commitment by the late spring. Budget problems were surfacing and they had to get a handle on the problem sooner rather than later. Rob told Barry that he was going to have to postpone the new school building project planning until May, so they agreed to cancel their meeting the next week.

🕐 Time-Out—So What

1. What one thing did you learn from Barry's story?
2. What is your experience with trying to make a change without others buying into it?

PARTING COMMENTS

Barry and Rob sat in the superintendent's office reviewing the morning. They were looking at the evaluation flip chart notes. Things went reasonably well, but again there was so much content covered. The group needed more time to think through many of the ideas and still had unanswered questions.

"Anything else on your plate that we need to discuss before I head out?" Barry asked, hoping that he hadn't done too much already.

"Yes. Wait a minute. I'm going to release a principal before we meet next. Any thoughts?"

"Why are you doing this?" the professor challenged.

"Remember, he started the year off on the wrong foot and has been fighting me at every turn. It's obvious he's not comfortable here. He was a favorite of the other guy and I'm not treating him the same way. I'm trying to treat all principals fairly. Too much partiality before! He doesn't seem to be accountable for either learning or his budget."

"So?"

"I'm going to call him in and suggest that he might be happier elsewhere. If that doesn't work I'm going to give him notice in March. The board members already know what I'm thinking about. This will be the first test for my position on personnel decisions with them after first informing them. I believe I've done my homework, but we'll see."

"I'll be interested in the outcome. So what else do you need from me?" Barry questioned.

"Does this make sense? What am I missing?"

"Have you advised him of your specific concerns, given him a chance to respond, and then agree on an improvement plan?"

"Well, no!"

"Have you practiced your Social Style learning on him? You are a Driving Style and he is . . . a what?"

"He's an Expressive."

"So?"

"I need to recognize that his growth goal is to check before going off half-cocked. And before you say it, I'll need to look to our Sit Lead model so that I can be specific on what I expect and then closely check on his progress. I told Susan that I would deal with it, so she could stay out of the line of fire."

Barry cautioned, "Rob, be careful how you handle this as all eyes will be watching. They are probably looking for you to be fair using some due process even though not required by law. I'm thinking, since you haven't done your homework, if he responds well enough to your direction, that you could give him another year.

"Let me think this over. It's sure food for thought."

"Another thing that we should review maybe next month is an implementation plan for the assessment of student progress. If you would like I can develop some more ideas around how we did the KSAs, standards, and assessment and some practical thoughts about Effective Schools."

Rob wanted help on his evaluation with the board, so he asked, "I really want to talk over my preparation for next week's closed board session. It's my past due midyear evaluation."

"What are you planning?" Woodson asked.

"I've developed backup for each goal that we did last November. It's very thorough."

"Okay. Also, I might suggest giving them the packet, but do a short executive briefing."

"Sounds like a good idea."

"Are you giving it to them in advance of the meeting?"

"What do you think?" Rob asked.

"No, what do you think?" his mentor challenged.

"The more comprehensive the information I give them now will indicate how conscientious and thoughtful I am. It may cause more questions, but it'll show I'm prepared. I'll try to stick to the briefing outline and encourage feedback when I finish each item."

"Good. Since this is somewhat informal, be sure to listen for clues about their priorities. This will help you plan for next year also. That is, if there is a next year," he teased.

"Thanks! There will be a next year! I feel better. I'll give you a call when it's over," Rob said.

"Please wait until the morning after. No more late-night phone calls," Barry said, smiling but serious. "Unless it's an emergency."

"I got it! Talk to you soon. And by the way I plan to have a small group over to celebrate our new house soon and would like you to join us."

Rob and Barry parted, recognizing the large amount of territory covered. Rob left to visit one of the high schools and Barry headed home wondering how much he had helped them better understand the power of strategic management.

🕐 **Time-Out—Now What**

1. In your organization determine what is missing in terms of student learning driving the mission.

2. Can you measure or determine your organization or department commitment to its mission?

3. If you were planning to plan what would you do first in creating a strategic plan?
4. Seek out more information on systemic management and change and share with your leadership group.

SUMMARY

The dilemma of the superintendent's role in school board elections was introduced and discussed. Some helpful hints about working with prospective board candidates were covered. How involved should the superintendent become in board politics is the key question.

The elements of a successful transformation of a district's focus are covered next. The dynamic change going from a teaching organization to one based on student learning is described. The transformation included the definition of a mission statement, developing core values, and projecting a vision. An example of training an entire school system was presented. A list of key questions to consider before starting such a process was answered using the example given. The chapter came to a close with the consideration of two problems. The first was the consideration of terminating an unsatisfactory principal without due process. Second, the superintendent got some help on preparing for his midyear evaluation.

MONTH 8—FEBRUARY

Strategies and Survival Skills

1. Prepare yourself on how you want to handle school board election politics.
   • Clarify this role with your incumbents in advance.
   • Consider establishing a nonpartisan board candidates briefing session.
2. Examine your own school system and determine whether the focus is on learning rather than teaching.

- Determine whether there is a system priority to know where you want to go.
- Is there a plan to get there?

3. Consider a proven model and strategy for use throughout the system to improve student learning.
   - Remember that the entire system in place may need to be part of the school improvement effort.
   - Be reminded that the system is larger and more comprehensive than the schools within it.

4. Have your ducks in order before starting the dismissal of an administrator.
   - Fairness and due process are requirements.
   - Be specific on your goals for improvement.

5. Make sure you have an annual evaluation plan in writing, either in your contract or in board policy or in both.

6. After setting performance goals with the board of education, be sure that you gather data to support what you have done.
   - Prepare the material in a professional manner.
   - Consider an executive briefing to keep the superintendent and the board on time and on task.
   - Confirm the procedure that you put in place early in the year.

TOOLBOX

Cook, B. *Strategic Thinking Presentation*. The Cambridge Group, 5795 Carmichael Parkway, Montgomery, AL 36117.

Haines, S. (2004). *The ABC's of Strategic Management: The Systems Thinking Approach to Creating a Customer-Focused, High-Performance Learning Organization*. San Diego, CA: Systems Thinking Press.

Pfeiffer, W., Goodstein, L., & Nolan, T. (1985). *Applied Strategic Planning: An Overview*. San Diego, CA: University Associates.

10

MARCH: MEASURING THE MISSION

Not everything that counts can be counted and not everything that can be counted counts.

—Sir George Pickering

The nation is over tested and under assessed.

—Doug Reeves

SHOULD AND CAN YOU MEASURE WHAT YOU DO?

In this chapter you will do the following:

1. *Learn how to more clearly define KSAs.*
2. *Understand the assessment needs of a system aligned with instructional standards.*
3. *Understand the need and purposes for assessment. Be able to define for your system the why, what, how, how well, where, and who of your learning system.*
4. *Understand the relationship among academic standards, curriculum alignment, and assessment.*

MARCH MADNESS

The weather was the pits again. A series of Pacific storms were cascading down the coast from Alaska, making a mess of the streets, flooding everywhere. It was a mixed blessing as Southern California was coming out of a 6-year drought in a big way. It had started to rain in October and hadn't stopped much since.

As Dr. Robert Moore, Paradise Valley's school superintendent, sloshed his way through the storm to Dr. Barry Woodson's office on the university campus, he was thinking about their last meeting. He remembered the exciting phone conversation he had with his mentor a few days ago. Rob was still feeling pretty good, but realized there was a lot to learn. The board had just finished reviewing his first 7 months as superintendent.

LAST WEEK'S EVALUATION SESSION REHASHED

When Barry picked up the phone in his office at home a week earlier, he recognized the phone number on the display. It was either Rob or Diane.

Rob heard the early morning wakeful voice of Dr. Woodson saying, "Hello, Rob."

"How did you know 'twas I?" Rob responded cheerfully.

"I'm a good guesser. Besides, I knew last night was 'the night' and you would be calling soon," Barry answered. "I suppose you want to give me a blow by blow?"

"I'm cool! It went so well that I'll just hit the highlights."

"Good!" Barry chided.

"Did you keep a copy of the list we made and used in the summer?"

"Right next to my heart! Seriously, I think it's in my file at the university," Woodson said, searching his memory, or what was left of it, and then asked, "Why don't you just review what the board said about the six or eight areas you worked on with them earlier?"

"Wise old sage, I did as you suggested. I kept to the outline that I had sent them prior to the meeting. Behind all of this was my decision on whether I wanted to come back for a second year, even though I have a 3-year contract. After our work together I feel confident that with a little guidance from time to time I can be a good superintendent. And more important, I want to continue being one here in this district."

"I'm not surprised about your decision. You're doing well as a rookie."

"I'll go down the list quickly," Rob continued, before Barry could say more and embarrass him.

He then covered the six major areas.

1. Bond the board into a positive working force with the best interest of kids as a priority.

    "Each of the five was pleased about the progress. They said I handled the recall issue well and cited the November board goal of stopping them arguing as a deterrent. They still don't love each other, but progress is being made. They felt more informed."

2. Assess the current budget, find some money for salaries, and increase the ending balance.

    "This was a big A+. They couldn't be more pleased. This was a big win since they made such a big deal out of the former superintendent's prowess in finance. Giving them a new balanced budget after salary settlements last fall really won me support from the two conservatives."

3. Successfully finish negotiations and begin working on developing a win-win model.

    "This and the budget went hand in hand. Not having as much acrimony with the unions was a plus. I did warn them that the honeymoon might be over now that we are headed into next year. I gave them some ideas for improving upon this."

4. Working through the principals, begin to review the district's commitment to learning and determine the level of commitment by the schools, administration center, and parents.

    "They had been getting regular updates on our progress. While impatient to some extent they were okay with where we are. I committed to this as a high priority for next year."

5. If needed, develop effective administrative training and staff development programs that would lead to creating a learning organization.

    "We haven't yet presented this plan. I told them the cost would be shown in the budget and we would be recommending a considerable increase in this area to include teachers and support staff. However, we are going to go slowly at first as we assess the staff's readiness level for some of it."

6. Continue planning for the new elementary school funded from the construction bond measure passed in May.

"I included the steps that we are taking, starting in May. I let them see where they would be involved."

Following this replay the mentor interjected, "What was the overall consensus?"

"The chair said they would respond in writing, but everything was on target and that I had exceeded expectations. They want more communication as critical events occur, because the press is looking to use anything for news. If they were better informed they could help the district better—and, of course, protect themselves from appearing uninformed or stupid."

Dr. Woodson sounded pleased with Rob's achievement. "It looks like continuing on the job is almost a given, if you don't mess up in the next few months. If rated satisfactory or better do you still want to work toward an automatic rollover year?"

"We might want to strategize about this later, but with the three majority board members up for reelection next year it might be a sign of positive support for the superintendent in the eyes of the public and even for those running against them," the rookie reasoned with some insight and then added, "If the vote is unanimous, it could build more confidence in the system to continue the way we're trying to lead it."

"Good. We can talk more, if need be, at our regular meeting," Woodson suggested as they said their good-byes.

🕐 Time-Out—A So What

1. What is your assessment of Rob's progress to date?
2. As a member of his board and on the basis of what you've learned this year, what would you want Rob to do more of? Less of?
3. What are his strengths?
4. Would you recommend that he try for a contract extension at this point?

MEETING AT THE UNIVERSITY

Rob had been lucky enough to find a parking space in front of the Education Building; otherwise, it would have been a long wet walk from the parking structure. A flash of lightning and a rumble of thunder caused him to move a little faster. Hanging onto his umbrella and cradling his briefcase to keep it dry, he hurried up the front steps, being careful not to slip.

The now more-seasoned rookie and the mentor were meeting in Barry's small office on the second floor.

Rob had come to the city for an all-day regional superintendent's meeting. Since he didn't want to fight the rush hour traffic, he had suggested they meet at the university for a while until the traffic mess slowed down on the freeway before he headed home to North County.

Following last month's orientation session with his mentor, Rob and his team had agreed to take a second small step toward developing a plan that would move them along the road to improving the teaching-learning process. They believed that looking more toward the *leading* indicators rather than the trailing or lagging indicators of effective student learning would give them a best shot at helping all their kids learn better. For example, Barry said that a leading indicator to be measured was time on task. Another was a safe and orderly environment.

They would start by encouraging or telling each school staff, depending on their readiness level, to select a couple of critical areas to start working on. They agreed that an operational strategy to use the criteria from Effective Schools would be a good place to start. However, the leadership of the Paradise Valley School District wasn't quite ready to move forward until they had done a lot more homework.

After their usual warm greetings, comments about the weather, and the beginning of baseball spring training in Arizona, Rob asked, "Did you get the e-mailed topics I thought we should cover today?"

"Yes, but truthfully haven't had much chance to look it over. I've been trying to catch up on grading this quarter's term papers and midterms."

"There are a few conversations I feel we need to continue—I want to know more about how you defined your KSAs (knowledge, skills, and attitudes) and more on alignment of standards, curriculum, instruction, and assessment. I assume these were effective practices?"

Barry responded, "They were and still are now that they are in place. It was a huge task!"

"Another point is more on Effective Schools implementation and, more to the point, on school improvement needs for us. The cabinet wants more clarity about this before making a commitment."

"I can do that," Barry added. "First, are there critical issues you need to deal with day to day that we need to talk about? I suggest we start with these since we usually end up with not enough time to do so. We're not always good time managers once we get into something big. We don't pay much attention to the big-rock practice. Urgent issues seem to get in the way as we predicted months ago. There's never enough time."

Rob wanted to take another look at site-based management, discuss getting his first budget started on the right foot, and strategize about the collective bargaining process starting this month since their three unions' initial proposals would be presented publicly at the next school board meeting.

But before they got into the agenda, Rob began telling Barry about the superintendents' meeting he just attended downtown. His disappointment and frustration showed. After the group did the real important stuff, such as reviewing plans for the annual June conference and golf tournament, another first-year superintendent asked about the No Child Left Behind (NCLB) act. She wondered what others were doing to gear up for another frustrating change laid on by the feds.

After listening to the griping for a while, Rob decided there was a bigger issue—that of NSLB, No Superintendent Left Behind. The negative reaction to NCLB was evidenced by both strong comments and the quiet body language from those who wouldn't say anything—probably the Amiable and Analytic Social Style. Rob had learned about these styles last fall. Since he didn't get too much help on this issue from the group with their other busy agenda, he needed to bounce some more ideas off Dr. Woodson.

⏱ Time-Out—A Reflection

1. Traditionally, how has your system handled federal mandates?
2. Are they readily embraced?

> 3. How was this particular change managed?
> 4. Where do your district's schools stand in the process or in any other state or federal assessment program?

BACK ON TOPIC

"Well Rob, where do you want to start on the journey to system improvement? You realize that the district needs to work through the mission, values, and vision piece first—even if you already have them. They need to be reviewed continually. Everyone has to be part of the act if it's going to drive success.

"To do it right it will take at least 6 months and probably more in getting a parallel input process with stakeholder groups working well. It depends on how quickly you want to bring the larger group along. Concurrently, some type of planning is needed to get each school and department deeply involved and committed. Otherwise, it's a piece of cake," he said, remembering his own struggling experiences—almost the blind leading the blind in those early days.

"I'm not sure we have the luxury of time with the state, forced by the feds, about to breathe down our necks," Rob said thoughtfully.

"Then I suggest you think about just doing what you have to in meeting the minimum now. Later it can be redone, if necessary, and improved upon. Survival is the first law in the federal jungle!"

"Now that makes sense. Do you know what your former district is doing? Do they have to do much more?" Rob asked.

"There is one school in Program Improvement (PI). They didn't have a subgroup scoring high enough in math for Special Education students. They missed by less than half of 1%. Now the feds are attacking our state's classification levels. Even in the largest district in the state, the state superintendent is going after them to change what they are doing. I read that Utah invited the feds out as we speak."

"How do you avoid PI?"

"Here are some obvious steps. Maintain 95% participation rate for all groups. If it is a problem take immediate steps. Launch an information campaign—go directly to parents. Appeal to minority groups that

NCLB is primarily about serving their children. Appeal to high school students' pride in their school's reputation," Barry offered.

"I'm not going to worry too much. Our several schools in trouble are symptomatic about what I've found wrong here. I've concluded for the most part that it's the district's lack of focus over the past few years. We'll need to go to the whip, beginning with our planning and change efforts starting later this spring," the CEO responded, showing he now understood the problem and challenge. He just needed the right tools to do the job.

"Good thinking. You need to know there are some glitches for even higher performing districts. NCLB is set on developing and defining a highly qualified teacher (HQT) for every student on the planet. My district didn't have the data they needed all in one place, so they had to create a process to pull all this data together. The real question now is how much difference does it make to the HQT criteria when a teacher who majored in chemistry is a most successful biology teacher and has been for 20 years? I know there are alternative methods of certification."

"That's another dimension of my problem. More things to reorder!" Rob said.

Barry kept going. "Apparently there is some data from the Northwest Educational Assessment group that indicate that California's criterion referenced test is one of the toughest among 16 states where data were available. What does this mean for your students compared to others?"

"I'm not surprised at this, Barry, with all the subject matter 'experts' adding to the mix. They think their subject is the only player in town."

"One of the biggest challenges is deciding how important it is to gear up to teach to the test. I know you are aware of this issue as we've all had teachers who have cheated or pushed the limits in preparation—just to look good. How do we prevent this pressure?"

"I'm going to put that question on a to-do list and ignore it for now."

"Rob, before we go further let me ask, what does being in the fourth grade mean to you?"

"What kind of question is this?" Rob responded, wondering where Barry was heading.

"Just answer the question!"

"It means that you've been promoted through the grades. You're 9 or

10. You're working on fourth-grade work. But maybe you aren't at this level academically and you're just sitting in a fourth-grade seat! Or maybe you're bored and can handle the sixth-grade work or at least some of it." Rob suddenly got it. "These tests are geared for a grade level and don't always measure what the kids really know. We need our own local comprehensive assessment programs to fight back. Need to keep assessment in balance. Need to know what we're measuring and why. Our public needs to know, also," he said, warming to the subject.

"That's part of it but let's go on, noting that learning how to learn may be more important than skills in test taking," Barry observed critically.

"Sounds good."

"In spite of all this I think what has been developing over the past 10 years without federal 'guidance' has put my old district in good shape with just some other minor adjustments for now. The new data ware-housing system I launched them on is now working well. It's called TIMS—Total Information Management System. I challenged the executive director, Charlie Garten, to find a way to make it happen. He used a partnership with a firm in North Carolina to put it in operation. Each student's school-life history is available at a touch of a button. From this, student data can be disaggregated and reassembled as needed," Woodson replied with a feeling of satisfaction, noting that many of the things he started were continuing.

"Barry, you know that we are nowhere near to this hi-tech position. Our grading system is online and the state testing results are all we are getting now, as I understand it. The regional center has some pilot projects in a few districts," Rob said somewhat dejectedly.

"I know that, but the big issue to me is not the why but rather the how we're heading down this road. This insatiable drive in Washington to improve learning for all is well intended, but I'm not sure it will survive in its present form. The pressure of too many failing schools and districts will force a political pullback, revision, and retrenchment. Just recently the secretary of Education is making concessions to some states, including ours."

"I can see that clearly, too," Rob joined in. "The larger districts keep making headline noises."

"A bigger issue is the forced concentration on the basics only. It might be a surprise to the president and Congress that all essential learning isn't always found in a basic's course or classroom. I'm not negating that each child needs to know how to read, write, and compute proficiently. But at what expense to those who easily master these skills and need to move on? What are we doing for their program of studies with all this time and emphasis on test taking? Most high schoolers don't really care. Their high stake tests are those enabling them to get into colleges and universities," Barry said with his big bias showing.

"Barry, did you see the students' and newspaper reaction to the new SAT scoring system—the new 2,400 point total with 800 points for the added essay part?" Rob said with a newfound interest.

"Yes, and this hasn't been factored in with the state-mandated high school exit exam—pass or don't graduate. Will there be big problems when a student has high SAT scores and doesn't pass the diploma test for one reason or another?" the mentor responded, anticipating some interesting fireworks downstream.

"Wow! I didn't think of that possibility!"

"Getting back on point, let me give you an example of a valuable learning they don't measure. In a high school band program there are nearly 300 students from a total enrollment of 3,000. They divide up in sections and practice with a student leader. They practice to make perfect. They spend hundreds of hours performing. Their grade point averages don't go down, but rather go up. Should we drop or cut back on this program to focus on the basics? I think not! I may be making too big a deal about what I see. How to balance this act is the $64,000 question."

"I'm glad you don't have really strong feelings on the subject!" Rob inserted, hoping to get a word in edgewise.

"Rob, the good news is that there's hope. Why don't we look at this as an opportunity, not a problem? Use this as leverage to move Paradise Valley's schools forward. Remember, you wanted to do this when you came on board 9 months ago. Are you still there?" his mentor wanted to reaffirm.

"Yes, of course, but there's so much to do! Where do I start?" Rob asked expectantly.

"Why don't I fill you in on what I left out at the cabinet workshop last month? You'll see that we chose to use the then new state mandate as a friend rather than something just to be tolerated. We were able to manage the process and get out of it what we thought was best for us."

"I like that approach. Go on," Rob encouraged his mentor.

"Let me go back to our mission statement," Barry said, digging through a stack of papers on the credenza behind his desk. "Ah yes! I found you hiding. Rob, take a look again."

Our mission is to ensure that each student, to the best of his or her ability will master the knowledge and develop the skills and attitudes essential for success in school and society.

"Rob, what thoughts occur to you about this statement?"

"It's almost like everyone else's. I know it drove your folks. Putting on my backwards thinking cap, I wonder what the body of knowledge was you wanted students to learn. And how did you define skills and attitudes? Was that the difference? Or was it your core values? You couldn't have used the state standards as there were none when you in innocence started this journey," Rob said smiling, remembering what Barry had said earlier about their long and rocky ordeal. "You changed what schools had been doing for centuries."

"No question about it! That's a key point! Of course, at first we had our out-of-date state frameworks and a board-approved curriculum defining what we were expected to impart. It was not aligned nor were tests measuring what was supposed to be taught. But we still had a semblance of local control! Finally, we realized we had to do much better than just the old ways."

"Did buying into 'All students learning' drive change?"

"Yes. Let me get on with the story and you'll see how it came together for us. The state revised one core subject each year, so every 7 years we got an update and criteria for buying new state-approved textbooks. Throw in skills and attitudes we now expected our students to demonstrate and there still were too many more unanswered questions. We hadn't even considered the concept of 'alignment.' However, allow me to take a shot at framing what helped me along the way."

🕐 **Time-Out—A What**

1. How well is your curriculum aligned with your state standards?
2. What issues are you still facing in passing the NCLB test in your state?

3. How do your system's mission, core values, and vision drive change?
4. What do you think will happen with the federal government playing a greater role in state and local assessments?

TAKING A LOOK AT THE LEARNING SYSTEM

Barry went to another pile and handed Rob a diagram.

"Let's take a helicopter view of the situation first, a systems look. This model is simple to understand but raises complex issues."

"I get to try and see the big picture first," Rob recalled (see Figure 10.1).

"Before we go into the content of the KSAs, look at the diagram again and focus on all the questions. While each learning organization has to or should answer each of the seven questions, not many have done so in a deliberately and consciously analytical fashion."

"Just quickly fast-forwarding my thoughts, this could be overwhelming!" Rob judged.

"In going beyond the driving force statement 'All students learning— whatever it takes,' we more clearly defined the elements (questions)

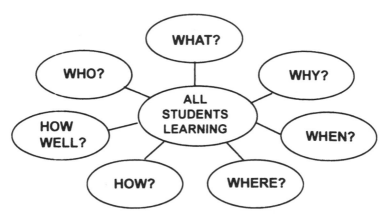

The ASL-Systems Model

Figure 10.1. The Helicopter View

that make the ASL-Systems Model come alive, giving it a sense of energy and hope. This model tries to provide a thorough description of all the elements that need to be brought to the table for discussion in a systematic way.

"To define the KSAs contained in the mission, we developed a picture or vision of what the unlimited stretch targets were to be in the core curricular areas. Essentially we believed that each student must meet minimum competencies and then be challenged through a multitude of learning opportunities to reach as far as the student can go while in our schools."

"I see this as commendable, but so time consuming. Where am I going to find the time and people?" Rob answered with a worried frown. He was getting more and more frustrated as he began realizing the gap between an idealized future and where he guessed Paradise Valley was now in this effort.

"Later. Don't jump to this now. We will take time to get a plan in place if this is what you want," his mentor answered, trying to keep the frustration at a low ebb for now, and then went on, "One day I was reflecting on the 'All students learning' battle cry and recognized that words just weren't enough. A sudden insight about the statement was causing me to think beyond it. What did it really entail? Then I framed my concerns using the seven defining questions you see in the diagram. I think any district with a rallying cry, or even asking what they are about concerning learning, can ask themselves these same simple questions that yield complex answers but can drive powerful change."

"I see where you are going. But let's finish the developmental story. First, tell me more of the journey," Rob said impatiently, wanting to get the complete big picture before going into the details.

Barry continued his historical tale.

"After developing a mission, vision, and core values with the rallying cry of 'All students learning—whatever it takes,' there remained these many unanswered questions as I looked into bringing lasting and meaningful change toward continuous improvement in the organization. I realized if you can't measure the impact of the change, you will never know when you get there. We finally remembered the need to identify critical success indicators (CSIs), or in systems thinking the Phase B box, answering the questions—How do we know when we succeed?

How do we measure what we do? How well or how close are we getting to the target?"

If you don't know where you're going, you're already there.

"Remember what I said last month, quoting our friend Yogi Berra, 'When you come to a fork in the road take it.' I could add, if you don't know where you're going, you're already there. We can't afford to do this. The destination must be identifiable at least in a future state. We need to know which road has the highest probability to get us there. We have to redefine that road and its many arteries for our system's health and welfare. The system in place will serve only as well as it has in the past, except the state or feds may take over a school or two. The development of a new road to learning for all is critical."

The development of a new road to learning for all is critical.

🕐 **Time-Out—A What**

1. What is the model trying to portray?
2. Are there other questions that need to be asked?
3. Do a mental check. Can you explain your answers to these questions?
4. Where would you go in your district to find the answers? In writing somewhere?
5. What does "All students learning—whatever it takes" mean to you?

"When we built a backwards thinking model, we tried identifying the end results we wanted. This proved troublesome. We didn't know how to measure product, only process. We really couldn't figure out early on how to develop the CSIs. Yes, we had standardized test scores and college entrance exam data, and we thought we were good. But we didn't have experience in measuring student academic progress in the early 1990s. We hit the ground running before most states were even thinking about academic standards in the basics of reading and math. We just weren't organized and we didn't know what to do, even though we were recognized as high performing.

"Just as important, we still weren't sure that there was enough organizational will to improve and get even higher performance. Remember the old saw 'Being good is the enemy of being the best.' We were in this mental state and needed strong leadership to push us to the critical mass tipping point. Now there were enough folks on board to tip the balance in the desired direction. It's in the neighborhood of 30% some say.

"We then developed a first cut of our academic standards and rolled them out to the schools. They were developed by groups of teachers under the able leadership of one of our directors. It took 2 years. But we weren't done! She left our district for a promotion, leaving our standards project incomplete. I found a very able teacher to finish her work. At this point we were beginning to understand the significance of alignment across our academic programs. Her efforts were helped along by a software program to aid in the alignment of standards. This meant our standards, the state's new ones, and those from the state testing program could now be integrated with much less time and effort."

"Are there software programs we should be looking at?"

"Yes. I'll give you a list later."

"Okay, continue."

"The alignment process was like a double-edged sword. Matching up content standards, grade level course work, test items, and resources created a clearer picture of what should be taught and learned theoretically, but it also revealed a need for stakeholders to revisit the curriculum and prepare to modify and make changes."

"That's a big commitment to time and resources. How long did it take?"

"Forever, and it is still going on. Once the new format is in place, then continuous progress toward seeing that the kids learn the prescribed curriculum is never ending," Barry replied, remembering all the work that had gone into this effort over 10 years, and it still wasn't finished.

He thought about telling Rob about the time it takes to reorient and reteach this to each new staff member every year, but decided that he would find out soon enough.

"It seems like a long and persistent trip," Rob said, recognizing the obvious.

"That it was and is. The journey is never over. It became a way of life for us. It should be the new way of life for most schools now in the 21st century."

🕐 Time-Out—A So What

1. What did you learn from this story?
2. Compare and contrast this journey to the one your district took or is taking.
3. Discuss.

"What about standards?" Rob asked.

"Let me share something I did earlier for our folks with the aid of the visionary teacher I mentioned earlier. I accidentally found her when approving a project funding request and moved her from the classroom into the Learning Support Services Division to continue with the work."

"That's the new name they created for the old Education Division after you went through the strategic management and change process wasn't it?"

"I think I told you everything changed to focus on learning and the support thereof."

Barry then went on to explain how, with the emergence of more state standards than could possibly be taught in a year, they had to come up with a way for better managing and embracing the content knowledge by using a unifying-theme approach for 12–K. Remember, they had their own, the state's, and those from the state tests to integrate. Their challenge was to put together all of the pieces of the puzzle in such a way that a user-friendly document and curriculum could be produced. This structured model he was showing Rob was an attempt to do just that.

"Here's an example of organized content and standards organizing the sciences—the interrelationships that will drive teaching and learning at high levels in all of the schools across the district" (see Table 10.1).

Rob then asked, "When are students expected to provide evidence for the state, the site, and district that they have made achievement toward reaching all of the identified standards in science—life, earth, and physical?"

"Over time we developed benchmark assessments. These summative assessments were given at specific grade levels and defined the level of performance, indicating how well the students achieved the standards," Barry responded with a sense of accomplishment.

"This is interesting. I suspect the high school classes where this is appropriate will use the same 12–K type unifying standards?" Rob asked.

"This model was used for all subjects as we worked on them." Then Woodson added, "First we did reading, writing, and math looking to grade 12–K alignment. We also set a grade-three benchmark that all students would read proficiently by year's end."

"That seems like real work!"

"Yes, but it's easier now with the aid of technology," he reminded his protégé. "As I mentioned, there are several software packages that can help. Be wary because many don't do what they claim and test items aren't always aligned with those of the state."

After this discussion Woodson got Rob back to his questions using another paper to provide information about the model's questions.

They still hadn't finished a discussion about the original learning model yet. The two of them kept going down side streets. Barry was gradually getting back to where they left off.

As Woodson's people started to respond to the seven key questions, they had to set out a way to define, align, teach, and measure the standards. This required them to define the components and create a collective, common language and understanding of the terms, their purpose, and use.

"I like the notion of unifying standards, 12–K. If we don't consolidate the hundreds of standards there is no way we can teach to them and expect students to learn them," Rob responded and then asked, "I suspect some of the unifying standards are only 8–K because of how the courses have been created at the high school level."

Table 10.1.   Discipline: Science—Domain: Life—Unifying Standard: 12–K

Students know that all living things are made of cells, which are basic units of structure and factions in which all life processes occur.

GRADE 3

What does a student at this level need to know to make appropriate progress toward achieving the unifying standard at or beyond a proficient level?

Students know that plants and animals are made of cells that have structures for growing, surviving, and reproducing.

What are students experiencing in the classroom that supports learning this content?

Third graders will
1. Identify plants
2. Describe characteristics of animals
3. Describe the life cycle of both plants and animals

What should a third grader be expected to do with skills and knowledge related to the standard?

Exit Performance Task
By the end of grade 3, students will design models of plants and animals to be used to demonstrate and communicate their understanding of how each grows, survives, and reproduces.

GRADE 7

What does a student at this level need to know to make appropriate progress toward achieving the unifying standard at or beyond a proficient level?

Students know that organisms are made of cells that act in similar ways. They know the function of cell walls, chloroplasts, nuclei, mitochondria, photosynthesis, mitosis, and differentiation. They use that knowledge to understand the levels of cell organization: cells, tissues, organs, organ systems, and whole organisms.

What are students experiencing in the classroom that supports learning this content?

Seventh graders will:
1. Identify parts and functions of cells
2. Describe cellular activities
3. Explain the similarities and differences of the structure and organization of plants and animals

What should a seventh grader be expected to do with skills and knowledge related to the standard?

Exit Performance Task
By the end of grade 7, students will design plant and animal models that will be used to demonstrate and communicate their knowledge of cellular functions and their understanding of cell structure

"Yes, of course. In science it gets harder to identify with the different course offerings, but it can be done. Reading may be a better example, because it isn't readily identified with one specific course. If we could wave a magic wand and make it so, every teacher should be helping with reading and writing in high school.

⏱ Time-Out—A Reflection

1. What did you discover?
2. Discuss the organization of the work. How would it work at your place?
3. Compare and contrast this model with what your district has been doing in curriculum and alignment.
4. What's missing? Explain how you would improve what your district has done or is doing.

THE WHY QUESTION

Finally, Barry got back to reading the ASL Learning System Model diagram and attachments discussing the seven questions.

"The why question discussion forces us to examine why we are doing what we are doing. We are chartered by the state constitution, of course. But what is our purpose in the real life of students we teach?

"The answer to this is best explained in the moral purpose of public education. John Goodlad (1990) said it well, 'We came to see with increasing clarity the degree to which teaching in schools, public or private, carries with it moral imperatives—more in public schools, however, because they are not schools of choice in a system requiring compulsory schooling.' It is this deep sense of a belief system in education that should drive us" (p. 698).

Barry stopped for a moment and said, "Some place I have Fullan's book. Let me read this to you, as I think this sets the framework for what we do. Up front we know that the schools were formed and the authority over them given to the separate states. We do what each of our states tells us to do. They define the state's mission through law and regulation. Let's look beyond this.

"I'm reading on pages 8 and 9 of Michael Fullan's *Change Forces*, where he quotes John Goodlad defining his four moral imperatives: 1) facilitating critical enculturation, 2) providing access to knowledge, 3) building an effective teacher-student connection, and 4) practicing good stewardship."

Barry set the book down and looked quizzically at Rob, waiting for a response.

"That's an interesting list, but is it practical? How would I use it?" Rob wanted to know.

"I think I would use it to start a discussion about change or strategic thinking for learning. It's a great conversation piece to get people to begin discussing what they believe. I'm convinced that we have to be committed to learning for all, and I mean all, to fulfill our moral purpose," Barry said with conviction based on his experience and beliefs.

 Time-Out—A So What

1. Reread Goodlad's moral imperatives. Discuss them in a group.
2. What do you like? Dislike?
3. How would you use this information?

THE WHAT QUESTION

"Rob, this challenges us to rethink what we are teaching and what the kids are supposed to learn. With all the help we are getting from the state and feds do we care? We should! What is the systems role in defining what is to be learned? Looking at the moral imperatives do we need to think more about how the local school system defines what goes beyond what the state measures? Are we going to sacrifice the learning opportunities for all by eliminating important things we are teaching youngsters only to get good state test scores? I hope not. But I challenge you folks, as you begin these conversations at the school level, to come to a conscious decision about it. In this I'm not raising the issue about competencies in the core subjects, especially in reading mastery at an early level and computation skill mastery.

"To meet the challenge of state mandates of standards and frameworks, we need to clearly redefine the 'what' for each curriculum strand creating common, but realistic, targets and competencies for all students. Even though the state is playing a major role, we are challenged to make our new system work. Without clear definitions, directions, assessments, staff development, and accountability systems, the 'what' won't happen!"

"Barry, wait a minute. I am confused. Even working in curriculum and instruction, I never supported the state's top-down accountability policies. Why do we put up with it?"

"Didn't I mention this before? I quit fighting the system and decided to use the energy and money from the state to make it work for us. I think the word *co-opting* is appropriate here. We couldn't fight it any longer because there was too much publicity—and it was partially the right thing to do."

Rob recalled those conversations and noted, "We talked a little about this before. You did your declaration of independence after you became a higher performing district but before the state's accountability system was in place. Your district helped shape it as I remember."

"Somewhat. I knew many key legislators from all our previous lobbying efforts. We sent key staff to meetings to help keep them from doing dumb things. It's been said that 'He who controls the agenda can rule the world,'" Barry added with a touch of humor.

"Let me explain more," Barry continued. "I reasoned this way. In California the 'big school board in the sky' is the state legislation with the approval of the governor. They set the funding levels for each of California's approximately 1,000 school districts with about 13,000 schools on the basis of historical data on funding levels in the 1970s and 1980s. We had to accept that funding reality. I always said 'until the Berlin wall first comes down it won't happen' to describe the chances for better funding to come along. And the wall came down in my lifetime. What a surprise! Maybe someday I'll see the school finance revision! This gives the state the right and obligation to demand accountability of some sort. Maybe it's long overdue and we have resisted far too long. But we should demand a good assessment system that works the way it is intended."

"It seems to me this is even more important in states where the fate of district finances is in the hands of the local voters," the rookie reflected.

"Why so?" the mentor quickly asked.

"The accountability reality is everywhere in the country. If a system isn't performing well, how long will the parents and electorate put up with it?"

"Good point!" Barry responded. "Even still, if the teachers aren't supporting the effort, they can mobilize the electorate and toss out supportive board members as their terms expire. I know of many cases where this has happened. Remember, where three incumbents are replaced, if they are seeking reelection, the superintendent isn't long for that world."

"Shall we move on?" Rob suggested.

Barry resumed. "The What question should be guided by our vision of what a successful high school graduate should look like. A few years ago we brought the entire community together to define what we want our graduates to learn and become. These outcomes are immersed in what we do and provided a vision for a well-educated high school graduate.

"If you'll excuse me, I should call one of my students before 4:30." Barry said.

"Okay. I need to take a walk down the hall anyway," Rob declared, realizing his discomfort.

THE WHO QUESTION

Who is the recipient of learning? Who is it that takes responsibility for teaching? The who is, first and foremost, all students, especially now that we have to measure performance of subgroups. In our system this is defined in the mission statement of pre-K through adult learning. Adults aren't yet subjected to a rigor of standards unless they are seeking the high school diploma or certification of the mastery gained.

The who of the provider of learning also is complex. It is the teacher, of course. An emerging point of view is that the learner is a primary provider. Teaching as a facilitator requires co-opting and energizing the learner as a monitor or manager of learning. In the new teacher's role as facilitator and coordinator of learning, we are changing the teaching-learning paradigm, as Joel Barker has so aptly described the paradigm change process. No longer can we just toss out information and hope some of it sticks.

However, do we need to look other places where students are learning and ask who is responsible for proper teaching being done? The roles of parents, peer groups, and the media come to mind. New technologies, the Internet, and distant learning are but a few of those—the who—that contribute to teaching our standards. Where are the new demands for our system coming from, and how can we use this information to improve what we do?

THE HOW QUESTION

The how question involves everyone in the system to make sure we keep our eye on the target and our energy on the main thing. (We must always keep the main thing the main thing.) Effective research-based teaching strategies, model lessons, easy access to supportive instructional materials, and coaching are each a critical part of how.

The how also creates a demand for a learning organization to respond and support teachers by modeling teaching and learning for all. This deals with Goodlad's notion of making effective teacher-student relationships imperative. The entire arena of what we are about must be defined. How do students learn, how do we provide meaningful feedback, how do we organize learning, and how do we organize the day are but a few questions we need to ask ourselves. And of course, we must decide on how we are going to do it!

THE HOW WELL QUESTION

Knowing that we reach our goals and that students meet academic targets is reassuring, but not enough. The assessment or measure of how well we do what we say we are going to do is the critical piece in our model. We need to not only define what we mean by how well but also establish both the criteria and the resultant measures.

What are our CSIs for the system, school, and for each student's learning process? Where and what do we measure? The state has again helped us in the enactment of grade level promotion standards that have to be part of the how well question. This entire issue of getting feedback information is further complicated by asking, Why are we measuring what we are now? We need to clearly understand who we are assessing, for what purpose, and how the data will drive change and improvement in the system.

Rob reacted to this last statement by raising his hand to stop his mentor just as if he were in class. "Barry, I've never thought of the stuff from this point of view. What do you have on this?"

"I recently read a paper by Margaret Wheatley and Kellner-Rogers. They, with tongue in cheek, state, 'everyone knows that you can only manage what you can measure.' But then they ask, 'Do the right measures make for better managers? Do they make for stellar organizations?' They answer their own question, of course. They basically say that measurement is important, but we need a feedback system using measurements to make the organization a quality organization."

Rob interjected with confidence, "Sounds like the circular feedback trail in the backwards thinking flow in the A-B-C-D-E model I'm getting more familiar with each month."

"There's not a lot new under the sun, but different folks just touch our old friend the elephant in different places. They indicate that in any living system feedback differs from measurement in several significant ways:

"Feedback
- is self generated,
- depends more on the context,
- changes,
- allows new and surprising information to get in,
- is life sustaining, and
- supports a movement toward the fitness and sustainability of the organization."

"I see not everyone is swept away with the number-crunching game," Rob observed.

"We want and need reliable, high-quality work through commitment, focus, teamwork, learning, and quality. These are the things that contribute to performance, not just aiming at good test scores or measurements," Barry said with some emotion.

"Back to the point!" Barry stated, before he began to comment on the chart. "The state funds the schools and sets state standards to assure the taxpayers that their money was spent on what it was intended for. In this state, he who has the gold rules! Do they have a legitimate reason to expect results from the investment of millions of dollars? From their point of view, of course they do. With the results from California's large city school systems so low, the political pressure is great to get much better results. They need some measure by which to make decisions or at least justify the ones they do make.

"After 2 years of resisting this notion I saw the light and accepted the fact that the state has the right and obligation to do so. Remember, the state's testing programs to meet state standards are big enough to measure what students should know and be able to do in today's or any day's society! Let's look at the chart" (see Table 10.2).

⏱ Time-Out—A So What

1. Review Table 10.2. What would you add or change based on your own understanding?
2. Compare and contrast these elements with what you have in your system.
3. If you need to add to your assessment system, where would you start?

"What's the best way to make sure the how well gets done? The superintendent asked, thinking it almost an impossible task to monitor each classroom.

"It's not easy, but that's why principals are supposed to be instruction leaders," Barry suggested. "They monitor the classrooms and with a good data-driven assessment system it *can* happen."

Table 10.2. Student Assessment

Who	What	Why
State Government	Benchmark status at selected grade levels with a state-developed testing system. Added a test to determine competencies to be eligible for graduation. They dipstick and sample only.	Responsible for defining the curriculum and measuring the success of districts as they determine levels of funding.
Local School Districts	Matrix sampling-assessment system should provide data for monitoring schools and provide data to improve instruction throughout. Data should be provided to measure student progress or lack thereof.	Need critical success indicators to measure progress toward strategic goals set for the year. It's more than student assessment. Those who monitor need valid data to help schools provide necessary resources.
Schools	Schoolwide, class, and student-specific data to monitor the learning process.	If all students are supposed to be learning, teachers and principals need to check frequently on progress.
Teachers	Teachers need immediate feedback on student learning to inform instruction.	To inform instruction daily. To have data to individualize instruction.
Students	A system that gives students timely feedback on their own results.	To help them become self-sustaining or peer team learners.
Federal Government No Child Left Behind	All students to meet national standards by 2014, so need an assessment system. States each have their own plans. The assessment is dipsticking and sampling only.	President makes it a federal mandate for federal funds, trying to drive higher performance at a defined level so no child will be left behind.

"Go slow early so you can pick up speed later in beginning this change process."

—Jerry Anderson, former superintendent, Brazosport, Texas

"Before I go on let me share a way to look at this. I got this at a SIA meeting last year. We had already been working on this issue before I retired. I think it's worth looking at. It doesn't directly answer your questions, rather, it suggests questions you should ask of your system."

Barry then told Rob that Rich DuFour and Robert Eakers suggested that by following the guidelines improvement on norm-referenced standardized tests scores should happen.

1. Is the curriculum aligned with the state test objectives?
2. Is the curriculum, in fact, being taught? By each teacher? How do you know?
3. Do students have opportunity to practice the kinds of knowledge, skills, or processes they will have to demonstrate on the tests?
4. How do we assess what students are learning and what can they do prior to taking the standardized tests? What plans are in place to focus on areas in which students are weak?
5. Have we disaggregated test results from these tests by grade level, subject area, and most important, individual classrooms? Have we identified pockets of low scores?
6. Have we analyzed test results to the degree that we can identify test objectives on which individual students score poorly?
7. Does each school have a plan for focusing on individual students who aren't learning; in other words, has each school developed a pyramid of interventions?
8. Are the results analyzed by teams of teachers to identify high-priority goals for the school improvement plan? If all of the goals of the school plan were achieved, to what degree would it significantly change student achievement data?

"Boy, you sure are a collector of ideas from others!" Rob exclaimed. "In my modest moments I claim I never had an original idea. I went places and saw good things I could integrate into the system. And it worked!" the mentor said, making a point he hoped Rob would remember. "We did do much of what is on the list. Commonsensically organized again!"

"Do you want me to go back and respond to DuFour's questions right now?" Rob popped off, referring to the handout Barry had just given him.

"Don't get huffy. Of course not! Think a minute. Is this a part of looking good on state tests for survival or can it be used to enhance student learning? You have to decide. DuFour was very successful driving high performance in his former high school district and is now on the road helping others," Barry explained.

"Give me a copy for our consideration. As you know, I'm not sure where we are headed. This may help if I can find time away from day-to-day crises to plan," Rob answered in frustration.

"Are you suffering rookie growing pains?" Barry commiserated. "Don't be impatient! The things we're talking about today could be elements or the foundation of a 5-year plan. I just want you to survive long enough to make it happen."

 Time-Out—So What

Reread the questions.

1. To what extent do you agree with this approach?
2. What elements are in place in your district?
3. To what degree are they making a difference?

Barry looked down at his bookmark on the original paper they were working from, getting them back on track once again, and continued with the fifth of the seven basic questions.

THE WHEN QUESTION

This is another complex question. It deals with time of year, time of day, and grade level appropriateness. With the advent of technologically based communication, we have a new set of opportunities and challenges in dealing with when. This brings into focus the need for continuous learning for organizational planning. For the schools to meet the demands of a changing society, we need to have an agile and responsive system in place. While we like to believe that the intended curriculum is taught between 9 and 3 in the classroom, research won't support this unless we make it so.

Now that learning is required, time has to be flexible.

Now that learning is required, time has to be flexible! There are scores of alternatives available to choose from as models for schools.

THE WHERE QUESTION

Learning can take place beyond the school walls. Consider the following: virtual schooling, online classes, home schooling, video games, and other alternative approaches. As suggested previously, we don't have much control over the where of student learning. We hope we are able to direct the intended curriculum in the proper direction. Students will be learning more and more away from the schoolhouse.

Is school a place or a process?

One fundamental question we need to probe is, is school a place or a process? If a process, where will it take place? As we get more creative with the individual needs of learners, the places will change. How is it changing for you?

"Rob, when it's all said and done can you answer this question?" Barry challenged the superintendent. "If you had to go to court and prove beyond a reasonable doubt that your students were learning, what would you take along as evidence?"

"This is the question, isn't it?" Rob agreed.

"The system needs to change to make sure learning for all is taking place—that the system is making headway in this effort."

⏱ Time-Out—A So What

1. What did you get from the discussion of the seven questions?
2. What two or three points made the most sense?
3. What do you think of the unifying-standards concept presented?
4. Review the ASL-Systems Model in Figure 10.1. What pieces are evident in your system?
5. If you had to go to court and prove beyond a reasonable doubt that your students were learning, what would you take along as evidence?
6. Could you win the case with what you now have?
7. If not, what are you going to do about it?

BACK TO THE EVERYDAY

Rob turned to Barry and said, "Enough! Enough! I'm over, oversaturated with good stuff. Can I get back to the 'other' things I wanted to talk about—the more urgent stuff?"

"Where do you want to start? Traffic has to be smoothing out. Do you have time to grab a bite?"

"I think I'll call and just say I'll be later than expected. Dinner's probably in the oven. It won't be the first or last time."

"Okay then, let's summarize," Barry suggested. Rob needed a break to call home.

After the short recess they had a quick look at Rob's other concerns. Barry agreed to call tomorrow and fill Rob in, if need be.

They talked a bit about the unions' initial proposals. They decided that the district should not overreact but rather thank the unions for their hard work and make a response at the next board meeting to fulfill the legal requirements.

On the subject of the budget they discussed how to approach the issue with the usual demand for higher salaries certain to be put on the table. Rob wanted to know how to "hide" money since neither he nor the business manager had been through this before. They decided that the three of them needed to meet real soon. The moral dilemma seemed to be that Rob had committed to be up front with the teacher's group. Now the reality hit him. Was the board ready to support this notion? Could they hold the line if the entire budget was open to public scrutiny? He hoped so, as that was where he was leaning. Board budget sessions were starting next week.

Finally, they agreed that they would exchange e-mail on planning more about site-based management as part of a total improvement plan they had discussed earlier. And they would for sure start first on this topic next month without fail!

🕐 **Time-Out—A Now What**

1. How would you approach initiating an improvement program in your district or school?
2. Who would you include on a core planning team in reviewing or instigating your system's or school's reflections and studies on the mission statement, vision, and core values?
3. What are the greatest deterrents to moving forward?

SUMMARY

After settling in at the university for their regular monthly meeting, the superintendent's midyear evaluation was discussed. This was based on the criteria he had established with the board in late summer. The next topic discussed was the NCLB act and its impact on a school district learning system.

The scene then shifted to a continuing history in the development of a standards-based curriculum in another district. A learning model was presented that contained seven questions that every school system should answer for itself. The CEO and superintendent should have clear answers to these questions for his or her system. A lot of time was spent on giving some explanation on these questions. Some philosophical thoughts from John Goodlad were introduced.

The scene then shifted to understanding more about the need for assessment and assessment models. A list of questions was presented that, when answered and implemented, would tend to improve norm-referenced state test scores. Helpful input from various experts was introduced that made a difference.

Timely topics on school budget, collective bargaining, and site-based management were briefly introduced.

🕐 Time-Out—Reflections

1. Do you have a personal vision of what you want your students to learn? How would you describe it?
2. How do you feel about a transition from teaching to learning in your organization?
3. Is this consistent with your belief system? If not, reflect on why.
4. On a scale of 1 to 10, how would you rate your school or district in pursuing learning for all?
5. How would you go about planning to plan in your situation?

MONTH 9—MARCH

Strategies and Survival Skills

1. Be sure to follow through on your board evaluation timeline.
    - In the interim keep steady flows of information going back and forth from you to individual board members.
    - Listen carefully for clues that might indicate troubling areas.
2. Keep abreast of all state and federal programs that would affect your learning system.
    - Be sure you understand programs such as NCLB.
    - Carefully determine the best way to move forward, or if you should at all.
3. Use opportunities created by the various legislatures to enhance your own systems goals.

- Try not to be a victim, but rather use mandates to leverage improvement in your system.

4. Look for holes in your standards and assessment alignment program.
   - Determine whether you're truly aligned or just going through the motions.
   - Do you have a clear sense of mission, a vision, and core values you can impart to others in the system?

5. Remember that basic skills are just enabling skills, not an end unto themselves.

6. Refuse to eliminate programs that yield high payoffs for learning such as music, art, athletics, and others for the sake of basics and test scores.
   - Make these programs work for you in helping kids master the basics.

7. Develop or find a process proven for making school improvement work in each school in your district.
   - Don't try to do it all alone. Use proven methodologies for your change process.
   - If you steal one, don't try to copy it and drop a readymade solution on the schools, rather, use it to develop a process for your system that is yours, that your folks create.

TOOLBOX

Barker, J. (1985). *Paradigms: The Business of Discovering the Future.* St. Paul, MN: ILI Press.

DuFour, R., & Eakers, R. National Education Service (NES), 304 W. Kirkwood Ave., Suite 2, Bloomington, IN 47404. www.nesonline.com.

Fullan, M. (1993). *Change Forces.* London & New York: The Falmer Press.

Goodlad, J. (1990). *Studying the Education of Educators: From Conception to Findings. Phi Delta Kappa* 71(9), 698–701.

Poway Unified School District, 13626 Twin Peaks Road, Poway, CA 92064. www.powayusd.com.

Reeves, D. (1998). *Making Standards Work.* Center for Performance Assessment. www.testdoctor.com.

Wheatley, M., & Kellner-Rogers, M. (June 1999). "What Do We Measure and Why? Questions About the Uses of Measurement." *Journal for Strategic Performance Measurement.*

APRIL: DO YOU KNOW HOW TO CHANGE? AND WHY SHOULD YOU?

Most people say they would die before they would change—and usually do!

—Mark Twain

BEGINNING A CHANGE PROCESS

In this chapter you will do the following:

1. Deal with a serious student situation.
2. Review some crisis management ideas in dealing with the press.
3. Get some more ideas on delegated site-based management.
4. Have the opportunity to review change theory and practice related to a district change effort.
5. Begin to integrate selected criteria for improving the system.
6. Learn how to use Herzberg's thinking in negotiations.

A PROBLEM IN PARADISE

Barry and Rob were working in the living room of the superintendent's new home, enjoying a late afternoon soda and snack. They had two flip charts marked up with planning ideas. While they were deeply engrossed in conversation, the phone rang. Rob ignored it and let it ring, knowing the answering machine would catch it or the caller would call back. When it started ringing for the second time, Martha, Rob's wife, picked up the phone in the den and, after apologizing for the interruption, handed the phone to her husband, telling him it was Diane and it sounded serious.

"Hi, Diane. What's happening?" he said, realizing it must be important for his assistant to call the house.

"Dr. Moore, I'm sorry to disturb you, but I think you need to know what we've just heard," an excited Diane exclaimed. "There's trouble at Paradise Valley High School, and the press has gotten hold of it. Something about locker room hazing. It doesn't sound good."

"What have you heard? Who's on this? Is Larry still there?" Rob asked, referring to the director of secondary education. He looked at his watch. It was just past 4 now.

"Joan Hartfield called for you," Diane said, naming the high school's principal. "She told me that a parent had just come to her with the story. The boy's dad was really upset. Something about anal penetration with a broomstick in the locker room. It seems some baseball players are involved."

"Call her right now and have her call me at home. Barry's still here," he said with exasperation in his voice. What now, he thought? Why me? The press will be all over this and we're not set up to deal with an ugly situation. He hoped *60 Minutes* wouldn't be showing up in his office, but there would probably be local TV cameras to get ready for.

Again he picked up his cell phone. He began calling school board members to inform them about what they were going to read and probably hear on the 11 p.m. news or earlier. Only three were contacted, so he left messages and asked the other two to call him as soon as they could.

Then he made two more calls. The first was to see if the school district's attorney would be free the next morning, and the second was to Don Halverson to let him know. Don reminded him about a public relations specialist they had met and chatted with at a couple of chamber of commerce mixers. She had offered to help them outline an effective community relations plan. He just hadn't had the time to do it. Then it was one of those important but not urgent items. But now! He would give Arlene Hogan a call tomorrow when he got to the office. Maybe he should hire her to help deal with this mess and more. Between calls, Barry mentioned that he had worked with her before.

Do you know how to make lemonade out of lemons?

Maybe it was too late for this crisis! Now may be the time to make lemonade out of this lemon! He'd done it before.

The now more experienced rookie gave Barry a brief overview of what he'd just heard. He added that although he had dealt with a few crises in his former position, he wasn't ready for this. He could only anticipate the worst consequences—and still in his first year!

Excusing himself, Rob picked up the phone and tried to locate the director of secondary education, Larry Ramirez. His secretary said that he had left for the day. Rob would try and catch him at home later. They needed to meet early in the morning.

Gazing out the sliding glass door at the beautifully landscaped yard the Moores had inherited when they bought the house, Barry reminisced about some of the crises he had experienced. There were several that he had to handle or had delegated. Among the toughest was when a parent claimed the water polo coach was having sex with his daughter. This came to the surface when the Navy dad returned from overseas and punched the coach out at pool side. After all the dust cleared, it became clear that it was the mother who had been involved with the coach. Some of the girls on the team didn't like the daughter and had spread untrue rumors about her.

Fortunately, the staff had been well trained to handle the press. He remembered some of the advice he had gotten early in the game:

1. Don't hide.
2. Acknowledge problems.
3. Make it yesterday's news as quickly as possible.
4. If you haven't already done so, view this as an opportunity to meet news reporters connected to the district.
5. Get reporters' names, affiliations, and other information for future more positive contacts.

6. Set up press conferences if appropriate—be accessible, professional, and honest.

When Rob got off the phone, Barry would bring up and review some of these ideas. Rob perhaps already knew this, but a quick review wouldn't hurt before he got personally involved in working this through.

As he reflected a smile came across Barry's face, remembering his ordeal with the so-called religious right protesters. He had to have one person arrested twice for interrupting staff in-service training sessions. Had to go to small claims court twice. The judges ruled in favor of the action the district had taken.

He remembered his anger and resentment about the concerted attack on the district by these few extremists. This handful of folks tried to overload the district with requests for data, hoping the district responses would give them more information they could use to further attack the district and superintendent. Even a former board member who had been recently defeated did the same. It was a mess for a while.

Every time the district responded with more than one sentence, it brought three more requests for data. They learned to send the requests for information back for specificity and clarity before responding. The district responses got real short over time. In his jaundiced opinion this religious right was neither. His opinion was printed in the paper when his anger got the best of him and he said it aloud, but it made the point. From this experience he handled the press better.

On advice from a fellow superintendent to solve this problem, he brought some of the more rational, conservative concerned parents in to chat. After listening for a while, he then better understood their fear. He was able to begin easing their concerns about the curriculum and modern practices, such as letting middle school students correct each others' papers under teacher guidance. When challenged individually, no parent actually said anything being done in the district was hurting their own children. They had been propagandized by the party line again about some alleged devious satanic practices contained on a list of about 30 issues to fight against. They even had Dr. Larry Lezotte on their hit list because he believed in equity for all students, and this meant that poor and disadvantaged kids would get the same chance as their own well-provided-for children.

After three sessions and out-quoting them when they brought up Bible scripture trying to make their case, many of their fears were calmed. In closing, he invited them to come directly to him if any problem existed with their own child. Most of these folks were well meaning but needed reassurance to ease their fear that their child would be okay. For the most part it worked. They finally stopped trying to create news through sensationalism.

🕐 Time-Out—A What

Think back on a crisis you've experienced or observed as well as what has been described.

1. How were the communication issues handled?
2. Would any of the suggestions given here have helped? How?
3. What did you learn from these experiences?

"Rob, is there anything I can do to help?" the mentor asked, coming back to the traumatic issue at hand after Rob got off the phone.

"Barry, actually, I'm okay for now. I've got to meet with Joan and see if Larry and the rest of the cabinet will be available early in the morning."

Rob wondered why his director of secondary education wasn't called, but maybe he had been. He hoped there wasn't a problem there between the principal and her director. He would have to look into this later.

The phone rang again. It was principal Hartfield. "What's going on?" Rob asked. After listening a few minutes, he said, "Have you talked to the kids and coaches yet? If not, be sure you take good notes. Before we react we need the facts. You'd better call in the police. Is your city-assigned school police officer available?" After a pause to absorb Joan's reply, he responded, "He's already gone? Call the police station and tell them what's been going on and see how they want to handle it. It's not an emergency, so tomorrow you need to mobilize for interviewing those involved." After listening some more, he told Joan that her director, Larry, would be there at 7 a.m. sharp to help outline a strategy for communications to parents and the press. This is where they had to initiate

damage control. As they hung up they agreed to be in touch early in the
morning.

After hearing only one side of the conversation, Barry made a suggestion, "Why don't you take a minute to think about how you might want
to see the outcome turn out and plan accordingly?"

"What do you mean?"

First, Barry reviewed the advice he had gotten and then suggested,
"For example, make a list of all the parties that need to be dealt with.
Board members, victims, perpetrators, other students, parents of each,
press, and whoever will need some communication. You might want to
review it with Larry and Joan before she goes to the school, so you're
both on the same page. This will not go away overnight. Try keeping the
damage to a minimum."

Since they had spent all afternoon discussing organizational change
and outlining a strategy to address the standards and assessment piece
he needed, Rob would need to shift his focus to this new issue. This was
in the important-urgent area of the decision matrix, he knew, but he still
didn't like it. This would be the first big student problem with public
relations implications he would be facing since he had been hired. He
now fully realized that unplanned stuff would be always a part of his life
as superintendent.

Knowing that Rob needed time to work this out and that he was in
the way, Barry thanked Martha Moore and said his good-byes. He got
an assurance from Rob that he would call if he was needed. Barry wasn't
too concerned since things like this happened to high school principals
and Rob was experienced handling similar problems.

REFLECTIONS ON CHANGE MANAGEMENT

Even as he worried about this new problem, Barry headed home thinking how pleased he was at the progress Paradise Valley was making
toward ratcheting up their commitment to student learning. They were
moving in the right direction.

To remember all he and Rob had covered, he began dictating in his
handheld recorder. This was a great tool he had recently purchased.
When he got to his computer, he just plugged it in and his voice-

activated software typed out everything. Of course, he had to remember all of the commands or he would have a deciphering problem again. With practice he was getting better.

His thoughts drifted back to what had been discussed. It started with the question that had been partially considered in their previous meeting in his university office. Rob wanted to move now toward some site-based management. He was still thinking like a principal rather than a superintendent. He reverted back to focusing on himself rather than detaching himself and taking the helicopter view. And when asked what that meant, Rob told him that he wanted to be told what the boss wanted, be given some resources to carry it out, and have the district office leave the school alone to do the job.

Barry agreed with this to a point. However, he reminded Rob that not all principals were ready and able to take on this responsibility. Again he reviewed the readiness elements, willingness and ability, and asked Rob if he knew how ready each of the principals were to make a specific change, even more so, did he have the support of the central office directors? Rob agreed that he needed to review more about the change process. He told Barry that he wasn't in that great a hurry as he only wanted something planned now to start next fall or a year would go by without moving forward. Barry then smiled and mentioned a saying he had picked up somewhere, Change is an unnatural act among unconsenting adults.

Change is an unnatural act among unconsenting adults.

WHY CHANGE?

While in agreement, Barry had once more pushed the superintendent to make sure Rob knew where he was headed. The mentor pushed by using the five-whys questioning technique. The answer to the first why was Rob wanted to improve the system. Again when asked why, Rob decided he wanted students to be more successful in the district's schools. Why? He wanted them ready for work or further schooling when they graduated. Why? Rob was getting testy at this point and said that he guessed it was based on his value and belief system and the reason he got into teaching in the first place. Why? Helping students grow and develop with sound leadership was a prime reason he offered.

"Nothing endures but change."

—**Plato**

Woodson had reviewed a few points with Moore. First, he reminded him again about clearly understanding the change process. They talked some about Ichak Adizes's (1993) definition of management: "To make decisions and implement the changes needed." He then shared some material on change he had gathered over the years.

He had reminded Rob that "To lead is to live dangerously because when leadership counts you must lead people through difficult change, challenging what people hold dear"—something he picked up from *Leadership on the Line: Staying Alive Through the Dangers of Leading* (2002) by Heifetz and Linsky.

Woodson had handed Rob a page from a report prepared by the Association of California School Administrators and released way back in December of 1994, which he thought still was on point about leadership and change today.

Preparing Strategic Educational Leaders for the Twenty-first Century

Modern education leaders can safely assume only two conditions.[1] One, they will almost always have to operate within the context of a larger organization or within a set of rules they do not establish alone. Second, change appears to be the only contemporary condition which is constant, and thus, organizations and their leaders must continually adapt.

What is now called for is a new executive model: "Strategic Leadership." Strategic Leadership is an enlargement of the currently fashionable "transformational leadership." Using much of the framework of transformational leadership—collaborative problem solving, building organizational capacity, etc.—Strategic Leadership expands the boundaries to encompass additional crucial elements that will assist education leaders to create and sustain dynamic, productive organizations.

Effective educational leaders exhibit important common characteristics and engage in common activities. Strategic Leaders:

- Are able to develop and articulate a vision of what the organization with which they are connected should be like.
- Possess the skill to know how to cooperate, when to motivate, and under what circumstances to inspire those with whom they work.
- Know about the major operational levers which can be employed to control or change an organization's course or direction.
- Continually gather and analyze data which can be used to guide or re-align the outlook or operation of an organization.
- Take the time to reflect upon the interaction of external environmental conditions and internal organizational dynamics.

Four macro socio-demographic, economic, and political currents are dramatically altering the conditions within which educational institutions, and educational leaders, must operate. These conditions are 1) increasing global interaction and economic competition and the need for a better prepared, more highly skilled workforce, 2) the ever-more-porous nature of national and international boundaries making it possible for ideas and cultural mores to spread with increasing rapidity, 3) the burgeoning heterogeneity of the nation's (and particularly California's) population, and 4) the intensifying web of politics in which education increasingly is caught. Association of California School Administrators.

"No man ever planned to fail—what probably happened was he failed to plan."

—Will Rogers

Rob made an interesting observation that information from the ACSA report seemed to be incorporated in the strategic change and planning model Barry showed them how to use last summer. Barry thought to himself that Rob got it, which pleased the mentor. The context for planning had to include some elements of school improvement and then be used for wrestling NCLB to the ground. Rob commented that he knew from his 8 months on the job that this would be leverage for doing things maybe sooner rather than later.

As they chatted more about changing the organization, Barry reminded his protégé that, even in dealing with the macro concept, always remember change occurs one person at a time.

Finally, when they got back to reality on the specific next steps in moving the staff forward, Barry added that Rob could always blame the need on the state or feds, and they both agreed somewhat humorously. Sometimes this got the job done or at least started. They needed to get data they could use to make informed decisions. But which data? This they would determine later after the principals and directors were involved more.

Then Barry had agreed to get some material on change for Rob and his team to review. After this, they would meet with the cabinet to consider some ideas about gearing up on school improvement. They agreed that a plan would have to be flexible enough for each school to do its own planning but within the guidelines that would be established centrally. Even though the system wasn't ready to forcefully commit to learning for all, Rob wanted to start changing the conversation and to shape the culture to achieve this end in mind.

Rob was insistent, even if some principal readiness levels were suspect, that a direct approach in defining the problem and getting them involved, however reluctantly, may have to be done.

THE CHANGE PACKAGE FOR THE SUPERINTENDENT

With his thoughts fully captured now for posterity, Dr. Woodson turned off the recorder, drove in his driveway, and pushed the garage door button. As he walked into his family room, he knew that he should begin getting materials on change together for Rob. Right after dinner he promised himself—unless there was an interesting movie on tonight. He could always get up early in the morning.

Being semiretired had its perks compared to the 16-hour days he used to regularly put in. As he rationalized, he thought that his best work was done early in the morning anyway.

Woodson woke earlier than usual. There had been no interesting movies on last night, but he did get hooked on a History Channel special, *Alexander the Great*, he had missed earlier. Not a paragon of good leadership practice, but Alexander did have a goal and commitment to get there, whatever the moral purpose was. There was not much else in it to inspire today's leaders.

"Failure is not fatal, but failure to change can be!"

—John Wooden, former UCLA basketball coach

In spite of his late night, his thoughts were about what to prepare for. After a glass of tomato juice, he went down the hall to his darkened office just as the sun was lightening the eastern sky and began digging into his old files. Breakfast would have to wait. Get this stuff off to Rob, do your 3-mile walk, hit the hot tub, and then you can have breakfast, he tried to convince himself. The first place he looked was in the old presentation outline file that he and his staff trainer had done in the past.

As he was sorting through the stack he thought about his own ignorance on this topic before he had a chance to meet with the gurus on change at a University Associates conference in San Francisco. He had been a superintendent for about 8 years and was still learning about the field of organizational behavior and development when this opportunity came to his attention. It helped organize his thinking and helped his group make fewer mistakes as they moved to change what they had been doing. Early on he had tried to involve people in decision making, but as a leader dealing in crises he thought he knew best. Now the game had changed, but the approach was still situational, based on the task, and the followers' readiness to implement the change.

SOME WORKABLE CHANGE MODELS

Barry always gave Rob more than was probably necessary, but he rationalized this by thinking the CEO could start filing these materials away for a rainy day. He even thought Rob might want to share some of the stuff with his cabinet. Ironically, it had started to rain again.

Looking in his file, he saw Curt Lewin's (1982) model that described the process like this: First, you have to unfreeze the behavior, then make the change, and then refreeze it with the new behaviors. Beckhard's (1987) work was next. He had described it as moving from an old state to a new state by using transition management. It required feedback from the new change group to the old to bring all the people along.

THE ROLLER COASTER OF CHANGE

Some of the best material he had seen about the psychological components during change describes the process in steps: shock and disbelief, depression and anger, hope and acceptance, and finally, reconstruction and rebuilding. Others use the terms *form*, *storm*, *norm*, and *perform* to express the same idea. Part of this was from Kanter's earlier work.

Then he found a chart called the "Roller Coaster of Change" that Haines had refined describing the various phases people go through when they are affected by change. The folks at the Centre for Strategic Management put it all together with systems theory, creating a more profound tool for systems thinking and management. Much of the work of the gurus Woodson had studied offered help for folks who needed to process their way through the cycle of the roller coaster of change (see Figure 11.1).

The change-cycle curve reflects the intensity of the change on the vertical axis. The length of time taken to process through to a satisfactory change is represented on the horizontal axis. It started with Rosabeth Moss Kanter's description of what occurs during traumatic change such as divorce, death of a loved one, or getting fired. She says that we all go through the four stages and how we do so is critical to keeping our emotional balance. Some don't make it and stay in an unhealthy state for a very long time. They just can't let go and move on.

This is a similar pattern that Paradise Valley will experience when it's announced that they will be gearing up to meet the new state accountability plan required by the feds. Changing the priority to embrace learning for all as a fundamental force and testing subgroups will cause the emotions to surface, as clearly indicated on the Roller Coaster of

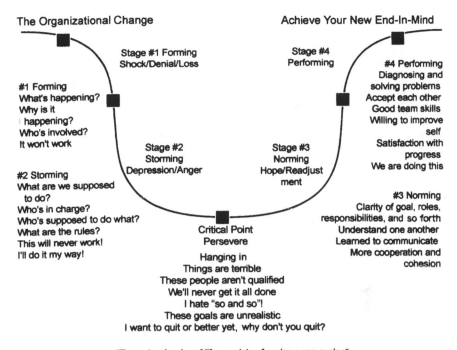

The Organizational Change   Achieve Your New End-In-Mind

Stage #1 Forming   Stage #4
Shock/Denial/Loss   Performing   #4 Performing
                                                        Diagnosing and
#1 Forming   solving problems
What's happening?   Accept each other
Why is it   Good team skills
 happening?   Willing to improve
Who's involved?   self
It won't work   Stage #2   Stage #3   Satisfaction with
                        Storming   Norming   progress
#2 Storming   Depression/Anger Hope/Readjust   We are doing this
What are we supposed   ment
  to do?   #3 Norming
Who's in charge?   Clarity of goal, roles,
Who's supposed to do what?   responsibilities, and so forth
What are the rules?   Critical Point   Understand one another
This will never work!   Persevere   Learned to communicate
I'll do it my way!   More cooperation and
                            Hanging in   cohesion
                        Things are terrible
                    These people aren't qualified
                    We'll never get it all done
                      I hate "so and so"!
                    These goals are unrealistic
            I want to quit or better yet, why don't you quit?

"The natural order of life consists of cycles upon cycles"
Adapted from Centre for Strategic Management, San Diego

Figure 11.1.   The Roller Coaster of Change and Systems Thinking.
Source: Haines, 2000.

Change. They will have to identify and work though these different emotions as they prepare to move forward for the benefit of students and the community they serve.

There was a lot more to this and Barry offered to send Rob more information. In this material he would include times and dates of work–shops on the topic. A saying came to mind characterizing what Rob had to do. "If it ain't broke, break it!" While many staff thought things were okay, the CEO's task was to create what Warren Bennis calls "Confident Uncertainty."

BLANCHARD'S SEVEN PIECES OF CHANGE

As he looked deeper in the file, he found Ken Blanchard's video of a workshop on change dynamics. It was a riot! He slipped it in the VCR and watched it again. Woodson had done 10 or more workshops in his own district and for others, doing the activity live. Then he would play for them Ken's pretaped debriefing and, every time, Ken would describe almost exactly what had happened at Woodson's workshop.

Renaming the activity "Blanchard's Seven Pieces of Change," Woodson began the exercise by having people stand face-to-face and look at each other for 2 minutes. After this, he asked the participants to stand back-to-back and change what they were wearing, moving things around, taking things off, doing whatever they could creatively to change their appearance. They then were to turn back and try to identify what changes their partner had made. They started with 5 items, then 10, and then were asked the third time for 10 more. This last set didn't really happen as too many people had already dropped out or · after a loud moan were about to. The folks were then asked to sit down.

Next, Woodson would suggest that Ken Blanchard had been watching and these were his comments on instant video. He then played the tape, stopping to point out what he observed that Ken agreed with. By observing the behavior of the group, Woodson could give them more personalized feedback than Ken did on tape, of course. However, the participants were amazed that Ken's seven observations were almost always right on target in describing what had happened.

There is a moral to the story or activity and some powerful learnings from the experience.

THE BLANCHARD OBSERVATIONS

During the initial phase of change

1. People will feel awkward, ill at ease, and self-conscious.
   This is illustrated by the obvious discomfort shown by body language and the relief suggested by the conversation following the 2-minute stare-down activity. Folks don't know where even to place the eyes, especially if the pairing was male and female.
2. People will think first about what they have to give up.
   While the directions don't preclude folks adding to their attire,

even by putting a pencil behind an ear, most often they struggled with taking something off or moving it.

3. People will feel alone even if everyone else is going through change.

   If you can imagine 40 to 200 people standing back-to-back in a large room, you will note that almost every one is facing someone else's partner. The directions didn't preclude asking for help from others.

4. People can handle only so much change.

   The first 5-item change session goes relatively easy. When the group is asked to do 10 more, grumbling starts, and some start to drop out. With the announcement of the last 10, the place goes into an uproar of resistance. At this point, they are asked to only sit down.

5. People are at different levels of readiness for change.

   This behavior is illustrated by the willingness to do the exercise in the beginning, some half-hearted attempts, and then avoidance by just talking to their partner, and finally some early dropouts.

6. People are concerned that they don't have enough resources.

   This is almost axiomatic in any change process. We need more money and more people. We don't think in terms of doing away with the least important and often unnecessary practices in the organization. In this situation people had all sorts of resources on tables or using things from others to make a change.

7. People will revert to their old behavior if you take the pressure off.

   This is a hoot to watch. The Expressives have their ties off, wrapped around their heads, pant cuffs rolled up, and whatever. The women got more comfortable taking off jackets and jewelry. They definitely look and feel more comfortable than when they arrived. But what happens? Almost everyone goes back to how they looked prior to this activity. As soon as the facilitator says, "Now let's ask Ken to debrief the session," before they even start to sit down, they change back to more formal dress (see Table 11.1).

He wondered how Rob feels about change. He hoped this little exercise would give him more insight. Paying attention to the remedies will work over time.

Table 11.1. The Seven Pieces of Change and Suggested Action

The Observations	We Can Help By . . .
1. People will feel awkward, ill at ease, and self-conscious.	providing enough information
2. People will think first about what they have to give up.	holding a mourning session to grieve what is lost
3. People will feel alone even if everyone else is going through change.	structuring interaction and helping others see linkages in the new setting
4. People can handle only so much change.	prioritizing the change and allowing time, even 2–5 years, to make it work
5. People are at different levels of readiness for change.	seeing change as situational with people and helping rather than labeling resistance in the process
6. People are concerned that they don't have enough resources.	helping them see other resources and opportunities beyond their own situation
7. People will revert to their old behavior if you take the pressure off.	managing the change journey by coaching and holding people accountable for the desired results

Source: The Ken Blanchard Companies.

Woodson put all the material together and sent it to Rob at Paradise Valley School District with a note to Diane asking her to make sure he saw it as soon as time permitted. They planned to meet in a few days, so hopefully Rob would have time to review some of the package. With the press on his doorstep and commotion going on over the hazing issue, he doubted that Rob would see this as an urgent priority.

🕐 **Time-Out—So What**

1. What's your take on this?
2. What do you know about change theory? List your ideas.
3. Think of a change you, your school, or your district has gone through lately and apply the Blanchard observations. What did you learn?
4. How did you react going through the change?
5. What would you advise now in retrospect that would have made it easier for you or your group in the process of change?

FOLLOW-UP ON HAZING

Two days later Barry decided to call Rob since he hadn't heard from him. The papers were full of the hazing story. The district seemed to be handling it well. The police were investigating, so the district was deferring to them. The high school athletic director was leading the school's own search for the truth.

Diane indicated that her boss was in and had a few minutes to chat.

"Dr. Woodson, we survived the first 48 hours without *60 Minutes* showing up!" he said with a sense of relief, before his mentor could even ask the question. "I think it's going as well as expected. We've spoken to one alleged victim and his parents. No one else has come forward and we believe that he was the only one where physical contact was made."

"How is the legal issue with the parents? Are they going to sue, if this proves out?"

"Not at this point, but our attorney warns us to expect it and to be careful what we say. It seems there was a time after fifth period and before the students reported to the baseball field that the athletic locker room was unsupervised. The entire staff has been advised not to talk about this for now."

"I'm glad it's under control. How has the working press been?"

"Not too bad. We gave them some air time. We deferred to the police investigation going on. They seemed to understand that we had to protect the victims' names. We told them we would involve them if, and when, we could say more."

Barry then asked about the change package he had sent over. Rob acknowledged receiving it but hadn't really absorbed it yet. He had asked Don to read it so they could compare notes later.

WORKING ON THE WORK

Before they hung up, it had been decided to meet in the central office the next week to go over some more ideas on change, next steps for implementing some aspects of site-based management, and planning first steps for improving instructional accountability. They still needed to work on negotiating a strategy that might reduce tension. They set aside working on a communication plan until their session in May.

NEGOTIATIONS WITH HERZBERG

A week had gone by without any more communication between them. The mentor realized that the rookie, now a much more experienced one, had his hands full.

Meeting back in Rob's office, they both recognized that they had been avoiding the discussion on negotiations for far too long. The deadline for the board agenda preparation was approaching, for the meeting where the board would need to present the new labor contract proposal for a first reading even though it was a perfunctory step.

Barry told Rob about what he had learned the hard way. Early in the game his position was win-lose as they had discussed earlier. In their initial request, the teachers' union presented a demand for a 10% raise, but he had recommended no raise in the board's proposal. In addition, they might throw in a merit pay proviso, to go into negotiations with lots of leverage. It was illusory, as they eventually had to hammer out a compromise.

A few years later, after reading more about Frederick Herzberg's (1967) motivation-hygiene theory, a light suddenly came on that changed the atmosphere. Rather than challenging the union in the old traditional way that affected the teachers' environment, where possible the district switched the approach to the motivating factors about the work itself. They avoided threats to the status quo. Usually, the union's first broadside to the school reps and teachers was about how unfeeling the administration was and they were going to have to fight this tragedy right from the start.

This insight came after the administration and superintendent had established a strong in-service program, did much in recognizing staff successes, and generally involved teachers in more decision making.

A key factor was Barry's establishment of his famous—or infamous—rappin' sessions throughout the organization. Even through contract negotiations, this meeting with teacher reps continued. They were carefully planned so no pressure was put on either the superintendent or teachers regarding negotiation issues. Trust in the superintendent was building and success in improved test scores had created a more receptive environment.

Barry gave Rob an overview of Herzberg's findings that were applicable for negotiations. First, he showed him the findings about what motivates people and what acts as demotivators.

Motivators—The Job Itself	Hygiene Factors—Environment (Demotivators)
Achievement	Policies and administration
Recognition for accomplishment	Supervision
Challenging work	Working conditions
Increased responsibility	Interpersonal relations
Growth and development	Money, status, security

Barry added that this was effective in keeping the emotional content under control initially and then into the future in many areas. He gave an example when Rob questioned him about how this changed the board's proposal. The mentor replied that instead of proposing 0% to counter the teachers' sometimes unrealistic 15–20% request, they said that they believed in a fair salary settlement without jeopardizing the instructional program and class size ratios in the schools. It established the board's agenda and it seemed to work. The union couldn't start off by telling their folks that the board was going to stick it to them again. They knew they would get some sort of raise and that their working environment wasn't to be touched. This took away another one or two nonmotivators.

Barry was quick to point out that, while money was a demotivator, it wasn't a motivator according to Herzberg's investigations both in hospitals and school districts. Also, this set the stage for the move to a more win-win approach that they had previously discussed.

🕐 **Time-Out—A So What**

1. Review your union's proposal. Does Herzberg hold true?
2. Review your district's proposal. How does it look?
3. What changes, if any, would you try to make?

SOME ELEMENTS OF DELEGATED SITE-BASED MANAGEMENT

When Rob came back into the office after being called away to make a decision on the upcoming budget discussions with the director of business, he was met with a statement from Barry.

"Rob, let's go back to the change you want to make with the principals. Do you want to begin implementing some elements of delegated site-based management that we discussed earlier?"

"This is what we've been talking about for a few months," Rob said. "Yes, because I believe in it. Remember my thinking is still that of a principal with independence, where the district office gives me the charge and then leaves me alone to do the work."

"Okay, then, what do you want to change in this first go-around?" Woodson asked, to get this rather complex item focused. To help, they had to be on the same page in defining what site-based meant for Rob. Woodson knew to be successful they had to start slow and simple. He remembered the old saw "How do you eat an elephant?" The answer is, one bite at a time. Rob needed to determine what size elephant he wanted in the process. What was the end in mind? And what would the small bites look like?

"Some budget items and a more active role in hiring teachers," Rob began. "I want to start implementing some school budget ideas, the personnel staffing unit plan (PSUP) and bottom-line accountability. Recall we discussed this way back in October."

"Good."

"I would like to invite more involvement by the school and staff in teacher hiring before school opens in the fall," the rookie stated in an assured manner. He wanted to begin changing a few things as soon as possible for them to take effect next year. There would be a few more things if he could get the teachers to go along with some of his ideas.

"Rob, what about your PSUP? I know that you and your assistant in personnel have used the system before. Why don't you give him the charge of being chief implementer?"

"That's a good idea, but I need to get principals to buy into the plan. We saw that in a change process folks will first be concerned about what they will lose, have to give up. Is that going to be true if I go with a PSUP?"

"What do you think, Rob? You know them better now," Woodson suggested, taking this problem monkey off his back and returning it to the superintendent's. Rob needed to begin the application of learning and integrating ideas for himself. "Think about Blanchard's seven change elements. See how they could be used here."

"I can anticipate some problems, especially with the one principal I've been working with."

"Rob, it is obvious to me that not all your principals are at the same readiness level. You need to bring them all in and talk. When I initiated a major change, I gave the principals and directors 2 years to get the necessary staff training and to begin the implementation process. Of course, that was far more complex as it was partly in response to the paradigm shift from teaching to learning. With fewer principals it may be easier. Let's review the seven pieces. How will most of your team see this? What are some going to have to give up?"

"Well, four or five will not like systematizing the budget as they are still getting extra favors this year established by the previous guy. I didn't find out about this until late fall and decided to let it ride for now. They will be giving up a favored position and believe they could lose dollars. They're probably correct!"

"A basic truth of management—if not of life—is that nearly everything looks like a failure in the middle . . . persistent, consistent execution is unglamorous, time-consuming, and sometimes boring."

—Rosabeth Moss Kanter

"Some will embrace this. Another group will say okay and wait to understand it. Still others may have always relied on the district to do this work for them. Some find it easier to let the big guys go first, so they won't have to work as hard and then can point fingers if things go wrong. Some won't like to face the staff in answering tough budget questions, if the principal is responsible," Rob added, drawing from his thoughts and experiences in his former district.

Barry said, "If you're set on this and the decision is made, then you need to be honest with them. Spend time describing the advantages and disadvantages. Carefully explain why you want to make the change and that you want them to help develop the implementation steps. Explain that you are not going to be so directive in all areas, but for now it has to be this way to get this in place almost immediately, for time is too short to debate the decision. Especially let them know how teachers will become involved down the line. Of course, this will scare some to death. You might go out on a limb and talk with them about where they see their own readiness as a group and then decide where each is as a site leader."

Rob then suggested a way to get started. He explained how to set the baseline funding at each level—elementary, middle, and high school. One way to minimize the shift was to fund each level where the most money was and standardize the level at this point so no one would lose and many would gain resources. He reminded Barry that this is regular program funding and does not include, for example, special education, Title I school grants, and other specially funded categorical programs or schools.

"Let's lay out the steps I need to take. I want to get started tomorrow," Rob declared with excitement.

"Okay. We'll put this through our backwards thinking model. You might want to work it through with your administrative cabinet also. I can get you started."

With this as a start Rob took the planning model back to the cabinet. After grinding on it for a few hours, the group would lay out the strategy and roles each would play. They would try out their thinking on a few principals first and then adjust before going to the entire group.

🕐 **Time-Out—A So What**

1. What is your current thinking on site-based management?
2. Where is your district in this movement?
3. How would you start to change thinking in a district that is top-down controlling?
4. How would you use the principles of Situational Leadership to implement more in your district?

FOCUSING ON IMPROVEMENT

"What about planning to focus more on improving the learning environment in the schools? Where should we start? I'm anxious to get principals involved sooner than later. The pressure of NCLB hasn't gone away. This year is the first year in which the new state plan starts to track the required data," Rob so aptly reminded Barry.

"Let's track back to a couple of ways to start the principals thinking more about the gap between where they are and where you want them to be."

"Sounds okay!"

"We have the research to support the identification of the leading factors that if in place will ensure the development of an effective school. This is a school driving to meet the learning-for-all value while ensuring equity for all."

"Yes, I remember our discussions and the criteria," Rob proudly responded while walking over to the board to write from memory:

1. Clear and focused mission
2. Instructional leadership by the principal
3. High expectations for success
4. Opportunity to learn and time on task
5. Frequent monitoring of student progress
6. Safe and orderly environment
7. Home-school relations

"Barry, where should I start?" Rob asked his mentor.

"With the end in mind, of course," came back the response quickly. "Numbers one and two will be a handful in the beginning. Some of your principals, if not most, will need to be guided in providing the necessary leadership. They must be on board with a clear understanding of the mission. Some you will have to be directive with and others use the appropriate styles. Ideally, the path to this new thinking should start with individual knowledge to change the individual's attitude leading to changing the individual's behavior. The totality of this should drive organizational change and is described as participatory change.

"However, for some who don't take to friendly persuasion, you may have to use position and coercive power. If principals don't respond, you might want to suggest a career change—and look for the roller coaster then.

"The coercive process starts with the power leader declaring what the change is. For example, starting next week you each will begin disaggregating all your test scores and come up with a plan in 2 weeks to improve student learning. This approach reverses what I just described. It starts with forcing group behavioral changes, hoping to get individual behavioral change by the principals—hoping to give them enough knowledge after the fact to develop an individual attitude change. Is this clear?" Woodson finished.

"Although time is short, I still like the participatory model best. I already told them I was laying on more site-based stuff but wanted them to help figure out what to do first," Rob declared, seemingly understanding what Woodson described.

"This is a 'tweener.' It's in the nature of 'I've made this decision, but I need your help in the implementation of it.' Just be clear on what role the staff has in decision making. No games or deceptions and you can get along fine," was the response.

"Got it!"

"I would suggest you begin with task groups deciding what data needs to be gathered for each area—your new baseline data," Woodson suggested. "Then I suggest you determine how the central office can help by gathering what you can through existing computer information systems to cut down on the site time and paperwork."

"I could get some of my group and some principals to chair the various teams I guess," Rob said.

"Good! I'm going to send you a workbook on how to identify the work that needs to be done for each criterion. Use it with your staff in planning. Once you get the steps in place, I would be happy to review it. I think your group can pull it off."

Still feeling frustrated, Rob asked, "How am I to assimilate all the change stuff you sent me? It's all a whirl now. I need to understand how you used it." Rob was showing his impatience. He wondered how he was going to sort it all out. He then asked what effect this exercise had on Woodson's district.

"Basically, the impact was on leadership. First, it made us more aware of what we experience when we go through change without always realizing it. It provided us with words and a language we could use to better describe what we were feeling individually," Barry remembered. "Systemic change comes from leadership, not programs, projects, and innovations. Good things began to happen as we integrated all that we were learning about leadership. This didn't happen overnight, as I've said before. More like 2 to 5 years. You have to plan the time for training."

"The jury is still out on what you've been teaching me," the superintendent responded.

"So let's review what you got from me today," Barry suggested, helping Rob to simplify.

"I gave you some ideas for join-up activities to help direct the group's thinking and start the process of changing mind-sets."

Dr. Woodson went on to review the roller coaster of change strategy. He told Rob that if we don't realize the way people respond to significant changes in their lives, the odds are that we won't get to lasting change or at least may get there the hard way.

The resistive forces are great in the bureaucracy itself, Woodson explained. In reading Dolan's work, he remembered the author using a sailing metaphor. "Sea anchors to change" was how he described this resistance. At various times, he suggests that the school board, the superintendent, the central office, and the teacher union are the main drags for change.

"Get the right people on the bus of change, the wrong people off, and the right people in the right seats, as Jim Collins suggests in *From Good to Great*. However, don't forget that in this context you need to know where the bus is going and why," Barry said.

"I like what you said before on systemic change. I think you were quoting something Larry Lezotte said when we were talking about this. Systemic change includes structural change—roles and responsibilities—and cultural change includes beliefs, values, vision, and myths. Did I get this right?"

"Rob, it seems that we've come full circle. We keep coming back to the systemic change model each time—the Five-Phase A-B-C-D-E of it. The need to visualize your future and plan how to get there is about the simplest way I can describe the process."

"I'll mull this all over and give you a call, if I need a refresher on any of it," Rob responded, overwhelmed but hopeful.

"Anything else on your mind for today?"

Let's see, we covered change, got started on site stuff, and dealt with beginning planning for the criteria. Still on the agenda for next time is the meeting on new-school planning and more on developing an effective communication plan."

"I'll get my ducks in line for this."

"Oh yeah! I'm going to keep you posted on the high school hazing issue. What else do we need to mention?"

"President George H. W. Bush said on April 18, 1991, 'To those who want real improvement in America's education, I say: There will be no renaissance without revolution,'" Barry added to the mix.

"It looks like his son, the current president, is following through big time," Rob observed, referring to the newest involvement through NCLB.

"Time will tell if this dramatic change will be supported. Does the American public have the courage and will to sustain it?" Barry philosophized.

"Most of us have to try," Rob said hopefully.

"To this I would add a quote from SIA, 'Join with us in the needed change process to "learning for all" or we will hold the revolution without you.' Also, we decided to support the organizational change movement from a teaching focus to one on learning."

As they gathered up their papers after setting a date for next month, Barry had a parting word. "Rob, I want to leave you with a thought for the day. Never be afraid to try something new. Remember that a lone amateur built the ark but a large group of professionals built the *Titanic!*"

Remember that a lone amateur built the ark but a large group of professionals built the *Titanic!*

SUMMARY

This chapter encompassed the change process and related problems as challenges. However, it started out with a student crisis that the leadership was unprepared to handle effectively. The story then returned to a discussion on why we should change. The leader's role and obligation for planning and change was emphasized.

The chapter contains many models known to be helpful in preparing an organization for change. Included were some join-up activities along with the roller coaster of change and "Blanchard's Seven Pieces of Change." These were introduced to help better understand the psychological elements during a change.

The chapter concluded with a description of some notions about moving toward more delegated site-based management and implementation planning for improving the learning system guided by the well-researched leading indicators found in Effective Schools.

🕐 Time-Out—Reflections

1. In the transformation from a teaching organization to one seen as a learning organization, how should the conversation be changed in support of the focus on learning rather than teaching?
2. Who are the clients for learning—students or parents? Do you agree that it should be the learners? Why?
3. What would have to change in your school or district to "make it so" as Captain Kirk would say?
4. Describe some issues that would come up during the change process and how you would handle them.

MONTH 10—APRIL

Strategies and Survival Skills

1. Be ready to handle crisis situations by having a plan in place.
   • Be sure key staff know how it's supposed to work.
2. Don't hide from the press and do acknowledge problems.

- Do this with the caveat that student names are confidential.
- Stay away from too much detail with the press, especially when the police are involved.
- Keep parents informed as much as you can.
3. Learn all that you can about sharing the leadership role with others.
4. Trust the schools to be able to make more decisions affecting them within the guidelines established.
    - Remember, it's delegated site-based management.
5. Acknowledge the difference between participatory and coercive change as well as all that can be learned from various change theories and models.
6. Remember to start with the end in mind and keep the helicopter view handy so as not to get bogged down and side tracked from the main mission of "All students learning."
7. Always ask, "What difference will this difference make" before you start and even throughout a change cycle.

NOTE

1. ACSA Commission on Transformation Leadership, Preparing Strategic Educational Leaders for the Twenty-First Century—A Consultant Report to *Fueling the Flame.*

TOOLBOX

ACSA Commission on Transformation Leadership. Preparing Strategic Educational Leaders for the Twenty-First Century—A Consultant Report to *Fueling the Flame*, (December 1994).

Adizes, I. (1993). *Adizes Analysis of Management*, [Cassette]. Los Angeles, CA: Adizes Institute.

Beckhard, R., & Harris, R. T. (1987). *Organizational Transitions: Managing Complex Change.* Boston: Addison Wesley.

Blanchard, K. The Ken Blanchard Companies, 125 State Place, Escondido, CA 92029. www.kenblanchard.com.

Collins, J. (1958). *From Good to Great: Why Some Companies Make the Leap . . . and Others Don't.* New York: Harper-Collins.

Haines, S. (2000). *The Systems Thinking Approach to Strategic Planning and Management*. Boca Raton, FL: St. Lucie Press.

Heifetz, R., & Linsky, M. (2002). *Leadership on the Line: Staying Alive Through the Dangers of Leading*. Boston: Harvard Business School Press.

Herzberg, F. (January–February 1967). *One More Time: How Do You Motivate Employees? Harvard Business School Review*. Boston: President and Fellows of Harvard College.

Kanter, R. (1984). *The Change Masters*. New York: Simon & Schuster.

Lewin, K. (1982). Workshop notes from Situational Leadership Training. Escondido, CA: Center for Leadership Studies.

12

MAY: IS THE MISSION POSSIBLE?

"Question: Which approach is better—improving what is, or creating what isn't? Answer: Yes!"

—Ken Blanchard and Terry Waghorn

CAN AND WILL YOU TRY TO MAKE IT SO?

In this chapter you will do the following:

1. Learn how to change a flat tire while going 60 miles an hour.
2. Learn from the change experts.
3. Learn about the elements of a positive communication plan.
4. Review what to do before 60 Minutes arrives.
5. Learn how to shorten the planning time in building a new school.
6. Share some thoughts on technology issues.

THE E-MAIL

Today was the fourth of the month and Dr. Barry Woodson had just finished paying his stack of monthly bills and then entered the amounts into his software program. Surprisingly, there was even a nice ending balance. As he looked at the remaining papers on his desk, he noticed an overlooked birthday card. Opening his checkbook one more time, he wrote out a check for his oldest son, a doctor upstate, celebrating his 40th. This brought to his mind the need to make plans to go visit. With school ending next month along with his teaching duties, he would have some time before summer session started in July. He hoped everything would be going smoothly in the Paradise Valley School System by then. He wasn't even sure what his future would be in helping Rob beyond this current school year.

He had two other clients—new superintendents—to begin working into his calendar.

While continuing to straighten out the mess on his desk, he heard the familiar ping from his computer. He opened his e-mail program, noticing that he had a message from Rob Moore. As he began reading it, he thought about reports the papers carried on the high school hazing problem and how the district was handling it. It was becoming yesterday's news, but wasn't going away entirely, as three boys had been arrested on criminal assault charges and sent to juvenile hall. As expected, this rekindled interest in the incident by the press so it made the headlines again.

Dear Barry   May 4th

Barry, I'm sure you've been following the hazing issue, so let me bring you up-to-date. Things seem to be going as well as expected. The police investigated and arrested three boys who seemed to be the instigators. According to what we discovered, this happened previously during fall football with no physical penetration, only threats as part of a sick initiation prank by two of the boys. Our own investigation is completed, and in our attorney's opinion, we seem to be liable due to lack of appropriate supervision in the locker room while the athletes were dressing for practice.

Since I've made it a habit when we are in error to try and resolve issues out of court, I will work to settle the legal and damage issues soon. But we will go to the wall when we believe we're in the right. We will try to get by with paying medical only, but these days there're two chances of this happening—slim and none!

To keep the board up-to-date, we had a special meeting with our attorney to share our probable exposure. They didn't like it much more than the rest of us did. The board is insisting on better locker room supervision plans, coaches setting high expectations with each new season and team—both boys and girls—and clarification of our expectations for both high school coaching staffs, reinforced by their athletic director.

I still want to develop a crisis management plan while this issue is on our minds. I really don't think we will forget it soon!

I need to get to a meeting now. Will chat later about topics for our get-together.

Regards, Rob

Time-Out—A So What

1. As superintendent, what advice would you give the principal for next steps in the process?
2. What would you have done differently?
3. Would you discipline the staff? Explain your rationale.
4. How would you add to the corrections suggested?

ANOTHER E-MAIL INTERRUPTION

Two hours later, as Barry was in the midst of outlining an article he was writing on the school change process, the computer's ping broke his train of thought. Usually, he wouldn't let this interrupt his concentration, but he was tired and losing it. He welcomed a break. Saving his work, what there was of it, he opened the e-mail program once again. After clearing out two spam messages, he found the one from Rob. He wondered what was on the rookie's mind this time.

However, before digesting it, he paused to think about their relationship. They were approaching the anniversary date of the exciting "now I am one" phone call for help. While the year's work together had gone reasonably well, Woodson felt they were in a critical place in their relationship. Was Rob getting too dependent? As mentor, sounding board, and coach was Woodson building independent strength in his protégé? Or hand-holding him too much?

All year long he had shared good successful practices. Rob seemed to have picked up the things that are important to Paradise Valley in these circumstances. Now Woodson thought that he should move Rob to more S-3 and S-4 levels, as described in the leadership training they'd done—participating and delegating more and letting his ideas come through instead of infusing others with his expert thinking. Woodson would have to guard against his own Driving-Telling Style and only troubleshoot enough to keep Rob from major disasters. Of course, he realized each interaction had situational components to consider.

Turning to the screen, Woodson read the message.

Subject: Projects to be Completed—May

Dear Barry,

The following still need our attention:

1. I'm running into some interesting behavior on the part of the school principals for some of the new ideas we want to implement next year. What more can you tell me about implementation of change?
2. The new school planning-to-plan meeting is scheduled on the 12th. Are you going to be able to attend? The cabinet and architect will discuss shortening the planning time line.
3. Don and I will be meeting with Arlene, our communication consultant, a week from Tuesday at 2 p.m. in my conference room, to go over some do's and don'ts in managing crisis and community relations.
4. We're having a big debate about our next steps for technology. Any ideas how we can sort this all out? We recognize that we have hardware and software issues along with training and replacement factors. Your former district was nationally renowned, wasn't it? Can you help me here?

Thanks in advance, Rob

A PHONE RESPONSE

Barry decided to call Rob rather than send an e-mail reply. This would give him much better insight as to how Rob was feeling as the school year was closing down. He needed more input from Rob on how to structure this month's activities. Barry was determined that he would be taking more of a backseat, listening and getting Rob to make the decisions.

"Diane, how are you this fine spring day?" Barry warmly greeted Rob's friendly assistant.

"Pretty good. And you?" she replied, sounding a little less than enthusiastic.

"You don't sound like your usual upbeat self," Woodson suggested, seeing if he could find out if her tone of voice was an indication of something wrong.

"Well, everything is coming down as we approach the year's end. I've been on a learning curve all year and now it feels like everything is about ready to dump on me," she replied with some frustration.

"Welcome to year end in the zoo," Barry replied, trying to cheer her up. "It looks like the dark before the dawn. Right now, trying to finish out the year's activities and plan for next year doubles your work. Don't be too discouraged. Recall that earlier I mentioned that once you get through a full year, it gets somewhat easier knowing what to expect when having experienced the routines. I know you've been writing notes and processes down on issues as they occur. Keeping a daily and weekly calendar ought to show results in year two. Having both you and the superintendent new to a district is hard but has advantages as you grow together without too many systemic biases to distract you. Keep the faith."

"That's some solace, I guess. Maybe it will slow down soon," she said hopefully. "I'll put you through to him now. And thanks for understanding."

After a minute or so pause Rob came on the line. "Barry, how are you? Did you get the latest e-mail?"

"Yes. That's why I'm calling."

"What's on your mind?"

"First, I may have to miss one or two of your meetings—the one on communications and the other on the new school planning. I could have conflicts at the university. If we can find time I'll be happy to debrief with you afterward," Barry stated. He had decided to back off some now and let Rob do his thing and then chat after the meetings. The two experts that Rob was planning to use would be okay. Barry knew the work of each.

"Barry, that's too bad. I think I've got the planning meeting under control and will take you up on debriefing after," Rob said.

"Can you expand a little on two items in the e-mail—the principal behavior and technology?" Barry asked.

"In a nutshell, a couple of principals are balking on the plan to implement some of the data collection before setting priorities for next year. They say they're too busy and their staffs are already overloaded," he said, sounding somewhat disappointed.

"Rob, that's not too surprising in any change process. Remember, one size doesn't fit all! Different strokes for different folks and different strokes for the same folks! These are two important concepts I got from Ken Blanchard. I'll pull some more ideas together for you to think about," Barry offered the frustrated CEO.

"That won't hurt any," Rob responded hopefully. "On the technology issue," he continued, "I need to see a plan or something to compare the scope of my problem here. In my opinion we are way behind the curve."

"My former tech guy is a genius. I can get you something from him. It may not be till late this month or early June," he assured Rob.

"That will be a relief. There's a big chunk of the capital outlay in the budget scheduled to go to technology and it doesn't look like we have a coherent plan to use it," Rob said with strong emphasis and then added, "I'm not going to start spending it without knowing where we're going."

"As long as I have you on the phone, is anything else happening I can help with?" the mentor asked.

"Let me think a minute and get organized." Rob looked up at his notes on the whiteboard where he had outlined his thoughts for Barry later. Then he proceeded to give his mentor a quick summary. He started a long monologue covering many items.

"1. Troublesome principal resigns for other job upstate—gives me an opportunity to hire and maybe move one or two around.

2. Staff has given me a heads-up about a possible drinking problem with another principal. I'm going to call him in and get his position. I know from family experience that alcoholism and lying go hand in hand.

3. Assigning the deputy superintendent to director of purchasing. Meeting to follow up on next steps. Will be effective July 1st. Seems to be a relief as we were going too fast and furious for him to keep up and contribute. Followed your advice and reversed

the Peter Principle kindly. Probably shouldn't have promoted him beyond his level of competence.

4. Schools—some problems in change process; we will need to speak more about this.

5. Yearly evaluation scheduled. Some board members don't think we need one, but I need to cement in place along with new goals. Finalize the annual public goals process—report on progress or not? My answer is yes. Need to establish a date, remembering three board members are up for reelection, so a contract rollover might need to be postponed.

6. Negotiations are scheduled for late summer. The win-win team has been meeting regularly to iron out minor glitches informally. It's better than working the grievance process. The joint group wants to make a report on progress at the June board meeting. I agreed to try it at least once. The trust level is still suspect, but getting better. This led to the summer schedule with a facilitator training and guiding us at the same time as we work the contract issues.

7. The teachers' union agreed reluctantly that they won't try to block me from starting the rappin' sessions the way I insisted. The fight was over who selects the teachers. I'm not ready to turn this over to use the union reps. I argued that the building reps don't always represent the mainstream. Nor are they necessarily the best teachers or most respected curriculum and instructional leaders. I wanted those who would be able to speak out and represent the real issues from the schools—the issues outside the scope of bargaining.

8. I'm copying some of the staff morale building ideas you used. I've started a program to recognize teachers that are retiring, those gaining tenure at the end of the year, and support staff with 5, 10, and so forth, years in the system. Diane jumped on the idea and started to pull all the data together. We're having what we've dubbed a Tenure Tea at my house in the backyard around the pool. This will be put on by the management team starting about 4 on the last Thursday of the month. You're invited."

Barry had listened for almost 20 minutes without saying a word. However, to keep from interrupting, he busily took notes. He had many questions and thoughts. Rob had been very thorough in his summary of key events.

Finally, he asked during a pause, "I like the Tenure Tea idea. I'll try and be there. But tell me more about the rappin' sessions with teachers that you're promoting. What problems are there?"

"As I spoke with the principals they were nervous enough without having poor teachers coming from their schools to spend time rapping on issues and, of course, telling the school's secrets. After talking to Don, I decided to let the principals pick their teacher reps in any way that made them feel comfortable. It was a trust issue. I probably violated change theory, but the principals didn't really oppose too loudly after hearing my rationale. They wouldn't dare! Just joking, I hope."

"And why are you doing this? I know I mentioned it was effective for me."

"I feel it will have a positive impact for both the schools and for me— better communication. I agreed to try it once at the end of this month to set the meeting protocols for next year."

"Why?"

"Too many good teachers have been isolated and not involved. I want to hear about what is going on in the schools from their perspective or that of their colleagues. I want direct teacher input on some new ideas that I may want to try later on. During dessert, after our luncheon at the Paradise Valley Country Club, I plan to have each building rep tell the group about one good thing happening at their school. I'm paying for half-day subs out of my budget."

"Sounds like you've got it under control. Go for it!"

"I decided to invite a union rep there to monitor and keep me honest. Their fear was that I'd use my power position to go around them during contract negotiations and probably bad-mouth their leadership. I did mention that I learned of this practice earlier in my previous district, where the teachers regularly went around my superintendent directly to board members. They didn't like this, as they were still skeptical about my intentions. Fearing the worst! Of course, I know my pleasant personality and keen logic will help them see me in a sound positive leadership role. I am ready to begin 'selling' learning for all by listening first. They did accept my counteroffer to debrief after each session with their rappin' rep."

"I'd be interested in following your progress next year," Barry concluded.

"Anything else, other than what I just told you?" Rob asked.

After quickly scanning his notes again, Barry asked Rob to share his thoughts about using the principal's resignation to make some other changes. Then he mentioned a program, Smart Start, that contained some ideas on effective leadership transitions along with staff training and development. Rob agreed to put these ideas on a future agenda. He hadn't thought too much about having an induction or development program for both the outgoing and new administrators in late summer and fall.

"I really like the way you are handling the deputy issue. Giving folks an out is reassuring. It helps to maintain self-esteem."

"I forgot to mention," Rob interrupted, "I'm letting him keep his current salary level for 6 months. I'm just a softy, I guess. The trade-off was that officially he requested the new assignment."

"Let me reinforce the importance of follow-through on the evaluation process, especially with the split board. There's a good personnel person at the county Department of Education that does this type of stuff to help school boards. I've done it also. I wouldn't suggest that I be involved because the board knows my role as your mentor and counselor. We need to keep the role of mentor and board facilitator separate from each other."

As they ended the phone conversation, Rob assured Barry that he would send him the agenda items he wanted to cover when they next met in 2 weeks.

THE NEXT MEETING AGENDA

Rob sent along the following, "Reminders for May Meetings." He added that this was rough, since they didn't stick to the agenda much anyway once they got together.

1. School planning process. Will give you a debriefing about our meeting.

2. Scheduled meeting with Arlene, the communication expert. If you can't make this one, I'll give an update.

3. Meeting with principals—I will find out what help they need for implementation of the PSU plan now beginning to take shape as well as new budget standards. An issue is what to do with carryover budget funds. Do we take the excess back or allow them to keep some or all for the next year's budget? How do we monitor balanced spending to meet school-defined as well as overall board goals? Or should we?

4. There is more than a little anxiety about pushing meaningful site plans for real change in measuring the leading indicators of learning as defined in the criteria. The principals and teachers are growing more unsure of what we are trying to do.

5. I've been asked to join "the" service club. Tell me what you did. What are the issues? I've spoken to about 10 or so groups since Christmas. Now the 2 most influential want me to join. Help?

6. What do I need to know about technology? What's out there that I should know about? You said you would work on this. May have to delay a month.

⏱ Time-Out—A So What

1. What suggestions do you have for getting the reluctant principals on board?
2. How would you counter their argument that everyone is too busy?
3. Any alternatives available? Explain.
4. What would you recommend on the school budget carryover issue? Let them keep it all, some, or none? Why and how?
5. What advice do you have on joining service clubs? How would you resolve the superintendent's apparent dilemma?

MORE THOUGHTS ON RESISTANCE TO AND MANAGING CHANGE

Barry thought he was reading some insecurity on Rob's part regarding his understanding of change. Wondering how to reduce this tension, he decided to mention some other ideas to help clarify. Probably, at the next meeting, he needed to guide Rob through one of his real problem situations modeling a logical thought process.

Barry recalled that about 10 years ago he had become intrigued with an interesting article Phil Schlechty penned about change dynamics. Barry thought he should go over this with Rob. He remembered his own cabinet pondering some snags in the restructuring process that characterized that decade. Mentally he noted that the only consistent thing now is that not much changes but change itself.

In those days, superintendent Woodson had just come back from visiting schools to help him get a better feel of the schools' attitudes about change that had been developing. The cabinet needed to stay involved, so he added "change" to the next week's agenda.

At this meeting, he revisited some information many in the group had heard before. It would be a good review. Often ideas and program elements gather rust when not used. Reintroducing them at appropriate times acted as a good reinforcement for adult learning.

Schlechty thinks restructuring requirements contain the need to be willing to go beyond hard data and without guidance from empirical research, Barry remembered. While this point of view was in vogue 10 years ago, times have changed somewhat; research is now available, so we have success models to help in embracing new thinking in the quest to meet federal pressure.

There is no wonder, he thought, change was nearly impossible these days. Too many uncontrollable changes in the air: new boards, superintendents, mandates, and new flavors of the month for quick fixes every time you turn around. Even after getting an infusion of new bucks earmarked for so-called failing schools, many were falling further behind. Organizational change, even in the best of families, is tough, let alone in those schools that have historically scored well below average in performance. These schools have so much to overcome, but there are living examples of success. Leadership, a systemic plan, and commitment seem to be the ingredients that work.

"Driving into the future with our eyes firmly fixed on the rear view mirror."

—Marshal McClune

Ending his reflection, Barry started to put together the material he needed for the meeting. Finishing a little early, he decided to make a dash for home, hoping to beat the rush hour traffic.

BACK IN THE DISTRICT

The Meeting

With the agenda in front of them the two were deep in thought. Finally, the mentor said, "Shall we deal with the site budget question first—the one on carryover? In my opinion there needs to be a balance between proper spending of resources and site autonomy. I would suggest that you set a dollar equivalent amount based on size to allow for carry forward to the next year's school budget. For example, each high school could have a limit of 1 1/2 PSUs, or about $110,000, to use later. In my experience, if you don't allow any carryover, the schools will spend every penny. Carryovers will allow them to double up their funds for a bigger project than they would be able to complete in just one year. A big technology project, for example.

"Barry, I'll discuss this with cabinet. I like it!"

"The personnel changes seem to be going well. I like what you're doing. Didn't know you were humane!" the professor teased.

"What did you bring to add to my wisdom on change? I'm concerned that the schools are fragmented. Some are moving forward and some dragging their feet. What's happening?" Rob asked, looking to his experienced mentor for help.

"I believe it's called change. Probably not everyone is ready for the new guy to move them where they may not want to go. You may want to rethink how you're pushing the envelope. What options exist for slowing down and rebuilding more solid agreement and trust?" the coach asked.

"I was hoping to get all 12 schools moving on this together, but it doesn't look like it's going that way," Rob reflected. "Maybe I should take victory out of the jaws of defeat and ask the few recalcitrant schools to come up with an alternative. I want to make darn sure they know they're going on the journey and their only option is when they begin. They need to know that neither I nor this mission is going away. Probably reteaching and reselling are in order. The ones lagging are some of our lowest performers. The worst case is that some school leaders will get on board later than sooner."

"What happens if some don't come on board?" Barry asked, pushing Rob some more.

"I guess there may have to be some leadership changes," he concluded, "me or them!"

Changing the subject slightly he asked what his mentor brought to the table to add to this complex issue.

"When the pace of change outside an organization is more rapid than the pace of change inside the organization, the future of the organization is at risk."

—Phil Schlechty

"Let me share an observation. 'When the pace of change outside an organization is more rapid than the pace of change inside the organization, the future of the organization is at risk,'" Barry said, quoting Phil Schlechty. "This is what's been happening for a few years and is now picking up steam with NCLB in the picture. Schlechty has written an article on what to expect from the people involved in any change process. I think it's worthy of adding to your plethora of information, at least now for awareness and possible use later. Remember it's you, the CEO, who needs to assimilate and integrate this into your organization's leadership culture. Pick an approach and make it yours."

Barry jumped right in and told the story about discovering Schlechty's concepts, before he handed Rob an article on point.

Barry started down memory lane. He was reminded that Phil had met with some of the benchmarking consortium superintendents a few years ago when the district hosted a quarterly meeting. Schlechty asked four questions and then provided ways of implementing change with five stereotype groups. Much of his questioning line was parallel to the systems thinking model, but it came at the issue from a slightly different angle.

1. What is the new circumstance or system that we are trying to create?
2. Can it be done?
3. Should we do it?
4. How do we do it?

For responses, each of the questions required different lessons-taught and follow-up staff development approaches. He suggested that the first situation requires concept development, the next a demonstration of previous successes, the third a values mission clarification process, and finally, the development of needed skills.

Using a metaphor of westward movement exploration, he then went on to describe the five types of roles encountered in a group or in the individual change process. The first, the trailblazers, will go where no one has gone before. They are first to volunteer to travel with Captain Kirk on the *Enterprise*. With a clear guiding vision, they are ready to go. In supporting them, they need to be recognized and have much personal and personalized support.

Next is the pioneer group, which is closely allied with the trailblazers. They need more assurance that the trip is worthwhile. They need stories and metaphors about success. They look to the trailblazer for some inspiration, but also need administrative support from the rear.

Settlers, the next to buy into the need for change, need more concrete support that parallels what is expected of them and where they're headed. Barry mentioned that this aligns well with social styles of communication. The expressives are out front and then come the drivers. The settler-analytic needs more data and assurance. Often these types need skill development training to build confidence that they can do the task. As an example, he thought about the need for teacher training on how to use data to inform instruction.

The stay-at-homes are the next group. They need a compelling reason to begin the change trip. If they feel that the present situation is so bad that anything looks better, they might begin. These possible amiables need security and to feel part of the main group. They don't like making waves. Their other motivation may well be that they begin to buy into a new and compelling vision.

Barry recalled that after they had developed a critical mass for the focus on student learning, this group began to come on board. He prodded them with guilt. How could it be that they couldn't support learning for all? Schlechty offers that he was most successful in a restructuring process by using benign neglect coupled with as much generosity as possible with them.

Are saboteurs critics or cynics? At one time did they venture out and get burned? They are somewhat loners, actively committed to stopping change. They don't want to go on another trip and don't want others to go. Some may best be handled by bringing them inside the tent early on and listening to their objections. Some are old timers, Barry reflected, that had seen too many start-ups and failures. Constant change in leadership and direction every year or so turned them into cynics. Those who have lived through failed innovation after failed innovation can be found in this group.

"You might as well add this to my file. At least it sounds like good reference stuff," Rob added with a sense of overwhelming resignation.

🕐 Time-Out—A So What

1. What does Schlechty's work mean to you?
2. How would you categorize yourself most of the time?
3. Can you identify anyone who you see as a saboteur? Describe this person's behavior.
4. Think about a recent change process you have led. Which of these five types can you identify in that situation?
5. What role did you play?
6. What advice do you have for the superintendent now?
7. How should he approach each school?

"Just maybe you and your cabinet might take another look at your principals through this lens and see if it makes sense," Barry suggested.

Even today it still made sense to the mentor as he observed the human scene of both coerced and participatory change in organizations. People don't change much over time, he thought somewhat whimsically.

GETTING FOLKS ON BOARD

Later, after sitting in on the communication strategy meeting, Rob asked if his mentor could take a few minutes to chat about setting up a better way to approach moving ahead on improving student performance in the schools. Rob mentioned to Woodson that he had decided to move forward on a broken front, something he remembered his mentor as doing. The issue was settled! Each school was going to work on this project! However, Rob had extended the time line for four schools. They needed more time to come on board.

"What's the problem?" Woodson asked cautiously.

"I need to review a model in place to get ahead of the learning curve—need to stay one day ahead of the students—rather, principals," Rob admitted a little hesitantly.

"Don't feel bad," Barry replied, "there's no need. Rather, let's look at the Lezotte stuff, *Assembly Required*, again and see what we can get out of it that might work."

"Sounds good. I have a few copies here. What should I look for?" Rob asked.

"Rob, let's go back to the beginning. We need to review his game plan. What are the essentials to sustainable school reform shown in chapter 1, 'The Essential Attributes'?"

"Let's see—he says that the effective model should have these six attributes. I'm going to list them on the board."

1. Focuses on results
2. Simultaneously considers quality and equity
3. Data-driven
4. Research-based
5. Collaborative in form
6. Ongoing and self-renewing

After they skimmed through the chapter, Barry asked, "Where do you need to start with your reluctant schools?"

"Now, I'm not sure they are convinced that I meant what I said about results. I'm going to ask Susan and Larry to get their school's disaggregated test data and start from there. They need to see that there is a problem at their schools. Maybe get the high schools to look at their real dropout rates by various groups."

"Are you convinced they understand the theories that underlie this methodology?" Barry questioned.

"Not sure! But we went through this for 2 hours in the orientation meeting," Rob replied quickly.

"I guess they were all enthralled, took copious notes, and gave you a standing 'O' when you finished laying it on them?" the mentor stated with a touch of sarcasm.

Ignoring the tone, Rob replied more seriously, "Of course not! I see that reteaching is in order. The two school directors are going to do the refreshment course this week," he stated with a solution seemingly in hand. "This should solidify their own thinking by teaching."

"Brilliant! Let's look at Lezotte's key concepts again before you rush off," Barry suggested (see Figure 12.1).

"This outline gives you a flavor of what he's developed. Go back again and reread his book if you need to keep one step ahead."

"Are there others in the field that could complement Lezotte's work?" Rob asked.

Woodson reached in his briefcase and took out a book. "Let me give you this copy of Richard Axelrod's book," Barry said, handing him a copy of *Terms of Engagement* he had recently reviewed. "There are

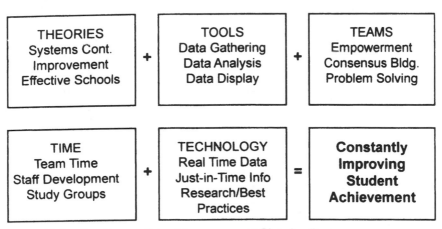

Figure 12.1. Continuous School Improvement Planning Program.
Source: Lezotte and McKee, 2002.

some good ideas for you in working with the schools." He then added that he had used this in class. According to the author the key points to success were accomplished by:

1. Widening the circle of involvement
2. Connecting people to each other
3. Creating communities for action
4. Emphasizing democracy and diversity of viewpoints.

"I'm sure these ideas are good and fit in with what I've been thinking for months. But I need to go back to taking small steps. I want to troubleshoot more on what's going wrong and why. I'll review the steps in moving toward schools becoming more effective, taking it one step at a time. I'll need them to make sure each school starts in a place where they can be successful," Rob said with sudden insight.

"I think you got it! What did you learn from the backwards thinking model that should shape the process here?"

"Of course, begin with the end in mind."

"Try showing the 'fall behinds' again how this process works and their expected role in solving this particular need," Barry suggested with strong emphasis.

"It means more late hours!" Rob said with a sigh. "It looks like widening the circle of involvement as Axelrod suggests and Lezotte emphasizes."

"Lezotte's engagement model reflects similar ideas, but is more focused. It still looks like you need more on building supportive relationships."

"Set formulas don't work—committed focus on mission does."

—Larry Lezotte

 Time-Out—A So What

1. Review Lezotte's key concepts. What do you think? Will it work?
2. In your school system, which data would be important to have to measure student achievement?

3. How would you get just-in-time student test data to help teachers do a better job?
4. How would you suggest that the two models can be integrated?
5. Compare and contrast this with Schlechty's work in the last section.
6. What advice would you now give the superintendent to get his principals on board?
7. What are some of the problems with integrating this with Situational Leadership?
8. Go back and reference the earlier chapters on Social Styles and Situational Leadership. How would you try to integrate these three programs?
9. What usable sense can you make of this in your own setting?
10. What grabs you as most usable?

"Thanks for this new data and thanks for the printouts. I'll be able to digest it later," Rob volunteered.

"Is there part of this that you see as helpful?" Barry questioned.

"I mentioned that a couple of leadership types aren't on board. The initial steps for identifying the needed data and measurements to ensure learning for all seem to have escaped their radar," Rob responded dejectedly. "I'm going to follow through using the directors as I mentioned."

"Your homework, if you choose to do some, is to select the most troublesome principal and put him or her through the four questions proposed by Phil regarding understanding and accepting this mandate. By integrating Social Styles, Situational Leadership, and Schlechty's work, you have good information to develop an action plan to work through," Barry suggested.

"What about my service club dilemma? What should I do?"

"What do you want to do?"

"Okay. Okay. Barry, I guess I need to put my thinking cap on. Again!"

"I'm not sure what your problem is," Barry said.

"Let's see. I visited and have spoken to most of them already this year. Two seem to be the most influential, with the most business leaders."

"Uh-huh—do go on."

"But do I really want to be tied down to one club along with the weekly lunch or breakfast meeting? Can I give enough time to the events and fund-raisers they do?"

Barry interrupted. "What is your main mission and will this add to or detract from it?"

"Probably detract now. But if I don't join I'll lose the opportunity to rub elbows informally and enhance good public relations, won't I?"

"Can you see a way to meet both objectives?"

"I'm not sure what you mean?" Rob asked, somewhat perplexed.

"I hear you say you don't have time now to commit 100% to their expectations. You want to maintain or create an opportunity for dialogue to promote the district and your ideas. Right?"

"Well, yes."

"Is there a third alternative?"

"What are you thinking?"

"Start your own lunches with the superintendent—maybe every couple of months. Invite key community and business leaders on a rotational basis. Talk about schools and listen. Encourage them to keep inviting you to speak to their organizations once a year. If your cabinet members and principals are so inclined have them join various groups so that the system can be represented. It's good experience for them anyway," Barry suggested.

"I like this thinking. I'll give it some more thought. Thanks."

They decided to call it a day after reviewing what had to be done by month's end.

STRATEGIC COMMUNICATION PLAN

Earlier in the afternoon, Dr. Woodson had joined the Paradise Valley cabinet for a training and exploration session focused on reviewing the year's experiences with the press and other public relations issues. One of his department meetings got rescheduled because the dean had to go out of town.

Rob was interested in what his mentor thought of this session.

"What did you think?" he asked Barry Woodson.

"Tell me what you liked. I've heard her present before," Barry said, as he was trying to get the superintendent to declare first.

"Overall, I liked it. I want to use her again," he responded thoughtfully. The "her" in this case was Arlene Hogan, communication consultant. "The need to have a plan in place made lots of sense. It's better than the locking-the-barn-door-after-it's-too-late, a process we just experienced. Why didn't I see this as important and urgent earlier in the year, I keep asking myself."

"You can't do everything at once," Woodson countered and added, "Something will happen again you won't be 100% ready for. That's why you need to be guided by your core values, the way you want to run this enterprise."

Arlene had gone through several steps in the planning process in working with the cabinet. They all thought it looked good. They needed to now find a staff person to help coordinate the work Arlene was to do with the district when Rob got her consultant contract approved by the board.

"I like starting with some suggested goals," Rob opened the conversation. "I'm getting used to creating the end game focus."

"Let me think about all this material and I'll get back to you later," Barry declared.

A REVIEW OF THE COMMUNICATION PLAN IDEAS

Barry Woodson was back in his office reviewing the notes and materials from the communication meeting. He assured Rob that he would review them and soon get back to the superintendent. The mentor didn't want to intervene on this. At first blush he liked what he saw. Rob would be encouraged to work this out for himself, or rather they would for themselves.

Starting at the beginning, he looked over the goals suggested. Arlene had started with the desired outcomes first.

Proposed Goals

1. To enhance the operating relationship among the school district, the school board, and the district's constituencies.

2. To define the roles and relationships that each partner within the school community plays. (Is the school board acting on behalf of the community, i.e., students, parents, etc., or should direct relationships be forged with these groups?)
3. To increase support for the district's mission and core values; enhance understanding of schools' accomplishment.
4. To accelerate the accomplishment of the district's goals—"All students learning"—by gaining support from parents, the school board, students, and community groups.
5. To achieve recognition by the media—newspapers, magazines, and television—for the excellence achieved and to use that recognition to build even stronger ties to the district's partners.
6. To mobilize the community and all its members to fight for increased school budgets owing to solid accomplishments.
7. To effectively manage crises using a well-conceived plan.

Objectives

The objectives of the program are designed to link the program strategy with the mission and core values. What we are suggesting is not new. What you are trying to do is to get ordinary people to work together in extraordinary ways.

Internal communications must be completely supported by the district's top management. Messages must be consistent and clear and should tie directly to the organization's strategy and critical success factors.

Specific objectives include the following:

1. To ensure that all employees become committed to the rebuilding and cultural change process.
2. To enhance the understanding of each person's role and signal rewards for those who operate in strategically new ways.
3. To communicate the values of working for the district.
4. To facilitate the flow of information and to reinforce progress through reiteration of the shared vision and values that will drive strategic success.

5. To build employees' sense of collective and individual responsibility for the district's future success.

6. To empower employees to participate in mapping and executing the change process so that they understand that their contributions are welcomed and recognized.

7. To ensure that the crisis management and media plan is understood by all the administration team.

The list seemed to be okay, he thought. Still, Rob needed to get someone in place who could work with Arlene and be trained to make the process work. He knew there was a lot more to it and it would take time.

 Time-Out—A So What

1. What did you like about the work done on the plan?
2. What new ideas were presented for you?
3. Are there key steps missing? Explain.
4. Would you be ready when *60 Minutes* arrives and asks to speak to you? How do you know?

THE NEW SCHOOL PLANNING MEETING

Just one week after the communication presentation, Rob Moore, Don Halverson, and Douglas Daniels, the business manager, were huddled together to consider a time-saving practice to plan for the new elementary school. They were 6 months behind due to change in leadership and the board election uncertainty. Douglas had been gathering data as he had had some experience in building new schools. In January he got the board's approval to proceed with the first step of hiring an architect and now they were considering a plan the architect, Jon Carpenter, was recommending. Jon would be joining them at any moment.

Jon had used this concept, essentially a 48-hour planning process, in an adjacent district. It saved several months from the traditional process most districts and their architects went through to get wide-based input.

The notion was to clearly establish the philosophy—the function. Kind of what the staff and community expected for their new school. The process centered on form following function.

Form should follow function.

Also, it eased the student relocation problem, as the new-school boundary issues were supposed to be settled at the same time. If not, at least it created acceptance and raised expectations.

After sharing his plans with the board, the superintendent was going to transfer a strong, deserving principal to the new school. She would be given an entire year to plan for the opening. This left two principal vacancies for the district. Don Halverson was starting the recruitment process.

When Jon arrived they got down to business. The architect outlined his proposal.

The plan starts with a presession dinner to train table chairs meeting with a group, which is the role a principal will play. The next day starts with the usual orientation of the group. Jon handed out the sample agenda to be used.

HORIZON VIEW ELEMENTARY—DESIGN SYMPOSIUM

Agenda—Day 1

8:00   Continental Breakfast
8:15   Welcome and Introductions—Design Symposium Goals
8:30   Succeeding in the 21st Century
9:00   Horizon View Elementary—Mission and Vision
9:15   Paradise Valley Historic District Mission and Goals
9:30   Brainstorming Session 1: "Vision for Learning"
        Forces at Work, Program Characteristics, Community
        Connections

10:15   Report Ideas and Concepts
11:00   Site Introduction and Tour
12:30   Lunch
12:45   District Goals and Strategic Initiatives
1:00   Brainstorming Session 2: Ideas and Concepts
        Planning Limitations, Design Opportunities, Facility
        Characteristics, Uniqueness
2:30   Report Ideas & Concepts
3:30   Summary of Brainstorming Sessions & Review of Next Steps
3:45   Closing Remarks, Distribute Comment Sheets
4:00   Conclusion of Planning Task Force Activities for Day One
6:00   Dinner—Design Session Snowcarding, Project Parameters,
        Design Concepts
8:00   Design Session: Conceptual Planning

Agenda—Day 2

8:00   Design Session: Conceptual Planning (continued)
3:00   Planning Task Force Reconvenes—Welcoming Remarks
3:05   Introduction of Design Process
3:15   Design Presentations
4:00   Discuss, Critique, and Identify Priorities
5:30   Discuss Next Steps in Planning Process
5:45   Adjourn

The ultimate objective was to select one of the three designs that were developed late at night on day 1. After processing on day 2, the architects get the go-ahead to finalize the design working with the design committee. Most of the functional activities were agreed upon, so now the first cut of the form had taken shape. The technical design would now move forward.

MISSION POSSIBLE

"Thanks for sharing the new school planning proposal with me. It really looks good!" Barry said in a very complimentary tone of voice. "Any follow-up issues we need to discuss?"

"It's a more generic problem rather than a one-school building project. For example, we will start planning for our third high school next year. It won't open for 3 years at the earliest. If we decide we want to incorporate what we know about effective learning and better school organization, how can we do it with existing staff? It's built-in overload," Rob stated the obvious.

"Several years ago, I ran into one of Blanchard's books, coauthored by Terry Waghorn. I'll get you the particulars as you may want to order some for your planning team. It's called *Mission Possible*. It's one partial answer to the question, 'How do you change a flat tire while going 60 miles an hour?'"

How do you change a flat tire while going 60 miles an hour?

"Sounds impossible! I remember you mentioning it in class. Give me a brief—I mean brief—outline!" he added with a point to make as they had a long agenda.

"Basically, they suggest that each staff member is part of either of two teams, the P team or the F team. The former works in the present on continuous improvement, short-term issues, while the latter looks at the future and real possible systemic change to meet the future changes in the environment or marketplace. They define the future as a period between 18 months and 5 years from now. This means the P team time zone is from now to 18 months.

"The members of the P team are more interested in improving the present rather than moving into the unsure future. More like long-range planners than strategic.

"They can start with thinking about their customers—students and parents—and their needs now. While we don't have much competition for our services now, it's growing, and the team needs to think about this. In dealing with questions, the team is encouraged to ask, 'If our present customers were to redesign our schools for us today, what would they turn us into?' At this point we can apply our systems thinking model to this effort. Do the vision piece and work backwards.

"The F team has the same three areas to ask questions of themselves. This time, the thinking gets strategic in nature, such as 'What strategic capabilities must we build to ensure survival or, better yet, market domination? How will we build them?' I know of one district whose children are being attracted to a neighboring one, causing them to lose revenue and enrollment, forcing a reduction in their teaching staff by undesirable layoffs each year. We're helping them to frame several issues using this thought process."

"This sounds intriguing! What about staffing the teams? You know they're going to ask about time and resources," Rob interjected.

"That's true enough. I can tell you how it was done in one district. This district had money for a consultant to work with them for 4 years. This was changing two high schools into one new one caused by declining enrollment. Basically, they worked in teams after school to accomplish this."

"It's tough to make predictions, especially about the future."

—Yogi Berra

Barry then talked about a different circumstance. He explained that another case centered on a new design for a high school based on best practices. It was designed around the form follows function notion. The delivery system needed systemic overhaul. The principal was selected and released full time to head the project. He was allowed to pick about 10 staff members for his F team. They were to meet on their own time but were given time to visit around the country to develop the best program they could create.

The second year, several more staff members were selected as part of the core group and the work continued. Then, the year prior to opening, they really went to work on implementing what they had decided was the best of the best. It's still working even though the staff has about doubled trying to keep up with the increased enrollment. They decided to open with only 9th and 10th graders, so the enrollment increase had to be part of the planning. It's easier to start a new change but harder to maintain over time.

Stephen Haines asks a provocative question on point in describing the difficulty of transition management. There are two tasks—one to manage the day-to-day operations and the other managing the transition process. Under stress and a heavy workload, he asks, which management activity loses out?

 Time-Out—A So What

1. Which loses out? Why?
2. Have you been part of a tire change, going full speed? How did you feel?
3. If someone told you it was important, would you take on a voluntary second workload, an F team role?
4. What would it take to motivate you to do so? What insight does this give you for motivating others?
5. How would you attempt to identify the future as an F team member in today's high expectation environment for school achievement?

Both Rob and Barry had much to think about. Rob was wondering why he kept asking his mentor for all this advice. But then he remembered that Woodson warned him that not all they had talked about was for instant reform. File it until needed, but don't forget it, he had cautioned Rob.

Barry noted that it had been a busy month. The school year was drawing smoothly to a close, but the issues that needed attention, Rob had discovered, would take years to fully address. Rob needed to get the right people and the planning in place to effectively and efficiently get the work done. The bottom line was an increase in student learning.

SUMMARY

May was a very busy month for the Paradise Valley School District. Items were postponed or flagged as needing attention before the summer break. The discussion started with a follow-up to the hazing crisis.

Then the superintendent created an agenda of items to be covered. Discussion ensued on personnel issues and how to work more effectively with teachers. Change was an issue, especially trying to move all the schools forward at the same time. But it just wasn't going to work out this way. Make haste slowly became good advice. A new strategy and plan were developed.

The superintendent was challenged to best use his time and resources over the issue of service club membership.

The work with resistive types chronicled by Schlechty and Block were presented in depth. A communication and media and crisis plan was introduced. The final sections contained a new-school-building planning process developed to shorten the time line. The final question, the chapter's title, Is the mission possible? was discussed using the work of Ken Blanchard on this topic. It was noted that this planning process has been used successfully.

🕐 Time-Out—Reflections

1. What are the key ideas you will do something about that you learned from the preceding discussions?
2. Which topics will be most helpful in the near term? The long term?
3. Identify a situation at your school or district and develop an improvement plan using some of the preceding concepts above.
4. Do you really understand organizational change? Explain.
5. What elements must we know about organizational change to find our own meaning to bring it to classroom level?

MONTH 11—MAY

Strategies and Survival Skills

1. Be sure to have a media and crisis plan in place before it's needed.
   - Identify all the key players that need to be informed.
   - Run a simulation as a practice exercise.
2. Know how to encourage strategic change and sustained short-term change at the same time.

- Learn as much as you can about the resistance to change by various types of folks.
3. Understand ways to get the troops on board.
   - Use the ways to build and sustain trust leading to achieving your vision.
   - Consider ways to reward staff.
   - Look at the means for working more effectively with teachers and their union reps.
4. Keep current on site-building strategies.
5. Don't be shy about reversing the Peter Principle.
6. Clearly understand your main mission and use your time to the best advantage.

TOOLBOX

Ackoff, R. (1981). *Creating the Corporate Future: Plan or Be Planned For.* New York: Wiley.

Axelrod, R. (2000). *Terms of Engagement: Changing the Way We Change Organizations.* San Francisco: Berrett-Koehler Publishers.

Baker, J. (1998). *Elementary School Design Symposium Workshop.* NTD Architects, 4719 Viewridge Ave. Suite 200, San Diego, CA 92123.

Blanchard, K., & Waghorn, T. (1997). *Mission Possible: Becoming a World-Class Organization While There's Still Time.* New York: McGraw-Hill.

Haag, E. (2004). Unpublished Presentation Notes. Haag & Associates. 19811 Fourth Place, Escondido, CA. 92029.

Haines, S. *Enterprise-Wide Change—Participant Notebook: Chapter IV. Smart Start.* The Centre for Strategic Management. San Diego, CA. www.cs-mintl.com.

Lezotte, L., & McKee, K. (2002) *Assembly Required: A Continuous School Improvement System.* Okemos, MI: Effective Schools Products, Ltd. www.effectiveschools.com.

Schlechty, P. (1993). "On the Frontier of School Reform with Trailblazers, Pioneers and Settlers." *Journal of Staff Development* 14(4), 46–51.

13

JUNE: THANK GOODNESS IT'S NEARLY OVER. WILL I SURVIVE?

WHAT NEEDS TO BE IN PLACE FOR NEXT YEAR IF WE ARE TO BECOME A DYNAMIC LEARNING ORGANIZATION? ANSWER: PLANNING, PERSISTENCE, AND PATIENCE

In this chapter you will do the following:

1. Discover more about a learning organization.
2. Find more ideas about staff development.
3. Review a technology plan.
4. Find out more about employee transition planning.
5. Look at creating the corporate future.

WOODSON AT HOME

The early morning sun, breaking over the back wall, caught Dr. Barry Woodson in the face as he sat at his computer staring out the window. Opening the sliding glass door to his sunroom, he went outside and rolled down the sunshade. He was not a morning person and usually didn't start writing this early, but his publisher was wondering if he'd dropped off the face of the earth.

It's going to be another great day, he thought to himself. Here I am trying to write and it looks like a golf day. Maybe I should go to the club and join the guys.

However, his conscience got the better of him and he returned to writing. Just 10 good pages a day was his goal, but he was almost a month behind schedule. Well, he rationalized, he could always write his book later. Publish or perish didn't bother him in his semiretired state anyway. Teaching, consulting, and working with the Paradise Valley School District changed his priorities this past year. Being this busy wasn't what he had in mind when he retired.

Here it is the first week in June and the school year is almost over. Barry was debating with himself on whether he should continue working with the Paradise Valley CEO. He decided they needed to address their relationship soon. Things were going well between them and he thought the school board was appreciative of his work with the first-year superintendent. Oh well! He'd just have to wait and not push it.

As he looked back, he decided that it was well worth it. Dr. Robert Moore, first-year rookie district superintendent, had done a good job. He hoped the board agreed with the mentor. He knew Rob's first annual performance evaluation was scheduled for next week and the extension of his contract was on the table. Rob was going to follow the same format as he did in his semiannual.

Woodson tried returning to his writing, but he couldn't get started as his mind kept wandering back to the unfinished district issues. The two of them hadn't even reached closure on the transition plan for the two new principals Rob was in the process of hiring. He needed to pull out the stuff he picked up from Steve Haines on Starting Smart, a transition process for moving into a new position.

In anticipation of an e-mail or call from Rob, he was preparing two papers for Rob to review—one on staff development and the other about his own experiences building a hi-tech school district.

In looking through his papers Woodson found a piece he had done earlier for a management staff development program. He would suggest that Rob read it before they shared it at the preplanning meeting for the cabinet workshop he'd been asked to lead in July. To date there was no further commitment by the district for future work.

To keep the topics separate he decided to send the material in two parts. First, he would address the staff development piece with some of Senge's ideas on a learning organization at the end.

He prepared an e-mail and an attachment for the superintendent.

Subject: Staff Development

Dear Rob,

While most private not-for-profit organizations claim they are people-centered organizations, stating that the people are the most important part of their success, it doesn't always seem this is the motive driving them. The not-for-profit service organizations, which don't manufacture anything or produce tangible products, can be seen as more people intensive. This doesn't mean they're people or customer focused either. However, more recently it seems to be that the strategic focus is seen more on the customer and meeting those needs in the fast-paced private sector.

Even in those areas where private enterprise is competing with government services, the focus on the customer is paramount. We've seen this at Federal Express when they started competing with the U.S. Postal Service and UPS. But what is the lesson to be learned for school systems?

We don't manufacture but rather hope that we can create a people-centered learning organization from top to bottom for our clients—students, parents, and staff. We want to maximize the learning process for our students. This means a commitment to make it happen and with this commitment to a staff development effort that we hope will change the culture forevermore.

As we keep the main thing the main thing then, all our efforts should be focused on the mission of "All students learning—whatever it takes." This, of course, means that the burden is on the CEO/superintendent working with the school board to advocate for a program that allows each member of the organization to grow and develop.

In a people business, as in any business, the training and development of staff is critical to success. While we aren't outsourcing too much of our services, there is competition out in the real world. So how do we compete with charters, Internet schools, and the scores of other alternatives now available to parents and students?

The answer is relatively simple. Provide a better product. See the customer in a new light. Learning is no longer optional. Sell the message and walk the talk. And, of course, talk the walk—sell. Can the current failing schools identified through NCLB make a positive difference in the future? Yes, but it requires a commitment to staff development.

The old approach must change to make the change happen. No longer can staff development be optional, self-choosing, and not aligned with the

central purpose of the organization. Assuming that there is enough commitment in the system and willingness on the part of the superintendent and
school board, improvement can be made and desired results obtained.

The first step is to know what the end in mind looks like. What do you
want people to know and be able to do? Sound familiar?

Now look at the following information for some ideas on how this might
be done.

THE PROFESSIONAL TEACHING STAFF

Some private-sector specialists suggest that an organization invest 5–6% of
their operational budget in staff development and training. Do we do so in
public education? Hardly! While we invest in conferences, training, workshops, in-service training, etc., the amount is probably in the 1–2% range.
We can't afford it? Can we afford not to invest? In my former district as we
became an accidental learning powerhouse, we didn't know that what we
did and were doing was the right thing. It was just commonsensically organized. It was simple: if teachers wanted to learn real stuff, not just complete
college units and nonrelative stuff for credentials and degrees, how could
we cause this to happen? We made it a priority of sorts. First, we decided
we needed to do more skill building. Not all teachers had learned how to
teach in college! So we started there. We saw that our early efforts were
making a difference, a difference in teacher attitude. This was among those
easy to persuade anyway. This began a 20-year odyssey that made a big
difference both in individuals and collectively in the organization.

The various programs were so successful that adult learning became part
of the culture. Teachers expected and, for the most part, got professional
training both in and outside the district. For example, during a stressful labor
contract year the union led a teacher boycott of all evening training at a local
hotel. Our mentor teachers had asked for a three-part series on presentation skills, which was part of their assignment. Out of 30 original sign-ups we
had only 20 show up the first night. It was such a great success that the next
two sessions had all 30 teachers attend in spite of the boycott. It was a
word-of-mouth endorsement by professionals. They would deal with negotiation support in another manner. Their personal development and organizational commitment as a mentor teacher was a higher priority.

In thinking through this topic, concerted effort must be made to do the following:

1. Understand what is needed in the system.
2. Develop meaningful and helpful training programs to get there.
3. Make it easy to attend along with some optional time.
4. Follow up and support the implementation of the training.
5. Retrain as necessary, remembering each year there are new people in the organization.
6. Train a cadre of trainers in-house.
7. Establish a trainer-of-trainer program for larger-scale and continuing programs to develop in-house expertise.
8. Send those with expertise to present at conferences, academic association meetings, and area workshops.
9. Remember Herzberg's work—work on those motivators.

MANAGEMENT TRAINING AND DEVELOPMENT

The superintendent should be a role model in this effort. It's a reflection of what the chief sees as important. Does the boss show up and stay through training sessions? Is he or she part of the program? Does the management staff go to training sessions off site together?

Continuous improvement requires the leadership to keep one page ahead of the staff. Well-trained and committed administrators make a big difference.

Where do you find the time to train? Find it! Evenings, after school, workshops during the workweek, and even weekends all have been successful. Be careful! Decide what knowledge and skill the system needs in a priority order. Remember different strokes! Not all have the same gaps in knowledge and skills. Differentiate.

Be sure there is a new management orientation plan. Begin before school starts and continue throughout the year. It's a heavy load for rookies but is essential in transmitting the culture and catching up the new folks to the skills you have identified as needed in your district.

Use administrators, including you, the superintendent, as trainers. This is another example of modeling the talk. Trainers often learn more than the participants.

Have some sessions open to all. Do cross-level and cross-function training where appropriate.

While these ideas are centered on management, these principles apply at all levels in the organization.

THE NEGLECTED CLASSIFIED SUPPORT STAFF

Try mixing in Social Style, Situational Leadership, and a few special self-help events apart from skill and job training for support staff. Don't leave them out. Honor their work and their need to be part of the organization. What is the role of the supervisor in training staff? Send staff to state and professional-organization workshops and encourage state, regional, and local leadership roles. Bus driver workshops and competitions should be part of the budgeted plan.

Be sure the support staff is part of the strategic plan. Have them develop their own level of commitment to learning for all. Train them on how to be part of the solution.

WHAT ABOUT TRAINING THE BOARD?

In California the state School Boards Association has a number of programs to help both new and old members. CSBA's Masters in Boardmanship Program is a 2-year program to help educate them. Encourage this even with questionable board members. The interaction with board members from other districts works for the best most of the time. You just have to filter all the new ideas board members bring home and want to start the next day.

Encourage board members to be part of any district staff development and planning programs you initiate. While there is a risk, the positive rewards are worth it. Rob, I would suggest you talk to them about what is expected of them beforehand. Use your one-on-one sessions to prepare them for this role. Are they a part of the process or observers? Remind them that sometimes they can intimidate staff and you want the staff to feel free to say what's on their mind. An out, of course, is that no more than two of five can attend without potential conflict in the open-meeting laws. Be sure they know that at times it's staff only!

When your board sees a powerful in-service program going on, most often they will be your advocates. And more important, they will understand what you are trying to accomplish when explained in a system improvement context. Remember, the leadership role in this should reflect that it's yours, not theirs. This must be established early on in your position and in your next position, if you have to leave. Finding a comfortable fit, defining your role, and standing tall will make it work.

THE SUPERINTENDENT TRAINING AND DEVELOPMENT

Where do you go and what do you need? After the first few years, I usually didn't find much value in any professional-association meetings. The conversation was seldom on learning and teaching or on organizational dynamics. There were times when two or three good ideas could be found. Go with an agenda in mind. What do you need? Talking to vendors on your specific needs can give you lots of good information. Stay focused on this agenda.

Be a taker and absorber of knowledge to store it, process it, and then give it back. Drive yourself to find out what you don't know. Accidental relationships with experts like Paul Hersey and Ken Blanchard have opened my eyes and avenues to both human resource development and organizational development. Keep your antenna up and ready to absorb what you're looking for. File good ideas away for later.

⏲ Time-Out—A So What

1. What part of the staff development concepts did you like? Not agree with?
2. Analyze the staff development program in your district in light of the work previously discussed. What would you see that needs improving in your district?
3. Under what conditions would you include board members as part of your training events? At all? Why or why not?

How does this all add up? When do I start building a learning organization?

In 1990 Peter Senge said a learning organization has identifiable characteristics. These characteristics are found in successful organizations. As I mentioned previously, we were one and didn't even know it. Each employee should feel his or her worth to the organization by being valued for training and development. At least, staff members need to know the administration cares and that these opportunities are sometimes required and some others available on a voluntary basis. If you want to reach a higher level of student learning, this must become a strategic priority. This includes time, budget, and other resources to make it happen.

Rob, Senge suggests the following five concepts in *The Fifth Discipline*. I hope you have a copy.

Building a shared vision: This idea carries with it the notion that you never actually arrive where your vision is leading you. It is the practice of unearthing shared pictures of the future that fosters genuine commitment to the organization's future and purpose. Keep the vision alive by being a spokesman and advocate.

Personal mastery: Learning organizations must be fully committed to development of each individual's personal mastery—the capacity to create a life in the way that is truly envisioned. It is developing the skill of continually clarifying and deepening this personal vision.

Mental models: Working with the various mental models found in the people in the organization. Recognition and communication of our mental models requires reflection and inquiry skills possessed by few administrators. It is the ability to unearth our internal pictures of the world, to scrutinize them, and to make them open to the influence of others. I tried to convey this to you throughout the year.

Team learning: The mental models that really matter in the organization are those that are shared. Individual learning is fundamentally irrelevant to systems, because virtually all important decisions occur in groups. This is the capacity to think together that is gained by mastering the practice of dialogue and discussion. The learning unit then becomes the group.

Systems thinking: This ties it all together. It offers a critical set of tools for understanding complex policy and strategy issues. Also, systems thinking is vital as a philosophy and set of principles that integrate all the learning disciplines. You've had a thorough dose of this over the past 12 months.

Rob, you can now see why I've been pushing you all year long about some of these ideas. By reviewing my own personal and organizational experiences without benefit of Senge's insight perhaps you have some better organized ideas of what needs to be done at your place. It's a long road and you now have a way—some tools to get there.

My whole approach last summer was to begin by an in-depth discussion of systems, which I've tried to keep alive all year. Then I added to the pot past experiences that integrated the many facets that we deal with on a regular basis. Having a clear understanding of what business you are in through strategic planning and then delivery of the results using strategic management is one way to be very successful, in my opinion.

Take a look at this material, share it, and then we can discuss it further.

Regards,
Barry

 Time-Out—A So What

1. Does Senge's material make any sense in light of our discussions about systems thinking? How?
2. What does it add to your knowledge about learning systems?
3. Describe how your district measures up to these concepts.

MORE ON TECHNOLOGY

After having a chef's salad with a soft drink for lunch, Barry decided to go back to the computer and face the task of editing the paper on technology for Rob. On reconsideration, he thought he'd only highlight some important issues. After taking some thoughtful time, he prepared and sent it along to Rob.

Subject: Some history and thoughts about technology written by my former district's executive director of technology.
Dear Rob,
How Did We Get Here?
Although the first computer use in classes began nearly three decades ago, there was no shared district vision for the development of educational

technology. In fact, no one was ready to look beyond the desktop for administrators and some teachers. Sixteen years later, the district superintendent, a strong believer in staff development, made the decision to hire a director of technology and a coordinator of instructional technology staff development to help focus staff on educational technology. The first 3-year technology plan replaced a long-ignored scope and sequence document, but it was never updated or reviewed after the first year. Strides were made in the networking and equipment areas, but the instructional impact was still inconsistent across the district.

After struggling 5 more years, a new director of technology was hired to create a new document. Staff participated in creating the new Learning Environment Plan, which takes advantage of the growing knowledge base in the business community and serves as the beginning of a strong implementation program for classroom technology use. Technology committees were organized at each site and strong business partnerships with large and small companies, including vendors, were created. The Learning Environment Plan was designed as a living document, reviewed yearly and approved by the site technology committees. Today, the plan is available on a website for the entire community to review and comment on for the following year's update.

The superintendent then mandated simple district targets—all teachers were to have e-mail and each learning area, especially libraries, was to have Internet access. Principals followed the lead and started attaching daily bulletins to e-mail or appearing on morning video broadcasts. A visionary plan that includes short-term objectives, coupled with strong leadership at the district and site levels, will go a long way in creating an atmosphere for success. So why was this a valuable approach and what does it reflect about leadership?

All of the work has changed the face of education in the district. The question is no longer "Should we have technology in schools?" but rather, "Where can technology help the student-learning environment the most?" With the data-warehousing application, staff will be able to research back 5 years and compare students who went through a learning experience with instructors who heavily used technology to students whose instructors did not use technology. Until this is done, we can at least claim the following results:

- Communication with parents has increased and improved in quality.
- Students use technology for an expanded school day.
- Virtual classes have given students flexibility with respect to creating projects.
- Virtual classes have given students flexibility in their personal schedules.
- Student access to resources is almost anytime and anywhere.
- Teachers can customize instruction.
- Students are having a variety of learning experiences.
- Students are better prepared for 21st-century skills.

The district's move toward new learning environments was not accomplished simply because it is a rich district. State funding is well below $5,000/student (below the state average), and the free and reduced lunch count is below 10%, restricting funding for technology and federal and state grants. Our success was attributable not just to financial resources, but to the planning, leadership, staff teamwork, and partnerships—including businesses, parent organizations, county office of education, and the city—that have shaped the environment that district students have available to them today.

Are students learning more? Are they learning better? Our assessments seem to indicate that indeed they are. Time and more data will tell us more.

IDEAS THAT GUIDE IMPLEMENTATION

Building the best learning environments for students is a goal for all educational professionals. Technology is changing these learning environments for the better and offering new ways for students to learn and grow. If properly shaped, this growth will continue throughout the students' lives. Here are some useful guidelines we've followed to help us move toward our goal and that may help you in reaching yours.

- Always think student centered and student learning.
- Create a 3-year plan. Listen to your community and seek input from students, staff, and parents.
- Update the plan yearly.
- Visit the Western States Benchmarking website.

- Ask vendors and community businesses how they view partnerships and student learning. Work with them to create a shared vision.
- Realize each new installation is a project and projects take time, need planning, and need to be managed.
- Use staff development as a curriculum development.
- Visit and talk with other districts—form a support network.
- Have an outside group do a technology audit before you begin your plan.
- Develop a good technology-support and information-system team.
- Read trade magazines—some based on business practices.
- Be careful what you wish for—plan, don't wish.
- Ask yourself on each project, Just because I can do this, should I?
- Secure district funding—remind everyone technology touches all aspects of education.
- Training. Training. Training.
- Never forget: Is it good for student learning?

Move forward on a broken front.

Barry looked at what he assembled, thinking, At least this is food for thought. Then he added a couple of more suggestions.

Rob, don't panic. I know there's not much technology in your district and it's not networked yet. Get a few folks together and begin planning. Do an assessment of what you have and then decide where you want to be. Beware of venders who have the perfect solution. I was most successful by moving forward on a broken front. This means that in the start-up phase don't try to have each school at the same place at the same time. It's too much to handle. Consider setting aside some money each year for internal innovative grants for the trailblazers to use. Be sure to focus these efforts on how these projects aid and abet the learning process or enhance the necessary support systems for managing the organization.

Good luck,
Barry

THE CELEBRATION

It was the evening following the school board meeting in June. Rob insisted that his mentor join him for a victory dinner at the five-star Paradise Valley Inn to celebrate the anniversary of their year together along with his new 4-year contract. He even offered to buy dinner as he was especially happy knowing he was going to get a raise. The raise would be the same percentage that the teachers would get after they settled on a new contract.

If you don't care where you're going, the wind doesn't make a difference, and if you are going nowhere, you're always there.

The management team was thinking about recommending a 4% salary increase for all employees. This had been budgeted and was there for all to see. They hoped they could bring it down within a percentage of this amount. The budget information was open to the unions this year.

As they were sipping a glass of wine, Dr. Woodson asked Rob to explain how the evaluation session went with the board.

"It went like clockwork—no surprises," Rob responded proudly. "I followed what we had done in March and just updated them. I even gave them an idea of what I thought the priorities should be for next year."

"Good work," Barry added with pride of his own. Rob was really doing well this semester.

"My observation was that neither side wanted to give the other any ammunition to use in the election next year. All five commented that they were hearing good reports from almost every segment of the community, starting with the teachers and administration staff—even parents commented on the new peace. The board meetings were now boring."

"What are your priorities for year two, ex-rookie? I don't know what to call you now. Congratulations—again!"

"How about superintendent Dr. Robert J. Moore, sophomore super-intendent!" Rob joked. "Or how about just the same old struggling Rob? I'm the same guy. I just know a little more."

"Well, how do you feel going into year two? As the year developed you seemed to like the job more than when you set that as a condition for seeking a new contract," Barry reminded him.

"I've come around. I think over time the mind lets you forget the bad stuff and remember the good times," Rob said thoughtfully and added, "seriously, this year has gone reasonably well, even though I didn't know what to expect. With the reorganization of the management team, we're stronger than ever."

"What did you set forth as your goals for next year?" Barry quizzed the superintendent.

"Nothing too surprising! You've helped me figure out how to define the mission and given me some tools of the trade to begin a new sense of direction for the district."

"Rob, how did the board feel about that?"

"I think this positive planned approach was key in getting them to focus together, which was a first for them after the years of squabbling."

"What else?"

"I continued some of the ones set in the fall—finish the new school, improve instruction, keep a good working relationship with the unions, and then added a strategic planning effort to get all our stakeholders to buy into the goals. This was the one objective from a year ago I really didn't work on. I committed to work on this next year.

"While I didn't write it down, I complimented them on their unified support of teaching and learning—and how much I enjoyed working with them, especially the past 6 months."

"How did they respond?"

"They seemed pleased. I built this through the superintendent's goals, which we had reported publicly last week at a special board meeting for this purpose. We had each administrator report on his or her area and responsibility. They loved it! It went well!"

They paused for another glass of wine and then gave the waiter their order. It was steak tonight.

"How do you really feel now?" Woodson pushed Rob, sensing there was something still bothering him beyond what he was saying.

"I still feel somewhat unsure. I had no idea what I was doing most of the time. Now that I've experienced a year, it really scares me. I found out how much I don't know!"

"Sophomore remorse already?" the mentor challenged with a big smile on his face. "I have to laugh. I remember the start of my second year. I know how you feel."

"I suppose I'm both tired and glad at the same time. I really haven't finished the first year and I'm thinking 3 months and 6 months downstream already," Rob smiled dejectedly in spite of his earlier bravado.

"None of this feeling sorry for yourself—which I know you're not. We're here to celebrate. Cheers!" he said again, toasting the almost-second-year CEO.

"I mentioned to the board that I wanted to continue with your services for another year on a more limited basis, probably on call with a smaller monthly retainer. I was surprised, but they agreed you really helped them and me both to keep the focus on the main thing. So cheers! You are stuck with me another year—that is, if you take on the assignment."

"I'll drink to that," Barry cheerfully said as he picked up his glass and took a sip of merlot. "I'd consider it an honor."

"Now that all the BS is out of the way, I have a few things to go over."

"No rest for the wicked!" Barry responded humorously. He appreciated Rob's trust in him. Thinking ahead he had decided to try to help Rob by reflecting back to Rob what the superintendent was saying. Of course, if a new topic they hadn't dealt with surfaced, he would try to provide direction.

"Here's what's on my mind now. If we can talk some of this through tonight, we might avoid another meeting this month," Rob said hopefully. This hadn't happened any month previously. Their track record didn't support wishful thinking. Too many surprises in this business!

Barry didn't respond, but rather sat there waiting for Rob to go on.

"I want to continue building cabinet strength, get some help creating a real learning organization, and go over your experiences in developing a NSBA-recognized technology-centered school district," Rob outlined and then paused.

Barry took the bait, as he couldn't keep quiet for long, "So what does this all mean? What do you want from me?"

"Can you share some ideas?"

"Of course I can! Tell me first what you want from your cabinet that it doesn't have," he asked, quietly trying to force Rob into backwards thinking once again.

"Got it! You want my end in mind! Each position has its own expertise. We will each have one more year's experience to build on. I want to see the cabinet as a well-functioning team in our roles as decision makers and leaders."

"How do you propose doing this?"

"Well, you may be part of the thinking. We have 3 days blocked out the last week in July before the principals come back. I already strongly suggested that vacations be taken the first 3 weeks in July except for the director of business services. We have budget issues to grind out sooner rather than later. And anyway, he goes elk hunting in October after all the school budgets are adjusted for enrollment in the new system we're initiating."

"What are you doing for vacation?" Woodson asked with a bias. He knew how easy it was to get trapped into covering for everyone else and not plan for yourself. He thought that Rob was thinking the same way. How important are we superintendents anyway? When do we feel comfortable enough to leave? Thinking back he remembered that his excuse for not taking vacations was that he attended many conferences and workshops early on and was out of the district enough. He did take a day here and there.

"I'm going to take the full 2 weeks at Christmas and a long weekend for skiing in February."

"Good! Be sure you do, now. Your family will appreciate it!" Barry said with a smile. He hoped he would.

"What about your schedule for late July?"

"You're on. I can work around my summer school obligation. What else?" Barry questioned.

"I know you gave me tons of stuff on becoming a learning organization. Should I start sorting this out—that is, first steps?" Rob asked with some concern and uncertainty.

"What do you remember about the indicators of a learning organization that I sent you? Think about it a few minutes, while I dig into my salad. It looks too good to avoid any longer."

During the silence Rob tried to remember Senge's points, as well as what Barry had told them his district had done by what he seemed to call accident or commonsensically organized.

Rob finished his salad and before the entrées came reviewed what he was thinking about the problem.

"Thanks for keeping quiet, or were you hungry? I can outline the five disciplines. Want me to rattle them off?" Rob said, still trying to make an impression with his coach.

"No, I believe you. The question really is, what do his concepts mean to you? Are you a learning organization by his definitions? Or do you want to become one? That is the big question," Barry said, driving home the point. "You have a choice. Carry your vision for student learning forward and bring the district along with you or not. What will it be?"

"Oh mentor of mine, I hope by now, with a year of your brainwashing, you know what I want to do or rather want be in 5 years," Rob responded quickly.

"In another district?" Barry shot back with a straight face.

"Possibly, but not until I've given Paradise Valley my very best. I'm, or rather we are, going to make a difference! We will become a powerful learning organization."

"I hope the difference makes a difference," Barry chided. He was rather pleased with the superintendent's affirmation and commitment. It made him feel that this past year's effort did make a difference.

"It will!"

The waiter interrupted with two steak-filled platters and a side of asparagus for each of them. This stopped the business conversation for a long while.

"Rob, on the technology question, I'm going to take the fifth—not scotch—and am not going to go through the technology morass tonight. We can do more later. Let's enjoy the rest of the evening," and then Barry quickly added, "I was superintendent before computers were invented, so our experiences will be different, but many of the principles won't change much over time."

"I thought you were superintendent before the abacus was invented!" the CEO popped off.

"Easy now," Barry smiled, "I was there with the Wright brothers, so don't get smart," he teased back. It was a 20-year adventure just as technology was taking shape for schools. Got to remember your roots—and more important, how tough the change process is.

"What else is on your plate, or rather mind, before the dessert and coffee come?"

The CEO then told Barry about the indoctrination of the two new principals.

After all the interviews the cabinet had agreed on two new principals, including the transfer of one of their top elementary leaders to the new school and giving her the challenge of the F team strategy. Rob wanted Barry to spend some time monitoring and coaching this transition process. The replacement for her was picked from the assistant principal ranks. This was one of their best and brightest at this level and they knew that he could handle a well-established school.

The final spot went to an outside candidate. What they were looking for was a strong, experienced principal, so one had to be brought in from a neighboring district. She would be assigned to the school that had struggled under weak leadership, where Rob had trouble getting the former guy to do anything. This would clearly be a big challenge, but she had experience in turning around the school she now headed.

"While I didn't know whether we'd get into this topic, I did try to recall some elements of Smart Start developed by the Centre for Strategic Management. Basically, it is how to handle the transitional change process more effectively. Typically the new executive is left to personal devices to maneuver through the organization. Contacts needed to accomplish the job are formed on the run, resulting in inefficiency and mistrust. Priorities remain unclear or are forgotten in the overwhelming press of handling teachers and kids—and the central office! An information overload is predictable. Productivity decreases as teachers and support staff try to analyze the new principal's priorities and style."

"Quite a memory there, Dr. Woodson," Rob interjected. "Did you stay up all night memorizing that or did you experience it?"

"It's commonsensically organized. Haven't you just gone through the process this year? Think back. That's a pretty good picture of you even though you had an outstanding mentor to guide you, Dr. Moore," Barry reminded him. "How easy is it is to forget bad experiences!"

"Cutting out all the baloney, how does this work?"

"It's the roller coaster of change all over again. This is a way to ease into the new role. It requires a 1-day transition meeting focusing on team building and direction setting with the new leader, the supervisor, and school site personnel."

"I suppose you can send me more detailed information."

"Of course, and you need to know it doesn't stop after 1 day. Continuous attention to integrating the new person in the job is an all-year event. Include what you have learned about Sit Lead in your thinking. Give specific directions and closely supervise until the new person shows that he or she can handle the tasks. It's not like we often do—sink or swim."

"It may be too late for this go-around, but maybe not. If we could do this just before school starts later this summer, maybe it would be beneficial," Rob said, thinking through the matter.

"If you're asking, yes, I could find time to go over this in more detail and pilot it at the school with the new principal who was selected from outside the district."

"Anything else for the good of the order?" Rob asked.

"Can't think of anything. Are we ready to hang it up?"

"I'll settle up then." Rob called the waiter over and handed him his personal credit card. Early on he had decided never to put dinner and drinks on a district credit card. Too many folks got burned by that practice. For that reason, he rejected the offer to have one. Instead, he asked for and got a monthly stipend to cover these occasions.

"Thanks for giving me the chance to be helpful this year. I'll plan on sending you some more stuff to pile on your credenza. Thanks for dinner and the conversation—and keeping me around. You'll need me less. After school starts you will be fine. I'll just be on call. We can go have a soda once in a while if you need someone to talk to," Barry said.

As they started walking to their cars Barry once again congratulated Rob on surviving his rookie year.

"I remember your challenge: know the good, love the good, and do the good! I think I've done pretty good for a rookie, haven't I?"

Just as Rob was shaking hands and wishing Barry a goodnight in the parking lot, his cell phone rang.

"Rob Moore here. No! Not again! I don't believe it!"

The End

SUMMARY

This chapter's emphasis was on staff development, personnel transition, and technology for the most part. Many good suggestions for staff development were discussed. A brief case study on planning for a technology-centered district was covered.

The rookie superintendent did survive and so did his mentor!

⏰ Time-Out—Reflections

1. Discuss the key factors you believe were instrumental in the superintendent's survival during the first year.
2. Think about what you want to continue doing that's good on your job.
3. What would you like to do more of, or start doing, in light of the suggestions offered?
4. What should you be doing less of or stop doing?
5. Prepare a strategic personal plan for yourself for the next 3 years.

MONTH 12—JUNE

Strategies and Survival Skills

1. Give serious consideration to becoming a learning organization.
2. At least develop a strong staff development program for all.
3. Keep it consistent with your mission and core values.
4. Consider all the factors in transitioning new employees and transferring the veteran.
5. Beware of gift horses—technology ones.
   - Have a plan.
   - Use experts if you don't have in-house expertise.
6. Get the board more involved in training and development.
7. Do a great job and get your contract renewed on your terms.
8. Good luck!

TOOLBOX

Garten, C. (2004). *Technology—Poway Unified School District.* Unpublished manuscript.

Haines, S. *Enterprise-Wide Change—Participant Notebook: Chapter 4. Smart Start*. The Centre for Strategic Management. San Diego, CA. www.csmin tl.com.

Reeves, R. (2005). The Reeves Consulting Group. rreeves@san.rr.com.

Senge, P. (1990). *The Fifth Discipline*. New York: Doubleday.

Western States Benchmarking, www.wsbenchmark.org.

14

AFTERTHOUGHTS: WILL YOUR DIFFERENCE MAKE A DIFFERENCE?

Those who follow the crowd usually get lost in it.

—Rick Warren

In this chapter you will be asked to consider the following:

1. Will I ever be able to make a difference and leave a legacy? Am I prepared or even thinking about doing so?
2. What are the career challenges and dilemmas facing you as a chief executive officer and superintendent?
3. Will I ever be able to achieve my impossible dream? And more important, do I have a dream?
4. What is your level of commitment to all students learning, whatever it takes? You are challenged to do something about it—starting today.
5. The survival skills and development of an action plan for self-improvement and preparation for your next big life-changing step.

THINKING ABOUT A LEGACY

With almost a joking attitude when asked the question, How do you want your epitaph to read? I most often replied that I want my tombstone to read "I made a difference in the life of Howard."

Who is Howard? He was a sophomore and I his principal when our paths first crossed. It was the late 1960s. He was an activist with the Students for Democratic Action and he was rallying all sorts of protests at the high school. The short version is that I persuaded him to form a legitimate on-campus club with a teacher-advisor and work inside the tent rather than outside on the fringes. Later, as a senior, he became student body president and went to college, earning a master's degree.

For more than 35 years I didn't give him much thought except as the headstone quote came to mind. Although at times I did wonder what had happened to him. Then out of the blue I received a phone call from Howard. In his loyalty to his former high school memories, he was back in the district raising hell again, challenging the superintendent's decision to change the school's mascot.

We talked. The life I didn't know how I had touched had joined the Peace Corps and gone to Micronesia. After 2 years he joined the Navy, later becoming a JAG officer. Because of his early overseas experience he was invited as a consultant and speech writer in the Reagan White House. He was even present when the mortgage was burned on the president's western White House retreat near Santa Barbara, Rancho del Cielo, the Ranch in the Sky.

The most touching point he made was that he applied what I had taught him, or rather what he had learned from me. The time came when he was able to apply this to work through some problems with one of his own children.

What's the point? Are you committed to making a difference in the lives of boys and girls? And will your difference make a difference? I came to realize later that this was my lifetime commitment. And maybe I had made a difference! What do you want your legacy to be?

"This is my life's most defining maxim: Success is the peace of mind as a direct result of self-satisfaction in knowing that you did your best to become the best you are capable of becoming—in all areas of life. It is difficult to be successful without a strong sense of spiritual well-being."

—John Wooden, former UCLA basketball coach

What are some career challenges and dilemmas facing you as a CEO and superintendent?

I've been around too many superintendents whose primary commitment is moving up to a bigger, more prestigious district just for the sake of moving up. Is this bad? Not necessarily so. If this is who you are, it works. As a rookie, or thinking about becoming one, have you looked ahead?

A good question to ask yourself is why did I go into teaching? For me it was about helping the kids I couldn't necessarily reach through church-related work. A personal drive to be better kept calling me to different roles. I got a lot of experience by moving around until I was faced with the challenge of a high school principalship. I wanted to be able to try my ideas out in a new school situation—and I did. This is where I began the drive to create an outstanding learning environment for our students. When I was able to define this as "All students learning—whatever it takes," I was captured by the vision. For nearly three decades as a school superintendent that was who I became. Even as I write this, the culture I left behind was so firmly established it became the belief system of those now in charge.

Back to the original question. Are you going to be a career hopper, or do you have a plan for growing and developing? Are you going to take the advice of your university advisors or the headhunters, starting small and then every 2–4 years moving on to bigger and better things?

A superintendent on the job for 2 years with a new 3-year contract has been contacted for a higher paying job. How does he process the issue? What advice would you give?

How are you going to make decisions about being drawn to a higher paying situation? Examine your own personal mission. Is part of it a consideration of future financial security? How does thinking downstream about retirement benefits figure into your decision? Is there a trade off with higher salary and loyalty to your current board? What did you commit to? Should you wait until the last year of a contract before trying to move on?

There is no right answer! It depends on you and how your value system works.

Do we need bigger challenges and opportunities to make even bigger differences? You need to consider this for yourself.

There's nothing inherently wrong with using this career path. Now that you know it takes 3–5 years to change the culture, are you going to make a difference? Think about it!

What other career challenges and dilemmas are facing you as a CEO and superintendent?

I hope the reading of this book will have clarified the aspects of leadership that you will find important to your own success. Listening to the interaction between Dr. Barry Woodson and Dr. Rob Moore through his first year's trials and tribulations may have given you a better picture of what leading an organization is all about.

The first question to ask yourself is, Do I really like being or want to be a school superintendent? Do or will I like working with the school board? One very able assistant I knew didn't like this aspect of the job, so after 8 years as superintendent he changed careers. When working with me, he was very comfortable letting me be the buffer between staff and the board. He just didn't like the politics as CEO.

Have you ever felt like the Lone Ranger? Attacking something that is wrong and no one is listening? Are you way ahead of the pack? Do peers have trouble understanding you and you don't know why? Does it feel as though they don't get what drives you toward excellence and trying to be the best? Do you clearly see what's going to happen down the road while others don't seem to see it at all? Are you the only one with the helicopter view of what it takes to lead the system to greatness?

Do you have the energy it requires to be a strong leader? Balancing career and family is hazardous to your physical and mental health. Can you balance all of life's priorities and be successful? Look at Covey's work again. What is in it for you?

Handling your career path has already been mentioned. It bears repeating here. Are you in the business to help folks get the most out of their job life? Building an empowered learning organization is a partial answer. Treating others as you yourself want to be treated still works! The focus on a school district's reason for being shouldn't be far from your thoughts. "What do students need to know and be able to do?" must be in your consciousness daily.

A final point here is trying to decide when to move on. Is it your choice or the board's? Often the chemistry isn't there or doesn't last for a variety of reasons. Or the composition of the board changes and you're gone within 6 months. Do you feel you can't make a difference anymore or are you just bored and want a new challenge? Be careful of your motives. Be true to yourself and as sure as night follows day you won't be false to anyone or something like it!

Often it is said "I know old George. He's had 1 year's experience twenty times!" And probably moved almost as often!

Be reminded of the Johari Window. Explaining how we process feedback, Joseph Luft and Harry Ingham used a four-paneled window to describe their thoughts on how we perceive ourselves and how others perceive us. They named them the public, the private, the blind, and the unknown windows. The growth objective is to make the "known to self" and "known to others" window, the public, the largest so there are no workplace surprises. This means we are open, listening, and processing feedback. We need to see feedback as a gift.

When all is said and done and you move on to your next superintendent challenge, will you be able to look back with some pride and say, "I left this place better than I found it. Student learning improved on my watch." Can you be proud of the legacy you left? Are people better for having shared their lives with you as CEO and superintendent?

"The first year I didn't know what I didn't know. Then I found out what I didn't know and that really scared me starting my second year."

—Ted Adams, veteran superintendent

FINAL, FINAL THOUGHTS

The questions and challenges in this afterthought will have to be addressed—either acknowledged in passing, just plain ignored, or productively resolved during your tenure as a school superintendent. You can avoid dealing with the issues, but eventually they will catch up to you when you least expect it. Be ready, if it hasn't already happened!

What do you want your world to look like 5 years hence? 10? What is your personal mission in life? On the job? Do you plan to make a significant difference or just move from district to district being a place holder—a good manager?

What drives you? Ask yourself the following:

Will I ever be able to achieve my impossible dream? And more important, do I have one?

Starting with an end in mind, reflect on the words in the first two stanzas in a song from *Man of La Mancha*. These words have inspired me to try to fulfill my own impossible dream.

The Impossible Dream

"To dream the impossible dream,
To fight the unbeatable foe,
To bear with unbearable sorrow,
To run where the brave dare not go.

To right the unrightable wrong,
To love, pure and chaste from afar,
To try when your arms are too weary,
To reach the unreachable star."

What does your unreachable star look like? Have you thoroughly thought about what you are doing, in considering a superintendent's job, or are you one? Whether you are a rookie, veteran, or a hopeful, what defines your moral purpose for doing what you're doing? Do you understand your own core values?

For those considering the CEO role, are you ready to meet the challenge? How are you preparing yourself? What are you doing in your current district? What is working? Is not working? Do you now have or need more tools to use?

It's about you and how you interrelate with those around you—the folks that make your system and subsystems work. You now know how important it is to have a core-value-based organization, something to frame the way you want to conduct business.

Has looking at the organization through the lens of systems thinking opened your eyes to new and exciting tools that are invaluable to the leader's success as a way of understanding and meeting your goals? You have been given practical real-life successful solutions to problems that many school leaders have shared.

I started my doctoral program career path because I worked for superintendents whose performance ranged from excellent to below ordinary—two way below. Mostly by those whom I considered less than effective, I was inspired to build a better mousetrap. Using the skills and strategies I have included in this book, I know that I contributed to a better education for students, and a good learning organization and environment for the adults.

Now go back and again read the words from *The Impossible Dream*.

What is your impossible dream? Does it have something to do with learning, not only for each and every student under your charge, but for the adults and the organization as well?

Are you ready to fight for literacy for all? For equal opportunity and equity for all? What did you write down as your core values? Do they need to be reshaped? Reviewed? Refined?

Let me ask you again. What is your impossible dream?

Are you ready to share your commitment to learning for all—whatever it takes? Where learning should no longer be optional, but required? Students can no longer just occupy seats. Learning for *all* has to become our target. Is this your "unbeatable foe"?

What does your "unreachable star" look like today? Can you see it? Describe it? How badly do you want it?

"Good enough wasn't, isn't, and won't ever be!"

—Peter Demyan, school superintendent

To really make a difference as the leader of a school system, I challenge you to focus on the quest of your mission, the purpose for which the system should exist. Don't flail at the imaginary foes. Define your windmills as real issues to fight and conquer.

Now read and reflect on the closing words of *The Impossible Dream*.

"This is my quest, to follow that star,
No matter how hopeless, no matter how far,
To fight for the right, without question or pause,
To be willing to march into Hell, for a heavenly cause.

And I know if I'll only be true, to this glorious quest,
That my heart will lie peaceful and calm, when I'm laid
to my rest.

And the world will be better for this,
That one man, scorned and covered with scars,
Still strove, with his last ounce of courage,
To reach the unreachable stars."

Copyright © 1965, words Joe Darion, music Mitch
Leigh. Andrew Scott Music, Helena Music
Company. ASCAP

What are you willing to march into "Hell" for? Again I ask you what legacy did you want to leave? A great career? Wealth? Power? Prestige? I strongly suggest that if you don't have an unreachable star, you probably won't make a significant difference in the lives of boys and girls.

I challenge you once more to dream dreams of what might be. Hang on to that dream as you lead. For if we, in leadership positions, don't have a learning focus, our systems will continue to fall short of reaching each and every child. And NCLB won't have made a difference nor will a multitude of other attempts to change the system in place over the past 50 years. And then will the world have been better because you passed this way?

Be a lifelong learner. Be a change agent for good things for kids.

"There is power in a vision of excellence so long as some of us share in that dream and believe in our hearts that we can make a difference."

—Unknown

🕐 Time-Out—A Now What

1. Be challenged to do something about it—starting today.
2. Be challenged to review the presented survival skills and develop an action plan for self-improvement and preparation for your next big life-changing step.
3. Dream the impossible dream, reach for that unreachable star!

"There are only two lasting bequests we can give our children— one is roots and the other is wings."

—Unknown

AFTERTHOUGHTS FOR SUPERINTENDENTS

- Review each month's survival skills and pick out the skills that you don't need any further help with and place them in one column and then list ones you need help with in another column. Reject those that don't make sense for you.
- Develop your own strategic life plan for the next 3 years starting with the end in mind.
- Build on your growth goals.
- Reread and refer to the appropriate chapters as necessary.
- How do you want your epitaph to read?

And finally, I would be interested in any stories of first-year experiences that illustrate what I've included in this book. What did I miss?

Also, I'm interested in new stories that could be used in future work. The names of the guilty will be protected!

15

AFTER, AFTERTHOUGHTS FOR SCHOOL BOARD MEMBERS: WHAT IS THE MAIN MISSION FOR THE SCHOOL BOARD?

In this chapter you will be:

1. Challenged to think about new superintendent transitions.
2. Able to review some ideas on effective board functioning.
3. Able to check your district's level of excellence.
4. Challenged to think about an impossible dream as a board member.

WHAT IS YOUR MAIN MISSION?

Take a few minutes and think through this question. Do you really know? What should it be? School boards often get into the morass of everyday problems when they lose a sense of mission and role. I've included some thoughts that might be helpful in your role as a school board member or for you as a superintendent to use as you begin a conversation with the board.

HIRING THE LEADER

The first part of this "After, Afterthought" chapter is provided in the form of questions for pondering and reflections for consideration, as you think about your most important role—hiring the best superintendent available at the time that matches your needs.

- What happens to communication when you have to change superintendents?
- How do you make a smooth transition between the old and the new?
- What programs need to continue, be dropped, or added under the new leadership?
- How do you minimize the loss in productivity during the first few months of a change in command?
- Is it possible to break the communication barrier during the transition and get productive results?
- Do you realize that in most every new hiring situation, you hire someone you believe will compensate for the perceived weaknesses of the predecessor, no matter how small?
- How do you protect against niche hiring—that is, hiring for the big deficit found in the former superintendent and not getting a well-rounded individual?
- What is needed to build the bridge between the new superintendent and the outgoing superintendent?

How is this accomplished? One way is to use a formalized system with the board's defined criteria for hiring the new superintendent: spend quality time with both the outgoing superintendent and incoming one and determine what's positive and negative, what should remain, and what should be improved.

In my experience, the outgoing and incoming superintendents seldom meet, especially if there has been some difficulty surrounding the former superintendent. If there is a problem necessitating the change in command, the two seldom chat.

It would be wise to spend a day with the outgoing superintendent to assess where the district has been and what he or she sees as the next steps for necessary improvement.

Next, spend a day with the new, incoming superintendent and share this data. Give the new superintendent a written analysis of the strengths and areas of concern. Develop a plan for the first 6 months as a desired outcome. Include goal setting for the year and a good feedback system.

Boards need expert help in not only the initial hiring process but also the equally important transition phase. Implementing and providing a yearlong mentorship opportunity as this book describes will increase effective relationships between the board and superintendent. This is even true initially on a more limited basis for the more experienced hire. The American Association of School Administrators also considers the mentoring of new superintendents critical.

EFFECTIVE BOARD FUNCTIONING

It seems to me that there are five areas that boards should consider when approaching the age-old dilemma of getting people working together on a board, especially a publicly elected one. By this I mean that each member represents his or her own interests and not everyone has the necessary background and experience in managing a large public enterprise. But working together for the good of the cause is critical if student benefits are to be maximized.

A review of the five areas may help provide some perspective.

1. Our context: environment (outside impactors)
   - external, customers, parents; internal constraints; structural, rewards; and policies and procedures
2. What we do: values, mission, and goals
   - assessment of current status, future ideal; board mission, strategies; vision; business plans; board goals; and values
3. Who does what: structure, roles, and responsibilities
   - organizational structure, individual roles and objectives, organizational structure support and expectations, superintendent and senior administrators, school and department management
4. How we make decisions that optimize quality and acceptance: processes, systems, and procedures
   - meetings, planning process, conflict management, problem solving, and decision making
5. How effectively we work together: relationships
   - Work style, communication style, strengths and limitations, process skills, and feedback

While this is presented in a brief outline format, it fairly well covers enough of the needs of an organization to provide hours of discussion and clarification. This process guarantees a shorter learning curve and optimizes effective understanding between board and superintendent. Through the process of examining this information together, can the relationship be clarified and more productive ways of working together be established?

SOME CHARACTERISTICS OF GOOD BOARDMANSHIP

Take a few minutes and think about these statements both from an individual point of view and from the point of view of the board as a whole.
As a board member, I believe the following:

1. I am committed to the mission and purpose of my school system.
2. I am able to make impartial decisions based solely on what's best for the district.
3. I am able to bring a level of personal expertise that will improve the board's ability to carry out and advance its mission of student learning.
4. I understand that part of my responsibility and legacy is to help encourage new board members to carry on and consistently improve the level of performance of the school system.
5. I always strive to work cooperatively with the superintendent and staff.
6. I realize that unauthorized time demands placed on staff by individual board members can have a negative impact on the organization and that time demands will work only through the board chair or superintendent.
7. I regularly attend board meetings, visit schools, and as often as I can, attend school district functions.
8. I keep well informed on issues and agenda items in advance of meetings.
9. I listen respectfully to other points of view.
10. I represent the school district positively to the public.

How did you do? Use this as a discussion vehicle for your board and superintendent. What implications do the combined findings have for board improvement?

HOW DO YOU KNOW HOW WELL YOU'RE DOING?

Every so often, maybe once a quarter, it might be a good practice to run through the following "Hallmarks of Excellence" check sheet on a formal basis at a board meeting or work or study session. It's like getting a tune-up for your car, before something not so desirable happens. This can be used at the same time a progress check is made on the district's strategic plan.

HALLMARKS OF EXCELLENCE

On a scale of 1 to 5, with a 5 indicating strong agreement, rate your system on the following:

In my district excellence is:

Circle one:

Disagree   Agree

A school district in which all school people are
helping kids to become something more than
they ever hoped to be.   1 2 3 4 5

A school district with a board that avoids getting
involved in day-to-day administrative decisions,
choosing instead to monitor the major decisions
of the central administrative team to ensure that
they are consistent with the mission and vision
of the school district.   1 2 3 4 5

A school district with a superintendent who
creates an organizational culture and structure

in which the talents of all school people may
flourish.   1   2   3   4   5

A school district with a superintendent who
preaches the school district's mission, who pays
attention to the school district's strengths and
corrects its weaknesses, and who talks about the
future and vision of learning for all to all school
and community people.   1   2   3   4   5

A school district that has become a learning
organization.   1   2   3   4   5

A school district that provides incentives for
developing innovations and programs that
improve students' learning and growth.   1   2   3   4   5

A school district that not only welcomes new ideas
but also rewards people who offer them.   1   2   3   4   5

A school district that integrates all parts of the
school system—strategy, human resources,
capital assets, reward systems, structure,
marketing, and promotion—into a cohesive and
manageable whole.   1   2   3   4   5

Add other hallmarks as you see fit for your situation.

AS A BOARD MEMBER, WHAT IS YOUR IMPOSSIBLE DREAM?

If you haven't read the words to this song already, go to the previous
chapter, "Afterthoughts," and read the lyrics to *The Impossible Dream*.
What is your impossible dream for your school system? Can you, and
more important, will you make it happen?

Remember Yoda's oft-quoted treasure, "There is no try, only do."

ABOUT THE AUTHOR

Robert Reeves has had more than 40 years of leadership experiences, some planned, some trial and error. As superintendent for nearly three decades he led the transformation of a struggling 10,000-student school system rife with problems to a large, 32,000-student, nationally recognized high-performing system. Many of the 32 schools in the system have become National Blue Ribbon Schools. Recently the National School Boards Association recognized the district as an award-winning technology-centered system.

Bob Reeves, after earning a doctorate in administration at UCLA, augmented this early academic experience with additional work with Drs. Ken Blanchard and Paul Hersey at the Center for Leadership Studies in Escondido, California. He was a consultant and trainer in Situational Leadership after first applying it within the school system. This early experience opened the door to other organizational development strategies developed by others as illustrated in *What Every Superintendent Should Know*.

He and his team were on the cutting edge of organizational transformation in applying the information to his leadership team. He and other top management staff modeled good teaching practices by becoming trained presenters for the practices used in transforming the system, without even realizing it, into what Peter Senge has now defined in *The Fifth Discipline* as a learning organization.

Reeves and Steve Haines, now chief executive officer of the Centre for Strategic Management in San Diego, drove a strategic plan, with the rallying cry of "All students learning—whatever it takes," to a new high in academic performance for California. The concept of a systems approach to organizational development followed to help keep them focused on the main thing: student learning.

The final big piece added to their repertoire of success was the work of Dr. Larry Lezotte, the Effective Schools guru, who helped them in the assessment of student learning.

With one of his associates he coauthored an article in *School Leadership* on tips for the new rookie superintendent titled "Now I Am One!" This was published by the American Association of School Administrators in November 2003 and helped lead the association to publish a compendium on mentoring superintendents released to the state associations in late 2004. He credits the encouragement from AASA as the prime motivator in creating this yearlong adventure of a rookie coached by his sage mentor.

The story, drawn from factual experiences, is a fictional account of how these successful programs can become valuable tools for any school leader.

Reeves also taught as an adjunct doctoral professor in the doctoral program at Point Loma Nazarene College as part of a partnership with Northern Arizona University. This provided the opportunity to transfer some of his seasoned knowledge to future school superintendents.

Nominated to the position by a state officer in a teacher's union, he has been a board of directors member and board chair for a continuing care retirement center for 9 years. He was able to apply the leadership skills learned to also transform that organization.

Now the chief executive officer and president of the Reeves Consulting Group, he spends time working with new superintendents and their boards during the hectic first rookie years and even beyond. He applies these same skills in working with chief executive officers and their boards in the continuing care field.

In 1984 he performed for more than a billion television viewers. A unique organizational and leadership opportunity was provided for a group of track and field officials. After being selected as the chief starter, Reeves was asked to train a 20-member group as the track starting team for the XXIII Olympic Games in Los Angeles. It can be truly said that he started Carl Lewis on three of his four gold medal opportunities. His motto was to be heard but not seen!

Made in the USA
Middletown, DE
29 June 2017